THE HISTORY AND RECORDS OF
QUEEN VICTORIA'S RIFLES
1792-1922

Monument erected on Hill 60 in memory of all Q.V.R. who gave their lives for King and Country in the Great War.

THE HISTORY & RECORDS OF
QUEEN VICTORIA'S RIFLES
1792–1922

COMPILED BY

MAJOR C. A. CUTHBERT KEESON V.D.

PRESIDENT QUEEN VICTORIA'S RIFLES
OLD COMRADES' ASSOCIATION

CONSTABLE & COMPANY LIMITED
LONDON : BOMBAY : SYDNEY
1923

REGIMENTAL BADGE.

INTRODUCTION

THIS is a Story of another Ten Thousand. Ten thousand of those gallant Lads of London whose praises have been sung by all our Leaders and all the Special Correspondents who have lived to observe and record their prowess on almost all the battlefields of the Great War. From August 4th, 1914, on which day the Order for Mobilisation was issued to the men then on the Roll of the Queen Victoria's Rifles, until the return of the Cadre from Germany on the 11th November, 1919, after five years of foreign service, just ten thousand men drawn from all ranks of life in London, the counting-house, warehouse, factory, shop, or bank, but very largely from the region surrounding Hanover Square where the Head-quarters of the Battalion are situated, passed through the ranks of the 9th London Regiment, Queen Victoria's Rifles, or "Q.V.R.'s" as they delight to call themselves.

The fighting value of the Cockney soldier has been recognised from the time of the Duke of Wellington to the present day. On all our far-flung battlefields he has played his part worthily, held his own with the dour Scot, the impetuous Irishman and the patient Provincial, and has never failed to come up smiling after the most bloodthirsty scrap. This, of course, alludes to the Regular Soldier. The Territorials and their predecessors, the Volunteers, had few chances prior to 1914 of proving their fighting worth, though the record of the City Imperial Volunteers and the Service Companies in the South African War had taught many of those who had come in close contact with them of what they were capable when properly trained and commanded. "The Volunteers," says Lord French, "met with little but derision. It was said that they only wanted to wear a uniform and play at soldiers and hardly anyone believed in the wonderful spirit which really animated them from the start." But they believed in themselves, took their training seriously, paid no regard to snubs or sneers, hoping that the recognition they deserved would one day come to them.

The sudden transformation of the Volunteers into Territorials, though it ultimately worked for their good and made it possible to send them out as complete units of a fighting force, did not for a long time ameliorate their lot. The age limit swept away at once a number of the "backbone of the Volunteer Force"; men who instilled into newly joined recruits that *esprit de corps* which had been its mainstay throughout its sixty years' history. More work was expected of Officer and man alike; compulsory attendance at Camp, the severance of cyclist sections from almost all regiments, and of Mounted Infantry contingents from a favoured few, all these things combined with the national lust for sport and pleasure which was so marked during the six immediate pre-war years, 1908–1914, did not make for the popularity of the Territorial Force so necessary to its well-being. In consequence, when war did come there was hardly a single battalion which was up to its establishment. This remark applies more particularly to the London Regiments; of those in the Provinces and Scotland the Editor cannot speak, but on the 1st April, 1910, according to the *Encyclopædia Britannica* there was a shortage of 681 Officers and 33,000 Other Ranks. And a considerable portion of these, according to so eminent an authority as Field-Marshal Sir William Robertson (*From Private to Field Marshal*, 1921, p. 140), " owing to inadequate training and other reasons could not be made efficient and by the terms of its engagement it (the T.F.) was not available for service outside the United Kingdom."

But the martial spirit of the Londoners, though it slumbered, was by no means dead. Thousands of men, still of fighting age, had passed through the ranks of the Volunteers and Territorials and when on that fateful 5th of August the call rang out they came tumbling over one another to join their favourite corps. The Q.V.R.'s filled up within forty-eight hours and in four days a second battalion was in being. The L.R.B.'s, Queen's Westminsters, the London Scottish, Kensingtons, Rangers, the Post Office Rifles, the whole of the twenty-six battalions of the London Regiment in fact. The H.A.C. and the Surrey Corps were not a whit behind, and in the space of a short three months Lord Kitchener was able to assure Lord French that a total of nineteen Territorial regiments were in France or on their way there, and that he was selecting two more to make up one per brigade. The first to arrive was the H.A.C. ; the London Scottish were in action at 10 a.m. on October 31st with a strength of 26 officers and 786 men and came out of it with a loss of 278, or about 34 per cent., eliciting from General Allenby the remark that : " Rarely, if ever, have second-line troops sustained unshaken so high a percentage of casualties." The once-despised Territorial had quickly developed into a first-class fighting man ; the Territorial Army stigmatised by Clemenceau as a " plaything " was considered fit to meet the most highly renowned and most formidably organised army in the world's history. Field-Marshal Lord French says of them in his book " 1914 " : " I say without the slightest hesitation that without the assistance which the Territorials afforded between October, 1914, and June, 1915, it would have been impossible to have held the line in France and Belgium, or to have prevented the enemy from reaching his goal, the Channel seaboard." Naturally implicit faith in their efficiency and stability was not accorded the earliest arrivals at the front, and their first experiences in action were gained by one company at a time in a regular regiment of the brigade to which they were attached ; later on the battalion took over a position as a whole and ultimately they were formed into divisions, London supplying the famed 47th, 56th, 58th and 60th.

High praise, too, was paid to the London Territorials by Field-Marshal Lord Haig at the Guildhall on June 13th, 1919 :

" The names of the London regiments illumine every page of the wonderful story of the great struggle through which we have just passed. Their deeds have won glory for themselves and their City in every theatre of war ; their dead lie on every battlefield. Wherever they have gone they have established the reputation of good soldiers, well conducted when in rest, sound and reliable when in action ; capable of enduring much, quick to learn and of never-failing cheerfulness. I think that everyone who has seen them in the field would tell you that the Londoner makes a first-class soldier. They have done well on all occasions and in all forms of fighting. I think that it is a moot point, and I have heard it disputed with some warmth, whether to a London or a Canadian Division belongs the credit of having taken the most prisoners in a raid during the period of trench warfare. It was a London Territorial Division, the 47th, that ultimately succeeded in clearing the last of the enemy from High Wood, in the days of the first Somme Battle. Few, if any, of the divisions that fought in France have a better record than the 56th Division. In all the fighting south-east of Arras, from the opening of our 1917 offensive, when they stormed Neuville Vitasse, at the northern end of the Hindenburg Line, as it then was, to the final attacks on the Hindenburg Line last year—and not least in their splendid share in defeating the crucial German attacks on March 28th, 1918, the 56th Division maintained and added to the great fighting record of London men. In the heavy fighting north of Zonnebeke, in September and October of 1917, the 58th Division did most gallant service under conditions of the utmost difficulty. In the following spring they greatly added to their reputation, fighting with unsurpassed courage and devotion, first on the right of the Fifth Army (where the most obstinate defence of Tergnier ranks among the most brilliant exploits of the battle), and, later, in the defence of the approaches to Amiens. Here, on August 8th, they took part in the great attack which launched our Armies on the road to final victory. The 60th Division was but a short time under my command, but we all know of its actions in Palestine. Truly may I say, that in choosing to-day to mark the honour you do to Sir David Beatty and myself by presenting us with these beautiful swords you have chosen well; for you have shown in the story of these past five years that in a just cause no man knows better than a Londoner how to use a sword."

The Records of the Queen Victoria's Rifles may possibly be of no historical value to students of the Great War. It was written for those who were in it and have come safely out of it for the fathers and sons of those who sleep in the fields of France and Flanders, and for the many thousands of men who at one time or another have been proud to call themselves " Vics "—not forgetting also those who were formerly as closely associated with the St. George's, Hanover Square, and the St. Giles's and St. George's, Bloomsbury. It was the outcome of a general desire of the rank and file that a Record

INTRODUCTION

of their experiences under stress of war as a unit of the erstwhile "Home Defence Force" should be compiled and preserved for their own enjoyment and for the encouragement of their successors.

In a number of the reviews of Regimental Histories that have been published during the past four years reference has been made to the difficulties that confront the compiler. It is no easy task as is popularly imagined, but on the contrary one of the most difficult and thankless a man can undertake. A call goes out from H.Q. for diaries, letters, reminiscences and accounts of anything that the narrators deem worthy of mention, photographs, papers, orders, programmes, menus, anything and everything; in due time they arrive, a full cartload of them. The whole heterogeneous mass has to be gone through in order that nothing valuable or important may be missed, the scanty fruitful wheat sifted from the plentiful but unproductive chaff. Modern battles are fought over a wide expanse of ground and very often men in the same battalion are furlongs, or may be miles, apart; they view objects from a different standpoint and consequently their stories differ, though all of them are true and trustworthy and must be made to fit in one with another. When all is nearing completion it is found that there are important gaps which should of necessity be filled in, and again the appeal for material goes forth. In some cases the most likely men approached plead forgetfulness, while in others those chiefly concerned are no longer with us, and yet again some writers gifted with a too vivid imagination have pictured scenes and incidents that will not stand the test of verification that is necessary in a Regimental History. In the present work whole chapters have had to be discarded altogether, or largely rewritten. Despite these drawbacks it has been possible to construct a fairly complete narrative from the time of mobilisation, embarkation and arrival at Havre on November 5th, 1914, of the progress through the fields of Flanders and France, the life in the trenches, the march even to the banks of the Rhine, to the return to London.

The regiment is largely indebted to Major R. H. Lindsey-Renton, D.S.O., who has been indefatigable in collecting MSS. from all who had a story to tell and for supplying details of events that came under his personal supervision. This officer has a record that is probably unique in the British Army of the Great War. Holding the rank of second in command of a company when he landed in France he served with the 1st and the amalgamated battalions until after the armistice on November 11th, 1918, as a regimental officer. He suffered neither from wounds nor severe sickness and only took the usual short leave at prolonged intervals. On several occasions he was in command of the battalion. He was mentioned four times in dispatches and was awarded the D.S.O. and the Belgian Croix de Guerre.

Other officers who may be mentioned in this connection and from whose diaries long extracts have been made are Major S. J. M. Sampson, M.C., the narrative being broken just after the fighting at Hill 60 where he was wounded, and resumed from January, to July, 1916, when he was again invalided ; Col. V. W. F. Dickins, D.S.O., V.D., who succeeded Lieut.-Col. Shipley, C.M.G., T.D., in the command of the 1st Battalion, and kept a daily record of events which has been largely drawn upon especially during the time of " The Great Push " on the Somme, commenced on July 1st, 1916 ; also of Lieut.-Col. P. E. Langworthy Parry, D.S.O., O.B.E., T.D., who succeeded to the Command of the 2nd Battalion on the death of Lieut.-Col. A. R. Berry, T.D., in March, 1917. Officer, Warrant Officer, Non-Commissioned Officer and Rifleman have all contributed to the making of the Records of the Q.V.R.'s as set forth in the following pages ; those who kept a diary have had it freely drawn upon ; those who have had a tale to tell have told it themselves in their own words, whilst those whose gifts of description and letter writing have rendered that not possible have also been made use of. Among the humblest—and the noblest—was poor Rifleman Snoswell who hated war with his whole heart but was determeind to do his duty to his country in spite of disabilities which necessitated an operation before he could qualify for foreign service, and died as a stretcher bearer succouring his stricken comrades in the fight at Hangard Wood on April 24th, 1918.

Invaluable, too, have been the letters sent home by the Adjutant of the Q.V.R., Capt. George Culme-Seymour, K.R.R.C., from November 5th, 1914, to May 6th, 1915. In the days of peace he strove hard to perfect the training of the regiment and in so doing he became a general favourite with all ranks. It is not too much to say that the Victoria's owe to Culme-Seymour and his predecessors from the K.R.R.C., from which celebrated corps their adjutants have come almost "from time immemorial," that high state of efficiency and discipline which led to their being among the first of the battalions selected for foreign service. Ever cheerful himself, Culme-Seymour—or George as he was usually called in the Mess—was always endeavouring to instil cheeriness into others, and, as his letters show, he always had a good word to say for everybody. His death on the night of May 6th/7th, 1915, was deeply deplored by all who knew him.

The arrangement and selection of the maps are entirely due to Col. V. W. F. Dickins and Major R. H. Lindsey-Renton.

In going through the mass of manuscripts nothing has struck the Editor more than the fact that with very few exceptions the writers have so little to say about the actual fighting. Day after day they will record the state of the weather, set down religiously what they have had to eat and drink, but for days to come not a single thing worthy of mention in regard to the war. For instance, a sergeant who laboriously kept a diary during the whole time he was out in France records nothing more exciting happening in February, 1915, than the following: "12th. Shopping with Sergt. S. R. in Bailleul. In Hotel Faucon. Had a drink. Names taken by Artillery Major for drinking spirits. 13th. S. R. and I at Orderly Room. Admonished." It was true that the Battalion had just come out of the trenches and things were comparatively quiet but the regimental casualty list just prior to the days quoted shows there really was a war on. Grousers there are in plenty but the British Tommy is a privileged grouser and would not be so continually happy had he nothing to grouse about. No doubt many will remember the C.I.V.'s marching song: "Grousing, Grousing, Grousing." But of real complaint, in the most trying circumstances, "in the wettest winter on record" (1914–1915), the records are singularly devoid. A note of cheerfulness and of confidence in their cause and in their officers, of loyalty to their companions and of contempt for the methods—not the fighting quality— of the Huns, the Boches, the Gers, or Jerry as they variously term their opponents, are all typical of their London blood and grit. At times they have a whimsical way of showing their sympathy. A young subaltern in a letter home writes : " I mentioned in the hearing of two or three men that I had not received any letters for some time. Two days later I received this little lot (enclosed). All signed by their nicknames. When one does not get a letter the men always send some. I've even known men to write letters to themselves."

The three weeks succeeding the landing in Havre were spent in acquiring battle training behind the lines and on November 29th the Q.V.R.'s had their first turn in the trenches, " A " and " B " Companies relieving similar units of the Royal West Kents and King's Own Yorkshire Light Infantry in the Wulverghem sector. It was not, however, until December 3rd/4th that the first recorded casualty occurred, when Rfn. Avila (2181) was killed in action. Their first big fight as a battalion was at Hill 60 on April 21st/22nd, when they lost 3 officers killed, 2 wounded and 15 R. and F. killed and 107 wounded. For conspicuous gallantry during this fighting 2nd Lieut. G. Harold Woolley won the first Victoria Cross awarded to a member of the Territorial Force. There quickly followed the 2nd battle of Ypres and from that time until Armistice Day the Q.V.R.'s took part in nearly all the chief engagements of the war, the battles of Messines and Loos excepted ; in the latter case they stood by for a special purpose which, however, never materialised. In the " Great Push " on July 1, 1916, they were told off with the 56th (London Territorial) Division to attack Gommecourt, and like the other battalions of the 169th Brigade, the Queen's Westminsters, the London Rifle Brigade and the 2nd Londons, lost heavily, as also did the sister brigades of the division, the 167th and 168th. The Victoria's casualty list as at first compiled ran :—

	Officers.	Other Ranks.
Killed	6	51
Wounded	5	290
Missing	5	188
	16	529

Unfortunately but very few of the missing ever came back.

INTRODUCTION

In the "great crisis at Arras" as Hindenburg calls it in April, 1917, in the battle of Cambrai in the following November, and in the great German offensive begun on March 21st, 1918, the Q.V.R.'s worthily played their part, in the last-named remaining at the Buttes de Rouy area from March 18th to the night of March 29th/30th, when they were relieved by the 10th London and moved back to an intermediate line along the banks of the Oise and through Biehancourt. On April 2nd this position was taken over by the 353rd French Regiment. At one time the Q.V.R.'s were practically isolated from the rest of the British Army. On August 8th they advanced with the whole Allied Armies and followed the retreating Germans until the latter, outmanœuvred and outfought, accepted the terms of the Armistice for which they had asked, and almost as suddenly as the war-cloud arose and burst in August, 1914, so did it come to an end at 11 a.m. on Monday the 11th day of November, 1918.

Of the 10,000 of all ranks who passed through the Q.V.R.'s 76 Officers and 1,385 Other Ranks are numbered among the dead. Seven hundred and thirty-seven were given commissions from the ranks—77 in their own regiment and 660 in other battalions. Of these latter the deaths of 91 have been traced in the Official List, making the total death roll 1,552. One hundred and thirty-four Officers and 230 Other Ranks were mentioned in dispatches or were awarded decorations of various kinds including the Victoria Cross of Captain G. H. Woolley.

The fortunes of the Q.V.R.'s in all these events have been duly chronicled in the following pages in order of date except as regards the 2nd Battalion, which arrived in France on February 4th, 1917. Accordingly its history up to Christmas of that year is told separately. Early in 1918 the 1st and 2nd Battalions were amalgamated and the tale proceeds. A short chapter is likewise devoted to the doings of the 3rd Battalion, which, after a career of about two years, became the 9th Reserve Battalion of the London Regiment, composed of the 9th, 11th and 12th Battalions.

The Regimental Committee, under whose auspices the History and Records are published, considered, in view of the fact that the 9th London Regiment is composed of the

Victoria, the St. George's and the Bloomsbury Rifles, each having a history and reputation of long standing of its own it would be desirable to include in the volume the principal incidents in their formation and career so that past, present and future members of the amalgamated battalion, and those interested in the history of the Auxiliary Forces might have them in a handy form. The Editor has attempted to carry out their wishes. Three generations of his family[1] have served in the Victorias, and it was with the fervent hope that in some shape or form it may benefit the dear old regiment he undertook the task of presenting its records to the public.

The thought that lingers in the mind of the Editor after the final revision of these records is aptly expressed by Field Marshal the Earl of Ypres in his book " 1914 " : "*I wonder sometimes if the eyes of the Country will be opened to what these Territorial soldiers of ours have done.*"

[1] The third, who was enrolled while still at school in December, 1914 served until the end of the war, finishing his duties as a Staff Captain with the Army of the Rhine. The Editor is proud to feel that his son's service in the war were considered sufficiently meritorious to justify the award of the M.C. for specific conduct in the attack on Hangard Wood on the night of April 24–25, 1918.

CONTENTS

PART I
THE FIRST BATTALION

CHAPTER		PAGE
I.	PREPARATION AND EMBARKATION	1
II.	THE FIRST DAYS IN FRANCE	13
III.	THE KING'S VISIT TO HIS ARMY	20
IV.	TRENCH LIFE IN THE FIRST WINTER	27
V.	1915—A BAD BEGINNING	31
VI.	CAMPAIGN LIFE IN FRANCE	38
VII.	THE SPRING OF 1915	44
VIII.	THE YPRES SALIENT	52
IX.	HILL 60	66
X.	"THEY HELD THE HILL"	74
XI.	THE SECOND BATTLE OF YPRES	81
XII.	THE YPRES STRUGGLE CONTINUED	91
XIII.	REST AND REORGANIZATION AFTER YPRES	102
XIV.	A CHANGE OF QUARTERS	112
XV.	FROM SEPTEMBER TO CLOSE OF 1915	119
XVI.	JANUARY, 1916	126
XVII.	A CHANGE OF DIVISIONS	130
XVIII.	PREPARATIONS FOR "THE GREAT PUSH"	138
XIX.	"THE GREAT PUSH"	146
XX.	THE BATTLE OF GOMMECOURT	160
XXI.	THE BATTLES OF THE SOMME	177
XXII.	A TALE OF THE TANKS	190
XXIII.	LES BŒUFS AND NEUVE CHAPELLE	193
XXIV.	NEUVE CHAPELLE AND THE MAUQUISSART CRATER	204
XXV.	1917—THE LAVENTIE POSTS	210
XXVI.	THE BRITISH ATTACK AT ARRAS	220

CHAPTER		PAGE
XXVII.	IN THE COJEUL VALLEY	231
XXVIII.	"THE GREAT CRISIS AT ARRAS"	238
XXIX.	THE THIRD BATTLE OF YPRES	248
XXX.	THE RAID AT DEMICOURT	257
XXXI.	BATTLE OF CAMBRAI	262

PART II
THE SECOND BATTALION

I.	IN THE MAKING	277
II.	FIRST EXPERIENCE OF THE REAL THING	284
III.	OCCUPYING THE OLD GERMAN LINE	291
IV.	BULLECOURT	297
V.	THE RAID ON MOW CAP	305
VI.	LIFE IN THE SALIENT	316
VII.	THIRD BATTLE OF YPRES	320
VIII.	THIRD BATTLE OF YPRES	335
IX.	THE CLOSE OF 1917	354

PART III
THE AMALGAMATION OF THE FIRST AND SECOND BATTALIONS

I.	THE AMALGAMATION OF THE 1ST AND 2ND BATTALIONS	365
II.	PREPARING FOR THE GREAT ATTACK	373
III.	THE GREAT GERMAN OFFENSIVE	380
IV.	"WITH OUR BACKS TO THE WALL"	393
V.	THE FIGHT IN THE WOOD	403
VI.	OFFICIAL DESPATCHES AND COMPLIMENTS	409
VII.	A LULL IN THE FIGHTING	417
VIII.	COMMENCEMENT OF THE ALLIED OFFENSIVE	421
IX.	THE HAPPY VALLEY	426
X.	EPEHY AND KILDARE POST	434
XI.	OPEN WARFARE AT LAST	445
XII.	TRIUMPHANT PROGRESS—ARMISTICE DAY	451
XIII.	TRANSPORT DIFFICULTIES	456
XIV.	CONCERT PARTIES	462
XV.	WITH THE ARMY OF THE RHINE	470

CONTENTS

PART IV
THE THIRD BATTALION

The Third Battalion	479

PART V
APPENDICES

APPENDIX I—
1. The First Volunteer Rifle Corps 491
2. The Royal Victoria Rifle Company . . . 504
3. Early Efforts to Obtain Recognition . . . 508
4. The Victoria Rifles 519
5. The St. George's Hanover Square Volunteers . 527
6. The St. George's Rifles (6th Middlesex R.V.C.) . 533
7. The Victoria and St. George's Rifles . . . 536
8. The St. Giles's and St. George's (Bloomsbury) Rifles 560
9. Territorials 571
   Queen Victoria's Rifles' Roll of Honour . . 576

APPENDIX II—
Decorations and Awards gained by 9th Battalion London Regiment (Queen Victoria's Rifles) 645

INDEX 655

ILLUSTRATIONS

LIST OF PLATES

PLATE		
I.	MONUMENT ERECTED ON HILL 60	*Frontispiece*
II.	REGIMENTAL BADGE	*To follow Title Page*
		To face page
III.	LIEUT.-COL. REGINALD BURGE SHIPLEY, C.M.G., T.D.	13
IV.	CAPTAIN G. HAROLD WOOLLEY, V.C., M.C.	70
V.	MAJOR THOMAS PRIOR LEES	74
VI.	CAPTAIN GEORGE CULME-SEYMOUR	98
VII.	{ LIEUT.-COL. T. O'SHEA, D.S.O. CAPTAIN F. W. ROE, D.S.O. (R.A.M.C.) }	142
VIII.	COL. VERNON W. F. DICKINS, D.S.O., V.D.	206
IX.	LIEUT.-COL. A. R. BERRY, T.D.	293
X.	THE BIG CRATER AT ACHIET (Q.V.R. BOXING)	296
XI.	LIEUT.-COL. P. E. LANGWORTHY PARRY, D.S.O., O.B.E. T.D.	358
XII.	MAJOR R. H. LINDSEY-RENTON, D.S.O.	384
XIII.	H.R.H. ERNEST AUGUSTUS, DUKE OF CUMBERLAND	492
XIV.	LIEUT. RANDOM DE BERENGER, ADJUTANT, DUKE OF CUMBERLAND'S SHARPSHOOTERS	498
XV.	SHOOTING MATCH (DUKE OF CUMBERLAND'S S.S. *v.* NOTTINGHAM RIFLEMEN)	500
XVI.	FLAG OF THE ROYAL VICTORIA RIFLE CLUB	508
XVII.	ST. GEORGE'S (HANOVER SQUARE) VOLUNTEERS, 1792	528
XVIII.	SPECIAL ORDER ISSUED TO ST. GEORGE'S VOLUNTEERS 4TH JUNE, 1799	530
XIX.	C.I.V. INFANTRY DETACHMENT OF THE FIRST MIDDLESEX (VICTORIA AND ST. GEORGE'S RIFLES)	544
XX.	IMPERIAL REPRESENTATIVE CORPS VICTORIA AND ST. GEORGE'S R.V.C.	550
XXI.	MEMORIAL TO THE FALLEN IN DRILL HALL	576

LIST OF MAPS

MAP		To face page
I.	HILL 60. (April 20–21, 1915)	72
II.	SECOND BATTLE OF YPRES. (April 24–25, 1915)	100
III.	CARNOY TRENCHES. (August, 1915, to January, 1916)	124
IV.	GOMMECOURT. (July 1, 1916)	176
V.	FIRST BATTLE OF THE SOMME. (Sept. 7–26, 1916)	188
VI.	FIRST BATTLE OF THE SOMME. (Sept. 30 to Oct. 19, 1916)	202
VII.	LAVENTIE. (January, 1917)	218
VIII.	BATTLE OF ARRAS. (April 10, 1917)	230
IX.	BATTLE OF ARRAS. (April 14, 1917)	246
X.	THIRD BATTLE OF YPRES. (August 16, 1917)	256
XI.	BATTLE OF CAMBRAI. (November 20–30, 1917)	272
XII.	BULLECOURT. (May, 1917)	304
XIII.	MOW COP RAID. (July 22, 1917)	314
XIV.	SPRINGFIELD-WINNIPEG OPERATIONS. (Sept. 8–9, 1917)	334
XV.	THE FIGHT FOR PASCHENDAELE. (Sept. 26–27, 1917)	352
XVI.	HANGARD WOOD. (April 24–25, 1918)	408
XVII.	TAILES WOOD. (August 10, 1918)	424
XVIII.	HAPPY VALLEY. (August 24–25, 1918)	432
XIX.	ST. EMILIE AND EPEHY. (Sept. 7–8, 1918)	438
XX.	KILDARE POST. (Sept. 22–23, 1918)	444

The Maps in this volume are taken from the Official War Office Maps and are reproduced by permission of the Controller of His Majesty's Stationery Office.

PART I
THE FIRST BATTALION

THE HISTORY AND RECORDS OF QUEEN VICTORIA'S RIFLES

PART I

CHAPTER I

PREPARATION AND EMBARKATION

SUDDENLY as the war-cloud burst upon the general public in the closing days of July, 1914, in even more unsuspected and dramatic fashion did the idea that they might be called upon for imminent active service dawn upon the officers and men of the Queen Victoria's Rifles. In accordance with the Territorial Force Regulations full preparations had been made for the Annual Camp Training, commencing with the August Bank Holiday, that being the most suitable date for London men to get away. In order that there should be no interference with the convenience of the holiday-making public, entraining had been arranged for Sunday, August 2nd, and an advance party consisting of Lieut.-Col. R. B. Shipley, T.D., Major V. W. F. Dickins, V.D., Lieut. Lindsey-Renton, and Major T. O'Shea (Quartermaster), and others had already proceeded to Lulworth and were awaiting the arrival of the Battalion when the following telegram was received from the G.O.C., 1st London Division:

"All units return London as soon as railway can take them, leaving rear parties to hand in equipment as directed by telephone. Communicate with railway. Men to disperse to homes on arrival."

On receipt of the message Col. Shipley and Major Dickins immediately quitted the camp and motored over to Wool Station, where on arrival they found that the 12th Battalion

London Regiment had detrained and were resting in an adjoining field awaiting further orders. Another train arrived with the 11th Battalion and was sent back at once, Col. Shipley going with it. Instructions were given to Major Dickins to return and clear camp at once, and to proceed as soon as possible to London with as many of the advance party as could be spared. While waiting on the platform at Wool Station a second wire was received through the station master stating that the train with the Q.V.R. aboard had got as far as Wimborne and had been sent back to London. What the speculations of the men were it is impossible to conjecture, but no doubt the grave rumours flying about for the three or four days previous gave them some inkling of the truth. Lieut. Lindsey-Renton remained behind at Lulworth with a small rear party to clear camp, and received a telegram saying:

"Inform all officers or N.C.O.'s in charge of rear parties that they are to strike camp and prepare carriers' notes for camp equipment and forward same to Portsmouth. The officer in command sub-district, Weymouth, will arrange hired transport to collect camp equipment as soon as possible. They are responsible for same until it is collected and put on rail."

Major Dickins, the Q.M., and a few others returned to London on the Monday but the remainder of the rear party did not get away until the following Thursday.

Upon reaching town on the Sunday evening the Battalion marched to H.Q., Davies Street, where the men were dismissed and told to parade next morning, when following a long route march to Ealing and back they were again allowed to go to their homes.

On Tuesday, August 4th, at 5.45 p.m., Orders for Mobilisation were issued and the following notice was sent to every man on the Roll of the Regiment:

Army Form 635.

TERRITORIAL FORCE EMBODIMENT. NOTICE TO JOIN.

No......
    Rank and Name.
        9th London Regiment.

Whereas the Army Council, in pursuance of His Majesty's Proclamation, have directed that the 9th County of London Regiment, Queen Victoria's Rifles be embodied on the 5th day of August.

You are hereby requested to attend at 56 Davies Street not later than 6 a.m. o'clock that day. Should you not present yourself as ordered you will be liable to be proceeded against.

(Signed) G. CULME-SEYMOUR,
Adjutant, 9th London Regt.

Date *August*, 1914.

Within three days every man on the Roll of the Regiment had reported himself with the exception of one who was away on his summer holiday in Norway and could not get back. He sent a cable to that effect and managed with great difficulty and much inconvenience to report himself within the week.

On the following morning, August 5th, the following Proclamation was to be found posted on every available space in London :

Army Form E. 634.
(Royal Arms.)

[Form to be used when the Territorial Force is Embodied.]

TERRITORIAL FORCE.

HIS MAJESTY THE KING having been graciously pleased to order by Proclamation that directions be given by the Army Council for Embodying the Territorial Force, all men belonging to the said Force are required to report themselves immediately at their head-quarters.

Printed for His Majesty's Stationery Office, by Hazell, Watson and Viney, Ltd., 52 Long Acre, London, W.C.

100,000   2—09   Forms

$$\frac{\text{E. 634}}{3}$$

6   14   56.

For a fortnight the battalion assembled daily at Davies Street, where kits were got together and equipment served out ;

drilling in the parks being varied by route marching to Richmond and other parts of suburban London. On August 21st it set out for Bullswater, in the Aldershot Command District, where it arrived on the 24th, halts having been made at Richmond and Englefield Green. At Bullswater more intensive and extensive training was the order of the day, everyone from the C.O. downward doing their utmost to get fit. A second fortnight was passed in this way at Bullswater until September 8th, when another move was made. That night the men were billeted at Bramley, on the 9th at Horsham and on the 10th/11th at Hayswards Heath. St. John's Hill Camp, at Crowborough, was reached on the 12th and here a stay was made until October 18th.

Concerning life here Major Dickins writing on September 9th says: "This is a lovely spot, very high up, and plenty of very fresh air, too much sometimes; the sun is hot during the day, but it is very cold at night. We do not know how long we shall be here; we are kept hard at work; up at 5.30; physical drill 6.30 to 7.30; then breakfast; C.O.'s Parade at 8.30 to 3.0; then dinner; Orderly Room at 4.0; Inspection of feet at 4.30; and 5.0 p.m. Inspection of Rifles, etc.; then tea. In addition to the above on Tuesdays and Thursdays night marching for about $3\frac{1}{2}$ hours, so we have a fair day's work and not much spare time."

Writing from Winchester on October 20th, Col. Shipley says: "Things have hummed along. Vernon (Dickins) is at Crowborough as Camp Commandant with machine-guns, transport and a few details. I brought the regiment round here on Sunday morning, leaving Crowborough 2.15 and reached here 8.15, dropping companies en route. We guard the line from Farnborough through here to just short of Eastleigh, and from Basingstoke, G.W.R., to Reading. It's a damned nuisance and infernal shame as the whole brigade was shaping well and we had just started battalion training, but now all training is knocked on the head and I have only just enough men to guard the line until I get 100 recruits back from musketry on Saturday. We took over from the Liverpool Irish Rifles. . . . Fleming is at Hook; Shea, Basingstoke; Sampson, Mortimer, G.W.R.; and Lees here."

The order to take over the duties of guarding the railways caused great disappointment throughout the battalion. Having volunteered for foreign service everyone was in hard training for the purpose, but they then feared that this would mean that they would not be sent abroad. This spirit is exemplified in a song much in vogue about that time as a Regimental Marching Song. In 1916 it was published in *Tommy's Tunes* (No. 56).

ONWARD, QUEEN VICTORIAS.

(*Tune :* Onward, Christian Soldiers.)

Onward, Queen Victorias,
   Guarding the Railway Line.
Is this foreign service ?
   Ain't it jolly fine ?
No, we're not downhearted,
   Won't the Huns be sick ?
When they meet us over there,
   All looking span and spick.
Hope on, Queen Victorias.
   Don't forget the fray.
We shall do our duty
   For a bob a day.

At last the welcome news arrived that the battalion was to proceed overseas. It was conveyed to the Officer Commanding, Lieut.-Col. R. B. Shipley, in the following documents :

[Copy.]

Secret.　　　　　　　　　　WAR OFFICE,
　　　　　　　　　　　　　　LONDON, S.W.,
121/348. (M.T.1.)　　　　　　*27th October,* 1914.

SIR,

 1. I am directed to inform you that the 9th (County of London) Battalion, the London Regiment (Queen Victoria's Rifles), has been selected for service on the Continent, and the necessary steps to prepare this unit for service oversea should be completed by 12 noon, Saturday next the 31st instant.

 2. This battalion will be concentrated forthwith and will be replaced on the Farnboro'-Eastleigh Section of the railway by the battalion of the 3rd London Infantry Brigade, now employed in guarding the line from Bulford and Andover to Southampton. This latter battalion must, however, arrange

to guard the portion between Southampton Docks and Eastleigh, as well as the section from Farnboro' to Eastleigh.

3. Subject to the concurrence of the General Officer Commanding-in-Chief, Southern Command, the 9th Battalion London Regiment may be concentrated at the Southampton Rest Camp. The place of concentration which is decided upon should be notified as early as possible to the War Office (Telegraphic Address—Dirmobize).

4. A copy of detailed instructions regarding mobilisation is attached, and all communications regarding it should be addressed to "Dirmobize."

5. A copy of this letter is being sent to the General Officer Commanding-in-Chief, Central Force, and the General Officer, Commanding London District.

I am, Sir,
Your obedient servant,
(Sgd.) N. P. BOOTH, Capt.,
For Director of Military Training.

[Copy.]

M.T.1. On 121/348.

The 9th (County of London) Battalion, the London Regiment (Queen Victoria's Rifles), has been selected for service on the Continent. It is to be held in readiness to proceed abroad at short notice. The necessary steps to prepare the unit for service overseas should be completed by 12 noon, Saturday next, the 31st instant.

The unit will proceed oversea at the establishment laid down in War Establishments, Part II.

All personnel proceeding with it must be medically fit for service, fully trained and 19 years of age or over. No personnel who do not fulfil these conditions are to proceed with the unit.

Will you please obtain a report by telegraph as to the number of officers and other ranks in this unit fulfilling the conditions stated above.

Arrangements are being made for the rearming of this unit with rifles sighted for Mark VII ammunition, and for the conversion of its machine-guns to enable them to fire the same ammunition. The necessary Mark VII rifles and ammunition will be sent direct to the unit. Any rifles sighted for Mark VII ammunition issued to the unit, in excess of the numbers of non-commissioned officers and men proceeding abroad, are to be returned to the Chief Ordnance Officer, Weedon, immediately, and are on no account to be transferred to the Reserve Unit. Similarly any excess of Mark VII ammunition should be returned to the Army Ordnance Department.

The clothing and equipment of this unit should be inspected immediately and the necessary replacements be effected without delay. Please inform us at once whether this battalion is in possession of complete web equipment, including packs; in the event of any deficiency the pattern of equipment in possession of the unit should be stated. In the event of any difficulty being experienced the fact should be reported to Dirmobize by telegram.

All 1st Line and Train Transport, vehicles, horses and personnel, of this unit is to be sent to DEPTFORD on Thursday next, 29th instant. They should report to the Officer Commanding the Horse Transport Reserve Depot, Foreign Cattle Market, Deptford. The Officer Commanding the Depot should be informed by wire of the probable hour of arrival and strength of the party proceeding.

At Deptford the transport will be inspected and the necessary replacements carried out and deficiencies made good. The transport will remain at Deptford pending the issue of further orders as to embarkation, and, in the event of the battalion proceeding abroad shortly, the transport will rejoin the unit at the port of embarkation.

(Sgd.) J. B. Wells, Captain,
M. 27/10/14. Staff Captain.

On October 30th the Battalion H.Q., which had remained at Winchester and all except a few details stationed at Crowborough, proceeded by train, picking up the detachments at various stations along the line, arriving at Southampton about noon. Here they were directed to go to "The Rest Camp." "The most unrestful camp I was ever in," says Col. Shipley. The weather was deplorable and the ground literally a quagmire. Here the battalion stayed until November 4th, during which time numerous outfitting and equipping duties had to be carried out. The men were supplied with the old long Lee Enfield rifle specially strengthened to take the Mark VII bullet. The latest pattern Army rifle taking the sharp nosed bullet was not issued until nearly a year later, by which time all who could had provided themselves with one culled from the battle field. It was a far more useful and handy weapon for trench warfare purposes.

There was much changing of equipment, water bottles, etc. which gave the Q.M. Stores the time of their lives, writes one of its staff. "The officers were issued a new equipment made of webbing, and many belts passed from hand to hand on account of differences in waist measurement. In one particular instance it meant the use of two sets made into one with the help of a sadler belonging to the A.S.C. Twenty-four hours' leave was granted to the whole battalion to enable the men to say good-bye to their friends and relatives, one half leaving at a time. When the day of departure, November 4th arrived there ensued a scene to be long remembered by those who took part in it. The battalion paraded and was marched through the town on the main thoroughfare to the Dock Gate the populace gave the boys a hearty send-off and remarks of 'splendid,' 'the finest we have seen,' etc., were freely heard They were indeed a body to be proud of, and officers and men alike were proud of themselves and of one another. Upon entering the gates the s.s. *Oxonian* was seen in the gathering darkness, and the men were marched straight aboard and led to their allotted quarters by their respective Company Q.M.S.'s. The vessel bore the appearance of a whitewashed maze, but investigation showed that it had been used for cattle or horse transport and the boxes had not been dismantled or altered for the transport of troops. The men, however were glad of the opportunity to drop their packs. Some little coaxing and persuasion were necessary to get the horses aboard but the task was completed in good time." During this proceeding the regiment was pleased to greet an old friend in the person of "W. W." (Major A. Wynn), formerly Q.M. and Secretary of the regiment, but for the past three months M.L.O. at Southampton. The Major wished one and all "Good Luck and a Safe Return." "The spirit and bearing of the men," writes Platoon Sergt. W. W. Crossthwaite, "were superb, and when the Colonel read out various messages from friends left behind, and particularly when he shouted, 'Keep your tails up, Boys,' there was a roar of cheering that warmed the hearts of us all. And what a battalion it was Nearly 1100 of as good sportsmen and adventurers as ever crossed the seas."

The men soon settled down to their strange surroundings, each hunting for a comfortable bunk for the night, and thankful for a few hours' rest and respite from the mud to which they had so long been accustomed. The *Oxonian* slipped away as soon as darkness fell, strict instructions having been given that no light was to be shown. The night was quiet but cold, and little inconvenience was experienced by anyone. No lifebelts were issued or directions given in case of danger or disaster, and some of those on board wondered what facilities were available for use in case of sudden emergency; a few boats there were, but these, it was stated, were for the crew, —if necessary the troops must swim. Everything, however, turned out well, the passage was calm and uneventful, though the men felt thankful when Havre was sighted about 6 a.m. on November 5th. Landing began about nine o'clock and continued without a hitch until the last wagon and the last horse were safely ashore. The battalion quickly moved off to No. 1 Rest Camp on the high ground two or three miles from the quay. After an inspection and re-fit parade and a general smartening up the men were dismissed to their allotted lines and tents. Most of them quickly made their way back to town for a general look round and to make the acquaintance of the French estaminet.

Next morning the battalion was again on the move, this time to the railway station, where it entrained at 4 p.m., the intervening time being occupied in collecting transport and putting it on the train. As they marched out of the camp the L.R.B.'s marched in.

The rank and file journeyed in cattle trucks, 40 to 50 in each; the officers six in a carriage, "not exactly comfortable," says one of them. The men started "Baa-ing and Moo-ing," and on some biscuits being served out they imitated the barking of dogs, taking all things as they came with their usual cheeriness. The journey lasted all night and 26 hours altogether, a halt being made for three-quarters of an hour at Abbeville for breakfast at eight o'clock. Company cooks were paraded and rations served out on the platform, the great difficulty being the deficiency of water, but at length a supply was obtained from an engine standing by—not too clean, but serviceable enough. Fires were kindled from broken bully beef boxes and soon all were on better terms with themselves. On the journey being resumed occasional halts were made, the inhabitants at such times being very persistent in their appeals for "souvenirs" and "biskeets." At the same time they most hospitably proffered hot coffee and vegetable soup or cigarettes. St. Omer was reached just before 5 and there the regiment detrained, the men feeling very thankful for an opportunity to stretch their limbs.

In the H.Q. carriage were the C.O., Col. Shipley, Major Dickins, the 2nd in Command, generally referred to as Vernon or Dickie, the Adjutant, Captain Culme-Seymour, equally familiarly addressed as "George," the Q.M., known universally as "Tim," the M.O., Captain Roe, R.A.M.C. ("Doc."), and Lieut. Cawston. Much speculation went on as to where their destination was likely to be, the "Movement Order," which was carefully handed to the C.O. at Havre Station by the R.T.O and "to be kept very secret," had the place of detraining written in cypher, unknown to all, and a couple of maps of the district which were produced were carefully scrutinised to locate the spot. Eventually the quest had to be given up and the party resigned themselves to their fate.

The battalion fell in by companies in the station yard while the train was shunted into a siding. Some time was spent in collecting the kit and baggage, and that at length being accomplished the order was given to march off in silence—a silence that all speedily found both oppressive and unnecessary. But they were new to the game at that time.

A word or two concerning the Transport Section. From the time the order was given to leave Crowborough on October 27th, "Dick" Shepherd, the T.O., had a very worrying, not to say rotten, time in endless inspections of the first line transport. At Crowborough most of the wagons and harness was condemned, also some of the horses had to be exchanged, and orders were given that all the first line and train transport vehicles, horses and personnel, were to be sent to Deptford on October 29th and report to the O.C. Horse Transport Reserve Depot, Foreign Cattle Market, Deptford. This was done and a further inspection took place, when most of the horses and material were replaced and deficiencies made good. Precisely the same thing happened at Havre. Fortunately the train here was two hours late in arriving, which fact enabled Lieut. Shepherd to get his men, horses and wagons assembled in due time. Then it was found that only thirteen trucks had been provided to take twenty-two wagons, and it was only after the use of much strong language and taking some of the wagons to pieces that the job was accomplished. Even then one wagon had to be left behind. This incident caused a vast amount of astonishment among the French railway officials, as they had declared it to be an "impossibilité," and they were obviously impressed by the T.O.'s determination not to be beaten.

The constitution of the battalion at this time was as follows :

Lieut. Col. R. B. Shipley, T.D. In Command.
Major V. W. F. Dickins, V.D. Second in Command.
Capt. G. Culme-Seymour (K.R.R.). Adjutant.
Major T. O'Shea. Quartermaster.
Capt. F. W. Roe (R.A.M.C). Medical Officer.
Lieut. F. B. A. Fargus. Machine-gun Officer.
2nd Lieut. H. Shepherd. Transport Officer.

"A" Company

Major T. P. Lees.
Capt. R. G. Warren.
2nd Lieut. G. Fazakerley-Westby.
2nd Lieut. J. Nichols.
2nd Lieut. K. W. Johnson.
2nd Lieut. J. B. Hunter.

"B" Company

Capt. S. V. Shea.
Capt. R. W. Cox.
Lieut. J. C. Andrews.
Lieut. E. W. Hamilton.
2nd Lieut. G. H. Woolley.
2nd Lieut. P. S. Houghton.

"C" Company
Captain H. Flemming.
Capt. H. E. L. Cox.
2nd Lieut. E. P. Cawston.
2nd Lieut. W. H. Carter.
2nd Lieut. R. B. Murray.

"D" Company
Capt. S. J. M. Sampson.
Capt. R. H. Lindsey-Renton.
Capt. D. W. Bolton.
2nd Lieut. A. L. Cowtan.
2nd Lieut. C. F. Griffith.
2nd Lieut. D. L. Summerhays.

O.C. Depot
Capt. J. E. A. Hunter.

Upon arrival at the Front the battalion was posted to the 13th Infantry Brigade, 5th Division; Commander, Major-Gen. Sir Charles Fergusson.

13th Brigade.

2nd King's Own Scottish Borderers.
2nd Duke of Wellington's West Riding Regiment.
1st Queen's Own Royal West Kent.
2nd King's Own Yorkshire Light Infantry.
1st Queen Victoria's Rifles.

LT.-COL. REGINALD BURGE SHIPLEY, C.M.G., T.D.

CHAPTER II

The First Days in France

THE Q.M., the R.Q.M.S., together with the interpreter proceeded in advance to the village of Arques, some four miles distant. The battalion following later found billets had been secured in the neighbourhood of the Town Hall in various distilleries and factories. On the 8th the battalion rested, no parade being held. On the following morning training was resumed in real earnest, lasting from 8 a.m. to 5.30 p.m. and largely consisting of digging, varied by marching and attack practice. Rations were drawn from St. Omer by regimental transport each morning. This routine lasted for several days, one day being much like another; the weather was cold and wet and the men frequently got soaked. Target practice took place almost daily. On November 14th, Lieut. Fargus had a narrow escape, a bullet from his revolver passing through the upper of his boot and lodging in the sole. He was considered lucky to have got off so lightly, the actual result being merely a bad bruise.

On November 14th, Field-Marshal Lord Roberts died in St. Omer and a Memorial Service was held there on the 17th, on which occasion the Queen Victoria's Rifles' buglers were detailed to sound the "Last Post," while a party consisting of Lieut. J. C. Andrews and 20 men, wearing the South African riband, marched in the procession. The remainder of the regiment lined the streets along the route.

Rumours of the regiment being ordered to the front spread daily, but still the training went on. As Captain Culme-Seymour wrote: "We are doing a lot of good and they are learning a lot. They need it." In due time the order to leave came and the battalion marched off at 10.45 a.m. on November 19th for Hazebrouck, a march of 11 miles, with snow falling all the time. Billeting there for the night a further trek was made next day to Bailleul, a distance of 10 or 11 miles. As the Q.V.R.'s were marching out of Hazebrouck a German Taube flew over and dropped three bombs on the town, killing a civilian. Bailleul was reached about 1.45 p.m. On the 21st the Taube appeared again and dropped a bomb close to the Q.V.R. billets, damaging the hospital and killing three wounded patients. A week was spent in Bailleul, the work done being chiefly route marching. On their first night there the men were quartered in a school, but a couple of days later their billet was changed to the " Graperies du Nord " in enormous glass houses with straw and hot-water pipes, which the men found very comforting. The grapes, however, had all gone !

On November 27th the battalion left Bailleul and marched to Neuve Eglise, being inspected on the road by Gen. Sir H. Smith-Dorrien, who in a speech to the men spoke very well of them and dwelt upon what would be expected of them. Two days later the Q.V.R.'s had their real baptism of fire, Major Lees (" A ") and Capt. Shea (" B ") taking their companies for their first turn in the trenches. Leaving Neuve Eglise about 4 p.m. they proceeded to Wulverghem, once a biggish village but then a mere mass of ruins. Here guides from the Royal West Kents and the K.O.Y.L.I.'s joined them to lead the way to their posts, " A " replacing the first-named and " B " the K.O.Y.L.I.'s. Their experiences are thus vividly described by the Adjutant, Capt. Culme-Seymour :

" The route for " A," old Lees, was quite easy and so I went with " B " and Stephen Shea. We were met by an officer in the village, which is not a village, but a mass of ruins, and he led us first to the Battalion Head-quarters, where the whole battalion will be in about six days' time. There were a few shells going over and a good many snipers at work, but beyond accustoming the men to the sound, etc., nothing happened. We had to walk through most awful mud, right up to our knees in places, and through a stream, though very small yet very wet. It was a bright night, moonlight, but with clouds every now and then, and we went along very slowly and quietly, the men doing very well and making no noise. When we got to the Battalion Head-quarters we halted, and Shea and I and others went in and discussed how the relief was to be carried out. There were front line trenches, support trenches and reserve trenches; Woodruff Cox and Houghton were put into the reserve trenches, which were behind head-quarters, and I went on with Shea and the remainder to the fire trenches. The support trenches were held by the K.O.Y.L.I., part of whom we were relieving. It took a long time, and at last we got to within 80 to 70 yards of our trenches and then we put them in by platoons at a time. There was a lot of sniping going on, some bullets going pretty close, but the men were quite good and did not bob or duck more than one could expect for the first time. Woolley was quite calm and chaffing with me; Stephen pretty serious. The German trenches were in most places from 300 to 400 yards off, and on the extreme right where Woolley's platoon was put; they were within 120 yards, so it was quite exciting. They all got in all right, and I came back with the lot that had been relieved.

" 'A' got in all right, too, but they had a much simpler job. I went back to the village and walked back here with Tim (Major O'Shea), the 'Bantam' (Capt. Leys Cox) and some others whom I had left at Battalion Head-quarters of the K.O.Y.L.I. We got back here at 9.45 p.m. and altogether I had had quite enough. The Battalion H.Q. of the K.O.Y.L.I. had been shelled like mad the day before and was all in bits, except for the room we talked in, and the other head-quarters, West Kent (who did so well), were in a cellar in the village. Old Dick Shepherd came too and did not care a damn. I was very pleased with the men, though, of course, there was no heavy firing. This evening I have been taking up the two machine-guns with Fargus, to relieve those with the K.O.Y.L.I., with Stephen Shea, but I only went to the dressing station this evening, and take up 'C' and 'D' to-morrow, to relieve 'A' and 'B.' They remain in the trenches for two nights and then have two nights' rest. In about a fortnight we go back beyond Bailleul for a rest. We had quite a lot of shells on the way in yesterday, and a lot of sniping, but this evening there was nothing but snipers, and very few of them. Muggy weather, slushy." Writing on December 1st, Culme-Seymour adds: " The Brigadier came down this morning and was awfully pleased, as he said our fellows were shelled pretty heavily on our right—one officer, I think it must have been Woolley, picked up a shell which had come into the trench and threw it out—a very plucky thing to do!" Major S. J. M. Sampson, "D" Company, referring to the same incident wrote : "A minenwerfer fell into one of our trenches this morning and was chucked out by one of our subalterns (Woolley) without its exploding."

"A" and "B" Companies remained in the trenches for thirty-six hours, and though they were heavily shelled and sniped there were no casualties. Two German snipers who got within 20 yards of the trench were killed. "Our gunners gave them a very hot time yesterday, Stephen Shea tells me (Culme-Seymour) and did some wonderful shooting. Stephen is doing very well and has got his men well in hand. The Brigade Major has just been down here and said that the Yorkshires with whom 'B' Company was, had given us a splendid chit saying that the way our men stood their baptism of fire was splendid and that it should be brought to the notice of the Divisional and Corps Commanders! Not so bad, is it? I am awfully pleased."

On December 2nd the following telegram was received. Begins, K.O.Y.L.I. wires : "I think the attention of the Divisional and Corps Commanders should be drawn to the steadiness shown by the 9th Rifles yesterday under peculiarly trying conditions for a first experience of the trenches,' aaa. ends : "Divisional Commander has been informed. E. Dutton, Capt., G.S."

The relief is well described by Sergt. Crossthwaite, "C" Company : "In the late afternoon we started for the trenches, most of us armed then with the long rifle and short bayonet, with a heavy pack and certain comforts not detailed in Army Orders ; 150 rounds, and a stout heart, although I think we had the look of men who were about to pierce the fog of war and face the yet unknown horror of it. Our company—Capt. Flemming in command—and a very gallant gentleman he was —got to Wulverghem, as the night, dark and wet, had settled down. It was a village ruined, dead and deserted, and the battered church tower loomed up ghostlike. Passing through we left the road and struggled ankle-deep over beet fields sodden with water, platoon after platoon plodding along in silence. Guides from the trenches met us hereabouts and soon, slopping along like spectres, we wheeled half left and came under long-range rifle and machine-gun fire. This, our first baptism of fire, I shall never forget; the 'ping' of the bullets, seemingly near and just overhead, the mystery of the night, the soft 'slosh' of marching men, the whispered command passed on. The going became worse as we neared the line, the beet fields being here intersected by deep gulleys crossed by narrow planks, slimy with mud, off which many a man slipped to the ditches below. Suddenly there loomed up in the darkness what seemed like a long irregular ditch and here and there a black head bobbed up, and from near the heads flashes from rifles lit out, but all else was silent, dark, and sinister. The column extended along the line of the ditch and waited, and then out crawled objects that looked like men—black, muddy and utterly exhausted. Platoon leaders took over, and our line stumbled through patches of mud and rubbish plump into a foot of black water with a wet wall of sandbags in front. Sentries were posted and the relieved garrison crawled out, slipping away into the gloom like grim shadows. I don't think we were very miserable that first night, the novelty of it all was so obsessing, but the iron entered our souls later, and the time came when we got to know trenches to which these were a home of rest. In this part of the line, beneath the Messines Ridge, there were no shelters, no dug-outs, no trenches even, but merely a shallow ditch with a sandbag rampart in front, held together by rude revetments, black mud below, bullets overhead, the smell of death and the horror of blackness—but we kept our tails up! On the left of our sector was a barn reputed to be occupied at times by a sniper, and right in front, as we observed when dawn broke, was the long skyline of the Messines Ridge topped by the German trenches. Between their line and ours, and distant only about 200 yards, was a gully, evidently the haunt of snipers—indeed these gentry seemed to be everywhere, as bullets would repeatedly enfilade a sector and not infrequently come from the rear.

"To clear up the front a volunteer patrol was sent out under myself for two nights in succession, and, acting on Brigade instructions, we searched the gully. There was a bright moon

c

and we were fired on from some dense bush in front, but we managed to crawl back without a casualty and with information that proved useful to the Brigade Artillery. This was our first adventure over the top and I should like to mention the cheerful bravery of my companions, Lce.-Cpls. W. R. Gittens and L. Jolly. We got some souvenirs from a dead German, who smelt most horribly, but the papers found on him were not of much use."

" C " and " D " Companies had to stay an extra day in the trenches. How they fared let Capt. Sampson of " D " Company tell : " 5th December, 1914. I am back from the trenches and am very well indeed. There was nothing like an action, but there was continued sniping, etc., and we lost one man killed[1] and one wounded, neither of them in my company. The battalion has, I believe, given a very good first impression to everyone. You know that life in the trenches is not pleasant, so I write to you exactly what happens without reserve, as I think you would like me to do so, even if it may be unpleasant reading, but you must remember that it is much worse to read of than to go through, and that I was perfectly happy and content the whole time. We marched off at dusk through the village where we are billeted, and two miles further on reached the next village (Wulverghem). This is in the zone of artillery fire and presented a most melancholy appearance. Every other house is in ruins and there is not a pane of glass in any window, and in the road great holes where shells have burst. It was of course dark and no artillery firing goes on much after dusk. The inhabitants have of course all gone and you can imagine how melancholy was the appearance of this silent, ruined and deserted place. From here we marched some two miles through fields ankle deep in mud, once well-kept farms, now a deserted No Man's Land, with here and there dead cattle and more shell holes. As we get near the trenches bullets buzz by overhead. It is, of course, dark and one cannot tell where they come from. At last we file silently into the trench, passing those whose places we are taking. Imagine a grass field, 120 yards across, with a range of farm buildings on the further side ; under the hedge on one side are our trenches, on the other side, 100 to 150 yards off, the German trenches

[1] (2181) Rfn. Avila.

are clearly visible in the moonlight. Here two armies have collided and dug themselves in six weeks ago. Since then they have carried on a kind of poachers' warfare, stealing up to one anothers' trenches and firing into them. The crack of rifles is almost continuous all night and bullets seem to be all round one's head, but it is quite extraordinary how soon one gets accustomed to it. Personally I never felt the slightest wish to duck my head or lie down, but felt strangely calm. The shots are simply fired on the chance of hitting someone and the chances of your stopping one are very small indeed unless you do certain obviously stupid things, such as showing your head above the top of the trench. I found my trench ankle deep in mud and falling down in parts, and we worked all night trying to improve it, as it had been shelled two days before and more protection from artillery fire was needed. I was either digging or looking through a loophole all night. It was a beautiful night, a clear sky and a full moon, so that it was practically broad daylight and the snipers were very busy. They are brave men and good shots, but it is extremely rare for them to hit anyone, and one has only to be careful. They are difficult to deal with actively though, and one comes to nelgect them unless one of them gives you a good chance, which is seldom. Things are quieter here than they were, and well in hand, and they do not keep the same people in the front trenches long, so as it is now much warmer I do not anticipate any very great hardship. They seem inclined to take us very gradually up to our fences, so to speak, so as to get us slowly used to things. Also Company Commanders are told they are very valuable persons, and are not to expose their precious lives unnecessarily, this because G. Griffith and I went out on a patrol, and I was told not to do it again. I do not quite like the idea of hanging back, but we shall see. We shall be wiser a week hence."

CHAPTER III

THE KING'S VISIT TO HIS ARMY

THE FIRST CHRISTMAS.

ON December 3rd the King paid a visit to the troops in France and in his honour a terrific bombardment of the enemy's lines was arranged. Several copies of the Special Orders of the Day were sent home to their friends by members of the Q.V.R.

Special Order of the Day
by
His Majesty the King.

Officers, Non-Commissioned Officers and Men. I am very glad to have been able to see my Army in the Field. I much wished to do so in order to gain a slight experience of the life you are leading. I wish I could have spoken to you all, to express my admiration of the splended manner in which you have fought and are still fighting against a powerful and relentless enemy. By your Discipline, Pluck and Endurance, inspired by the indomitable Regimental spirit, you have not only upheld the tradition of the British Army but added fresh lustre to its history. I was particularly impressed by your soldierly, healthy and cheerful appearance. I cannot share in your trials, dangers and successes, but I can assure you of the proud confidence and gratitude of myself and of your fellow-countrymen. We follow you in our daily thoughts on your certain road to victory.

GEORGE, R.I.

December 5th, 1914.

In those early days of the War sending letters to the papers was not tabooed in the strict manner that was subsequently enforced, and many communications from the rank and file found their way into the columns of the London and Provincial Press. Writing to friends an officer of the Q.V.R. whose name we think it wise to withhold, though we shall make large drafts on his "Diary," says: "After reading and censoring the men's letters I have come to the conclusion that the biggest lies about the War are contained in letters from the front." Nevertheless, though those letters may not be quite so accurate as those written by officers, many of them possess an interest all their own and as such may be considered worthy of a place in the "Records" of the Queen Victoria's. Moreover, some of them have special interest, picturesquely portraying as they do the feelings of the citizen suddenly called to take up arms in earnest.

From many specimens the following have been selected, all dealing with events about the date with which we are now dealing. Under date of December 4th "A Member of the Q.V.R." states, in a letter which appeared in the *Daily Telegraph* of December 21st: "We had our first severe test on Sunday and Monday and have succeeded in pleasing the brigadier, who has complimented us on our steadiness. It is not really so dreadful after the first few minutes of funk, and up to now the small part we have played has been creditable. I think we shall come out of this safely and with credit to the battalion, and am glad to say that the men are keen and eager. The country around is a terrible scene of desolation and the wanton destruction is terrible to witness. It would be impossible for me to try and describe the inhuman way these poor, simple peasants and farmers have been treated. Where we are taking possession the people are reappearing and living in the ruins of their former homes. They have perfect confidence in our soldiers, which is not misplaced, for a more thoughtful lot of men it would be hard to find. Tommy out here is a very different man to the one we know at home. Here he has big responsibilities to face and great danger to encounter. He is a splendid fellow under such circumstances. The officer commanding my platoon is a splendid young man—an old Cheltenham boy.[1] We are all very proud of him and I hope he gets safely home. P.S.—Just been shelled out by shrapnel, but all well."

[1] 2nd Lieut. J. Nichols.

Writing on December 5th Rfn. Bushell says : "We have been right up in the firing line for three days—only 400 yards from the German trenches. We lost 1 killed and 2 wounded. The poor chap who was killed fell into my arms shot through the head. We were only supposed to be in the trenches for forty-eight hours, but they couldn't relieve us, so some had to go across an open space and bring up water and grub at night. The snipers were pegging away all the time, but we got back ' all correctly.' The ' Jack Johnsons ' are awful, but I saw the quality of the British Artillery the other afternoon, and the Germans got hell. They brought our guns up just behind us, and suddenly opened fire on the German trenches. I have never seen such a sight in my life. They simply banged shells into them every moment and we could see the earth being shot up to the sky and the shrapnel bursting all over the trenches. I venture to think that no regiment could have behaved better than our fellows. Every man was splendid. The villages round here, houses and churches, are a mass of ruins. The poor people have lost their all. Please God that people in England are not called upon to suffer as the people have here. If men could see what it means there would be no lack of recruits to prevent it " (*Daily Express*).

We cull another sample from the *Evening News* of three days later " from a private in the Q.V.R." " In the trenches, very bored and very dirty. Twenty-four hours in a bomb-proof dug-out, and now twenty-four hours in what is humorously termed the firing line. I haven't fired a shot yet. About 350 yards away a little scrap of earthwork shows on the side of a wrecked farmhouse. It is to be supposed that the Germans are there, but they are as doggo as we are. An idiot of a sniper is merrily peppering away somewhere quite close. An aeroplane (French, I think) came over just now and got potted at by the Germans. You hear a bump and a sound like an overhead electric car a long way off ; then see a spark somewhere up in the air and a little tuft of smoke, and your aero sails blandly on, the shell having burst about 500 feet too low. Had a royal time yesterday. Jolly little cubby holes, floored with straw, on the safe side of a hill about half a mile from the firing line, two men to each shelter. Bully beef, biscuits, chocolate from home, potatoes, cabbage and turnips from a field close by, cheese, tea, tobacco, the book you sent me and a jolly little coke fire in a bucket just outside. Awfully snug."

Another letter, from Rfn. L. C. Ebers, who unfortunately was killed a few days after sending it " to a friend at Stockwell," declares : " Our fellows were remarkably calm and steady in the trenches, and quite prepared to give the ' Huns ' a business-like reception. Before the battalion left for the firing line it was addressed by Gen. —— who was pleased to have us to give much-needed rest to other troops. The change was effected under cover of darkness, and without a hitch or a casualty. Our position was shelled the first day and projectiles burst within a few feet of us. It was really excellent the way those guns were silenced, our gunners finding the mark with deadly accuracy. In our part of the trench our chaps placed their hats on a sort of ledge at the back of us. A sniper spotted them and apparently thought they were fellows watching the effect of our shells on the German trenches. He started potting at those hats and made some very good shots. One bullet I found underneath one of the peaks. If anyone had been wearing it his number would have been up! " (*Evening News*, 12th December, 1914).

December was not a particularly eventful month so far as the Q.V.R. were concerned, but it was an extremely trying time for the young and inexperienced soldier who had to spend three or four days at a time in the trenches. And such trenches ! It must be remembered that the winter of 1914–1915 has been described as the wettest on record. On the 8th and 9th the companies were either actually in the trenches or were exercised in the art of trench-digging. While engaged in the latter " D " Company was unlucky enough to get two men wounded. On the 11th the battalion marched to Dranoutre, where they went into the Divisional Reserve. It was on the 16th of the month that the battalion for the first time as a whole went into the trenches, the General in giving instructions describing them as " absolutely awful—the worst I have ever seen." The officer commanding the party which took over the advanced trench described it as " a dirty ditch about 3 feet deep and 10 feet broad, on top of a hill, with no shelter of any kind and up to your knees in mud and water." Only an occasional reconnoitring party left the trenches at night-time and all the fighting that took place was the constant bombardment of the guns and the irritating, but generally harmless, shots of the sniper; unless a man carelessly exposed himself he was secure from the latter. During the four days the battalion remained in the trenches the total casualties according to the War Diary was 3 killed[1] and 5 wounded. In another of his interesting letters Capt. Culme-Seymour, in writing of these four days, says: "We came in for the first time as a battalion the day before yesterday and got one man wounded on the way in, close to the farm. Three companies are in the first line and one behind here in reserve. The Head-quarters are in this farm, which has buildings on both sides of the road. Head-quarters consists of the Colonel (Shipley), Vernon (Major Dickins), the Doc. (Capt. Roe), self and Cowtan (Lieut.) who looks after signalling, telephone, etc. Our servants are here, four runners from each company and the signaller and stretcher-bearers. Either we stop in a room in the farm, where we live by candlelight, day and night, or else in this 'dug-out' which is behind the farm. The German trenches are about 1000 to 1200 yards off, and from the farm we can see them and ours perfectly easy. Some of their trenches are within 30 yards of ours, and none of them further than a 100 yards. In front of our trenches and behind them, too, are lots of bodies of Frenchmen whom it is impossible to bury. The Germans originally held the trenches we have got now, and then the French drove them out but could not get any further, and so the Germans are on top of the ridge, and we are a short way down this side." The weather was very bad at the time and the men suffered much from foot trouble. The mud was awful. The men were constantly sinking in it up to their thighs. "They took five hours digging out a man who was up to his armpits." On the 20th the battalion was relieved and marched to a ruined village about a mile back. "We had fifty-three men this morning and last night who were unable to march back and had to be taken to the field ambulance, and that is less than any other battalion has had in that section. The men did very well and stuck it very well."

On the 22nd the battalion moved to Lindenhoek and once

[1] (1804) Rfn. L. C. Ebers; (1979) Rfn. H. B. Nicholls; and (2905) Rfn. E. S. Fryer.

more went into the trenches, but were relieved the next day by the 1st Devons. On Christmas Day there was a church parade at which the Rev. Fox preached a short sermon. "Mountains of parcels" had arrived and were duly distributed. On Boxing Day there was a football match between "A" and "C" Companies, the latter being the winners. In the afternoon Princess Mary's gift was served out. On December 27th the battalion was at St. Jean Capelle. On the 28th we find it recorded in a diary "Teddy Bear Coat issued." It seems odd that no further remark is made in any of the papers received concerning what must have been a very welcome issue. On December 29th the Q.V.R. moved once more, on this occasion to Neuve Eglise, going into the trenches at Wulverghem the next day in succession to the K.O.Y.L.I.

In a letter which was published in *The People* Rfn. S. Gubbins tells how he spent Christmas Day at the front : " To start with," he says, " I think every man had a good time under the conditions. We have been on and off in the trenches for the last two weeks and started our rest on Christmas Eve. On Christmas Day we had a church parade, football match, a good dinner with Christmas pudding and then messed about generally, finishing up with hot punch round a big fire at night. The officers of our battalion have subscribed together 150 francs for a football competition. Our company are in the final against ' C ' Company. They started to play it off this afternoon, but had the misfortune to burst two balls, so will finish the game to-morrow. When they were stopped 'C' Company were leading by 1 goal to 0." In a letter which was published the following week in the same paper, Rfn. Potter says : " 'We really had a most delightful evening,' as the song says. Up at 10 a.m., a good breakfast of bacon, bread and butter, jam, etc. Dinner of roast beef, etc., and a good helping of hot Christmas pudding (jolly fine stuff !). Tea, bread, etc., pudding, cake and biscuits. Then a concert, during which we had figs, nuts, grapes and cigars. So altogether we had a jolly time, despite the unfavourable circumstances."

Sergt. H. E. Soundy, in a carefully and regularly kept diary of the daily doings, says, referring to the Christmas festivities, December 25th : " Bright and frosty morning. Spent a very happy day in the mess ; chicken, beef and pudding, mince-pies, sweets, wine and two bottles of champagne given to Sergt.'s Mess by the Captain. Visited by the Colonel in the morning. All talking of home and saying we were having a happier time than our people imagined. Retired to our straw in the barn at midnight."

The remaining days of the year passed uneventfully. December 30th was spent in a route march of three hours and in instructing the men in the use of hand grenades, and next day the battalion left again for the trenches near Wulverghem, which they took over at about 4 p.m. from the K.O.Y.L.I.

CHAPTER IV

Trench Life in the First Winter

DESCRIBING life in the trenches in December, 1914, Capt. Sampson says of the men : " They have been awfully cooked more than once as we have gone short of sleep and they are carrying a lot on their backs. Then mud up to the waist is not very rare and up to the knees quite usual, and when you are covered with wet mud caked all over you it adds a good many pounds to the weight. We are having some cases of sore feet in consequence, but not many, and after a few days' rest the men are all right, though the everlasting mud and rain presses them a bit. I am quite satisfied with them though, as it is a trying first experience for town-bred people." Captain Culme-Seymour confirms this : " The men's feet were awful after being in the trenches, all swollen up, and it is awfully hard for them to get their boots on again if they take them off." Captain Lindsey-Renton, in a letter written on January 11th, 1915, after describing the formation of the trench by the engineers, goes on to say : " One would have thought this was pretty safe from being flooded though pretty useless if shelled, as almost any shell could, and did, knock it over, but as a matter of fact it was flooded. We went into the trench on Wednesday evening, needless to relate it was raining, and most of the time we were in the trench it rained continuously. All went well comparatively speaking, though the trench was frightfully muddy, until Thursday afternoon, when I noticed some water coming through an opening in the parapet at the back which was used as an egress from the trench. The water quickly became ankle deep and I called for some sandbags to block it up. They took a little time in coming, and when they did arrive the water was nearly up to the knees and still rising. When it got up to my knees I saw something had to be done, so I went along to Sampson and suggested that they should evacuate the flooded portion. On leaving the trench I found that all the ground behind was flooded to a depth of about three feet, the river (Douvre) which flowed past the end of our trench having overflowed its banks. It was a rotten job getting along as the ground was full of shell-holes and ditches from which earth had been taken with which to build the parapet. When I came back to the trench after a few minutes to tell the men to move, the water in some parts of it was well up to the waist, so you can imagine I got wet 'some.' Then, too, with two more days in the trenches and no change of clothes .... One poor fellow fell into a hole right up to his neck in water. I was able to take the men back for the rest of the night and the next day into reserve, but lying in a damp funkhole with rain, drip, drip, dripping through the roof does not help to dry one. I fortunately got my socks off and partially dried them, but not my breeches, and I can assure you that wet breeches are not a joy. . . . Lots of the men lost all their equipment in that trench. A party had gone off to get rations and when they got back found all their things under water, so that they have only got what they stand up in. It must have been a humorous sight to see me with a sort of broom handle for a walking-stick slowly pushing my way through the water feeling for holes with my stick and the water washing round my waist. The R.E. have provided water-proof boxes for the men to stand in with a small board across the corner to sit on. As we generally found them floating in the trenches, the men call them boats ! "

It is not surprising, then, to find one grateful N.C.O. writing : " All hail ! the 1914 rum that saved our lives and thawed the deadly chill that crept round our bones, but in spite of its valued aid we lost scores of good men who went sick with trench feet and rheumatism and who had to be sent back to the base or home."

Lce.-Cpl. H. Jones, giving an account of his experiences to a friend in London, wrote : " We have had our second experience of the trenches, and, compared with our first, it was absolutely hell. The way to the firing line seems of necessity to be through mud and water, but anyhow we got there without any mishaps, and filed into purgatory. A plank had been laid down the middle and you stepped off it into filthy mud and water up to your thighs. The Regulars we relieved had done twenty-four hours in them and were 'whacked to the wide.' We were of course wet, muddy and tired when we took over, but did our job, and did it as best we knew how; in fact, our fellows are more surprising every time, the way they stick it.

"The Germans kept sending up star shells like a Brock's benefit night, made the place as light as day, and then opened a fusillade. One, however, burst over their own trenches, and we spotted them building wire entanglements, and opened a rapid fire on them, and then with a maxim got them A1. The enemy had built some very elaborate entanglements, and were evidently funky of an attack. We gave them a hot time with our firing, and blew their loophole plates out and their head-cover to pieces. Then they shelled us with shrapnel and 'Jack Johnsons.' One of the latter blew one of our fellows right out of the trench, and he ran along the top and got in again quite unhurt. A chap in my section had his rifle blown to pieces in his hand; another had a cigarette blown out of his mouth, but the luckiest was a chap next door to me. A bullet came through the bank, went through his waterproof, overcoat and tunic, but only bruised his shoulder. When it hit him he said, 'They've got me," and went on smoking his pipe. The night came along and at 4.30 we got ready to shift, and crouched in the rain in full marching order for five hours before the relief turned up at about ten o'clock. We were done up by the time we had trekked back to the reserve trenches, after fifty-six hours of the firing line. They gave us hot tea—the first hot drink since Wednesday dinner-time—and we went to sleep directly.

"Talk about scarecrows—mud and filth to the eye-brows, wet, togged up in sleeping caps, etc.—we must have looked a crew Next day we spent in the reserves, where things were quiet, and we cleaned rifles and scraped a little off ourselves and slept. Rations included sardines, which the Captain had bought us. We found a bantam and brought her with us for the section's pet. She is as tame as anything already, and is near me now roosting on a post as calm and as confident as can be. In the evening we were relieved, and those who could marched back; the rest went in carts.

"All of us had terrible feet, owing to standing over our boot tops in mud and water for so long, and the sick represent one half our number now, but everyone is still very cheerful. Nearly all of us lost things, because if you dropped anything the mud swallowed it up directly. After this if anyone calls a Terrier a Saturday afternoon soldier when I'm about there will be trouble."

Major Dickins gives an account of a visit which he and the Adjutant paid to the front-line trenches on New Year's Eve, in which he says : "Leaving the farm at which we had our H.Q. about 10.30 p.m. we made our way through mud which was in many places over our knees. The night was fine and still and quiet reigned on both sides. On arrival in the front trench we found the men very cheery but of course in a dirty and muddy state. The Germans could be heard singing hymns or songs of a seasonable character and all seemed fairly peaceful. We passed along the whole of our line, wishing the men a Happy New Year, etc. But little firing was to be heard, and what there was came from the next sector on our left. We next visited the support line, commanded by Capt. Shea, and wished him and his men best wishes for the New Year and then returned to H.Q., arriving there about 3 a.m. very tired and dirty after a tramp of nearly five hours. There was a nice fire in the hearth, and after a good warm we went to our room which was up a flight of five stairs. There was an old French bedstead with just a mattress on it. I got into an old sack still wearing my dirty, wet and muddy boots and breeches, rolled on to the bed and was soon in a sound sleep." As we shall see he had a rude awakening.

CHAPTER V

1915—A Bad Beginning

MAJOR DICKINS continuing his narrative says : "I was awakened in a great start by the terrific noise of a shell which burst in the yard and was almost immediately followed by another which fell and exploded just outside. Jumping out of bed in a great hurry I forgot all about the sack which I had pulled up to my waist and fell head first down the five steps into the passage. A number of other shells came in rapid succession and hit the barn adjoining the farmhouse, in which were two platoons of Capt. Sampson's company in reserve. These shells did considerable damage and unfortunately caused us many casualties, 11 killed and 36 wounded. We (the H.Q. party) took shelter in a very small cellar whilst the shelling continued, which occurred several times during the day. At dusk we moved H.Q. about 300 yards back to another farmhouse, called Martyn's farm. Here we were shelled again the next day, but no damage was done, most of the shells going wide of the buildings."

It was a matter of wonderment to all how the Germans knew anyone was there, but it was surmised that the men in moving about must have exposed themselves outside the farm during the day or have been showing lights at night. Capt. Sampson displayed great coolness and pluck, dashing into the blazing barn and bringing out injured men on his back. For this gallantry he was awarded the Military Cross. Capt. Roe also exhibited great courage and skill in attending to the wounded while still under gunfire.

The killed were :

2290	Cpl. W. Gough.	1578	Rfn. J. R. Clarke.
2355	Lce.-Cpl. R. W. Mourant.	2067	,, R. G. Galley.
931	,, L. Morgan.	1980	,, C. Martin.
2127	,, F. H. Turner.	1749	,, W. Santler.
2532	Rfn. F. Allsop.	1687	,, W. Uglow.

Lce.-Cpl. A. E. Hoeller died of wounds on January 5th.

To add to the misfortune the regiment suffered the first officer casualty of the war, Lieut. Frederick Arthur Brian Fargus, the machine-gun officer, being shot dead by a sniper. Capt. R. Woodruff Cox, who was a witness of the occurrence, thus tells the story : " ' B ' Company's sector was situated in front of a semi-ruined farmhouse known as the Petite Douvre Farm, and the actual trench of which I had command was close to the Douvre River. The trench consisted of a high command parapet of very indifferent construction and in a bad state of repair and in only a few places raised to the height of a man's shoulder. One of our machine-guns under Lieut. Fargus was placed near the centre. The trench at that time was in a very muddy state and most of the men were squatting on the fire-step or on wooden boxes, sheltering behind the parapet. I was seated on one of these boxes just below the parapet near the Douvre River end of the trench. I noticed Brian Fargus inspecting the gun position, and with his usual disregard for personal safety he exposed himself once or twice and a sniper hidden in the Petite Douvre Farm had one or two shots at him. When Fargus had finished his inspection he came along the trench in my direction, the sniper potting at him from time to time as his head showed over the parapet. On reaching me I warned him that he had been spotted and got him to sit beside me on the box, and we discussed the situation generally. At the end of five minutes' conversation Fargus found his position somewhat cramped and shifted slightly. At that moment I raised myself so as to see over the parapet from behind some sandbags. Brian Fargus put his hand on my shoulder saying something about getting along and raised himself to practically a standing position. Almost at once a shot was heard from the direction of the farm and poor Fargus dropped dead behind me shot right through the centre of the forehead. He was buried at night close behind the trench he was in when he was hit, at a place called 'the willows,' it being practically impossible in those days to carry the body to the rear owing to the awful condition of the track across the fields."

Lieut. Fargus had been an officer of the Q.V.R. for over three years, having been gazetted to that rank in December, 1912. As machine-gun officer he had shown marked efficiency, and his death was greatly regretted by his comrades. He was twenty-seven years of age and was in practice as a solicitor. He was the younger son of Mr. and Mrs. Henry Robert Fargus of Milton House, Strawberry Hill, Middlesex.

The Q.V.R. remained in the trenches for three days, being relieved on January 4th by the K.O.S.B., and returned to Neuve Eglise, where next day another bit of bad luck befell them. About midday the Germans began shelling the town, which they had left unmolested for a couple of months. One huge shell exploded in the main street just outside the headquarters, killing 7 riflemen and wounding 15, 4 of whom afterwards died. These are the figures entered in the "War Diary," but other reports quote an even larger number of casualties resulting from this single unlucky shot. Company Q.M.S. Shore had no fewer than forty-two wounds. Wonderful to relate he recovered and is a frequent visitor to the headquarters in Davies Street and is proud to show everybody a key he had in his pocket to which he says he owes his life. A local curé and a few other men were literally blown to pieces. The curé's hand, it is stated, was afterwards found hanging from the telegraph wires.

Killed :

1770	Rfn.	C. Arthur.	1767	Rfn.	H. G. Hart.
2269	,,	C. R. Bowden.	1803	,,	W. A. Methopher.
1927	,,	T. R. Brand.	1547	,,	W. C. Kneale.
2250	,,	A. E. Alwin.	2512	,,	F. Vernon.
1611	,,	H. S. Dunn.	675	Lce.-Cpl.	W. Webb.
2628	,,	G. S. Dixon.			

Among others who had a narrow escape on 5th January at Neuve Eglise were the O.C., Col. Shipley, and the Second in Command, Major Dickins. They had been attending to some orderly room work at H.Q. in the main street and were standing at the door discussing which way they should take before lunch, it being just about twelve o'clock. "We decided," says Major Dickins, "to go up the street and had only gone a few paces (subsequent measurement proved the distance to be 37 yards) when a large shell came over and fell in the centre of the street just thirty-seven paces down the street from the H.Q. door. So had we chosen to go down the street instead of up as we did the shell must have fallen bar on us. It was quickly followed by five more."

During this salvo of shells C.S.M. Mark Brawn, " B " Company, showed remarkable courage and devotion to duty. The one that fell in the street burst forwards and wounded most of the men in the lower parts of their bodies. The killed nearly all had their legs blown off or badly shattered. C.S.M. Brawn did all he could to relieve the unfortunate sufferers.

In connection with this disaster " A gallant action by London Bank clerk " was recorded in the columns of *The Times* of January 12th in a letter from a platoon officer of the Queen Victoria's Rifles to the mother of one of the wounded Rifleman R. H. Cleverly (No. 2061). The letter runs " Rifleman Cleverly was wounded this afternoon by the bursting of a shell in the road in which he was walking. . . I should like to mention that his corporal, Brown, very pluckily went out into the street to find him and brought him back to the hospital. This was a plucky act and shows excellent comradeship. He will be a great loss to the platoon for he was a good soldier and a wit—a fine quality for a soldier on active service. However, we have much to be thankful for, as many who were standing near him were less fortunate. Before the war Corporal Brown was a clerk in the Union London and Smith's Bank, and Rifleman Cleverly was at one time a clerk in the same bank.

Two days subsequent to these mishaps, Rfn. H. J. Wright (Machine-gun Section) thus describes them. " Things have been awful with us ; we returned from rest last Tuesday week and on the Thursday our boys went into the trenches for three days ; some went right into the firing line, and some stayed about a mile back as supports ; one half-company of the supports were in a barn when a German shell hit the place with terrible results ; we lost 9 killed and 32 wounded. This was New Year's Day, and, as you may well imagine, everyone was much affected and felt it very much. To add to this one officer in the trenches was killed, shot through the head by a sniper, and naturally we were awfully glad on Sunday night when another regiment relieved them, and the rest came back safe and sound, although two fellows were buried for a few minutes by shells blowing the trench in on them and had to be dug out.

"On Tuesday last, the 5th inst., I went with our Quartermaster to a town about five miles back to draw clothing, etc., for the troops from the Army Ordnance Stores, and whilst driving back we heard that our lot had been shelled out of this village. We hurried along to see what could be done, and arrived just in time to see the boys round the graves of nine men who had been killed, and the Chaplain was reading the short burial service. The news we received was awful, as in addition to the killed, there were fifteen more wounded in our lot alone, and I don't know how the two other regiments suffered. Two of Debs' [1] fellows I know well were killed, and Dallender and Luscombe, of C. and E.'s [2] are both on their way to England wounded. Dally got it badly in the legs, sides and arms, but I hear that he is sure to recover all right as the wounds are not big or deep at all; and Luscombe got it in the head. Shedlock had a marvellous escape, pieces of shell went right through his cap and pocket, and he was not touched at all, only severely unnerved. I am glad to say that the boys were just marvellous, and whilst other shells were still whizzing about they were out dressing and bandaging the wounded who lay all over the road. One of the two Debs' men killed was fine. He heard the first shell burst right across the square, and said, ' I must be off, some of the poor fellows will be wanting me.' (He was a stretcher-bearer out here.) And no sooner had he put his head outside the door than he was blown to pieces by the third shell. This shell burst outside our billet and Arthur of Debs' was killed by it; he is one of our gun team. The firing did not last long as the English R.F.A. near here got into action and, we hear, silenced the German battery. But at any rate we have had no more trouble from them since.

"Last night the boys returned to the trenches again. We went part of the way with them with the wagons, etc., and now I am roasting a nice piece of beef which we shall take up tonight to them." The letter, after requesting that it shall be sent on to relatives, concludes with these words: "One

---

[1] Messrs. Debenham, Ltd.
[2] Messrs. Cox and Edwards, Old Cavendish Street.

does not like to keep writing of these things ; it brings back horrible sights too much, and it's not good to get affected that way on this game."

The following General Special Order was issued to the IInd Army Corps on January 1st :

IInd Corps Head-quarters

Special Order

1st January, 1915.

The day has arrived when, with much regret, Gen. Sir H. L. Smith-Dorrien, having assumed command of an Army, has to relinquish that of the IInd Corps, and he cannot do so without expressing to all ranks his gratitude for the loyal support which they have given him during the eventful months which have elapsed since the commencement of the war.

During these months the Corps has been engaged day after day and night after night in desperate fighting, continuous to a degree never known before in the history of the world, against a very brave and resourceful enemy.

Gen. Smith-Dorrien is indeed proud of the grand name which the Corps has earned for itself, whether in advance or retirement, attack or defence—if not always decisively victorious, yet invariably holding its own, and never defeated.

He is in the very deepest sympathy with all units in the heavy losses which they have suffered ; but it is a satisfaction to know that these casualties, great as they have been, are nothing to what the enemy have experienced, and without them this war could never have progressed as it has towards the successful issue which is in view.

It is indeed a great honour to have commanded such magnificent troops, who under any sort of trying condition—nerve-shaking shell-fire, overwhelming fatigue, extremes of heat and cold, continuous rain, mud, frost and snow—have always maintained their indomitable fighting spirit and have not only never complained but have shown a cheerfulness which at times they can hardly have felt. The one dominating aim of each individual has been to sink all personal feelings and to defeat the enemy.

It is a satisfaction to Sir Horace to hand over the command to Lieut.-Gen. Sir Charles Fergusson, who has already brought so much credit to the Corps by his handling of the 5th Division, which he had to relinquish on promotion some two months ago. It is a further satisfaction to him that, as the Corps forms part of his new command, he by no means severs connection with it.

W. H. RYCROFT,
Brigadier-Gen., D.A. & Q.M.G., IInd Corps.

CHAPTER VI

Campaign Life in France

WE have heard a good deal of hardships and discomforts, let us see how the men fared in regard to food. "I thought it might interest you to know how we live here," writes a rifleman in a letter "specially contributed" to the *Evening News* of February 6th. "Our usual rations consist of bread, bacon and jam for breakfast, tinned meat and vegetable rations for dinner, and 'toto,' as we say, or what remains, for tea. At times parcels are received from home, and then, of course, more toothsome morsels than the above are consumed. When parcels do not arrive at the critical moment, or when the contents of those received are prematurely disposed of (which perhaps is more often than not the case), by way of variation some of the boys provide themselves with delicacies in the shape of chops, eggs, etc. Boiled rice and jam also seems to be in favour, on account of it easily being carried and cooked. Fires are at times allowed, this depending, of course, upon the nature of the trench occupied, but when heat from this source is unobtainable, either being forbidden or impossible, owing to lack of fuel, our resources are by no means at an end. A piece of rag stuck in a tin of vaseline serves as an excellent cooker, and many a chilled sentry has benefited by hot tins of cocoa prepared in this manner. Candles, too, have done yeoman service in our culinary arrangements. You may marvel at our patience waiting for a mess tin to boil over a couple of candles, manipulating the tin so as to bring it constantly within the heat of the flame, but the thought of something hot crowning our efforts gives no limit to our endurance. When reaching billets we make up for lost time, and when billeted in a town or village it is a common sight to see troops crowding out butchers' shops, purchasing chops, steaks or sausages. Laden with these fresh viands, and having specially missed company dinner for the purpose of accruing an extra large appetite, we invade the local cafés and get the meat cooked, and with the addition of chipped potatoes sit down to a meal of which a Gog or Magog might well be envious. Thus you see in the food line, taking the short rations with the long, the average is not so dusty. You may ask, ' How do the men get on who do not speak French ? ' I can assure you what Tommy lacks in knowledge of foreign languages he makes up with in power of persuasion. It is humorous to listen to some of the boys trying a hand, or rather tongue, at speaking French. ' Avez vous—knife ? ' followed by vivid gesticulations illustrating the uses of the article desired, is but one attempt of a private to get what he wants. I could not help laughing the other day when a pal asked me to have a coffee. He preferred it with milk and I without, so the order was given ' Un café au lait and un without au lait.' These little incidents and many others are of everyday occurrence and are really most amusing."

At 10 a.m. on January 6th the battalion was inspected by Gen. Sir Charles Fergusson, G.O.C. IInd Army Corps, who " gave us very high praise." In his letter to the Adjutant announcing his visit the General wrote : "He had heard nothing but praise of the battalion and very high praise too." At four o'clock the same afternoon the Q.V.R. again paraded for the trenches and took over support dug-outs at Wulverghem. There they remained until 7 p.m. on the 8th. The weather is unanimously denounced as awful, much rain, with the trenches too wet to be occupied. During the three days only one casualty is recorded. Referring to this Capt. Sampson states : " Still our casualty list approaches three figures and the wastage from sore feet and rheumatism is heavy, so that the battalion is greatly reduced in numbers. We had rather a doing this time as we had very heavy rain and the trenches were wetter than ever. One of mine ran down to a river which suddenly flooded and the occupants were up to their waists in water, so we had to clear out of it temporarily. You should have seen us coming home ! mostly dead tired, many of the men lame from cold feet and all 'of us wet through and covered from head to foot in mud." Concerning the enemy's feelings he adds : " I certainly do not wish to remain here for twelve months, and I do not believe the Germans can conceivably last as long. I know what the wastage is here and I do not doubt it is just as heavy with them, and they are fighting half Europe. I have never yet seen a German, though I have sat for days within 50 yards of them, which seems so comic, but they do not seem to have any attack left in them." It was not very long before he was disillusioned and was sent home with a "Blighty."

On the evening of the 9th the battalion was relieved by the K.O.S.B. and were billeted for the night in Neuve Eglise. On the 10th they left for a rest at Bailleul, where they occupied "a large brick building—very draughty." Another diarist calls it a prison. From the 10th to the 15th the time was spent in a medical inspection, short route marches, inter-company football matches and a much-wanted clean up. A cheerful sergeant under date of January 13th records: "No parades. Went to No. 2 Hospital for 'pull throughs' and oil bottles. Rained all day. Had best meal since leaving England—pork and cabbage, roast beef, beans and potatoes, cheese, biscuits and beer. Ragtime singing in evening."

For a short spell there seems to have been an improvement in the weather conditions and the rest was enjoyed by all. Capt. Culme-Seymour writes : "It's very nice and peaceful back here (Bailleul). Tim and I are in the same room with two beds and very comfortable. Downstairs where I am writing now we've got a very nice small sitting-room with a fire. We have our meals in a small estaminet just round the corner. A beautiful day, quite hot sun, and a strong wind, such a change from continual rain. There's a clock just outside here which chimes exactly like Big Ben but, of course, not such a deep note. Sounds so strange. Very nice people in this house and do all they can for us. There are any number of people here living an ordinary life—yesterday—Sunday—with all their best clothes on and only a short distance off—the shells, etc." The welcome week's rest came to an end all too soon ; on January 16th the battalion marched to Dranoutre and the men billeted in Revetsburg.

Writing on January 18th Capt. Culme-Seymour says : "A white morning. Hard frost and snowing—great big flakes. Cowtan went off last night to Paris, until Thursday morning. We are only 430 men for the trenches now, a pretty big drop since we first landed. But I hope some of the sick will come back soon, and then there's the draft to come. 'C' Company are having a 3-mile cross-country race this afternoon for their men. Awfully good idea I think. Just been round 'A' Company's billets. They are a very happy party. Old Lees is in great form, and Nichols, too. Dick and the Doc. have been in tremendous spirits the last two nights. It's a great thing to have fellows like that about."

On the 19th, "almost at a moment's notice," and "in order to start a new arrangement between brigades," "A" and "B" Companies under Col. Shipley and Capt. Culme-Seymour went into the trenches at Wulverghem once again and were relieved three days later by "C" and "D" under Major V. W. F. Dickins and Capt. Cowtan as adjutant. It appears to have been a fairly quiet time, nothing but "one casualty" being recorded. Sergt. Sim has the following entry in his diary: "January 20th. Path making all day. January 21st. More rotten path-making." On the 22nd we find him in charge of a listening post and the next day's entry runs: "German first line trenches 400 yards off. Saw more of the bounders than on any previous visit. Used Holloway's glasses." January 24th brings a change for the better: "Relieved Jones and 3 men at listening outpost. Discovered German outpost 20 yards away. Returned to trenches at 6.15, very cold. Damn the outpost! Ration, salmon, bread, butter, jam, ham, and very nice too. Relieved 6.20 p.m. by Dorsets."

Rfn. F. E. Ellis ("C" Company) in a letter to his parents at Croydon, also tells of the weird first experience of a listening post. "The first night I was detailed off to be listening patrol; had to go out in front of the trench and gather what information I could. Not alone of course; there were four in all, two on and two off. Sounds a bit thrilling to you, no doubt, but somehow I didn't feel a bit nervous. We managed to get within a few yards of the opposing patrol; in fact we could see them smoking. We, however, weren't taking these risks. *I've* never been so quiet before in all my life. I think it took about an hour to get there, but the return journey lasted very few minutes."

Night found the weary Q.V.R. back again in Bailleul for a further rest. Culme-Seymour, who seems never to have known what fatigue was, thus describes his strenuous preparation for the much-needed rest : " January 25th. Slept jolly well last night. Tim and I in our old billet and very comfortable. I have arranged for a football match nearly every day and on the other day a cross-country race. We have taken a room for the men where they can write and read papers. A large room, and we are getting a piano, so they will be very comfortable. Sent up to near Neuve Eglise last night a cooker, or field kitchen, for the men on their coming out of the trenches—so they got soup and hot tea, and for the rest of the way they marched home singing like mad. Wasn't it splendid ? It's the spirit I love to see. We've got concerts every night—company ones. The old sort of songs, all very sentimental."

On the 28th he sends an extract from the " Summary of Information[1] sent in yesterday " : " The German Emperor's birthday was celebrated this morning by a salute from one of our heavy batteries against the house south-west of M. which has been suspected of being a battalion head-quarters. Eighteen lyddite shells were deposited into it and exploded with effect ; as a result many Germans were seen running in and out. Subsequently the house itself exploded ; it no doubt had been used for a depository for bombs and grenades. The effect of this explosion was followed by a *feu de joie* of innumerable smaller ones, so that the occasion seems to have been fairly suitably celebrated ! "

On January 30th the long-expected draft from the 2nd Battalion arrived, Culme-Seymour notes " and Shea with them. Two hundred and twenty-four men, some of whom have been sick. The new lot are a jolly good lot—splendid-looking fellows most of them. They are invaluable to us as it will make us up to about 150 a company for the trenches. We go into the same place as before on Monday, two companies at a time. Rather glad, as they are good trenches, and last time we had no bad feet to speak of. When Stephen Shea was in hospital he was next to one of the 2nd Seaforths. At Christmastime when there was all that friendliness with the Germans he went out and talked to them and particularly to a German Colonel. The latter knew everything about our reliefs. Where the K.O.S.B.'s were, who was on their left, and knew a Territorial battalion was on their right. That was us, and he said the latter were very good and never showed themselves.

[1] Commonly called *Comic Cuts*.

Words he used were—'D——d good they are too.' High praise coming from such a source."

It is stated that four officers arrived with the draft. Major Sampson, who was away on leave when it arrived, writing on February 2nd says : " I found that the new draft had arrived and I had received two officers (Russell Jones and Burchell) and sixty-two others, also ten men back from hospital, so my company is filling up again." This it will be remembered was the company (" D ") that suffered so heavily in the barn on New Year's Day.

On January 31st Col. Shipley in acknowledging the receipt of a case of " Comforts " sent to the battalion by the Q.V.R. Old Comrades' Association, wrote the President, Col. W. M. Tanqueray, V.D. : " Please accept and also convey to the O.C.A. the best and heartiest thanks of myself and the whole battalion for the generous gifts advised in your letter of the 22nd inst., which have now all come to hand. The knives and matches are especially welcome, but every single gift will be greatly appreciated. Yes, thanks, I am quite fit and sometimes I wonder at myself. We have been in Bailleul for eight days' rest, but, as we have had to stand by to run out at fifteen minutes' notice we haven't been able to benefit by the rest much. We had seven bombs dropped round us on Wednesday, killing a poor babe and wounding two women. We go back to the trenches to-morrow night for two spells of three days each. The weather is damnable, snow and slush, and I tell you, the men won't have much comfort. As far as I can I make them work most of the night improving the trenches, and unless attacked or heavily shelled the majority sleep during the day. To my mind this trench work is the most damnably demoralising work extant. I am glad to say the regiment has earned a good name for itself, although I say it as shouldn't. Sir Charles Fergusson, taking over the corps, said he heard nothing but praise from all officers. Tommy generally refers to us as ' Queen Vics—they're orlright ; they are sports they are.' The Belgians and French call us ' Black Buttons ' and say ' Black button soldiers, good soldiers.' I am very proud that the old battalion was one of the first Territorial Battalions to take over a section of the trenches as a unit. Most have sent half-battalions in at a time."

CHAPTER VII

THE SPRING OF 1915

ON the first day of February the Q.V.R. went into the trenches again. Writing the day before, Capt. Culme-Seymour describes the method pursued : " We go into the trenches to-morrow, two and a half companies in at a time. The Colonel and I go in for to-morrow and Tuesday night, then Vernon and Cowtan do two nights, then the Colonel and I again and then the other two, and after that back here again. Snowing again to-day, quite a lot, but it has thawed a lot this evening." From Major Dickins' diary we learn that the first detail consisted of B. C. and half " A " Companies. On February 3rd " C " and half " B " Company were relieved by " A " and " D " and half " B " Companies, Major Dickins and Capt. Cowtan taking the place of Col. Shipley and Capt. Culme-Seymour. On the 5th " A " and half " B " Companies were relieved ; on Sunday 7th, " D," " A " and half " C " Companies went in, and so on until Tuesday 9th, when " D," "A" and half " C " Companies were relieved by the 6th Cheshires (15th Inf. Brigade) and the whole battalion marched away again for Bailleul.

The month of February appears to have been exceptionally quiet. The usual turn in the trenches followed by an acceptable rest was all the battalion was called upon to do and casualties happily were few. None of our diarists has anything exciting to record. On the 6th Capt. Sampson writes : " We got back last night from two days in the trenches with only two slight casualties, both of them men who came out in the draft, so they have not seen much of the war. One of them was hit in the foot on the way up to the trenches and had to go straight back. We had two very fine days and clear nights and it seemed a pity to have to spend them in a hole in the ground We had some shells rather close the first day but no harm was done. The new draft behaved very well and seem good fellows, as also the draft subalterns." All ranks speak highly of their quarters and express their satisfaction with their confortableness ; recreation-rooms had been provided and in addition there was a cinema hall and by day the football matches. There is mention also of " nightly concerts " with the news that " the new draft have brought all the latest choruses with them and have quite a repertoire." Capt. Sampson reveals for the edification of his people what he had for dinner on February 11th : " In the trenches I had for dinner, hot soup, hot Irish stew, bread and cheese, washed down by rum and hot water, and finished off with a cigar—not bad for trench life ! "

On that day the battalion was inspected by Brig.-Gen. R. Wanless O'Gowan. One entry describes it as " nothing exciting," and another as " short and sweet." On the 9th Sergt. Sim records that they were " shelled with Jack Johnsons and shrapnel for one and a half hours, fifty shells bursting near dug-outs. Robby Lowes killed.* Smith and Hall, junior, wounded. Relieved by Cheshires at 8 p.m." On the 14th the same N.C.O. says he was " warned for cow-burying at Revetsberg." On the 23rd he records : " Cpl. Bishop wounded in jaw. Much shouting and firing on our right. Night also foggy. Patrol and 8 men under Lieut. Holms. Franklin shot in foot. Cpl. Densham missing." The missing Corporal was found next day, wounded in the thigh.

About the middle of February Col. Tanqueray, the President of the Q.V.R. Old Comrades' Association, sent out more " comforts " for both officers and men, and in acknowledging their receipt Col. Shipley wrote him as follows : " B.E.F. 14/2/15. My dear Tanqueray,—On behalf of myself and my N.C.O.'s and Riflemen please accept and convey to the Old Comrades' Association our sincere and heartfelt thanks for your kind present of knives, coffee and candles. The latter arrived yesterday and will be very useful. Vernon, Lees, Flemming, Sampson, all wish to be remembered to you ; Shea has gone to the base sick with influenza, and Roe, the two Coxes, Renton, Johnson, Nichols, Cowtan and Cawston are on leave at home, so we are a small mess. This eight-day rest I have taken a large and fairly comfy room and we are running

* (2509) Rfn. A. R. Lowes.

a regimental mess, as when away only company officers' messes can exist and one doesn't see much of the junior members. We are still on the same line of trenches; it is ghastly work. I am awfully sick as they propose to turn me out of the farm I have had my Battalion H.Q. in and put me in a cellar and a dug-out with no place for my company runners or signallers. Anyhow I am fighting for it, and have hopes. We hope to receive a second draft (100) to-morrow, which will help us along. So far casualties are: 1 officer, 35 O.R. killed, 80 wounded, 320 sick to base. I hope to get eight days' leave in about a month's time if I can; the wretched C.O. is the last person supposed to require leave. I am glad to say the old regiment has done very well and earned a good name all round, although I tell you as shouldn't. All brigades out here are to have one Territorial Battalion put to them. Something like fifty are out here now. Yours ever, R. B. Shipley."

This was followed four days later by another letter running as follows: " My dear Tanqueray,—Your very generous gift arrived safely under escort last night, and we all drank your jolly good health in the best liquor we have struck since Davies Street. Many, many thanks for your kindly thought of us and the good red wine which we all appreciated. As luck has it we were to have gone into the trenches yesterday afternoon but the powers that be have kept us out and we are standing to to move at short notice wherever wanted. I am hoping to receive the 2nd draft (100) before we move as we are short. It is absolutely appalling how the rifles vanish; our casualties are just over 110 k. and w., but sick tot up to 320. Anyhow, our officers are good, Warren, Bolton, Andrews, Hamilton feet, Shea influenza, all going; then 5 lately joined, so are full. I tell you I was jolly glad to get Roe and the six others back last night. I get absolutely rifle mad nowadays, can't stand losing a single man for sickness or any other cause, as with the sector we hold we are undoubtedly weak and I grudge every loss; it's silly but one doesn't want to be caught napping or short-handed. I hope to put in for leave in March after all the others have been—at the moment all leave is stopped— and I'll try to look you up and have a chat. One of the most interesting things is to watch men and see how they turn out in the trenches; it is surprising how some fellows we thought nothing of have turned out jolly well. Those two Redgell boys have done awfully well, Sergt. Parker ditto, Fairall, Andrews, have all distinguished themselves at one time or another. All the Mess send their affectionate remembrances and grateful thanks for your welcome gift. Yours ever, R. B. Shipley."

On the 19th February the 13th Infantry Brigade, less the Q.V.R., left Bailleul for Ypres. The Q.V.R. were then attached temporarily to the 15th Bigade, and left Bailleul for Dranoutre on the 20th. " A " " B " and " C " Companies went into the trenches the same day, " D " being left in reserve at Dranoutre. The Q.V.R. were sorry to part with the 13th Brigade if only as a temporary measure, having been on such friendly terms with all the battalions composing it. Since joining the 13th in November, 1914, they had shared all their fatigues and hardships.

On 23rd February after a long spell in the trenches the Q.V.R. were relieved by the 6th Cheshires and marched to Dranoutre through a storm of rain and snow. In his diary under date of February 25th, Capt. Sampson says : " Yesterday and to-day we have had heavy snow and are lucky to be out of the trenches. The three companies who came out the day before were rather unlucky, as they had one killed and seven wounded, one of them dangerously. There was a thick fog and they were repairing the parapet in front of the trench when the fog lifted and a machine-gun got to work upon them." Reporting upon this incident Lieut. Nichols wrote : " No. 1 Platoon, ' A ' Company. On Tuesday, February 22nd, at 8 a.m., a working party of No. 1 platoon were working in front of parapet under cover of a mist. The mist suddenly lifted and some Germans opened fire on party. Rfn. Spittle, one of party, was hit in front of parapet and Sergt. Pulleyn, who was making his way back stopped to bandage Rfn. Spittle. He stopped with him for ten minutes when the latter died. By this time the mist had lifted entirely and some snipers had the place marked. At 9.30 a.m. Sergt. Pulleyn, who had been lying in a hole full of water, made a final effort and succeeded in getting the right side of parapet. Had he not stopped to attend to Rfn. Spittle he could have regained the trench immediately." Major Lees forwarded this report to the Adjutant with a covering note " hoping that Sergt.

Pulleyn's action will be brought to the notice of the Officer Commanding."

Major Dickins records the arrival on February 24th of a second draft of 113 men from the 2nd Battalion; also that on the 27th Col. Shipley and Lieuts. Shepherd, Carter and Summerhays went on leave. The last entry for the month is: "Casualties to date, 73 wounded; 33 killed."

On February 27th the 15th Brigade was relieved by the 84th, the Q.V.R. being temporarily attached to the latter.

With the coming of March things began to get a trifle livelier, or rather more deadly. The shelling in the trenches is described as continuous and heavy. It opened quietly enough. On the 1st Culme-Seymour, optimistic as ever, writes: "Another month begun and another finished, making it all the nearer to the end of the old war. Peace has got to come some time and it can't be put off, I feel sure, much more than six months at the outside. Last night I was awfully busy and soon after I had finished the Brigadier and the Brigade-Major came and I went round the trenches with the latter." On the same date an entry in one of the diaries mentions for the first time the use of cavalry as infantry: "19th Hussars relieved Q.V.R. in 11a fire trench and 10b support trench." Describing the next night's work Culme-Seymour says: "Round the old trenches again last night taking a colonel man around. It was quite a lively night as we had a biggish working party in behind the parapet and the Germans must have seen them, because they opened a very brisk fire, but no one was hit, Near here Burchell got a graze on his head and had to go off and another man was hit in the arm. Nothing exciting at all, all day!"

On March 3rd the Q.V.R. had a stunt of their own. Sergt. Sim calls it "Sham attack at 1.45 a.m., M.G. and rifle. German got wind up," and Sergt. Soundy: "In reserve. Heavy rifle firing about 2 a.m. this morning silenced by our guns. Afterwards heard the cause of their firing. The Adjutant was in the firing line and said as they had been potting at our working parties we will wake them up. So he 'phoned back to the artillery to send one or two shells over and then ordered our fellows to yell like the devil and fire thirty rounds rapid. It did worry the Germans." The author of this little "worry" tells his own story : " Last night we had rather fun. I went up and got on to a battery and when they opened fire I ordered all our men to cheer and open rapid fire. We gave them a regular doing and they were so surprised they didn't answer for about five minutes and then one had to keep down for a bit. We must have done them a lot of harm, I think, and we only lost one man killed.[1] The men were delighted and it was a very good thing to do to put some spirit and go into them. They have all been rather too much ' live and let live ' lately, with the result that the German snipers kept on bothering us. After last night and all early this morning there wasn't a sound."

From the 1st to the 11th March the battalion was either in support at Dranoutre or in the front line trenches at Wulverghem. On the 5th Sergt. Soundy records : "Allemands excited over something ; about 1.15 a.m. opened fire with rifles ; sudden spasms, accompanied by a T.M. (trench mortar). They sent three shells into Wulverghem." Next day they shelled and set fire to a farm about 1000 yards from the Q.V.R. A 'large quantity of ammunition was stored there and was going off all day. Sergt. Sim enters : " Billy Hoskins shot.[2] Frozen feet." In the War Diary it is stated there were two killed and one wounded. On March 7th there was a good deal of shelling, and Lieut. Kenneth Johnson received a nasty wound in the hand that caused him to be sent home for a time. On the 8th Sergt. Sim was once more in the firing line, and says : " Went to sleep about 8 a.m. until 12 ; had dinner ; another rest ; just about to put some water on for tea when a shell burst just outside our ' abode ' and nearly shook our insides out. Ninth day without wash or shave ; looked a proper tramp."

Writing on the 11th Capt. Sampson says : " We had great fun in the trenches as a Territorial regiment from South Wales (1st Monmouths) which had just come out was attached to us for instruction. We took them about in parties and then they were put into the trenches in among our men. We did the ' seasoned warrior ' turn to the life, and they were very grateful and impressed. They are mostly colliers and expert

---

[1] Rfn. Kidby killed in action 3/3/15.
[2] Rfn. Wm. Hoskins killed in action 6/3/15.

with a spade. They are dead keen, have good officers an[d] will do very well when they have got accustomed to bullet and shells, which does not take long."

On March 11th a move was made from Dranoutre to Bail[leul], when the battalion went into billets at St. Jean Capell and from thence two days later into trenches in a new sector a[t] St. Yves, north of Ploegsteert. Everyone was impresse[d] with the new trenches. According to Capt. Sampson they ar[e] "quite the best we have ever struck," and to Sergt. Sim[s] "The cushiest trenches we have ever seen." Capt. Lindsey Renton writes: "You have no doubt often seen in the pres[s] about wonderful trenches, dug-outs, etc., well, we've struc[k] them this time. They are absolutely the show trenches. [You] could walk from the reserves in rear to the fire trench i[n] evening clothes without soiling them or getting damp fee[t.] The way up is what they call a 'corduroy road' made of [a] number of short planks nailed into two long ones, the latte[r] being placed on the ground so that one walks on the short one[s.] I have told you that 'D' Company were in reserve. The[y] are in a most charming position, hills on almost every side s[o] that the enemy can't see you. The men are in excellent lo[g] huts which have been built in the heart of the woods, an[d] they say they are more comfortable than they often are whe[n] at rest. Peasants come round every morning with eggs, milk bread and oranges. All this within rifle range of the enemy [if] they could see you. The officers' quarters, where I am writin[g] this, is a charming place (here follows the description of a[n] Armstrong hut); all this in the most delightful sylvan su[r]roundings. I went round the trenches last night to see wha[t] they are like, preparatory to going in, and found them far an[d] away the best we have ever seen, strongly built, perfectly dr[y] with most excellent dug-outs—the one I was to occupy was [a] palace." Everyone wondered how long they would be allowe[d] to remain in this Elysium. It lasted but two days! Cap[t.] Lindsey-Renton concludes his letter: "Just our luck. Ju[st] as we had got really to appreciate the place and rejoice ove[r] our luck we got orders that the brigade we had relieved we[re] returning and we were to get out."

March 17th found the regiment back in Bailleul. Thre[e] men had been wounded on the 16th and one on the 17t[h]

The battalion was relieved that morning by the Dublin Fusiliers. In a letter dated the 19th Capt. Sampson says: "There have been two biggish fights at St. Eloi and Neuve Chapelle and although they are both a long way from here they involve shufflings up and down the line which interrupt the routine of reliefs. . . . We have been attached for some time to each of two regular brigades and a battle royal is now going on between them, each of them asking the Corps Commander to attach us to their own Brigade. 'Fighting continues,' as the dispatches would say. We hope it will end in our going again to the trenches we have just come out of, but at present it seems unlikely. The places there had all been officially given London names and one was, for instance, ordered to be at 'Hyde Park Corner' at a certain time. We were told there were very few casualties there, but we had seven men hit in the battalion, of whom one died."

CHAPTER VIII

THE YPRES SALIENT

CAPT. CULME-SEYMOUR, writing on March 19th, says : "The weather is getting warmer and drier and we are calling in all the men's woolly waistcoats." Three days later the regiment marched to Ypres, a distance of about fourteen miles, and was quartered in the Cavalry Barracks and the Regimental H.Q. in the Rue des Chiens. The town is described by Capt. Sampson to have been "much battered by shell-fire, but the civil population has returned in amazingly large numbers." The children were constantly playing in the open streets, imitating the noise of bursting shells. On the 25th Sergt. Shuttleworth, "a very good fellow," was wounded rather badly, a rifle bullet striking him in the chest and coming out near the kidneys. On the following day the battalion moved into huts at Ouderdom. A new subaltern, by name Read, is recorded as having arrived. According to Culme-Seymour : "We are in the 28th Division now—Gen. Bulfin, and in Plumer's Corps, the Vth—and the 13th Brigade. Wanless O'Gowan again." A football match between the K.O.S.B. and the Q.V.R. took place on March 30th. "They beat us 2-0 Awful wind blowing and the teams were pretty equal." In the afternoon, says the same authority, "We go into Ypres and the trenches to-morrow. The Brigade is in for twelve days or thereabouts. We have three trenches and relieve ourselves, two companies at a time. Expecting orders in detail every minute from the Brigade, but suppose they're having their tea, so we will have to wait. We've got beautiful thin bread and butter for tea and cocoanut cakes. Bought in Poperinghe, which is a quaint old town, quite quiet and not touched at all. A regular sleepy old town if it wasn't for the soldiery who always turn night into day as far as they're allowed. Princess Pat's Canadians are a magnificent crowd—will do anything. We are going to be in 22 Lombard Street when we are in Ypres. It has been the Brigade Headquarters, but the Brigadier says we can have it—very nice of him."

The Q.V.R. went into the trenches at 5 p.m. on March 31st.

Although there were rumours of a big attack by the Germans on April 1st, 1915, the centenary of Bismarck's birthday, the day passed quietly. A third draft of 72 N.C.O.'s and men arrived from the 2nd Battalion, some of them going almost at once into the trenches. From the 1st to the 5th " A " and " C " Companies were in the trenches, " B " and " D " relieving them on the latter date ; and so on until April 10th when the Q.V.R. were relieved by the Norfolks (15th Brigade). On the 2nd, Lieuts. Carter and Cawston were wounded, happily not severely. In the ten days 5 rank and file were killed and 16 wounded. The battalion then went into hutments at Ouderdom for a rest. Referring to his spell in the trenches Capt. Sampson writes : " We have just done five days in the trenches. It is not really longer than usual, as we decided to do it in one dose instead of two, as the going to and from the trenches is tiring and there are generally one or two casualties on the way. It would be too long in bad weather, but here the soil is sandy, so that the trenches are dry. . . . The trench I was in was very quiet in the daytime as they could not shell it, the reason being that it was under a hill, at the top of which, from 70 to 100 yards away, was the German trench. The result is that they cannot lob shells on to our trench without lobbing some of them on to their own, which even a Hun resents. We were extremely lucky, having only one casualty in the fire trench and one going up to it. A third was hit on the way back, but the shot only struck his entrenching tool, and he got off with a bruise on the place provided by nature for bruises !

" We are on historic ground here. There has been extremely heavy fighting on the ground where the line of trenches now is. Every building is wiped out by shell-fire, only the foundations and a pile of brickbats where a house once was, and in the woods there is hardly a tree whose top has not been lopped off by the fire. It is as if the seven plagues of Egypt had swept down the zone for half a mile each side of the trenches leaving behind it dead trees, dead horses and dead men. We get accustomed to all these things and hardly notice them, but when one is out of the trenches again one begins to think sometimes what this country would be like if there were no war, and then one realises what a pity it all is. Here as I write all is peaceful enough except that a captive balloon hangs in the air close by observing for artillery and occasionally one hears the bang of a gun. At night, if it is still, the sound of rifle fire is like crackers being pulled at a party, with the occasional boom of a trench mortar, and we can see the flares when they go up from the fire trenches. Their long-range gun could shell us here (Ouderdom) if they tried, but they won't, as the camp is too scattered and heavy shell too precious."

The Hill, it must be remembered, was the now famous "Hill 60." Hill is, perhaps, rather an exaggerated term for what was really only a slight eminence about 60 metres in height, forming a small open space of ploughed land, surrounded on all sides by woods. It was the highest point of the Klein Zillebeke Ridge about three miles distant from Ypres. The Battn. H.Q. were in the railway cutting about 300 yards or less behind the fire trenches. They were dug into the bank of the cutting, and, says Culme-Seymour, were "quite comfortable with different little rooms for different people. . . . From the trenches the R.E. are mining under the German trenches, which are about 60 yards off. They are getting on well and can hear the Germans walking about above them. They won't blow them up though for another ten days or so. (It was actually sixteen days.) It seemed so weird to see in the back of the trench large pits with men and ladders in them, and to think that they went right along to underneath the trenches opposite us. There are signs everywhere of the hard fighting there has been round here—all villages and houses in ruins and in front of the trenches dozens of bodies of Frenchmen and the Prussian Guard which it is quite impossible to bury, as if anyone goes outside either trench they are almost certain to get hit at once."

From other letters written by the Adjutant a weird coincidence comes to light. On March 25th he writes: "One of the men here who betted we would leave England on the actual date we did leave long before anyone knew we would, is now laying 30 to 1 on the date we will be back in England, and it's April 5th. Wonder if he will be right ! " In a letter written on April 6th we get the sequel. " We had another man killed yesterday, looking over the parapet in the daytime. Funnily enough it was the man [1] who prophesied the battalion would be home by 5th April ! " As there had been a number of casualties due to snipers taking advantage of men thus offering a target, Culme-Seymour goes on : " I am organising a new sort of sniping squad and intelligence squad to spend their time in sniping at the German snipers, and also to find out all they can about them—circumvent them and send in reports. I think they'll be very useful. I'm going to put Cawston in charge of them when he comes out of hospital." A week later he reports that he has formed the squad. " A good lot, ready for anything." In the same letter (April 13th) he records : " Great excitement last night as about 11.10 p.m. a Zeppelin came over and dropped one bomb after another. Awful row. But they were all from 150 to 400 yards off us. No one was hurt, but it made some enormous holes in the ground—about 20 feet across and about 10 feet deep. I was in rather a state as we were playing the 12th County of London next day, who were with us at Crowborough, at football, and I was afraid they would chuck one on to the football ground, but thank goodness they were beyond. We should never have been able to fill in the hole, and everyone is awfully keen to play. . . . The enemy's trenches in front of ours are going to be blown up on Friday, and the K.O.S.B.'s and West Kents, with the supporting battalions of the 13th Brigade, are going to attack and push forward, so I don't know what trenches we'll occupy next time." The great match was lost, 2–0.

About this time we get testimony from home as to the value of the Territorial regiments as a fighting force. In a manifesto addressed to " Men of London," Viscount Esher, President of the Territorial Force Association of the County of London, says : " The Kensingtons, the Westminsters, the Victorias and others are names inscribed for ever on the battle roll of England " (April, 1915).

[1] (1525) Rfn. V. C. Fusier.

CHAPTER IX

HILL 60

WE now come to the famous fight for Hill 60. It was believed that the Germans were preparing a great offensive and Sir John French had determined to anticipate it. The Hill it will be remembered had been carefully undermined for days, five galleries being driven into and under the hillock. To the 13th Brigade was allotted the task of carrying the position after the mines had blown the defences to atoms. The regiments forming the brigade were the

2nd K.O.S.B ,
2nd Duke of Wellington's West Riding Regiment,
1st Queen's Own Royal West Kent Regiment,
2nd K.O.Y.L.I. and the
Q.V.R.

The K.O.S.B. and the West Kents were to lead the assault under Major Joslin of the West Kents. At 7 p.m. on 17th April the mines were fired and 250 yards of German trenches seemed to be struck by an earthquake. The trenches and their occupants had ceased to exist. The West Kents followed the Borderers, dashed into the debris, where a terrible struggle ensued in the dark. German reinforcements poured in, and fighting continued all through the night and all the following day with varying fortunes. By 6 p.m. on the 18th the Germans had succeeded in recovering part of the southern edge of the Hill. The West Kents and the Borderers, pushed back over the crest, were relieved by the Duke of Wellington's and the Yorkshire Light Infantry. "These regiments, supported by heavy artillery fire, darted forward and drove the enemy out at the point of the bayonet, fifty-three prisoners (including four officers) being captured. They were supported by the Victoria

Rifles, the second oldest volunteer corps in the Kingdom, now the 9th London Regiment, who fought with great gallantry."[1] Describing the fight Capt. Culme-Seymour says, in a hastily written note : " We've got the hill all right but we've lost a lot and I only hope and believe they lost more. . . . I went to the Lille gate this evening to see the party off which was taking up rations to our machine-gun team and all the time wounded men kept passing us, chiefly hit in the head, judging by the bandages. Tremendous bombardment again this evening, and we got notice a few minutes ago to be ready to move off at short notice to support. I've put the battalion at fifteen minutes' notice. The Prussians are against us and, of course, pretty tough fighters, but they're up against the best crowd in the whole world and I believe we'll do them all right. Nichols (Q.V.R.) is doing Staff Captain and had a very narrow escape to-day, I hear. The brigade staff are in our dug-out where we were the other day, and he was standing just outside with a lot of men. He left them and was just stepping inside when a big shell burst outside and killed the whole lot. One shell went on top of the dug-out and burst up one of the beams, but no one was hurt. The whole cutting is full of men killed and wounded, and of course it's the same in the trenches. We've got lots of men though and are quite all right. Everything will probably quieten down to-morrow. They made continuous counter attacks all last night, and two companies of them which were attacking at one time were wiped out by our (Q.V.R.) machine-guns."

" A " and " C " Companies spent the night of the 19th in the cutting, " B," " D " and H.Q. being in support. A number of men were employed in carrying much-needed stores to the new front line. In doing so they suffered a number of casualties. The Regimental Transport lost 3 horses in Ypres and had a cooker-cart buried under some debris. They immediately received orders to clear out. Writing late on the 20th Culme-Seymour states : " We were ordered up as the enemy made a counter attack and I am now writing in a dug-out. We have got two and a half companies up in front and for the present the rest are here. We had some very narrow shaves and Sampson has just been wounded."

[1] *The Times History of the War.*

A member of the Machine-gun Section, which it will be remembered took part in the first attack on the Hill, writing from hospital at Ballymena, says : " On Thursday April 16th the order came to the section that they had to man and take three guns to a position N.E. of Ypres. I was one of the chosen few. On Friday night we marched out of camp at 10.15 The Colonel gave us a speech. We were the first of this regiment to take part in an attack. Hence we considered it a great honour. Again, we were the only T.F. gun section that took part in the business. Well, we marched up behind two companies of the Royal West Kents and two companies of the King's Own Scottish Borderers. These two regiments were to make the first attack on the German trenches, or what remained after Hill 60 had been blown up. We sang like blazes the whole way. It was as dark as pitch ; you couldn't see your hand in front of your face. We took up a position in a trench to the right of Hill 60. Our orders were ' to fire like the very devil ' as soon as the last explosion was heard. The object of this was to draw the attention of the Germans in front and to prevent them reinforcing the hill. The explosion was timed for 7 p.m. on the Saturday. We spent most of Saturday in building alternate gun positions. About 6.30 we had the order to stand to. Everything was as quiet as possible. The sun was just setting and a more peaceful spot than Hill 60 was difficult to imagine. Punctually at seven a loud explosion was heard. Hill 60 was like a volcano. Simultaneously with the explosion our artillery started to shell and rapid fire was opened all along the trenches. You never heard such a din in all your life. It was like one continuous roll of thunder. The rifle-fire sounded like hail on slates, only much louder. We got into action in fine style. I was filling belts as hard as I could go Suddenly there was a terrific crash just in front. The Germans had spotted our gun and put it temporarily out of action Three of our chaps were buried and the gun was on top of 'em Soon got 'em out and was able to get the gun later. They kept up rapid fire and shelling for about half an hour. It seemed like years. We'd no idea how the attack had gone ; we'd no idea as to how many we'd lost. About eight o'clock things quietened down. Later we heard that the Borderers and Kents had taken the trench with very little loss (seven casualties) and that we'd only one killed in our section. It was after the K.O.S.B. and the Royal West Kents had taken the trench that they lost so heavily. The Germans had the range to a T. They shelled like blazes and made seven counter attacks during the night. Each attack was repulsed. About ten o'clock on Sunday morning things quietened down considerably and until the afternoon things were normal. During Sunday we repaired damage done to our trench and took a look at the German trenches opposite. They were badly blown about and we noticed that they made no effort to repair 'em. Hence we expected an attack on our lines. About 2 p.m. they started using their 'stink' gas. They put most of it on the Hill and on a place called 'The Dump,' on which we had a host of dug-outs. We got the waftings of the gas. It makes the eyes water and irritates the throat. It's devilish stuff. To be in the gas region must have been hell. It's the only word that describes it. The K.O.S.B. and the R.W.K. must have been heroes by the way they stuck it. Sunday night was a repetition of Saturday, only far worse for us, as the Germans had brought up more guns than ever. They knew Hill 60 was going up. We could see their trenches with ease from the end of our trench which faced the hill. On Sunday our chaps had to clear the enemy from the hill altogether. After they had been dislodged from the fire trench they took up a position just over the ridge. The K.O.Y.L.I. and the Duke of Wellington's made the charge. They got the Germans off the hill altogether, and, by gad, didn't the beggars run. Our new gun position faced the hill and we were able to blaze at 'em like the deuce. We got rid of 20 belts of 300. I believe nearly every shot was effective. We simply mowed them down like grass. On Monday things were the same as Sunday—stink gas as usual. Tuesday ditto. On Tuesday evening they spotted us and put over shrapnel like blazes. The first shell got an Exeter chap called Cox. I was just tying him up, when one got four of us ; I got it in the neck, another chap in the arm, another in the shoulder and one was killed. We knew it was all up as soon as they got Cox. They simply rained shrapnel on our gun and then they didn't hit it. I got tied up and went to sleep in a dug-out ; my neck was jolly sore. At Havre my wound showed signs of festering and I got packed off to Ireland to be operated on. With my usual good luck the wound became healthy and I've not to be operated on. I'm a lucky beggar, for the lump of iron narrowly missed some awkward spots."

" At the time of the great explosion the Q.V.R. were in rest billets five miles away," says Capt. Sampson, writing on April 22nd from No. 7 Stationary Hospital, Boulogne, "listening to the distant gun-fire and watching the flashes. The Germans made three counter attacks that night, losing very heavily, but their last attack retook a part of the new trench consisting of one of the craters formed by the explosions. On Monday (19th) evening this was retaken. On Sunday morning early we were called out of our rest billets at short notice and marched into Ypres, where we were billeted and our men employed to carry supplies of all sorts up to the fire trenches, an unpleasant job, in which we had a few, but not many casualties. Early on Monday morning we moved out of Ypres into reserve trenches and spent a quiet day there, having only a little carrying work to do. There was no fighting that day. However, on Tuesday morning the Germans opened a very heavy cannonade, shelling the fire trenches and our batteries, and also flinging huge shells from a 15-inch howitzer into the unfortunate town of Ypres. We were in a safe place about one and a half miles from the town, and these great monsters came roaring through the air and on their impact sending up a huge column of black smoke and debris, and causing a concussion which even at that distance struck one's ears almost with the force of a blow. In the afternoon I had the honour of a few minutes' talk with General Smith-Dorrien, who said he had watched the doings of our battalion and we had done 'splendidly.' He said he thought the Germans would attack again. All day the cannonade went on and about eight o'clock the Germans counter attacked again and continued to do so all night, keeping up a tremendous artillery bombardment on Hill 60 and the ground in rear of it. We at once got orders to move up through this zone of fire to a place about 400 yards in the rear of the hill. Off we started, the C.O. and Seymour in front, then I and my company ('D') followed by Major Dickins and Capt. Cox with "B" Company, hoping for the best, but knowing we were in for it. We had some casualties on the way up, but the air seemed full of shells and it was wonderful we did not have more. Once a group of shells burst all round us in front, and we were almost blinded by the gas escape, but uninjured. Finally, we got to our rendezvous (Larch Wood) and after a long delay I was able to collect my company and get them into the dug-outs of sorts, where we were fairly well protected from the rush of shells. All this time hand-to-hand fighting was going on in the trenches. Soon 'A' Company (Major Lees) was ordered up into the fire trenches, and at about 1 a.m. I got an order to take my company up. The men fell in silently and as steadily as possible, and off we set along the railway cutting and from there up a communication trench. After I had gone a few yards up this I found it had been blown in and that it would take a long time to get the company over the various obstacles. So I went through a gap into the railway cutting to divert the rear half of the company along the cutting. Finding this feasible, I went back to the subaltern in front, who was in the communication trench, told him what I was going to do, and then returned along the cutting to do it. As I was going back, a shell burst very close to me, and a bit of it hit me on the side of the head. I was able to give Summerhays my orders and tell him what to do, and he took the company on. I hear that later on he was killed after doing very fine work. He had been as cool as a cucumber all night, and was a splendid little man whose loss I feel very much. A rifleman tied me up. I was quite able to walk back to H.Q. and later to the dressing station two miles in rear. I lost a good deal of blood in the first few minutes but it soon stopped, and I was in no pain and very thankful to find myself still alive."

The story is well taken along by an account contributed to *The Great War* by a " Private of the Queen Victoria's Rifles," to whom fell " a large share of the fighting " : " Lieut. Summerhays takes his place (Capt. Sampson's). We are all unaware what is in store for us. A roughly made communication trench from the original fire trench to the summit of Hill 60 is traversed. We are soon busy fighting. Dawn (21st) gradually appears and the enemy begins bombarding with hand-grenades. One by one I see my pals fall. Maisey and Pearson a little way on my right are lying—never to move again. Lieut. Woolley takes command after Major Lees and

Lieut. Summerhays have been killed and the remaining officer of the Bedfords in sight. What a roar and tumult. Maxim-guns are hammering away, shrapnel bursting above us and blinding flashes follow the explosion of hand-grenades. My rifle becomes too hot to hold and I throw it aside for another. A bomb explodes a few yards away on my left among the Bedfords. What happens to them I don't know. I feel no longer a human being. Simply mechanically I continue firing. A glance to the rear—Cpl. Peabody is attending a wounded man. Lieut. Woolley appears at the mouth of the communication trench and encourages us by saying reinforcements are coming up. A blinding flash, and something hits me full in the face—a feeling as though someone had smacked the bristle side of a stiff brush in my face. My hand instinctively goes up—no, there is no blood. Only fine particles of earth have reached me, but Devereux and Wickens are both wounded from the same explosion, and grope their way to the rear.

"The Devons begin to arrive, and as they come up we make our way to the rear—crawling on hands and knees along the low, badly damaged communication trench into the original fire trench, and from there to the communication trench leading on to the railway cutting. Passing the Northumberland Fusiliers on our way, we reach another communication trench, leading from the railway to the support dug-outs, which are in what was once a wood. But few trees are left—mostly short stumps, for the tops have been blown off. Here we are gathered into some sort of order, and go across a couple of fields to some more dug-outs.

"Till now my nerves have stood me well; but as I recall the fearful sights I have witnessed, and realise the majority of my pals are gone, I give way and break down, sobbing like a child on its mother's knee. Presently I pull myself together and have a little food. It is about 11 a.m. (Wednesday, April 21st). I obtain permission to return to the wood to secure my pack. With some difficulty I locate the position of the dug-out Devereux and myself had occupied the previous night, but I happen to spot the packs. The dug-out had been transformed to a shell-hole, and it was lucky for us both we weren't in it at the time; my haversack is missing."

Major Dickins, who was with "B" Company (Capt. Woodruff Cox), says : "Just after passing Zillebeke we came under the most terrific shell and rifle fire. There was a hedge running across our front with a deep ditch. I ordered the company to line the hedge and get into the ditch so as to obtain cover. The ditch was about 4 feet deep and half full of the most foul-smelling mud I ever experienced, but this did not deter the men from jumping into it—in fact I have never seen a movement done so promptly before. Shells of all calibres were bursting round us, while the sky seemed filled with flashes and explosions ; the noise was terrifying, and on our right machine-guns were rattling out their fire. Fortunately for us we were under the cover of the railway embankment and these bullets were going over our heads. During this alarming and nerve-racking time C.S.M. Mark Brawn showed most marvellous courage by walking up and down exposed to fire and encouraging the men to keep steady and under cover. For this and similar gallant acts C.S.M. Brawn was awarded the D.C.M. We stayed in the ditch about twenty minutes when the shelling slackened and we then made our way up the hill to Larch Wood, where we joined 'D' Company who had gone up before us. In the circumstances our casualties were slight."

Lce.-Cpl. H. D. Peabody (1764) also has an interesting tale to tell : "We went up on fatigue, taking up ammunition, and as we came back Major Allason (Bedfords) asked for reinforcements for Hill 60 and refused to let us go. He told us that we could get rifles and swords on the hill if we had not got them. We then went up on hill, Major Lees taking over command. Major Lees decided that we should make a charge to the front of the crater where the Germans were supposed to be. The charge was made and only one German was found there. In the meantime the East Surreys went along the communication trench and occupied the right half of the hill. There they remained until morning, when their bombs had given out. Our own men had to retire when they were blown out with bombs, but they lined the rear of the crater and kept up a steady fire on the front to stop the Germans from occupying it. Just as dawn broke the Germans bombed and shelled us very heavily. Major Lees gave orders that where the bombs were falling very heavily then we could move left and right, but must be ready to line the crater again if the Germans came or in numbers. Shortly afterwards it was pointed out that the East Surreys were giving way on the right[1] and Major Lees went across to stop them vacating the trench, and in doing so was shot. On our left the Bedfords stayed in the trench until their ammunition gave out and it was impossible to get more to them owing to enfilading fire. They therefore vacated that trench and we saw no more of the Bedfords up there. This left about 30 East Surreys on the right and about 70 to 80 of our people. Finally Lieut. Woolley took over control of the company. Just before this an officer of the Bedfords silenced the German bomb-throwers by returning the bomb-throwing heavily; unfortunately, however, he was hit in the knee. At the same time Lieut. Woolley and Sergt. Warrington threw bombs. (This was between six and seven o'clock.) On the right about 6.30 the Germans turned a machine-gun on part of the trench and we had to move away from that part. Shortly after they opened very heavy shell-fire on it and blew it to smithereens. A guard was kept at the end to watch the Germans coming down the communication trench on the right. Soon afterwards this guard was blown out of position by shell-fire, and the East Surrey's officer who was there gave orders for us to move to the left and assist them. Cpl. Peabody was in charge of this guard. On arrival there Lieut. Woolley gave orders that as there was no room for us in the firing line we were to get what shelter we could, and, if the Germans rushed, to line the right crater. Gradually the firing line was thinned down, leaving about 40, and as Lieut. Woolley was in sole

---

[1] In justice to the Surreys we must add the following extract from Conan Doyle's *British Campaign in France.* " Soon after midnight in the early morning of Wednesday, April 21st, the report came into the Brigadier that the 1st Surrey in the trenches to the left had lost all their officers except one subaltern. As a matter of fact every man in one detachment had been killed or wounded by the grenades. It was rumoured that the company was falling back, but on a message reaching them based upon this supposition, the answer was, 'We have not budged a yard, and have no intention of doing so.' At two-thirty in the morning the position seemed very precarious, so fierce was the assault and so worn the defence. Of 'A' Company of the Surreys only fifty-five privates were left out of one hundred and eighty, while of the five officers none were now standing, Major Paterson and Captain Wynyard being killed, while Lieut. Roupell, who got the Cross, and two others were wounded. It was really a subalterns' battle, and splendidly the boys played up."

control, all other officers having been wounded, the N.C.O.'s took control of sections of the line. About eight o'clock the Germans opened heavy shell-fire all along the firing line and at nine o'clock, when the relief came from the Devons, we had between 20 and 30 men left. Lieut. Woolley handed over to the Devon officer, but as he was very upset I explained as clearly as I possibly could the exact situation of the Germans in the trenches, and also gave orders for all men to leave bandoliers behind for relieving regiment, and reported to Lieut. Woolley."

Rfn. Harold Sendall, a friend of the writer of the last extract, in a letter to his father written a week after the battle, says: "The Germans all day Tuesday kept up a heavy fire on the road leading to the firing line, so when five o'clock came and we were told to fall in we knew that we had clicked for something and sure enough we had. The enemy artillery followed us up all the way. We started to go over the fields and as the darkness fell the nearer we got the more terrible became the fire. We got to an old farm building and lay down in a ditch half full of green slimy water and very glad we were of the shelter it afforded. After some time word was passed back, 'Get ready to move,' for we had now come to the worst part of our journey. Over the next quarter of a mile I will draw a veil, all I will say is that never have prayers been more earnestly said; it was hell, no pen of mine can describe it, all I know is that the dear Lord brought me safely through. I had several escapes. Wednesday morning came at last and we were moved still further up, and the sight we saw I shall never forget. Of the 'Bump' itself H—— will tell you a bit about what the Queen Victoria's did, and I am proud to belong to the finest Territorial battalion in France. Our losses are very heavy and our splendid Major (Lees) has also fallen. One of the boys I left Crowborough with, Rfn. Maisey, has been killed and numbers of my friends have been wounded. Before I close this letter I must tell you about Harry,[1] he is an absolute hero in every sense of the word; he will soon be a sergeant and you could not have a better man."

Rifleman Sidney Seymour, who before enlisting in the

---

[1] Cpl. H. Peabody, who for his services in this action was awarded the D.C.M. Sergt. Pulleyn also received the medal.

Q.V.R. was well known in North London football circles as playing for the Grange Park and St. Mary's clubs, and as an entertainer whose talents were in frequent request at Enfield Club concerts, writing to a local newspaper gives a graphic description of the scene : " It was while my company were in the trench just at the rear of the first line that things started We had only rifles and bandoliers, but, nevertheless, had ' to get on with it ' ; we went up to the front right into the thick of things. 'Twas an awful sight. The trench filled with dead and wounded, bullets pouring across, shells bursting, grenades and trench mortars hailing in. How anyone came out of that place alive is truly remarkable. The magnificent way our boys held the ground was a sight to see. A mere handful of ' rabbit-shooters ' keeping back the German hordes. Aye and so effective were we in doing so that they gave up attacking, and back they went. I myself was knocked about by a shell which burst near me, but fortunately nothing was broken I lost the use of my left arm and side for about eight hours and was badly shaken. So unfortunately I did not see the thing through. Sergt. Pulleyn and Cpl. Peabody were the only N.C.O.'s who went right through, and the manner in which they conducted themselves was splendid. 'Twas a bad day for us as the company at roll call numbered 26 men and 1 officer. Corporal Peabody did fine work in attending the wounded. I had an awful shock the next morning as he did not turn up for some hours after we were relieved. When he did arrive he broke down just as we all had done. The strain was awful and to see your pals go one by one adds to the horror. We cried like children and were completely broken up. Our dear old Major gone, our Captain, two Lieuts. and nearly all our fellow comrades ; the only consolation was that we held the position and kept up the traditions of our Army. Never shall I forget that inferno, and how gallantly our boys, as Peabody puts it, ' stuck it '—and died. After this our little battalion still kept working, and we were in it again the day after. 'Twas another grand sight to see the boys under that deadly artillery fire marching on as though in Oxford Street. Here again we all had wonderful escapes. Thank God we did not have to do that charge. We could hardly lift a rifle."

" We had a pretty thick time of it up at Hill 60," wrote

Cpl. H. E. Asser. " It was some fight, I can tell you. When I heard the word to reinforce the hill I followed the man in front of me along the support trench and round the corner up the communication trench, which there was only about four feet high, and open to machine-gun fire from either side, with shrapnel bursting about and ' whizz-bangs ' flying over by the dozen. We screwed our way along the narrow trench, passing many wounded coming back. At the end of the trench we were at the bottom of the crater. We saw the top of the hill and began scrambling up. It was all loose, sandy soil, because that part had been recently blown up. Our part of the hill ran up at about sixty degrees and was some twenty-five feet high. We were soon amongst those at the top and our job was to keep up a rapid fire on their trenches. You fired like blazes until your rifle boiled and you fairly ached. Then the man behind stepped in and took your place until his rifle was the same ; then you had another go. All this time they were sending their little black hand-grenades, but they all burst outside our trench—they could not chuck far enough. We were flinging ours, which are a very different kind, right into their trench. What did the damage was their trench mortars— filthy things. All you know is a tremendous report, and the thing has burst, probably in the trench, and two or three men roll back in the crater and others are wounded, some badly, some not. The low groans above all the rifle and shell-fire are horrible to hear. I lost many pals, and it was an anxious time to see who were left when the relief came for us. We had had four hours, but some of our chaps had been up much longer."

Sergt. E. H. Pulleyn, who acted so bravely on February 22nd, again distinguished himself on the hill. Major Lees and the party under his command, it will be remembered, arrived on the ground about half-past eleven. "The night was dull and a slight rain was beginning to fall. Already many of the men had fallen, but at last close to the huge crater made by the British mine they made a stand and began to dig themselves in. Towards midnight Sergt. Pulleyn was ordered to take a platoon to the very top of the hill, 20 yards distant, and fill a gap for the support of the regulars on either side of the hill. The few yards intervening were fully exposed to the German fire, for the enemy was then under 30 yards away.

Sergeant Pulleyn and his sixteen men advanced. They had not gone 10 yards when six fell. The eleven remaining went on under a terrible rain of bullets and hand-grenades and reached their position. They had not been there two minutes when five more men fell. The six who were still unhurt remained under what cover they could for a few minutes, until, realising the utter impossibility of maintaining the post, the order was given to retire. They returned, bringing their wounded, to the original position, and now they were not more than fifty men holding on firmly to that dearly bought hill. The Germans dare not advance over the crest, but the cross-fire was terrific. The hours went by and the enemy fire scarcely slackened. The 150 were reduced to 30, but they held on. Suddenly Lieut. Woolley, an officer of another company, appeared in the trench. He knew of the terrific onslaught during the night and heard from the wounded that all the officers had fallen. So quite calmly he left a secure position and made his way alone as dawn was breaking to take charge of that gallant little band. They held their place, and when relief came at nine o'clock in the morning there were only 20 men left. But they had held the hill " (*Daily Graphic*).

The terrible nature of the bombardment is also depicted in the *Evening News* of May 10th by another " Private in the 9th County of London Regiment." "The Allemands were not going to let us have it all our own way, and at four o'clock they started a hail of shell-fire, which is supposed to have been the heaviest during the whole war for the area concerned. At times they must have been coming over five hundred to the minute, and it is a marvel that any of us came out of it to tell the tale. Four other men and myself were in an open trench and I would not have taken a 20 to 1 bet on our chances of coming through intact. However, thanks to a merciful Providence we emerged without a scratch. The shelling went on for twelve hours, then sobered down a trifle. At eight o'clock when it was pretty well at its height we had to reinforce at a different point. We had to cross a railway line in a deep cutting and it was absolutely hell with a capital H. The shrapnel and high explosive shells, hand- and rifle-grenades were bursting all around us, and dead men, stretchers, equipment, and so on looked ghastly in the flashes. We stayed in our next position till we were relieved two and a half days later."

In Culme-Seymour's account he says : " We had a great fight, but no time to write properly as we've only just arrived (April 22nd) and must get men settled in. We are in huts which are only just being finished. We had a baddish time. Such an awful bombardment. Later in the night we sent up two companies to the front line to counter-attack, as some of them had got into the trench on the top of Hill 60. Lees took three platoons up and drove them out and held on. The poor fellow was killed early in the morning—shot in the head and heart while directing the men what to do only 10 yards or so from the Germans. Summerhays was killed early and poor Westby we've never found, and there is no doubt he must have been killed. Sampson was wounded before we started to counter-attack and Woodroffe was wounded later. We lost about 130 men besides killed and wounded. We were all jolly glad to get back. The battalion did splendidly ; in fact, there's no word good enough for them. When we got outside Ypres just now Smith-Dorrien was there and spoke to the battalion. Tremendous praise he gave them. Woolley did gloriously, being on the hill with about 20 men when there were only 6 regulars with him. They—the latter—didn't come up, but Woolley and our lot did, and no doubt at all saved the hill and kept it, although they lost like mad until they were relieved, and then Woolley was the last to leave. I'm going to put him in for a V.C. Isn't it all splendid ? Rather short of sleep as you may imagine. I got a whack on my left knee from a splinter coming out to-day and a shrapnel bullet hit a small larch tree about three inches from my head this morning. I'm sending these home. So here we are all right and resting."

We now turn to Lieut. Woolley's own account of the affair : " At dusk we were ordered to go up to the Larch Wood and went by way of Zillebeke Lake and village. There we met a barrage of tear shells and 5·9's and a good deal of random rifle fire, so going was difficult, but we had remarkably few casualties. Sergt. M. Brawn kept my men amused by explaining to them that the show was well worth a shilling a day. When we arrived at the wood we found 'A' and 'D' companies had been sent up to the front with stores. They got mixed up in the counter-attacks and made some progress, probably occupying the German support line. Information came back that they were short of S.A.A., so Capt. Cowtan was ordered to take up Nos. 7 and 8 platoons (Woolley and Houghton) with a fresh supply. We started about 10 p.m., but it was about midnight before we had struggled up the communication trench which was blocked with wounded stretcher-bearer parties, messengers, etc. The C.T. was narrow and very much knocked about. As I was leading, a man, I think it was a 'runner' of 'C' company, just in front of me, was hit by a bullet in the thigh. He couldn't walk, and as the trench was too narrow to allow us to pass I tried to bind him up on the spot. He saw it was difficult and would keep the S.A.A. party waiting, so he asked us to leave him at the bottom of the trench and walk over him as they needed the ammunition very badly on the hill! We managed to get him moved to a wide spot and he was properly bandaged up there. I heard afterwards that he was all right.

"My orders were to report to Major Lees and bring back a written report on the situation, so that if necessary Nos. 7 and 8 platoons should stay up to help hold the front line. At the junction of the C.T. and trench 39 Major Allason of the Bedfords, who was detonating bombs, directed me up to the hill and I took on the leading men with a few boxes of S.A.A. and soon found Major Lees. There was a comparative lull except for rifle fire. Major Lees said he could not tell what the situation was himself and asked me to go round the hill with him. The craters were full of men in support. Just in front of them we met Westby and Summerhays; both were very cheerful and went over the ground with us. In the dark it was very difficult to tell much about the position, but Major Lees was quite satisfied that he had plenty of men to hold on with, and in fact thought it would be better to withdraw some by day as they were too crowded in the craters.

"I started back with his message and promptly got lost in a network of derelict trenches, shell-holes and barbed wire. I had just put myself right and picked up a party of four men also lost, when a heavy barrage was let down on to our old front line about 15 yards in front of me. I had to lie doggo

THE FIRST TERRITORIAL V.C.
CAPTAIN G. HAROLD WOOLLEY, V.C., M.C.

for some time, then went on and found Major Allason, who told me Nos. 7 and 8 platoons might return, so I passed down word and they began to file back. Just at that moment a messenger came down to say that the German counter-attack had driven our men back, so Major Allason ordered me to call back the two platoons to go and help. I passed the message down, but apparently Major Allason stopped the men going up with me, until he had more detailed information, for when I arrived on the hill and reported to Major Lees I found only three men with me. However there were plenty of men in the craters.

" Major Lees went off to the right towards Trench 38 to try and reorganise the men. I remained in the right crater and began bombing with Hales grenades. Almost at once a message came that Major Lees was killed. The bombs quickly ran out and someone found a box of jam-pot bombs. I had no matches to light the fuses and borrowed a box from Summerhays, who just then came into the crater. Soon after he was killed, but I did not see him. The jam-pot bombs were not a success, but at intervals more Hales were sent up by Major Allason and most of them I sent on to an officer of the Bedfords (Lieut. Kennedy) in the left crater—he worked there for a long time throwing bombs, standing in a very exposed position in his shirt sleeves. The sergeant who was helping me was killed, and soon afterwards a bomb exploded on my head but only tore my cap. One of our M.G.'s was sent up and took up a position in the left crater and worked extremely well, which encouraged us a lot as the German M.G.'s were very active, but before long it was knocked out.

" Hall was sent up to ask how things were going and I told him we should hold the craters all right, but soon afterwards the Germans started to shell us with field guns they had brought up to the ' Caterpillar,' about 300 yards away on the other side of the cutting. These just tore away the lip of the crater, causing very many casualties, and also caught the wounded, lying at the back of the crater, who tried to go down the C.T., or rather track, to Trench 39. I started to go to the other crater to consult with Kennedy about asking for more men, and on the way met another officer of the Bedfords wounded badly in the arm. Just as I reached Kennedy the German field gun switched on to that crater and the first shell broke his knee. Assisted by one of his own men I got him bandaged up, and our S.B.'s, who were doing splendid work, carried him back.

"I was now alone with both craters and the ground to the right to look after, so went from one group of men to another —they were huddled up in little groups where the crater lip or parapet was not blown away—cheering them up and keeping them firing. Ammunition was getting short and rifles jamming, so we had to collect rifles and S.A.A., plenty of which was lying about the craters. I had just left the left crater when two shells knocked out most of the remaining men; the wounded struggled for the C.T. at the back and the rest began to go back with them. Luckily I was standing so as to bar the way and the men in the right crater beckoned to them to come back as well. So I examined each one and sent the unwounded and slightly wounded back, and they manned the left crater again. That was our most trying moment. Fortunately the guns on the 'Caterpillar' ceased fire shortly after; probably several of their shells fell short and the Germans could not help killing their own men. Their fire was most discouraging, for we scarcely heard a round fired from our own batteries all the while. About this time a messenger came up from Battn. H.Q. to tell me that all Q.V.R. men were to go back to the Larch Wood, but that would have meant deserting the crater as there were only a few Regulars, Bedfords or E. Surreys, on the left, so I said we would wait for a relief.

"Soon after a young officer of the Devons arrived from Trench 41 in the left crater and reported to me that he had three men of his platoon left, but that they were cut off as the parapet on either side of them was blown away and three M.G.'s were raking the parapet above them. I told him to get them to crawl along into the left crater which was very thinly held. There were now just two small groups of men in the left crater, one in the right and another in the gap towards 38. The Devons' officer told me that his battalion was coming up to relieve us, which was good news as the men were very badly shaken. I had previously sent back word asking for reinforcements, but without result. Probably the messengers were too excited to deliver the message. I did not like to send more messengers as they did not return, so I arranged with the Devons' officer to go back myself and report the state of

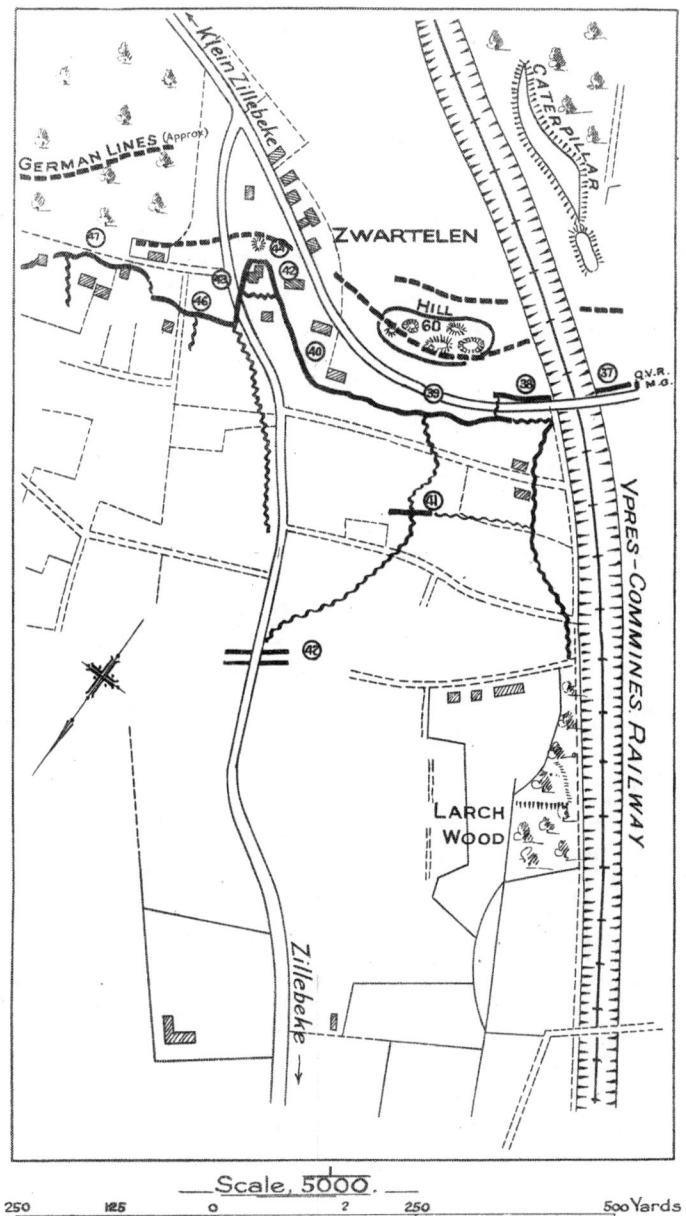

HILL 60. APRIL 20ᵀᴴ-21ˢᵀ 1915.

things to Major Allason. He told me that a relief was coming up at once and the news bucked up the men a lot.

"But the relief never came. So after a while I again went and told Major Allason that I did not think the men in the craters would last much longer. I found two officers of the Devons with him and their men in the C.T. all waiting. Naturally their progress up had been very slow and difficult and they had had about 80 casualties coming along the railway. I arranged to take up 30 men to hold the craters by day, and led the captain up, the men following. When we reached the crater I found only the captain with me, and his sergeant-major came along with a message that the men had been sent back to the trench on the right. I at once went to see what was wrong. They had been called off to 38 trench, as a platoon there waiting for relief saw the party coming and sent a guide to bring relief to themselves. I explained to them that their relief was coming in time and took my party back. Meanwhile in the C.T. to 38, blocking the whole trench, I found 60 trained bombers of the Northumberland Fusiliers ! They had been specially sent up to help on the hill, but their officer had been killed and they were misdirected. In consequence they had been waiting for some hours in the C.T.—trained bombers, with a plentiful supply of bombs—when we had been urgently needing them. I ordered their sergeant to take fifteen of them to help the Devons in the craters and sent the rest back to support. It then only remained to see the Devons properly established and bring off the Q.V.R. men who were left—about fourteen of them altogether.

"The situation was now comparatively quiet, but the Germans continued to shell the C.T. and railway cutting and we had some difficulty in getting back to the Larch Wood dug-outs. When we arrived there I think it was about 10 a.m. I never saw Lees, Westby or Summerhays after they were killed as I never really had the opportunity to look for them. I did not know till later that Westby was missing. I am sorry I cannot give the names of the men on the hill who helped me, but they belonged to other companies and I knew none of them."

CHAPTER X

"They Held the Hill"

MAJOR THOMAS PRIOR LEES was the second son of Mr. Alfred Lees and Mrs. Lees of "The Pines," Bedford, and was born in 1874. He was educated at Bedford Modern School, passing from there as head of the school to Clare College, Cambridge, where he was eighth Senior Optime and took his Degree of M.A. He entered the Home Civil Service Senior Division and at the time of the mobilisation of the Territorial Force was Assistant Secretary of the Civil Service Commission. He was gazetted 2nd Lieutenant in the Victoria and St. George's Rifles on March 22nd, 1899. From the first he was a hard-working conscientious soldier. He obtained a "Special" Certificate at the School of Instruction, Chelsea Barracks, was gazetted Captain in March, 1905, and Major in August, 1913. He passed "Distinguished" in Tactics and in other subjects. As our record shows he was trusted and beloved by the men under his command. The following extracts are taken from a letter sent to his family by Col. R. B. Shipley, O.C. the Q.V.R. : "He died like a hero, having retaken and made good a position of primary importance, which the enemy were on the point of reoccupying. I believe his death to have been instantaneous as he had a bullet mark through the head and was wounded in the chest. His last gallant charge was as he would have wished it, to the assistance of the Bedfords. The last words I heard him speak as he led his company off into the trenches, ' Now remember, if anyone is wounded the others must carry on, not stop with him ; if I am hit, go on.' We have recovered his body and are burying it close to the dug-outs we are occupying. Our total casualties in the fight were 2 officers killed, 1 missing, 2 wounded, 15 Other Ranks killed and 107

Major Thomas Prior Lees,
Killed at Hill 60.

wounded. Westby is missing and I still hope to hear is wounded and gone back. Summerhays is killed; Sampson and Woodroffe both slightly wounded. Everyone behaved superbly, thank to examples such as your brother's. It was his initiative and courageous behaviour that enabled us to hold on to the position and make it good. We are still cheery and tails well up. We have collected most of your brother's effects. They will be sent on in due course. We can only at present put up a rough cross to mark the position of your brother's grave, but it will be recorded in our register returns. I cannot even attempt to tell you what a stupendous loss this is to the regiment and myself, but we must console ourselves by remembering and trying to emulate your brother's unswerving devotion to duty and the unflinching gallantry shown by him in all times of stress ; in short, his life so earnestly devoted to others will live in our memories for all time."

Cpl. H. F. A. Hooper (No. 2349, " A " Co.), who was an eye-witness of the occurrence says : " On the morning when Major Lees was shot the Bedfords were on the extreme right of trench ; the East Surreys being on the left of the Bedfords. Sergt. Pulleyn went and reported to Major Lees and he immediately came over. On his way he had to pass an opening that was enfiladed by the enemy and he was shot. One of the Bedfords collected all Major Lees' papers and handed them over to Sergt. Pulleyn, who brought them straight to Lieut. Woolley together with his revolver. Lieut. Woolley gave them to Sergt. Pulleyn and told him to take them to headquarters."

Very little has transpired concerning the death of Capt. Gilbert B. J. Fazakerley-Westby. Early in the morning he was seen in the crater talking to Major Lees and other officers. Shortly afterwards he was missed and was never seen again. He was the only son of Capt. Jocelyn Fazakerley-Westby, D.L., J.P., late Scots Greys and Lancashire Hussars, and Mrs. Fazakerley-Westby, of Mowbreck and Whitehall, Lancashire. He was gazetted 2nd Lieutenant in 1911, Lieutenant in July, 1913 and Captain only a short time before his death. Col. Shipley, in a letter to his sister, wrote : " Both to the regiment and to myself your brother's absence is a great loss which will be felt by one and all. His quiet, unselfish devotion to duty and his love of his men endeared him to all, and this together with the gallantry he showed last week, will remain with us as a brilliant example for all to emulate." The family of Westby dates back to before the Conquest and appears in *Doomsday Book*. Capt. Fazakerley-Westby was a fine type of Englishman, standing over six feet high, and a perfect soldier whose heart and soul were in his profession.

2nd Lieut. Dudley Leycester Summerhays was the younger son of Mr. T. C. Summerhays, J.P., Alderman Surrey County Council and Mrs. Summerhays of Woodgate House, Wimbledon. He was educated at Westminster School, which he represented in the school team at Bisley for the Public Schools' Challenge Cup. He was intending to practice as a solicitor, but on the outbreak of war, assisting first in the Remount Department, he joined the 5th East Surrey Regiment (T.F.) as a private, afterwards receiving a commission in the Q.V.R., and proceeded with the battalion to France on November 4th, 1914. He was the last officer to join the battalion before leaving for France and only just managed to scramble on to the *Oxonian* as the vessel was leaving the quay at Southampton. Although he had only been with the Q.V.R. for such a short time he soon became most popular, was always cheery and was loved by all. He was a most promising and conscientious officer and keen to do his duty. Lce-Cpl. Nichols (No. 1977, 14 platoon, "D" Company), an eye-witness, contributes the following report of his death : "I was standing by Lieut. Summerhays in the trench on the crater and the enemy were throwing hand-grenades very heavily. One which exploded on the parapet killed Lieut. Summerhays instantly. Lieut. Woolley was directing operations and certainly stopped a panic which would no doubt have led to a rush for the communication trench."

Among the many gallant riflemen who fell during the fighting on Hill 60 was Rfn. H. Brian Brooker, No. 1 Platoon, " A " Company. His platoon was ordered to advance, charge across the open and occupy a small German trench. He was the first man in the trench and was immediately killed. In a letter to his parents 2nd Lieut. W. Upward wrote : " We all mourn the loss of a good soldier and International Sportsman."

" Brian " Hooker was a well-known footballer, being the

regular right back in the Surrey A.F.A. Team. Playing first for the Weybridge Elementary Schools eleven he subsequently had the satisfaction of representing his country as well as his county. He was given his place in the English Team in March, 1909, when a French Team was encountered at Ipswich, when England won by twenty goals to nil. He visited Bohemia as a member of "The Old Grammarians Team." He was also a good all round man in the cricket field. At the time of his death he was twenty-six years of age.

The desperate and prolonged fighting for the possession of Hill 60 will for long be an epic in the history of the British Army, so many famous regiments having at one time or another held the crest just before and during the second battle of Ypres. Closely and honourably interwoven in the story is a testimony to the fighting value of the Territorial Force as exemplified in the glorious part played by the Queen Victoria's Rifles, the 9th (County of) London Regiment, one of the oldest and most celebrated units of the London troops whose gallantry and bearing in some of the most trying episodes of the war have been sung by Field-Marshals Lords French and Haig, and by special correspondents without number. As has been said, the hill stands little more than sixty metres above sea-level and is about 250 yards long, but its importance arose from the fact that its crest overlooked all the ground between the British trenches and Ypres. "But Hill 60," says Sir Arthur Conan Doyle, "was a secondary matter. What was really being fought for was the ascendancy of the British or the Prussian soldier—that subtle thing which would tinge every battle which might be fought hereafter. Who would cry 'enough' first ? Who would stick it to the bitter end ? Which had the staying power when tried out to a finish ? The answer to that question was of more definite importance than an observation post and it was worth our 3,000 slain or maimed to have the award of the God of Battles to strengthen us hereafter." One by one all the officers of the Q.V.R. had fallen and even the N.C.O.'s who remained began to waver. Left to themselves the little remnant of men knew not what to do, when suddenly, just before the dawn, there had appeared from the communication trench 2nd Lieut. Woolley, who, hearing from passing wounded of the loss of all the officers, had voluntarily left a secure position with the reserve and proceeding along took over the command. Encouraging the men with the report that relief was on its way up, and hurling grenades at the Germans, who were but from 10 to 20 yards off, he induced them to hold on. This little " handful of Territorials, under a boy-officer, Woolley of the Victorias, were the only troops upon the top, but it was in safe keeping none the less " (Doyle). In the afternoon of the 21st the fire gradually died away and the assaults came to an end. Hill 60 remained with the British. The weary survivors were relieved and limped back to their rest camps in the rear singing, according to Sir A. C. Doyle " rag-time music," while the 2nd Cameron Highlanders, under Col. Campbell, took over the gruesome trenches. The Victorias had " stuck it " and their brave boy-officer was awarded the V.C., the first to be won by a member of the Territorial Force.

Lieut. Geoffrey Harold Woolley is the son of the Rev. G. H. Woolley, of Danbury Hill, Essex, and was studying for the Church when war broke out. He immediately joined the Queen Victoria's Rifles and was gazetted 2nd Lieut. on August 26th, proceeding to France with the battalion on 4th November, 1914. " When we went up," said an officer of the relief, " we heard someone calling encouragement to the men, and a figure kept leaping up on the line to throw grenades at the Germans." It was the heroic Woolley ; and no man more thoroughly earned the V.C. The official record of the coveted decoration runs : " For most conspicuous bravery on Hill 60 during the night of 20–21st April, 1915. Although the only officer on the hill at the time, and with very few men, he successfully resisted all attacks on his trench, and continued throwing bombs and encouraging his men till relieved. His trench during all this time was being heavily shelled and bombed, and was subjected to heavy machine-gun fire by the enemy." The poet of the 2nd K.O.S.B., Lce.-Cpl. T. Morgan, who also fought on the hill, in a parody on " How would you like to be me," wrote :—

> " We then got relieved by the 9th Q.V.R.'s,
> Who came up in close column with no guide but the stars,
> One of their officers gained the V.C.,
> And we all wish him luck, for a hero was he,
>   Tra la la, tra la lee,
>   The first Territorial to win the V.C."

Lieut. Woolley was gazetted to a temporary captaincy on June 17th, 1915, and was later awarded the M.C. He has since been ordained, and is now a master at Rugby.

The gallant conduct of the troops engaged in this severe contest was warmly praised by Sir John French, who issued the following Special Order : " Gen. Sir Horace Smith-Dorrien, 2nd Army. 21st April, 1915. I congratulate you and the troops of the 2nd Army on your brilliant capture and retention of the important position at Hill 60. Great credit is due to Lieut.-Gen. Sir Charles Fergusson, commanding IInd Corps ; Major-Gen. Morland, commanding 5th Division ; Brig.-Gen. Wanless O'Gowan, commanding 13th Brigade, and Brig.-Gen. Northey, commanding 15th Brigade, for their energy and skill in carrying out the operations. I wish particularly to express my warmest admiration for the splendid dash and spirit displayed by the battalions of the 13th, 14th and 15th Brigades which took part under their respective commanding officers. This has been shown in the first seizure of the position, by the fine attack of the Royal West Kents and the King's Own Scottish Borderers, and in the heroic tenacity with which the hill has been held by the other battalions of these brigades against the most violent counter-attacks and terrific artillery bombardment. I must also commend the skilful work of the Mining Company, R.E., of the 59th Field Company R.E., and 2nd Home Counties Field Company R.E. and of the Artillery. I fully recognise the skill and foresight of Major-Gen. Bulfin, commanding 28th Division, and his C.R.E., Col. Jerome, who are responsible for the original conception and plan of the undertaking."

EXTRACT FROM ADMIRAL NAPIER'S LETTER,
1ST MARCH, 1919

. . . As far as I can make out the little collection of graves must have been badly shelled, and it appears to have been carefully tidied up since, and such crosses as were left replaced. But there are many graves, I should think one-third, with no crosses and another one-third with crosses marked " Unknown Soldier "—and about one-third with names on. A few of the crosses are standing up but most of them are laid on the mounds. Although the ground is tidied up as well as possible it is desperately muddy, but no doubt grass will grow now that it is left in peace. It is railed in with a wire fence. I do not think there is any question of moving any remains, except some single scattered ones that would be in the middle of ploughed land or something of that sort. At least that is as far as I could ascertain.

. . . the railway cutting at Hill 60 is now half filled up by the ground slipping down, and no signs of railway left.

(Graves referred to, those above railway cutting just behind Larch Wood and the support dug-outs near Hill 60.)

The summit of the historic mound is now distinguished by a plain stone pillar bearing a bronze plaque upon which is inscribed :—

> This Memorial is erected
> by
> Queen Victoria's
> Rifles
> To the Glory of God and
> in everlasting memory
> of their Comrades who
> fell in the battle of
> Hill 60
> on April 20–21, 1915.
> Also of all other Q.V.R.'s
> who gave their lives
> for their Country in
> The Great War
> 1914–1918.

CHAPTER XI

THE SECOND BATTLE OF YPRES

ON Thursday 22nd of April commenced the second battle of Ypres, memorable for the first use of asphyxiating gas by the Germans. "The northern section of the salient from the crossing of the Yperlee Canal at Steenstraate (west of Bixschoote) round the north of Langemarck to the Ypres-Poelcappelle road was now held by the French Colonial Division under General Putz. Poelcappelle was in the possession of the enemy. Where the French trenches ended, the Canadian trenches began. Their division occupied a line of some 5,000 yards extending from the Ypres-Poelcappelle road along the Grafenstagel ridge to the Ypres-Roulers railway in the region of Zonnebeke. The division consisted of three infantry brigades, the third was in touch with the French, and the second was on its right. South of the Ypres-Roulers railway a British Division was strung out from Brookseinde to the western outskirts of Bercelaere, whence our line curved through the woods to Hill 60, and beyond it to the Comines-Ypres Canal. Thus the Allied forces formed an arc-like figure, the chord of which was the canal from Steenstraate through Ypres to a point a mile or so south-east of Hill 60 and a mile west to St. Eloi. The aim of the Germans was to destroy the French Colonial troops defending the northern section of the arc and to cross the canal north and south of Steenstraate and at this village. If they succeeded in these operations they would turn the left flank of the Canadians, who would have to retreat or fight an enemy in front and behind them. If they retreated to the Yperlee Canal, the bulk of the British troops from Brookseinde to the Ypres-Comines Canal near St. Eloi would either be cut off or have to make their escape under the fire of the German artillery, through the encumbered streets of Ypres.

That city would fall into the hands of the Germans and the Kaiser would then be able to proclaim the annexation of Belgium " (*The Times History of the War*).

The 13th Infantry Brigade was resting three miles west of Ypres at Vlamertinghe. The Q.V.R. had that morning left the railway cutting and made their way to Ypres, being met on their way to that town by General Smith-Dorrien, who addressed them by request of Sir John French.

After they had reached Brielen news came that the Germans had broken through by means of a " gas attack," at Langemarck, on a 6-mile front on a line held for the most part by French Colonial troops, and were advancing rapidly. " It was nearly 5 p.m. Suddenly an aviator reported that yellow smoke had been seen on the German position between Bixschoote and Langemarck. From their trenches the Turcos perceived a white smoke rising some three feet from the ground. In front of it appeared a greenish yellowish cloud, higher than a man, which drifted towards them. At every 50 feet or so along the German front there was a battery of 20 retorts, and the Germans had at last turned on the chlorine gas " (*Times History*). The Q.V.R. were turned out from their resting-place at Brielen during the night and were ordered to join the 13th Brigade, which was bivouacked near Vlamertinghe. In the early morning they marched to Farm, south of Elverdinghe and were ordered to attack on the east bank of the Yser Canal. They remained on the canal bank during the night and moved forward on the 24th to trenches at Wieltje, being heavily bombarded the whole time. On April 25th a fourth draft consisting of forty men arrived from the 2nd Battalion. From the 23rd to the 25th the regiment was involved in very heavy fighting. Major Dickins records in his diary : " Two officers wounded, 21 R. and F. killed, 76 R. and F. wounded, 5 R. and F. missing, 6 died of wounds." On the 26th the battalion was relieved by the 12th Brigade, returning to Elverdinghe. Writing on that day Capt. Culme-Seymour says : " We are back at last anyhow for a day or two, and I'm all right. A crowd of reinforcements came up as we went out and lots of guns. It's been a big fight, and I think it's the last desperate effort on their side. We lost 102 since Hill 60, and 131 at Hill 60. Everyone is a good deal knocked up, naturally.

There's such crowds to tell you, and I must wait until to-morrow to get the sequence of events right. We've been right in it and it really was awful, but I kept quite all right through the help of God. Herbert Flemming was within 3 yards of me when he was hit. I had just been explaining the situation to him and telling him where I wanted all his men, and that second he turned away to go and get them, when the old ' coalbox ' came. I was nearly deafened and fully expected to find myself hit— but I was unhit then and also at many other times. The men were magnificent and never hesitated. When I got in this morning about 7 a.m. I *very* nearly broke down with relief, but just managed not to. One or two of the men couldn't help themselves. There were some awful sights and it seems extraordinary that there is anyone to come out—but of course there always is. The Canadians were splendid and fought like tigers. Two battalions were wiped out. Our machine-gun sections practically were, too. Only five men and no guns left. We have only got 200 men altogether left and got a draft of 30 in to-day with Sampson's brother. We can't get much news, but from what we can gather the Germans have been driven back about three miles. There is a tremendous cannonade going on everywhere now. We are still in the shell area but comparatively immune, as there are so many other far more important things for the enemy to shoot at. It's a beautiful day. What a life it is! The Canadians' 3rd Brigade Staff yesterday were in a farm close to us and were frightfully shelled—never saw such a bombardment—set fire to the whole place and I'm afraid a lot of the wounded there must have been burnt. There were stacks of ammunition there, too, and it went on going off for about half an hour. Our Head-quarters was full of wounded. I had a short sleep this morning on getting in and feel much better now, and after a good night's rest I'll be as right as rain. Once or twice I felt very excited and made the men laugh, and I think helped them, as there were one or two very sticky times. The Germans came on at an awful pace and took a lot of stopping. I've got to get very busy making out a list of casualties and with getting some new machine-guns. Leslie Cowtan, Lloyd and Woolley were all awfully good, though Woolley was not in this last time as Hill 60 had shaken him up a bit, but he's all right now and ready for the next time. Herbert (Flemming) was not bad, I think, though hit in three places. The men really want a good rest, but I doubt very much if they'll get it. The Doc. (Capt. Roe) is all right, only a bit tired, and has done *awfully* well and worked splendidly under shell-fire the whole time, he's been splendid and quite calm."

The farm used as Head-quarters by the Canadians was known as Canadian Farm. When the buildings took fire the news spread about that they were stored with ammunition and that many Canadian wounded were inside. Lce.-Cpl. Yates of the Q.V.R. hearing this rushed into the blazing building and brought out a number of wounded men. For this gallant act he was awarded the D.C.M.

Capt. Culme-Seymour continues: "April 27th. Our kits are still at Ouderdom, and all parcels are there but we have sent to get them to-day. I'm afraid the casualties we are losing now are enormous, but they must be losing as much. We should have done, and be doing, much better if it wasn't for these beastly gases. Filthy smell it is and you *can't* keep your eyes open. They have issued us with cloths now to put over one's nose and mouth, and we carry them in our haversacks. You have to damp them first. Our machine-gun was smashed up on our way to the trenches, just before Herbert (Flemming) got hit. A shell pitched into the middle of them. We only had 5 left out of 21, but most of them were only wounded and will come back later. We lost about 60 before we got to the trenches, and 102 altogether. When we got up to the supposed trenches I found them all occupied and had to cram in fellows where I could get them in and order others to dig themselves in. They did splendidly and set to work with a will. Not surprising considering the shells that were flying about. . . . I got runners from each company and Leslie Cowtan to help me." Later: "Bombardment still going on. The fight won't be over for a day or two yet, I feel sure. It's a big thing. God grant we smash them, but they've apparently still got big numbers."

The said Capt. Leslie Cowtan has also an interesting account of the same incidents: "We got orders to get back to the huts, so started off and got back to beyond Ypres, where Sir John French was to inspect us, but we were late in getting there, so the commander of our Army, Gen. Smith-Dorrien, did so, and was very kind and said a great many nice things about us and what we had done. From there we went to our huts at Brielen and were just getting settled down when thousands of French began pouring through. . . . So there was no rest that night. We packed up and moved a few miles and joined up with the rest of the Brigade and spent part of the night in the open fields. Next day, Friday, the brigade was ordered to attack north of Ypres in conjunction with the French, so off we started again, very tired and weary. We arrived at the place in the afternoon and stopped for several hours in the middle of the day for rest and food. The attack developed and we were in reserve and, thank God, were not called upon; however, we had to spend that night in the open on the banks of a canal, still in reserve, and during the night carried up ammunition, and shovels, etc. Next morning, Sunday, confident that we had done our share the last week, we looked forward to going back for a long rest, in fact our brigadier said that he hoped to relieve us during the morning, but suddenly things went very wrong indeed a little further south and almost due east of Ypres; there the Huns had made a big push. It is there where very big fighting is going on and was going on when we arrived on Saturday morning. We had orders to occupy a second line of trenches and so again were not right in the thick of it, but in (taking up) this position we had to advance under very heavy shell-fire and lost a lot. Eventually the poor weary Q.V.R. arrived at the position and found it already occupied by Canadians, and so had to dig for life and make a trench. Up to this time I had been with the company, but having got the men up there, Seymour wanted me to stay with him, and so I remained at Head-quarters and helped him. All Saturday we were shelled but did not suffer so much, and stayed there all that day and night and all Sunday and Sunday night.

"During this time we were holding the second line. The Canadians were fine men, wonderful fellows, absolutely calm, and I have never seen such courage. In front of the line we were holding there was a line of troops attacking, and so we were not subjected to rifle fire, but only shell-fire, and plenty of that, I can assure you. There is not much to describe in this, for one just sits and waits. Well, having gone through these days and nights of work, about 4 a.m. yesterday we had instructions to leave our position and get back to a farm near the huts we went to after Hill 60, and so very tired and weary we wandered back to this farm where I am writing now, arriving about 8 or 9 a.m., and so yesterday we ate and slept ; last night I slept again and now do feel much more rested and fit. A great many friends have gone. Flemming was wounded in the leg, and Kinnison, our machine-gun officer, was also wounded. . . . Apart from officers' casualties, three have gone sick, so that altogether the battalion is a bit down. . . . During these strenuous days the regiment has absolutely behaved in a wonderful manner, the men dead tired but still doing what they ought to do and doing it properly. Before Hill 60 show started our reputation was made ; at Hill 60 it was absolutely cemented for all time, and since then—well, we have done better still. It is certainly a very fine regiment, and what it has done will not be forgotten, I hope."

The following extracts from the diary of Rfn. B. C. Stubbs (" B " Co., killed June 23rd), bears witness to the awful time the regiment was going through : " April 24th. Hurried off to another part of the line where Germans had also broken through. Journey made under terrific shell-fire and half battalion is now gone. Position taken up in reserve trenches to be held at all costs. Very exciting, but keeping calm and cool. Never prayed so fervently before, but am quite prepared to face whatever is to come and, please God, we shall stop them. Shell-fire is awful.

" Sunday, April 25th. Reinforcements up at dawn and attack in open order started. At first successful, and then to our horror saw our chaps retreating in disorder and Germans behind them a mile to our front. Most awful fifteen minutes of my life—shells everywhere—men being blown to pieces, and we are unable to help, but bound to wait for Germans and drive them off. Then our chaps rallied and to our joy turned the tables, driving them back into woods and holding them there despite shells and foul gas bombs. Stayed there all day, shelled whole time. Evening position unchanged and we must stop here.

" April 26th. At dawn hear more reinforcements are up

and we can go. Thank God it's over and the position safe. Trench strength of battalion is now 230 rifles, which will show what we have been through (normal strength about 1,000)."

Cpl. Harold Sendall also has a few words of interest to say about the strenuous days following the fight for Hill 60. Writing on April 30th he says : " After this " (General Smith-Dorrien's address) " we moved on to some huts which were being constructed 'while you wait' sort of style, and it was just about sunset when we got in them, then, believe me, we had not been there half an hour when we heard an awful row ; the Germans had broken through, just up the road it was said ; out we came and dug ourselves in on the side of a hedge. Then, after a bit, back to the huts again, and again, just as we were getting to sleep, marched to a field where our transport was stationed. Here they gave us some tea and some grub—how welcome it was to be sure ; we stayed there until Friday midday (April 23rd), then off again to the farm where we are now billeted, a rest under the trees, and then told to parade 'without packs' ; then our troubles started again. We took part in an attack as general reserves ; the attack was a success, so, fortunately, we were not wanted, but when it was dark my platoon had to take ammunition, etc., to the supports, the way the wounded were coming back. We had two men injured on this journey, I think. That night it was very cold ; we slept on the banks of a canal. The next day was, I suppose, the worst of the lot ; we left for the firing line again, not far from the 'bump,' how we got there no one knows. Our officers were just great, I can't say what would have happened if they had not kept cool. The Germans for a start sent over some 'Jack Johnsons,' they are sent with a view to make you run, then comes the shrapnel to catch you as you run ; the stink of the shells and the poor fellows calling for help was terrible, but we won through ; then, when it was dark, dug the trench we were to hold ; we held it all Sunday (April 25th) ; it was here that another chum of mine was, I am afraid, mortally wounded by a piece of shrapnel in the eye, Rfn. Perry, one of the best.[1] We saw some German prisoners, one only sixteen years old. The welcome relief came at dawn on Monday, we were too done for anything else. We got back

[1] Rfn. Horace Smith Perry, died of wounds, 27/4/15.

to the barn at last, hardly able to drag one leg after its fellow, the spirit was willing but the body could not back it up. Tuesday and Wednesday were mostly passed in slumber, so all we want now is a good long rest before we go up again ; let's hope we may get it."

On April 25th the Q.V.R. were at Wieltje ; the following day they were relieved by the 12th Brigade and went to Elverdinghe. On that day Lieut. Nichols was wounded at Brigade H.Q. Then came the two days that " were mostly passed in slumber." The 28th, we learn from Capt. Culme-Seymour, was a perfectly lovely day—hot sun and no wind. He goes on to say : " They keep on catching spies here and found three this morning with telephone apparatus on them. They probably have now suffered the penalty. I sent Woolley's name in this morning for V.C. or D.S.O. He did magnificently on Hill 60, and it is entirely due to him and a few men with him that we were able to hang on to the hill during a very critical time. Everyone was awfully done when we got in here. Tim (O'Shea) met me and shook hands and neither he nor I could speak. However, we are *quite* all right now and getting perfectly fit again. . . .We are better off for men than I thought and have got about 370 for fighting. So many regiments have lost such a lot ! Dick (Shepherd) still in hospital. There's a big pond in front of the farm here and all the men are bathing. I am going to have lunch with ' C ' Company to-day. Woolley commands ' A ' now, Cowtan ' B,' Leys Cox ' C,' and Renton, who has come back, ' D.' Lees is such a loss ; such a splendidly calm, quiet fellow and such a sound soldier—and the men loved him."

Culme-Seymour gives us some particulars of Nichol's injury. According to him it happened on the 28th. " Poor little Nichols was wounded yesterday. He was still with the Brigade Staff and was in a cellar with them when a shell came in and burst and broke his leg. I hope he'll get on all right. Always so awfully cheery and never depressed. He's done awfully well." He has also something to say of the men and things in general. " We've got them (the Germans) held all right now. It was a bit critical when the French went, but the Canadians did perfectly splendidly and saved the situation, while other troops were hurried up. I can't think it will go on for very long now. The Germans are still fighting splendidly, though, and seem to have lots of artillery. Leslie Cowtan is a very good sort, indeed—he always keeps cool and keeps his head and carries on just the same in spite of shells, etc. . . . The rest of the brigade are in some support trenches and dug-outs not very far from St. Jean and are, I believe, absolutely done up. The Brigadier has been trying hard to get us a proper rest and if this show dies down will, I hope, be able to get one. This isn't really an absolute rest as shells are continually falling on either side of the farm, trying to find the guns about 300 and 400 yards each side of here. Give us the guns and shells and lots of men and there isn't a shadow of doubt it will end in no time. Quite quiet at present—very little shelling, only desultory, so imagine the swine have failed once more in a desperate attack. What thousands they must be losing! What prisoners we've seen are quite boys. Their infantry can almost be considered a nonentity—it's their artillery that matters and we've got to get on top of them in that branch. We've managed to buy three chickens to-day and some *vin rouge* at one franc a bottle, so we shall have a jolly good meal. We've got no orders at all of any sort, so can't tell how long we'll be here or what we'll do next. But sufficient for the present that we are getting a rest and some sleep. The last is what everyone wanted. I think I only had at the outside six hours for practically nine days! It's so extraordinary how one can do it, but one gets used to it. Sergt. Clayton—that splendid fellow who sang so well—was killed. Wasn't it a pity? Such a splendid fellow he was and worshipped by everyone."

Sergt. Walter John Clayton was a well-known member of the London Stock Exchange. He was the youngest son of Mr. and Mrs. C. H. Clayton, of Hillside, Ditton Hill, Surrey, and was for many years captain of the Surbiton H.C. Familiarly known as "Jack," his commanding stature and cheery temperament, apart from his brilliance as a player, made him an outstanding personality. He was a clever amateur actor and singer.

CHAPTER XII

THE YPRES STRUGGLE CONTINUED—DEATH OF CULME-SEYMOUR

OF the terrible nature of the fighting in this second battl[e] of Ypres, Sergt. Crossthwaite has much to say, bu[t] several of the incidents he deals with have alread[y] been described in the preceding accounts. "Near the south sid[e] of Wieltje," he writes of April 25th, " we came to more ope[n] ground and were in full view of the German artillery observer[s] who at once turned on such a murderous barrage of heav[y] stuff, 'Black Marias' and shrapnel, that it seemed impossibl[e] any man could live through it. No. 9 platoon was practicall[y] wiped out, John Davies, Farrar, Wilkie[1] and the remainder o[f] their section being killed by a direct hit. No. 10 followed i[n] short rushes and men fell fast, but the survivors pressed o[n] through the blinding smoke, the ground torn with flame an[d] the red shrapnel bursting overhead. About half the platoo[n] won through and doubled to a hedge parallel to the Germa[n] position. Orders were passed along to dig in behind the hedg[e] as rapidly as we could, as the enemy was seen to be advancin[g] and there was little time to spare. There were no picks o[r] shovels, so each man got to work with his entrenching tool an[d] dug for himself a hole. The ground was very hard and th[e] roots of the hedge struck across at right angles, but, incredibl[e] as it may seem, every man was up to his shoulders inside a[n] hour. In the course of the night these holes were joined u[p.] It was a marvellous bit of work, done as it was by weary me[n] exhausted by the stiff advance. No sooner were we dug i[n] than we saw dense masses of greyish figures emerging from wood about 500 yards in our front. The battalion got int[o] action, and right and left of us we could hear the whirrin[g]

---

[1] ? Wilkinson. All three killed in action, 24/4/15.

of machine-guns. Well below us, say, 300 yards, and to our right, a battalion was extended along a wide field and I never saw anything to equal the cool machine-like discipline of their firing line. The Germans advanced out of the wood to within, I should think, about 200 yards, and then this firing line got to work on them. Their rapid fire was like that of a machine-gun. I could see the men falling fast but the line remained glued to the earth and the enemy broke before it. I never found out the name of that battalion but I take off my hat to it whatever it was. . . . I think it would be about five or six on this afternoon when I saw Captain Flemming hit. He was walking away from us about 100 yards to our rear, on his way to another platoon, when a shell—one of the variety we called Black Marias on account of the thick smoke it made—struck just behind him. He seemed to jump in the air and half turn round and we fully expected that he had been killed outright, but although badly wounded he was still alive and when dusk came he was taken down, to the great grief of the company which he had led so well for many months."

Capt. Flemming joined the ranks of the Mounted Infantry section of the Victoria and St. Georges R.V. at the time of the South African War, and on the dissolution of that section, when the Volunteers became the Territorials, he was given a commission. He was sent home and was received into the Fishmongers' Hall Hospital, where he died on the 7th of May. He was accorded a military funeral at Hampstead Cemetery, the 3rd Battalion Q.V.R. supplying the Guard of Honour and Firing Party. A number of past officers of the regiment attended.

"When darkness fell," continues Sergt. Crossthwaite, "I got permission from Capt. Cox to send a couple of my men to reconnoitre a farm we had seen on the way up. They came back in about half an hour with a pail of buttermilk and a big steak pie which had been abandoned by their former owners on their flight southwards. We had a glorious tuck-in, as we were nearly famished, and while we were discussing this little godsend a Canadian Colonel strolled up and said, ' Well, Sergeant, you seem to have struck oil some. Do you mind giving me a bit of that pie as I have had nothing solid for a day or two.' So he joined in and we gave him a tot of rum, too. He told us most of his battalion had been wiped out and that the Canadian Division he was attached to had made their big stand just about the place where we were entrenched. Later on in the evening the Adjutant came round and told us that the Canadian General had congratulated the Q.V.R. on the splendid work they had done that afternoon. They had filled a very dangerous gap in the line in the nick of time, and got to work so quickly with their digging and firing that the Germans had not realised that the position was held by barely one-third of a battalion extended in a thin line with no guns and no supports. They did not find it out until it was too late."

"The Private in the Queen Victoria's Rifles" whose contribution to *The Great War* we have already noticed referring to those eventful days says: "About midday on Saturday, April 24th, orders arrive to be ready to move. We tramp across fields, recently ploughed and sown, passing the village of St. Jean on our right. Everywhere troops are on the move. An enemy aeroplane has seen what is happening and soon shells begin to drop—not a few here and there, but a perfect hailstorm of metal. Troops are moving up everywhere. Order is kept marvellously considering. We stumble along as quickly as we can. I don't know who is leading us, or where we are making for. The air is thick with smoke and breathing becomes difficult. Presently we reach a partly built rampart and are told to spread ourselves out as much as possible, and dig ourselves in behind it. Operations are soon begun. Higher up a shell has burst among our men; another bursts within a few yards of the spot where I am working. I have just time to fall flat—surely that can't have missed me?—Yes, I am quite all right, though Chalmers has got a nasty piece in his thigh. We are only digging a few minutes when orders come to advance toward a farm building. Making our way in our own time we reach a pile of mangle wurzels—I stay behind this for a breather. Half-right from this about 200 yards away, is a trench, and it is there we are to make for. Having recovered my breath I make a dash. The enemy have evidently spotted us, and a machine-gun is soon busy. Gad, I never heard so many bullets whistle past me before! I reach a sort of 'don't care' mood and plod across to the trench as best I can, for I am absolutely whacked. I reach it in safety, and flop down on some straw in the bottom, thoroughly exhausted. The trench is held by Canadians, but they are very few, and my company links up with them. Apparently this was originally a support trench, but owing to the enemy having been successful in taking some trenches of ours in front of a wood, this position is now a front line one. We arrive just after the Germans had made an attack on some other trenches, and had been repulsed, and as they retreat across an open space, between a farm building and the wood, we are able to pepper them well from our position. The range was 800 yards, but I think we accounted for a few —anyhow, not many reached the wood. This is the first occasion on which I have had a real target—and didn't I enjoy it, too. As darkness came, we began to get busy improving the trench. There was a plentiful supply of good turf to be dug behind the trench and very soon we began to make ourselves a fairly safe shelter. Rain, however, began to fall, and this did not cheer our spirits. Dawn arrives (Sunday, April 25th). About 7 a.m. heavy rifle fire opens from the wood, which is half-left from our position, and presently we observe the cause —a kilted regiment is advancing to attack. The bark of a dog sounds above the rifle fire, and, sure to behold, there is the figure of a big black dog running ahead of the Scotties. What a fine sight !—for an enormous lot of the poor chaps are falling. The distance is far too much to cover (about 800 yards), and in broad daylight, too. Very soon the attack is given up, and those who are left make their way back. Things quieten down a bit. I snatch an hour or two's well-needed sleep. About 2 p.m. the enemy start shelling some farm buildings about 15 yards in the rear of our trench, but about 100 yards from the spot where I am. They are sending over some very heavy stuff. My pals must be having a pretty hot time up at that end. The farm buildings are used as a head-quarters by the Canadians. The range is soon found, and smoke issuing from the buildings shows us a fire has occurred. Soon ammunition begins to cackle off, and this goes on for some hours. A lot of stores, etc., must have been lost. The bombardment lasts about three-quarters of an hour, during which I count ninety shells that have been sent over. News comes along that one of the shells dropped on the parapet of the trench further up on the right, and Cpl. Beard and Rfn. Monker had been injured. Dusk comes on and, being anxious to fill my bottle, I volunteer to get some water from the pump at the farm. I take another fellow with me and we pick our way through the ruin to the pump and begin filling the bottles. There are a lot of other fellows (Canadians) also on the same search; others are in search of whatever they can find in the way of spare rations, etc. Suddenly another shell comes over, bursting beyond the buildings. Fellows scuttle away like rats; my pal and I make hasty tracks for our trench again. Having reached it in safety I sit down and laugh, for it is really most amusing to see everyone suddenly dart away in all directions, dropping the tins of jam which they had been confiscating. The rest of the night passes peacefully and we are able to continue the work of fortifying our trench. Roberts, unluckily, gets a stray bullet in his arm. But it is a nice clean wound. The grey dawn (April 26th) begins to appear and with it a heavy mist. About 4 a.m. our Adjutant appears and tells us to hurry and get ready to be relieved. It is most essential to get away before the mist rises, for it is now almost broad daylight. We file out and are led across fields, reaching the village of St. Jean, through which we pass. What havoc and devastation has been done! A few days ago people were living here, and now, roofless houses, shattered walls, shell-holes dotting the cobbled road. Furniture is lying in the streets, the smouldering remains of a motor-ambulance stands on the side of the road; dead men and horses are lying everywhere, and not always the whole body, alas. We leave the road and go across country once more; at last, striking the canal, we move along the banks. This embankment is now a mass of dug-outs, for it has been heavily shelled since we were last here. All had seemed so undisturbed before, and I plucked cowslip which grew among the grass. We rest a few minutes when we have crossed the pontoon bridge, and then continue our march to the farm near Elverdinghe. We are all played out by this time and many have had to fall out on the way."

The following Special Order for the Day was issued by Lieut.-Col. Shipley on April 28th, and was read not only to the 1st Battalion in France, but to the 2nd and 3rd Battalions of the Q.V.R. then training in England :

28/4/15

Special Orders for the Day.

The Field-Marshal Commanding-in-Chief has received the following message from the Secretary, War Office. His Majesty sends the following message :

" During the past week I have followed with admiration the spendid achievements of my troops including the capture and retention of Hill 60 after heavy fighting, and the gallant conduct of the Canadian troops in repulsing the enemy and recapturing four heavy guns.

I heartily congratulate all units who have taken part in these actions."

The appreciation of the services of the battalion expressed by General Sir H. Smith-Dorrien, Commanding the 2nd Army, after the return of the battalion from Hill 60 will be in the recollection of all ranks. Since then the battalion has had to undergo another trying ordeal with a further heavy list of casualties. The Commanding Officer endorses every word the Army Commander said and wishes to convey to all ranks his great pride in having the honour to command such a magnificent body of men. The long list of casualties which are inevitable the Commanding Officer very deeply regrets, and wishes to offer his sympathy to all those of his comrades who have lost their friends. In such operations as these it is difficult to pick out individuals who have particularly distinguished themselves when all have done their duty so nobly and without the slightest hesitation. He, however, wishes to call attention to the services of the undermentioned and to thank them in the name of their battalion for the invaluable services on Hill 60 and during the operations East of the Yser Canal.

Capt. W. F. Roe, R.A.M.C., and all Stretcher Bearers.
  2nd Lieut. G. H. Woolley   "A" Coy.
    830 Sergt. G. R. Warrington "A" ,,
   2349   "   F. Hooper   "A" ,,
   1867 Lce.-Cpl. F. A. Swoffer   "A" ,,
   2233   "   P. G. Clarke   "A" ,,

66	Sergt.	M. Brawn	"B"	Coy.
1435	"	S. L. Ramus	"B"	,,
3366	C.S.M.	Sherriff	"C"	,,
2073	Rfn.	A. Payne	"C"	,,
882	Sergt.	H. E. Soundy	"D"	,,
2170	Lce.-Cpl.	C. H. Rose	"D"	,,
1293	Sergt.	G. Arnold	"C"	,,
306	A/C.S.M.	E. W. Andrews	"A"	,,
1061	Sergt.	E. H. Pulleyn	"A"	,,
1760	Cpl.	H. D. Peabody	"A"	,,
1876	Rfn.	A. B. Ashford	"A"	,,
2361	Lce.-Cpl.	G. F. Telfer	"A"	,,
892	Sergt.	R. Browett	"B"	,,
2375	A/Sergt.	H. J. How	"B"	,,
2519	Lce.-Cpl.	N. Bell	"C"	,,
450	C.S.M.	F. T. A. Brehaut	"D"	,,
2087	Lce.-Cpl.	H. J. Fippard	"D"	,,
2160	Rfn.	J. Darrell	"D"	,,
2925	,,	C. A. Spooner	"D"	,,

The well-earned rest came to an end all too quickly, but the men got the benefit of three full nights' sleep. At 6 p.m. on Thursday, April 29th, orders came for the battalion to go into the trenches again, and two strong Companies made up from the remnant of the regiment marched to Wieltje under the command of Capts. Leys Cox and Lindsey-Renton, where they were put under the command of the O.C. the King's Own Yorkshire Light Infantry. Having crossed the canal by the pontoon bridge they were met by guides. The guide for Capt. Lindsey-Renton's company, one of the K.O.S.B, very soon lost his way, first going into the line held by the French where an officer directed him elsewhere. Eventually the company got on to a good main road along which they marched There were no signs of any other troops beyond an officer standing at a cross road. The guide led on without in any way indicating where he was going or how near he was to the line Just then a Very Light went up from the German line which appeared to be but a short distance away. The officer ran up from the cross road and informed Capt. Lindsey-Renton that he had gone well beyond the British line and was walking straight into the Boche position ! The guide had led them through the very gap in the British line which they were to have occupied and but for the warning given by the officer the company would have marched right into the arms of the Germans. On this night and the following day the casualties in the regiment numbered 3 rank and file killed and 7 wounded. Amongst those who fell on this occasion were Rfn. G. Clarke and Gillate. The following details of their end were contributed by Lce.-Cpl. Norman Bell : "It was after the Canadians had been driven back and we were advancing again. A party of us had to go out to dig a trench right in advance of our lines, at night-time of course. After digging in one place we had to cross over some open ground right in front of the German position to get to another part of the trench. We ran across and some of our men jumped down into the trench, when we found that one named Clarke had been hit. Gillate immediately dropped his spade and ran out to try and help him, only to be hit himself. We got them both in and found that Clarke was dead, and that Gillate had three bullets in his body and only lived about twenty minutes. I was so struck by the manner of his death that I thought I would like his people to know, otherwise he will remain one of the ' nameless heroes ' of this terrible war." Geoffrey Wyndham Gillate was the son of Mr. E. Unwins Gillate, of 57 Venner-road, Sydenham, and was twenty-two years of age. He was educated at the Aske School, Hatcham, and was an employee of Messrs. Pawsons and Leaf, Ltd. His body lies in a graveyard at Ypres.

On the 30th the whole brigade came out of the line, but there was to be no " rest." From May 1st to 11th the Q.V.R. were mostly in support, changing their quarters almost every day. All the time there was continuous heavy fighting, but it proved a very important fortnight in the war career of the Queen Vics. On May 6th Lieut.-Col. Shipley went sick with a damaged knee and handed the command of the regiment over to Major V. W. F. Dickins ; two days later Lieut.-Col. Shipley was invalided home. On the 5th with the aid of a gas attack the Germans had retaken Hill 60 and repeated attacks by our old friends the K.O.S.B., the K.O.Y.L.I. and the West Kents failed to regain possession of it. The strength of the Q.V.R. at this time was but 320. On the morning of May 7th the

Adjutant, Capt. Culme-Seymour, of whose interesting letters we have made so much use, was killed. The sad occurrence is thus described by Capt. Leslie Cowtan : " As you know, Hill 60 was retaken by the Germans and counter-attacks were made by that poor old brigade—the 13th. The K.O.S.B. tried in vain and then the K.O.Y.L.I. tried a little further down with ourselves in support. It was while that attack was going on that George was killed. The attack started at 2.30 a.m. and about 3.0 a message came down for one company to go up in support. My company (' B ') was detailed and off we started and got up, but found hundreds of men there, and so I stayed in a communication trench leading to the support trench I was supposed to be in. There I intended to wait until the support trench got cleared a bit of K.O.Y.L.I. and then put my men in. George came along and saw me and we had a talk about the position of the attack generally, and he decided that I had better get my company back to better cover than the communication trench and come up again later if necessary, as the communication trench was very shallow and bullets raining over the top. Then from me he went on to see the Major of the K.O.Y.L.I., who was directing things—and then apparently he was not satisfied and decided for everyone's sake that he would go and have a look for himself in the fire trenches. It was without doubt a most essential thing to do, for the situation was almost impossible to work out without first-hand news. And then he went into 39 and 40 trenches, then occupied by the Cheshires, and it was there that he was shot. He didn't linger or even have time to think, for he died at once."

Gen. Sir Charles Fergusson, Commanding 2nd Army Corps, wrote : " I have heard a little from an engineer officer who was actually with George at the time. The whole story, so far as I can gather and from what I know, is as follows : We lost some trenches the night before and a counter attack was ordered. The Germans had got a footing in our line of trenches and had made a barricade at each end to cut us off. The attack was made in front by the Yorkshire Light Infantry, and the Cheshires were ordered to co-operate from the right flank, to blow down the barricade at that end and work up the German trenches. This was in the middle of the night. The 9th London were in support in a little larch wood about 300 or 400 yards

Captain George Culme-Seymour.
Adjutant, Q.V.R.

from the trench in question. The Yorkshires attacked, but there was some uncertainty as to whether the Cheshires were getting on and a company of the 9th London was ordered up in support. They were also told to find out what was going on and send back word, and George said he would go up and find this out. He got along to the barricade where the engineer officer was trying to plant his explosives to blow it up. While they were doing this the Germans came up to the other side of the barricade. George called on the men behind him to drive them back and was apparently climbing over the barricade, or at any rate dashing out to lead them, when he was shot dead. It was quite instantaneous; he had no suffering. They brought him back and he was buried behind the little larch wood." " Our old larch wood," as he termed it in the very last letter he sent home; written on the eve of his death. His burial is thus described by Sergt. Crossthwaite : " We buried him, under severe fire, just north of and near the boundary of Larch Wood. Major Dickins read the burial service over the body and Capt. Roe, the M.O., and four sergeants, among whom were McMoran of the gun team and myself, as representatives of the regiment, lowered him into his last home. I don't think there was a man of us who did not break down, so great was our love for and admiration of the gallant soldier who had so much to do with the making of the battalion. It was an irreparable loss."

The following letter, written by Sir Charles Fergusson to Lieut.-Col. Shipley after he had left the battalion, was received by Major Dickins : " IInd Corps, 8/5/15. My dear Shipley, I hoped to have come over to see you to-day, but the activity of the Germans keeps me tied to my Head-quarters for the time being. I do sympathise so with you in the hard time you and your fine battalion have been going through, and more especially in the loss of poor George Seymour—I know well how you must feel it. He was as gallant a soul as ever stepped, and his loss means much to us—I have written to his poor little wife, who is a niece of mine, but of course have no details to tell her. If you ever have time, I wish you would scribble me a note to tell how it happened, and where he is buried, so that I may be able to tell her something. I wish it had been possible already to pull your battalion out into a better resting-place, and as soon as it is possible it will be done. But they can give me no outside troops at the moment and we have to struggle on as best we can. I know your battalion has done its utmost and will continue to do so, but I know well how exhausted it must be.—Yours very sincerely, (signed) Charles Fergusson."

Capt. George Culme-Seymour was the youngest son of Admiral Sir Michael Culme-Seymour and gained his commission in the King's Royal Rifle Corps from the Militia in October, 1899. He served in the South African War, taking part in the operations leading to the relief of Ladysmith, locked up in which was a battalion of the K.R.R.C. under the command of Col. W. Pitcairn Campbell, a former Adjutant of the Victoria and St. George's V.R.C., and the present Honorary Colonel of the Q.V.R. He was also present in the actions at Colenso, Pieter's Hill and Laing's Nek, and was awarded the Queen's Medal with five clasps. His work and influence in the early days of the war were invaluable and helped largely in making the battalion all that it proved itself to be in the actions and incidents we have described. He was thirty-seven years of age and left a widow and two children.

The duties of Adjutant were taken over by Capt. Cowtan until May 15th, when he went sick and was succeeded by Lieut. J. C. Andrews, who carried on up to the 25th, when Capt. Ormrod, Royal Welsh Fusiliers, was officially gazetted Adjutant. This officer, however, returned to duty with his own regimental unit on June 22nd, when Lieut. J. C. Andrews was appointed his successor.

The first "ranker" in the Territorial Force to gain the V.C. was Lce.-Sergt. Douglas Walter Belcher, a former member of the Q.V.R., but at the time of winning this great distinction belonging to the London Rifle Brigade, which he had joined on the outbreak of war. The official record states : " On the early morning of May 13th, 1915, when in charge of a portion of an advanced breastwork south of the Wieltje-St. Julien road, during a very fierce and continuous bombardment by the enemy which frequently blew in the breastwork, Lce.-Sergt. Belcher, with a mere handful of men, elected to remain and endeavour to hold the position after the troops near him had been withdrawn. By his skill and great gallantry he maintained his position during the day, opening rapid fire on the enemy, who were only 150 to 200 yards distant, whenever he saw them collecting for attack. There is little doubt that the bold front shown by Lce.-Sergt. Belcher prevented the enemy breaking through on the Wieltje road, and averted an attack on the flank of one of our divisions."

One of the men with Lce.-Sergt. Belcher, Pte. E. Hodgkinson, was given the Military Medal. Both Belcher and Hodgkinson were shortly afterwards given commissions in the Queen Victoria's Rifles. Lieut. Belcher, V.C., later served in an Indian regiment. In 1922 he rejoined the L.R.B.

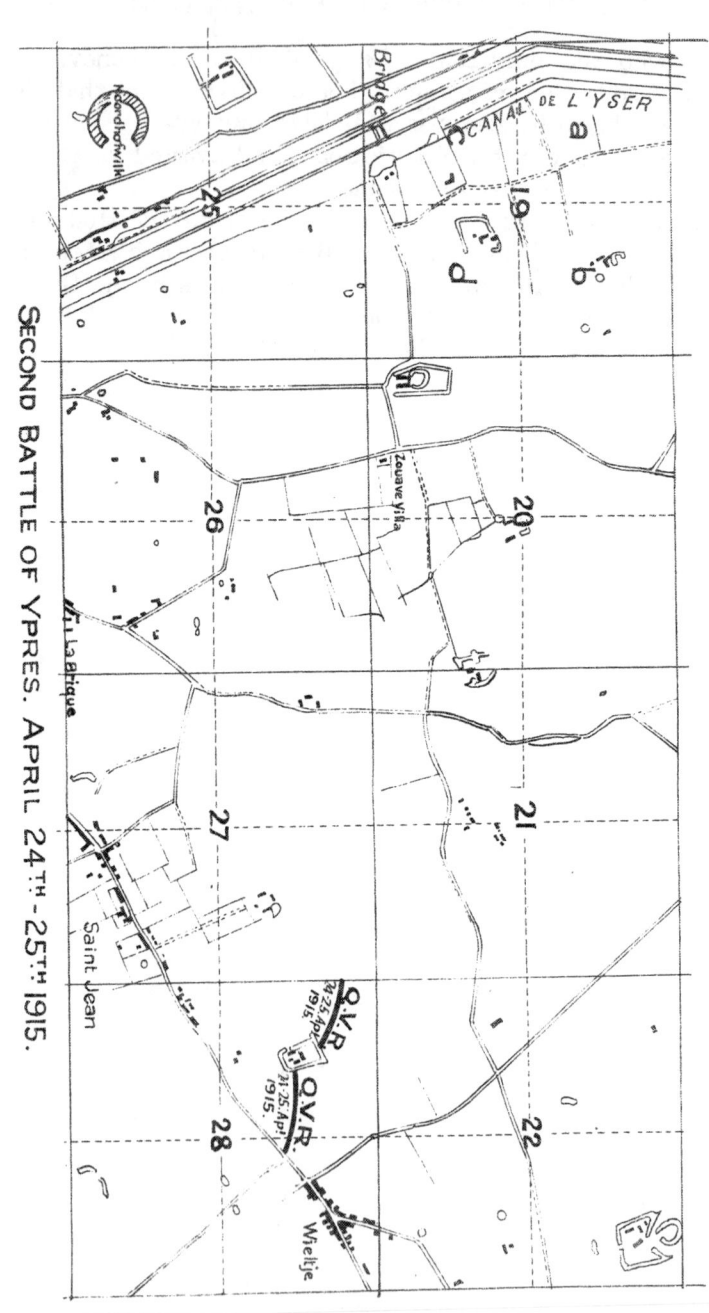

CHAPTER XIII

Rest and Reorganization after Ypres

IN spite of their gas, terrific bombardments and repeated assaults, although they occasionally made a little headway, the Germans were held and enormous losses inflicted upon them. Fighting continued all around the City of Ypres, which was itself heavily shelled throughout the battle, particularly on May 11th when over hundreds of incendiary shells descended upon the ruins, and again on the 13th when, according to Sir Herbert Plumer, " the heaviest bombardment yet experienced " opened. The Germans attacked on a wide front but were everywhere repulsed ; fresh British troops were brought up, a counter-attack made, and the original position regained. By nightfall the enemy had completely failed, the ground being covered by their dead and dying. By May 17th not a German who was not killed, wounded or a prisoner remained on the left bank of the Yperlee Canal.

On May 8th the Q.V.R. had been pulled out of the fighting line and from that day until the 13th were stationed in dug-outs on the west end of Zillebeke Pond or Reservoir. It was according to Sergt. Crossthwaite : " One long nightmare of hiding in foul and muddy holes either in the wood or on the railway embankment ; standing-by at night with endless fatigues to the trenches with ammunition and engineering stores, getting scraps of sleep during the day and much wind-up sometimes, muddy and lousy and utterly fed-up."

On May 11th Lieut. J. C. Andrews, who had been suffering from an attack of " trench-foot " and had done two months' training with the 2nd Battalion in England, rejoined the battalion. He was accompanied by Lieuts. J. C. Holms, E. J. A. Lane, L. Duncan and S. J. Holloway, and on the 12th arrived a further draft of 140 men from the 2nd Battalion.

Lieut. Andrews was appointed Acting-Adjutant and was shortly after given the temporary rank of Captain, ante-dated to January 8th.

The 13th Brigade at this time was under the command of Brig.-Gen. Wanless O'Gowan, with Capt. Hunter, K.R.R.C., as Brigade-Major, and Capt. Street, Devonshire Regiment, as Staff Captain.

On the 13th May the battalion was relieved at 11.10 p.m. and marched to a rest camp at Scherpenberg, arriving at 4.50 in the morning.

Let a new-comer on the scene, Lieut. H. P. Rashleigh, who had joined up on May 4th, relate his sense of the relief, apparently as welcome to him as it was to the bitter experience of the past couple of months : " Here we are, out of the hurly-burly for the time being. We spent five days altogether in those dug-outs (near Zillebeke Pond) behind the firing line, sleeping and doing nothing in particular all day, and sending up fatigue parties by night to the firing line (Hill 60). At last, yesterday, a message came round that we were to be relieved. We sent up a fatigue party of 75 to carry sandbags to the firing line at dusk and soon after their return we started off, one company at a time, at intervals of ten minutes. The whole march was about twelve miles and the first part, of course, entirely in the dark. I found it rather a stiff march, because of the weight of my pack, which rather caught me between the shoulders. After three or four miles we halted and, as we were well out of the danger zone, the remainder of the march was carried out by the battalion as a whole. About five miles short of our destination we had a halt of three-quarters of an hour and tea was served out. I don't think I ever enjoyed myself so much. We arrived here (Scherpenberg) at about six this morning. We are in huts, in rather pretty surroundings, green woods and so on. We, four officers in ' D ' Company, share a hut about 20 feet by 15, roof sloping almost to the ground on both sides. We have a servant each, and a fifth to do the cooking. On our arrival they brought us hot soup, followed by hot meat of some kind, and potatoes. Then we had some fruit which one of us had had from home. Then we went to bed—on our valises—which were spread on straw at one end of the hut, with blankets, and slept the sleep of the just, till 1 or 2 p.m.; then shaved, washed and dressed with solemn deliberation befitting the occasion. I think we may be here ten days or a fortnight, but it does not do to be too sanguine—the men at any rate (and most of the officers) badly needed this rest; they have had a bad time during the last month or so, especially before I came out. I refer to the fighting on Hill 60, where we had a lot of casualties."

"Rest and Reorganisation" was the order during the six days spent at Scherpenberg. Each company made its own arrangements, submitting the programme for the day to the Orderly Room. Instruction chiefly consisted of platoon and company drill, musketry practice and a course for machine-gunners. On the 20th a move was made to Ouderdom (F. Camp), where more company training was indulged in. On this day Major V. W. F. Dickins was placed in temporary command of the 13th Brigade. Two days later the huts at Ouderdom were vacated and the battalion marched to Chateau Blanc near Kruisstraat, where the men went into dug-outs in H.23.a and b. "This time they really are some dug-outs," says Lieut. Rashleigh.

Digging and fatigue parties of 100 per company were provided nightly, one company, in turn, resting in support dug-outs in the chateau grounds for forty-eight hours and providing carrying parties. On the night of the 23rd, writes Sergt. Crossthwaite, "C" Company was detailed for night digging near Hill 60: "We got away as dawn was breaking and ran slap into a gas-cloud travelling east from Ypres. We saw a green mist about twice the height of a man creeping along the ground and until it reached us we had no idea it was the deadly stuff that the cowardly Huns had loosed. There was soon little room for doubt, however, as it gripped one by the throat and made breathing almost impossible. We must have been a long way off the cylinders, but even then we suffered a lot as we had absolutely no protection. Just as the column had been thrown into this confusion the Germans put shrapnel over and we had 22 casualties (1 Officer, and 21 Other Ranks. War Diary). Luckily we were near a line of cottages and so got protection from both, but it was a near thing. When the order was given to take cover I rushed into a cottage where a Belgian woman was in bed and she shrieked blue murder, thinking I was a Hun! I was sick for four days after and still at times feel the effect of the foul stuff."

The battalion left Kruisstraat on May 26th and proceeded to trenches Q2 and Q3 at St. Eloi, the H.Q. being in a partly ruined convent in the adjacent village of Voormezeele. These trenches had been occupied by the Liverpool Scottish. "The distribution," says Capt. Lindsey-Renton, "was as follows: 200 men, practically a company and a half, in the front line (Q2), one company in support in Q3 and the remainder of the battalion in reserve in dug-outs and shelters in Scottish Wood (H.35.b). Battalion H.Q. in the convent in Voormezeele. The battalion held these trenches without any outside relief but had to arrange its relief within itself. Q2 on its northern side was practically a support to Q1, but on its southern flank became the front line. All these trenches were overlooked by the famous 'Mound of Death,' where there had been heavy fighting in March. The work in the sector was heavy as even when the men left the trenches and went back to Scottish Wood for a rest there were fatigue parties every night which took every available man away. The trenches were but breastworks really and required a great deal of labour to get them into good repair. During the time the battalion was in the sector it used no less than 87,000 sandbags in making and repairing the breastworks. The battalion dug a communication trench from H.35.b central through Elzenwalle to Voormezeele to give covered protection for approach by daylight. The Transport and Q.M. Stores were near Dickebusch. Major R. W. Cox was in charge of all men while in Scottish Wood and acted as a battalion rear H.Q., keeping up a continuity of control and organisation in the reserve area. Owing to its height 'the Mound' gave the enemy excellent observation over all our trenches and necessitated our building up the trenches to afford cover from view. This especially applied to the communication trench between Q3 and Q2 which was much exposed. The corner by the church in Voormezeele was a very awkward place to pass along at night as it was continuously raked by rifle and machine-gun fire, and anyone having to pass the corner did so hurriedly. An object of interest in the vicinity of the trenches was a bus which in the early days of the war must have been hit by a shell while conveying troops from Voormezeele to St. Eloi. It was in pretty good condition. A house standing near was known to all as ' Bus House.' "

" Life in Scottish Wood was not free from disturbance. Being only 3,000 yards from the front line it was rather close up for a ' rest ' area and frequently received a dose of whizz-bangs. Luckily they usually fell in the eastern portion of the wood while the troops were stationed in the west, but as some people were living in wooden huts the arrival of a shell was always disturbing. On one occasion eleven men were wounded by shrapnel while washing. While here we had our first experience of plagues of flies and other winged creatures ; there was especially a green fly of the size of a ' bluebottle ' that infested the trenches in swarms and in places completely covered whole portions of the parapet. We also soon appreciated the necessity for stringent sanitary precautions which had not previously existed ; in fact, could hardly exist, in the conditions of the winter months. One night the Germans exploded a mine in the trenches on our left and at the same time put down a fair barrage with artillery fire, and although the mine was not on our front a good many shells came over and caused several casualties." (War Diary: Other Ranks, 3 killed, 2 wounded.) " Although it was summer time we suffered a good deal from our old enemy, flooded trenches, more especially in the communication trenches ; the one leading from Voormezeele south in the direction of ' Moated Grange ' and the east towards Q3 was often flooded to a considerable depth."

Writing on May 28th Lieut. Rashleigh reports : " One of the fellows (? Hallett [1]) was shot yesterday morning while on sentry duty ; there was apparently no chaplain to be had so Renton asked me if I would officiate. We had a stretcher and six men and a corporal—they all took turns at carrying— and the funeral took place about a mile behind the firing line (in Voormezeele), and we got back at about half-past one or two. Except for that one casualty we are having a very quiet time here. From the officers' point of view the routine is something like this—the men have to ' stand to ' when ordered ; when not standing to we post sentries, so many to

[1] Frank William Marmaduke Hallett, killed in action, 27/5/15.

each section of the trench. The officers have to go up and down their particular section of the trench at irregular intervals to see that the sentries are alert. By night one officer is not supposed to sleep at all. I get my sleep usually between about 3.15 a.m. and some fairly late hour in the morning—this morning it was 11.30 a.m. So you see we are having a fairly easy time at present. I sleep in a large dug-out with Renton. Sammy (Lieut. Sampson) comes in for meals—he has left his knife, fork and spoon behind at Kruisstraat and has to depend on charity in this respect. We lunch to-day at 4 p.m., tea at seven, dinner at midnight. Besides looking after sentries we are supposed to make arrangements for repairing the trench in various ways—a never-ending job."

On June 6th Major Dickins was gazetted Temporary Lieut. Colonel and two officers arrived from the 2nd Battalion. On the 15th Lieut. Holms was promoted to Captain. Two days previously it was announced that Sergt. Burgess ("D" Co.) had been awarded the D.C.M. for distinguished conduct on January 1st when the shell burst among Capt. Sampson's platoon in the barn.

Writing to Col. Tanqueray, the President of the O.C.A., on June 18th, Col. Dickins says : " Many thanks for sending me the copy of the resolution passed by the Q.V.R. Old Comrades' Association congratulating Woolley ; I have made it known to the regiment here. Also please accept my thanks on behalf of the Q.V.R. for your kind thoughts and proposing to send us out 100 more knives ; they have not turned up yet, but no doubt will do so in due course and will be very acceptable. To-day being the anniversary of Waterloo we expected things to be a bit lively, but so far nothing much has happened. I am seated in the garden attached to my H.Q. in a ruined village and a few shells are going over my head and bursting about 50 to 100 yards away, but one has been under fire so long that you take very little notice of it. If it gets too bad or a bit too close I have a dug-out in the garden to retire to and wait events, with a telephone to the trenches and guns. The latter I can turn on in 30–40 seconds. It is very hard work running and commanding a battalion here, there is such an enormous amount of official correspondence to do and some awful conundrums to answer, in addition to having to visit all the trenches and supports every day and night, by either Andrews, who is my Adjutant, or myself. We have been in our present trenches for a month, so I expect we shall move again soon. The weather has been very hot and the whole country smells and stinks of dead bodies, horses, cattle, etc., many in the fields still unburied, which are very difficult to get at, and then only by night as they are in places constantly under fire; the ruined villages smell very badly from the quantity of refuse about, but it speaks well for being inoculated against typhoid fever as we have not had a single case in the battalion."

During the whole time the Q.V.R. were at Voormezeele and Scottish Wood the German snipers were very active and a number of casualties occurred. The total for June was 3 killed and 40 wounded.

Among the killed was Rfn. Bernard Castle Stubbs, No. 2655, who joined the regiment in September, 1914, and was attached to " B " Company on February 24th. During his short term of service he kept a diary, from which we have given one or two extracts concerning the battle of Hill 60 and subsequent fighting. He was a member of the Fenchurch Street office staff of the Union Castle Line and his death at the early age of twenty-four closed what was a very promising career. He was educated at Slough, where he was distinguished both in his classes and in the school sports, and was head boy of the school during his last terms, as well as captain of the cricket and football teams, the holder of a cup fives championship, and the winner of the swimming medal of the school. He later captained the Old Boys' football team. On June 22nd Rfn. Stubbs was wounded by shell-fire in the head and died two days later. (His diary of the war was later privately printed in Chicago.)

Early on the morning of July 11th Trench Q3 was heavily shelled by the enemy, 8 rank and file being wounded. On July 13th Temporary Lieut.-Col. V. W. F. Dickins was gazetted Lieut.-Col. and permanently to the command of the battalion.

" During the fifty-seven days we held this line," says Sergt. Crossthwaite, " we were toiling day and night at repairing and strengthening the weak spots in the ramparts, what time the Engineers were steadily sapping forward to a German outpost position called the 'Mound of Death,' a huge thick bank of earth midway between our lines and those of the Germans. This mound was at the time in the hands of the Germans, who no doubt had run up to it a communication trench from their front line, and as it made a good rendezvous for their snipers the brigade had orders to 'shift' it. All through the period from the end of May to the middle of July the saps crept on towards the 'Mound of Death'; night after night Q.V.R. toiled heavily along trenches of mud and slime, laden with timber and sandbags to feed the ever-working moles of the Engineers. As dawn broke on the morning of the 17th July the Engineers exploded the mines underneath the mound. The company ('C') were standing-to and as our artillery put shrapnel over the enemy trenches we saw a huge spout of rubbish vomited from the earth. Up it rose to a height seemingly about 200 feet and dark brown in colour—a loud roar followed, the sides of the mound slipped downwards and out. What losses the Germans suffered we never knew, but the attempt was, I should think, only partially successful as the shape of the mound was affected at the sides only."

On the same day that "the Mound of Death" was blown up, the Germans exploded mines under Trenches Q1 and R. Both the Q.V.R. in the former and the K.O.Y.L.I. who were garrisoning the latter, losing heavily. "We heard of eighty casualties," writes Sergt. Crossthwaite, "and the remnant were brought down the C.T. from Q1 to Q2. In the front line there were, as we heard afterwards, quite 160 casualties including our own, which up to then were light in comparison. We kept up a very rapid fire with rifles, M.G.'s, and shrapnel as a barrage in anticipation of a rush, but night came and the attack did not develop. We had a pow-wow at night in Capt. Cox's dug-out and all arrangements fixed up in case of further trouble. On Sunday morning 18th July our artillery, which was not very effective, shelled the Germans and in return they gave 'C' Company, who were occupying what was now the front line, as bad a time as ever they experienced. Bullets were ripping the top of the sandbags in broad daylight, when out from the rear and left of the mound arose in the air a long 'sausage,' like a tube, which floated horizontally and advanced with a zigzag motion to our line. It came on slowly, deliberately and wickedly, hawk-like hunting for prey, and hovering over the left of Q2 suddenly dropped vertically. The explosion was the most terrific I ever heard and its effect equally appalling. Two dug-outs, fortunately empty, were blown clean out and every sandbag and trench in the neighbourhood smashed flat. Following this aerial torpedo the objective was searched with shrapnel. For three terrible hours the bombardment went on, the torpedoes searching along the front. We got the men under what cover we could, some behind the buttress at Hyde Park Corner and some in the trench connected with Queen Victoria Street. At the height of the shelling Capt. Cox rang up our battery, pointing out the location of the gun which was projecting the torpedo and asking for immediate help. The reply was that the supply of 'H.E.' was nearly exhausted and shrapnel only available! The platoons occupied the trench in the following order: from the left 9–10, 11–12 and 9–10 had the worst of it. We had about 20 casualties and indeed were very lucky to escape with so few. Two direct hits were made by the torpedoes— right in the trench—but the others fell just short or just beyond. After the second hit all of a group of men between platoons 9 and 10 were rendered stone deaf by the explosion, their clothes torn to ribbons, some wounded, some half mad, and one poor chap with his left hand hanging by a piece of skin. We were ordered to prepare for a charge, as the report got about that the Germans were coming over and everybody felt relieved to know that at last we could get to work and get a bit of our own back. It had been a cruel strain and greatly would we have loved to go forward with the steel, but Fritz was bashful and did not follow up his first success. The company came out of it well on the whole but, to my mind, it was the stiffest bit of 'wait and see' work that we had up to then experienced. I had my proverbial luck again and came through all right, but the narrowest escape I had was towards the end of the day. I was taking a drop of rum round to some of the relief just off duty when a 4-inch shell struck the sandbag wall behind which I was standing —plonk. It did not explode and I and the rum were left in possession of the field. I had an extra tot to steady my nerves."

The weather for the whole of July proved to be exceptionally fine, rain being reported only on the 10th and 17th. The battalion left this comfortable sector on July 21st, on which date it was relieved by the H.A.C., and marched to Reninghelst, where the men rested for the night in huts and proceeded next day to Steenvoorde. "This march," says Capt. Lindsey-Renton, "will never be forgotten by those who took part in it, everybody getting wet through and through. Having been in the St. Eloi sector for eight weeks where the longest march was from one and a half to two miles, the men were not in good marching trim, and everyone arrived at Steenvoorde thoroughly worn-out and drowned." A stay was made here until July 30th, the men doing company drill, particularly route marching and march discipline. On the 26th the brigade was inspected by the G.O.C. 2nd Army, General Plumer. Welcome reinforcements of 10 officers and 50 men arrived respectively on July 14th and 16th. The total casualties for the month were 2 killed and 39 wounded, all rank and file.

CHAPTER XIV

A Change of Quarters

ON the last day of July the regiment left Steenvoorde at 8.30 in the morning and marched to Goodewaersvelde station, where it entrained for Corbie via Calais, Boulogne and Amiens. On arrival at Corbie a further march led to billets at La Neuville, after an eleven hours' journey Only a two-day halt was made, and on August 3rd Ribemont was reached, at which camp the 13th Brigade was inspected by Sir Charles Munro, the G.O.C. Xth Army Corps, during the afternoon. The day following "we fetched up in the quaint old town of Bray which," says Lieut. C. O. Tabberer, "we were to know and to love in the future as a home from home." Here guards were posted on the roads round the town and machine-guns emplaced for anti-aircraft work. Gen. Ninous, commanding the French troops, expressed a desire to see some British troops on parade, and it was arranged that "C" and "D" Companies, under Capts. Leys Cox and Lindsey-Renton should be inspected by him on the outskirts of the town. The inspection took place on August 6th, the men being in full kit. Gen. Ninous expressed his admiration of the steadiness of the troops on parade and gave the order, "En Repos," but Gen. Wanless O'Gowan, who was also present, explained that British troops did not stand at ease while being inspected. Ninous said, "L'immobilite c'est parfait," and added that the French troops could not be got to stand still. Just as the inspection was nearly over a car drove up and another French general, the Divisional Commander, alighted and said he, too, must inspect the parade, and a fresh inspection took place for his benefit. One of the things prepared was the firing of a new rifle grenade, but when the time came for it none of the grenades would explode. It had been arranged that following the inspection the companies should march past, but just as they were getting ready to do so another car drove up with yet another general, this time the French Corps Commander, and he had to be in the show too. All three generals took up a position at the side of the road while " C " and " D " Companies marched off, the last-comer, taking the salute, while Gen. Ninous, for whose benefit the show had been arranged, had to take a back seat. The next day, however, he was repaid the compliment he had paid the battalion, for it furnished a Guard of Honour on his departure from Bray.

During the first week of their stay at Bray an " Entente Banquet " was given by the sergeants of " C " Company to the sergeants of a French regiment which was about to take its departure. Sergt. Crossthwaite gives the following account of it : " The French sergeants, who are much more important birds than British sergeants, and have each a batman, brought along their wine—the red wine which is part of the French Army issue even as rum is ours—and they brought too their henchmen bearing many gallons of soup maigre, and we reinforced the banquet with our own stew made by the company cooks and our own rum and a bottle or two of whisky, which we begged (or stole) ; anyhow we won them. It was a great feast and we had a happy time together ; we got them all well down. We tempted them with rum and then poured in a terrible hail of whisky tots so that at the last they were kissing us and blessing us as they were led away. They told us many curious things, amongst them, that for many weeks there had been a sort of mutual truce, and casualties were few and far between ; how two milch cows in the meadows at Carnoy supplied milk to the officers' Mess 1,000 yards behind the line. Now, they said, the rest was over and they were going to a warm quarter, and that things would wake up too in the Bray sector as something ' Verry beeg ' was expected shortly. A servant of one of the Frenchmen astonished us very much. He spoke in the Newcastle dialect with a touch of broad Cumbrian that was as the breath of the North to me. He had been an onion seller from Brittany before the war and knew all the pubs and haunts from Carlisle to the East Coast. We could not get him down—he was too used to it."

There was no falling off in discipline or indeed of that smartness which is characteristic of British battalions, Territorial or otherwise, wheresoever they may be, and the rivalry of the various regiments to be " the Ace " of the brigade was of the keenest. One day the Brigadier came into the Q.V.R. Headquarters and after chatting with Col. Dickins for a time said : " I don't think much of your sentry outside ; he is not well turned out or smart. I have just passed the sentry outside the Blanks' Head-quarters and he is one of the smartest sentries I ever saw in my life." The C.O. expressed his regret and his intention to deal firmly with the delinquent, and soon the Brigadier went off. Incontinently the C.O. decided to go and have a look at the Blanks' model sentry. On his way he met the Colonel of the Blanks. " Good morning," said he. " I hear you have a wonderful sentry and I was just coming to have a look at him." " Oh ! " returned the C.O. of the Blanks, " but I was coming to see *your* wonderful sentry. The Brigadier tells me he never saw a better and he has been getting at me about my sentry not being up to Q.V.R. mark ! "

A stay was made at Bray for a fortnight, the battalion being exercised in Company Training which included swimming instruction. The pond at Bray was ideal for the purpose and more than one company held competitions and exhibitions. On August 9th, 2nd Lieut. Lane and 2 O.R. were sent on a trench mortar course at Valheureux, and on the 12th Lieut. Upward and 2 O.R., to the Vth Divisional Salvage Corps. On the 13th, 3 officers and 75 men were sent out at ten o'clock at night for digging in Cable Trench. Two days later the battalion moved to Bronfay Farm, where they took over from the K.O.Y.L.I, and for three nights supplied mining and carrying parties for the R.E. On the 18th it left Bronfay for Carnoy, where it relieved the K.O.S.B.,' "A" Company occupying trenches 46 to 49 ; " B " Company 50 and 51 and " C " Company 52 to 54. " D " Company was stationed in dug-outs in Carnoy, where were also the H.Q. In taking over these and the usual " trench stores " it was found that the latter included a couple of cows which had been taken over by the K.O.S.B. from a French battalion. These cows supplied " D." Company with fresh milk during the whole of its stay at Carnoy, a luxury which was much appreciated. These cows were provided with a dug-out and were well looked after by a K.O.S.B., who used to take them out for exercise and grazing in the valley during the day, where they were out of sight of the Hun and fairly safe from rifle fire but necessarily exposed to shell-fire, to which they seemed to pay no attention.

On August 20, a draft of 20 O.R. arrived from England, and on the same day four men were reported as " Gassed " while working in a mine. Rfn. Leather has a story to tell concerning his adventures in a mine. " We were billeted about that time in Bilon Wood," he says, " just east of Bronfay Farm, and No. 2 Platoon with 2nd Lieut. Meakin in charge were ordered to go on a mining fatigue at Fricourt, lasting from twelve midnight until eight o'clock the following morning. It was my first time in the line and I was rather keen to see what it was like, but the keenness soon left me. After marching for some time we came to a communication trench, where we were met by a R.E. corporal who supplied each man with a wooden plank to carry to the saphead. It seemed to me that we marched miles along the trench, but presently we arrived at the front line and went on until we came to a big mine crater. Here we met some sappers then belonging to the 2nd K.O.S.B. but shortly to be transferred. They fairly put the wind up me by telling us that ' Jerry ' was only seven yards away. A little later I found out this was quite correct. For the first two hours the sappers did nothing, while I dozed in the shaft just under Jerry's front line. Then the sappers started working and we with them. The work lasted an hour and stopped as abruptly as it began, the workers being only too pleased to have a rest. Suddenly we heard something tumble down the shaft. We heard a cry for help and began hauling up the basket used for the removal of the excavated chalk, which was found to contain one of the sappers unconscious. He had been climbing up the shaft when he was overcome and fell some 30 feet or so. Another sapper started to climb, but just as he got nearly to the top he commenced swaying and just managed to clutch the rope, which we hauled upon and managed to get him out. It seemed that they had run into an old German sap that had been blown up some time before but was full of gas. As there was nothing more to be done and as it was nearly daylight we sat down outside talking. The Duke of Wellingtons were holding the line next us and a sentry who was on duty just by the saphead asked us if we would like to see a German. Of course we would ; so one after another we four looked through a periscope and could just discern the nose of a German peering between two pieces of chalk. The periscope belonged to a platoon officer of the D. of W. and was one that could be closed up and carried in the pocket. We had to climb up about 3 steps to reach the firestep, the trench being very deep, and I think the noise we made in doing this must have attracted Jerry's attention, for he fired, and being only seven yards away blew the periscope to pieces as the D. of W. man was looking at him. That started a sniping match between them which finished with the D. of W. having a bullet through his cap. (N.B. There were no tin hats in those days.) I heard later from the D. of W. himself while we were resting at Bray that he got Jerry in the end. Both these incidents put the wind up me terribly, but what capped the lot was just before eight o'clock as we were sitting down and smoking waiting the order to go without any warning a terrific explosion went off just behind the front line. I had heard my first ' Minny ' go off ! It was the first of hundreds as I learned later to my sorrow. As I left the trench I gave a sigh of relief and went back to the wood to some hot tea and ham."

Life at this time seems to have been passably comfortable, especially for the commissioned ranks. Lieut. Rashleigh who had been away on leave, writing on August 20th, says : "We are in dug-outs some way behind the firing line. They are the best dug-outs I have seen so far. This one—Renton's—is about 10 feet high, 15 long and 7 broad, and has in it a table, washstand, 5 chairs and a (sort of) bed, besides shelves. We 'D' Company officers, use it as a day room. The one Eccles and I sleep in is considerably smaller and we share it with an officer, of another company, one Farmiloe. We sleep on three beds, i.e. straw on wire-netting stretched two feet or so from the ground, and these beds practically fill the dug-out, so we have to eat, etc., in this one. The rats and mice are rather tiresome at night. We try to keep them down by organising rat hunts in the evenings. The men enjoy them tremendously, but last night our total bag was only two."

On August 24th, two companies were withdrawn to Carnoy,

where they took over trenches from the Devons, and were followed next day by the rest of the battalion, the succeeding week being spent in either trench or dug-out, in improving trenches and parapets and constructing dug-outs for Headquarters at Carnoy. During this time 2 men were killed and 1 wounded. Referring to the Carnoy trenches, Lieut. Tabberer writes, " It was in the trenches and in the advanced post that young Truscott[1] was killed, and a further casualty was suffered in the company in the last afternoon of this tour. I remember somewhat of a depressed feeling but hoping that we should get away without any more casualties when an orderly came running to say that Sergt.-Major Fairall had been hit. I hurried to the spot which was at the junction of the trench between ' B ' and ' C ' Companies. He had been hit as he was moving away from the loophole through which he had just put five or six successive shots. He was famous in the regiment as a first-class shot and a sniper, and the pathos of it was, that he had served his time and was soon to return to England."

Company Sergt.-Major Fairall (killed 24/8/15), was 41 years of age, and was the second son of Mr. George Fairall, of 36 Grange Road, Ealing. He joined the Victoria and St. George's Rifles in the early 'nineties and took a keen interest in the work. He gave early promise of becoming an expert shot, his first important success at Bisley being the winning of a St. George's badge in 1901. In 1912 and 1913 he was champion shot of the regiment, winning the St. George's Cup and gold jewel on both occasions. He got into the " Three Hundred " for the King's Prize on several occasions and in 1913 succeeded in winning his place in the " Hundred." He was also a member of the English Twenty Club. His skill with the rifle was indirectly the cause of his death. He had been at the front for ten months and for some time before he was killed was one of the leading snipers in the Q.V.R. Major Woodruff Cox, in a letter to his father, stated that the enemy appeared to have located C.S.M. Fairall's position, for a bullet passed right through the loophole into his side and through his heart. He survived but a very few minutes and died quite peacefully. The last resting-place of this gallant warrant officer is at

[1] (1038) Rfn. W. H. Truscott, killed in action 23/8/15.

Carnoy, four miles N.N.E. of Bray, where he was buried by his comrades, the funeral service being read by the Brigade Chaplain. Sergt.-Major Fairall was highly respected by every man in the Q.V.R. and the various clubs associated with it, he was also well-known in connection with the London Diocesan Church Lads' Brigade, in which for five years he held the rank of Major. In a letter to his father, Lieut.-Col. Shipley wrote, " Your son was a bright example of unselfish manliness to all of us in the regiment who were privileged to know him ; his cheery good humour and devotion to duty endeared him to us all. Personally I feel the regiment has lost one of its right-hand men, for his influence was always exerted on the side of right and his ideals were of a very high order ; it was largely the good work put in by him and his friends that enabled the battalion to earn the excellent name it has gained." Major Woodruff Cox also wrote, " Your son was greatly appreciated by all who served with him. He was always on the spot and a good soldier ; his place will be most difficult to fill and the remembrance of him will never be forgotten by the whole battalion and particularly by his own company."

CHAPTER XV

FROM SEPTEMBER TO CLOSE OF 1915

SEPTEMBER, 1915, is memorable for the great British offensive round the mining district of Loos. Long prior to the actual battle, preparations were made along the whole British line extending right away from Zeebrugge, which was bombarded by a Naval force under Vice-Admiral Bacon, to the French Army in Champagne. Enormous reinforcements in men and guns poured in from England, the troops were exercised in every imaginable way, in making and destroying trenches, wire entanglements, bombing with rifle- and hand-grenades, and rehearsing every movement that should ensure success. During the whole of the time thus occupied the Q.V.R. were stationed at Bray and Carnoy. On September 4th Lieut.-Col. Dickins went home on leave, handing over the command to Major R. W. Cox. On Thursday, 9th, Captain Holms was killed and one rifleman wounded. Captain Holms[1] of " A " Company was sitting on or near the Talus Bois, near Carnoy, making a sketch of the enemy trenches. He must have been observed by a sniper, who fired and wounded him mortally. He was taken to a dug-out, where he died the next day.

Everybody, of course, knew there was " going to be a move on," and rumour was rife among the Queen Vics that they were to be " right in it " this time. Col. Dickins returned and took over command on September 19th. He summoned the officers and described the scheme they would be called upon

[1] Capt. John C. Holms was the eldest son of Capt. Douglas and the Hon. Mrs Eileen Holms, of 19 Prince of Wales Terrace, Kensington, and grandson of the late Lord Russell of Killowen. He was born in November, 1891, and educated at Beaumont College and Corpus Christi College, Oxford. He joined the Q.V.R. on the outbreak of war and was given a commission on September 6th, 1914. He joined the battalion in France on May 11th, and was appointed temporary Captain on June 15th.

to carry out. It was to be " a side show " to give a finishing push to the Boches when they were got on the run ! Interminable fatigue parties were the lot of the regiment during the period of waiting. All the time they were at Bray and Carnoy the routine was as follows : 1½ companies in Bray in billets ; ½ company in dug-outs at Carnoy in support ; 2 companies in trenches Nos. 36 to 41 ; improvement of fire trenches, parapets, etc. ; construction of new Battalion H.Q. dug-outs, and working for R.E. On the 23rd, the Battalion H.Q. were removed to Bronfay Farm and 2 companies of the regiment were moved to Carnoy and the remaining 2 to Billon Wood. From the 24th to 29th—while the Battle of Loos was being fought—their work consisted of carrying and digging fatigues. On the 30th, Bronfay Farm was taken over by the 9th Gloucester Regiment and the Q.V.R. went into billets at Chipilly. On this day one rifleman was killed.

" September 28th may be considered to mark the end of the Battle of Loos, as originally designed by the Allied commanders. No great results were obtained by the fighting, which had cost the British Army very heavy casualties. The reasons for the comparative unsuccess were many. In the first place there were not sufficient reserves immediately available to back up the early successes of the British and consolidate the positions won. This gave time to the Germans to rally and counter-attack. Perhaps the unexpectedly rapid advance of the British had something to do with this. Secondly, the French advance took place six hours after the British. This left the right of the latter exposed to a flank attack. These unfortunate events may have been, and probably were, unavoidable, but the result was that a battle, which if fought under more favourable conditions might have changed the aspect of the war, was to all intents and purposes a failure." (*The Times History of the War*.)

The Battle of Loos and the capture of the Messines Ridge were the only big operations that one or other of the battalions of the Q.V.R. did not take any active part in from the 5th November, 1914, to the Armistice on the 11th November, 1918. The little bit assigned to them in connection with the battle of Loos did not come off.

Incidentally might be mentioned here the death of Major

Wyndham H. Dickins, a very well-known member of the Victoria and St. George's V.R.C. He was a younger brother of Lieut.-Col. V. W. F. Dickins, and until the Territorials supplanted the old Volunteers was in command of the Mounted Infantry Contingent of the Corps. He came forward on the outbreak of war and was gazetted a Major in the 12th Pioneer Battalion of the Sherwood Foresters and was fatally wounded at the Battle of Loos on the 25th September, 1915. He was hit by a small piece of shell in the back, which severed the spinal cord, and he died in the train at Abbeville on his way home to England. He had only been out in France with his battalion about six weeks and this was his first action. He left a widow and two sons.

The first week in October according to the Regimental War Diary was spent in Company Training, route marching, attack practice and road-mending. Several of our diarists note that football had begun again and many concerts held. It was while at Chipilly, writes one of them, "that we began to put up our little badge of 'Q.V.R.,' permission having been obtained some time previously from the Brigadier and the Divisional General and a supply procured from London by Col. Dickins— black worsted for the N.C.O.'s and men and bronze metal letters for the officers." Another recreation was fishing, for which Captains Waller and Leys Cox had a great reputation, but tradition says that neither of them scored a bite. On October 8th H.Q. and "A" and "B" Companies moved into billets at Bray and "C" and "D" to Etinhem, and on the 10th from the last-named place to Bray. The H.Q. and one half-company went into dug-outs at Carnoy and 2 companies relieved the 2nd K.O.S.B. in trenches 36 to 41, the companies relieving one another in the trenches in turn. The remaining men were occupied in mining and carrying fatigues, the construction of H.Q. dug-outs at Carnoy and of the support line. On October 15th, the enemy exploded a mine at Fricourt, one man of the Q.V.R. fatigue party suffering from mine gas and shock. The following day Sergt. Burgess, D.C.M., was killed. He was in command of No. 15 Platoon and went out before dawn to examine the condition of the wire in front of his trench and was hit by a stray bullet and killed instantly. His death was a great loss to the men of his platoon, by whom his qualities were admired and respected. He had been given the D.C.M. " For conspicuous gallantry and devotion to duty on January 1st, 1915, in searching for and tending wounded under heavy shell fire and remaining in a barn, which was being heavily shelled, till all the wounded had been got out." On October 18th, one man was wounded, and on the 23rd, Captain Waller, while out in front with a working party, was badly wounded in the leg, necessitating his return to England. At the same time one other man was killed and one wounded.

On October 25th, a mine was exploded by the enemy, killing three men of a mining party supplied by the Q.V.R., and causing much suffering to three others from mine gas and shock; four days later a severe vibration was felt by those in the dug-outs at Carnoy, the result of another mine being exploded. On the 30th, Capt. G. H. Woolley, V.C., returned from leave in England and took over the command of " B " Company. November proved to be another quiet month, the whole of it being spent in billets and trenches alternately at Bray and Carnoy. On the 3rd, the appointment of a new Brigadier was announced, viz. Brig.-Gen. L. O. W. Jones, D.S.O., Essex Regiment. Regimental duties as before consisted chiefly in mining and carrying fatigues, cleaning and repairing trenches, etc. Casualties were very few, being for the whole month : 1 killed and 5 wounded. On the 21st, a Sunday, an enemy patrol of three men was encountered at a listening post occupied by Rfn. Nicholls and Rfn. Rose, both of " D " Company at 37 trench. They accounted for the whole patrol, two being killed outright and the third dying later from the effect of wounds. The bodies of the killed and the wounded man were brought in, but very little information was obtained from the latter beyond the fact that the regiment to which they belonged had recently been transferred from Russia. Their equipment was described as " new ; boots good and clean ; clothing indifferent."

In the course of this month gum boots were served out to the men and proved very welcome, for the weather had been atrocious. Stringent precautions were also ordered to be taken to prevent frost bite and trench foot, and the orders were strictly enforced. The state of the trenches is said by one writer to have been awful, " full of mud, not liquid, but sticky, which made going about in waders and gum boots difficult, for where the mud was very deep the hands had to be employed in extracting one's limbs or the boots would have remained behind. If you stood too long in one place you required a traction engine to drag you out." Lieut. Rashleigh thus recounts an experience of his : "The trenches are in a semi-liquid state. The whole company, I am informed by a kind friend, are laughing over a predicament that I fell into in the early hours of this morning (December 2nd). I was coming back from Renton's dug-out and had to go through a piece of trench where the liquid mud had partly solidified. I had on waders which act very well when the mud is liquid, but on this occasion one foot, the left, stuck fast. I couldn't move it, at least the boot. Eventually a rifleman came along and had a try at getting out the boot, but met with no success. I then took my foot out—socks only—and stood on one leg while he tugged at the boot again. Nothing doing ; so off he went to get me another boot. After a considerable, and uncomfortable, interval another rifleman, sent by rifleman No. 1, appeared with a left boot, which I proceeded to put on, only to discover that the effect of standing still so long on my right foot had wedged that down in its turn ! So a right boot had to be fetched and finally I was free, leaving the first pair of boots to their fate."

A similar predicament befell Col. Dickins one morning when visiting the front-line trenches in company with the Adjutant. The mud was deep, and the C.O. being a fairly heavy weight he sank in above his knees and was quite unable to move, and there stuck smoking his pipe until a relief party of five men with shovels and planks came to his assistance.

On Thursday, November 4th, a memorial service for members of the Queen Victoria's Rifles who had fallen in the war was held in St. George's Church, Hanover Square. It was conducted by the Rev. R. H. Sinclair, Chaplain to the Regiment, and was attended by about 300 officers and men and a number of friends and relatives of " Our Glorious Dead." A printed Order of Service was issued to all attending the service and contained the names of 7 Officers and 132 Other Ranks with the dates of death up to the 16th October.

December passed very much after the fashion of the preceding month, the battalion being alternately in billets at Bray or in trenches and dug-outs at Carnoy, performing the same old round of duties, in the same old rain, in the same old way. On the 9th and 10th the War Diary records that : "Headquarters' dug-outs and vicinity were considerably shelled with light shrapnel by enemy at 11 p.m. to 5 a.m." Casualties nil. On Sunday 19th it was discovered that in front of the trench occupied by "D" Company a small sap existed in the enemy's line. Patrols had reported the presence of a German post in the sap, and also, erroneously as it transpired, that the wire was weak. At an early hour in the morning a strong patrol of 14 men all belonging to 14 Platoon, under Lieut. Eccles, with Sergt. McKenna and Lce.-Cpl. Eames, were sent out to bomb the post and bring back a prisoner if possible. Part of the patrol got inside the wire, which was found to be very dense. They were perceived by the enemy, who opened fire on them with a machine-gun at about 15-yards range. Eccles was wounded in three places, 2 men were killed and 3 others wounded. Eccles gave the order to withdraw, when he found a wounded man inside the wire, and despite his own wounds, with the assistance of Eames, picked up the man and, though being under heavy fire and bombs, managed to get him through the wire and back to safety. The bodies of the dead had to be left behind. For this exploit Lieut. Eccles was awarded the Military Cross and Lce.-Cpl. Eames the Distinguished Conduct Medal.

On Christmas Eve the artillery on both sides was reported to be more active than usual, though as far as regards the Q.V.R. there were no casualties. We miss the cheery letters from the rank and file describing the Christmas festivities of a twelvemonth back, but that was a thing of the past. The Censor had forbidden the publication of letters from men on service somewhere about the beginning of July, 1915. The information contained therein might have led to our undoing !

It must not be supposed, however, that there were no Christmas festivities. On the contrary we constantly hear of concerts by the " Whizzbangs " and other troupes. Details alone are scarce. Lieut. Tabberer, on returning from leave after a month spent at the Third Army School, writes : " I found myself arriving in Bray during the course of the ' B '

MAP No. 3.

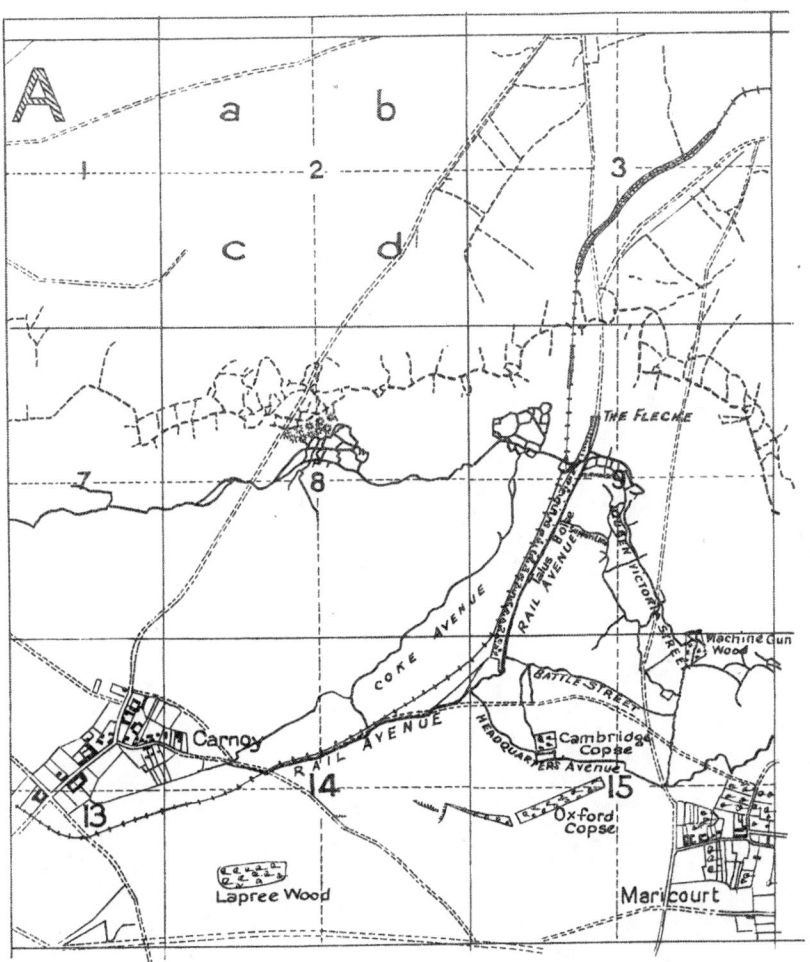

CARNOY TRENCHES. AUGT 1915-JANY 1916.

Company Christmas concert on the Tuesday after Christmas. It was indeed a pandemonium; shrieks of applause for the performers came from all sides. I can remember seeing Cpl. Hockley waltzing up and down the stage with a saucepan as fiddle. Afterwards we returned to our own pleasant billet and there was another Christmas dinner. We had Basil Clarke (M.O.), Gerald Forsyth, Old Mack[1] and one or two others in. It *was* a gay evening." Three days later he says: " We were all dreadfully scared in the Head-quarters dug-out by the apparition of a fiery head at the end of a trench, suspended in the darkness. The batmen had pierced holes in a pumpkin and had inserted a candle !" On New Year's Eve a warm greeting was sent over to the enemy trenches, who returned the compliment. Just in the thick of it a telephone message came through from Head-quarters: "The Commanding Officer wishes all ranks a happy New Year."

In a letter written on December 9th Lieut.-Col. V. W. F. Dickins asks Col. W. M. Tanqueray, V.D., President of the Queen Victoria's Rifles Old Comrades' Association, to convey to the members of the Association the heartiest thanks of the battalion for the nine cases of writing-pads and envelopes which had duly arrived that day. "The battalion," he adds, " is upholding the traditions of the old Corps in every way and is doing good work. The weather is awful and we are having rather a rotten time."

The casualties for December were: 1 accidentally killed through the collapse of a dug-out, 1 accidentally wounded, 2 killed and 7 wounded of Other Ranks, and 1 Officer wounded.

---

[1] Lieut. K. L. Mackenzie (Transport Officer).

CHAPTER XVI

JANUARY 1916

HONOURS AND AWARDS

WHAT all friends of the Queen Victoria's Rifles considered to be a good omen was the mention in Dispatches on the first day of the year of Lieut.-Col. Dickins, Capt. J. C. Andrews and Capt. R. H. Lindsey-Renton, and this was followed on January 13th by the announcement that H.M. the King had been graciously pleased to make the following (among other) awards :

To be Companions of the Distinguished Service Order :

    Major (Temp. Lieut.-Col.) Dickins, V.W.F.
    Major W. F. Roe, R.A.M.C. (Our old friend " the Doc.")

Awarded the Distinguished Conduct Medal :

    No. 66   Co.-Sergt-Major Brawn, M.
    No. 3268.   Co.-Sergt.-Major Sheriff, A. J.
    No. 983.   Lce.-Cpl. Yates, A. J.

C.S.M. Sheriff was also awarded the Cross of the Order of St. George (4th Class), Russia.

How the news was received by the battalion in France is told by Major S. J. M. Sampson : " A Subaltern has just walked into head-quarters and electrified us all by congratulating the C.O. on being awarded the D.S.O. He has been the first to see *The Times* to-day and neither the C.O. nor anyone else knew of it. Great rejoicings ! Our doctor (Lieut.-Col. Roe), who was with us last winter, has it too, for work done with the battalion, which he has now left. So also has the Major of our Field Ambulance. The quartermaster produces a piece of ribbon within a few hours (wonderful man), and it is duly affixed to the Colonel's chest ! The other two D.S.O.'s come into dinner a few days later, neither of them yet be-ribboned, and are greatly delighted when the C.O. presents each of them with a piece of the ribbon. Altogether a pleasant and successful evening. The Mess President has raised a case of Veuve Clicquot (*goût* Anglais) which certainly adds to the general harmony of the proceedings."

In reply to a letter congratulating him on his decoration Col. Dickins wrote on January 23rd : " I consider the regiment has won this great distinction by the good work and splendid behaviour of all ranks during the time they have been out here and that it is as much theirs as mine, only I happen to be the lucky one that wears it. We are now out of the trenches for a short rest, for how long I do not know, but to be away from shells and rifle fire for a time is a treat. If only the weather would clear up and be fine it would be very pleasant as we are in a decent part of the country and I get a good ride every day. The men are looking much better for their rest from trench life. They have drill every morning, and football, cross-country runs and boxing in the afternoons. There is no doubt about it the old Vics have done jolly well, especially at Hill 60 twice, second battle of Ypres and the Yser Canal, when with the Canadians, and also during the fourteen months in defence in the trenches. I do not think there is any Territorial regiment out here that has been anything like so long up in the firing line all the time as we have been, and only twice during the fourteen months having a short rest of seven days each time. I am glad to say everyone seems very well and we shall all be very pleased when the war ends and we can get back to some home comforts again. Many thanks for your promise of toasting the Brn. serving in H.M. Forces at the Victoria Rifles Lodge on the 26th inst. I wish I could be with you ! "

Major Sampson, who it will be remembered was wounded at the attack on Hill 60 and was invalided home and who returned to the battalion in France on January 3rd, 1916, notices changes that have taken place in the general conditions of men and things during his eight months' absence. " Everything is different from last year," he says. " Dug-outs for everyone, respirators, plenty of bombs and other luxuries. Machine-guns seem active on both sides, but there are very few shell-holes and no shelling in progress, only the mud is still with us. The trenches are interesting but complicated. They were made by the French from whom we took them over last summer. The Hun is ' under dog ' here, instead of ' top dog,' as he used to be at Messines and Ypres. The gunners strafe them daily and use about twice as much shell as theirs. In fact, there is no doubt that all along the front of the British Army things are much better. All ranks are much more optimistic, though some are rather war-weary."

The battalion remained at Bray and Carnoy until January 10th, when word came that the whole Division was being relieved and that it would go out of the line for a long rest. On the 10th the Q.V.R. were relieved by the 2nd Wilts Regiment and returned to Bray, leaving that place on the following day at 6.15 p.m. and marching to billets at Sailly Laurette, which was reached just before nine o'clock. Rumour for once proved to be true. A stay was made at Sailly Laurette until the end of the month, the time being expended in cleaning up, instruction in innumerable courses for officers, attack practice and open order drill, etc., and, of course, football and athletic sports.

"The French people," says Major Sampson, "must be tired of having troops billeted upon them, but they are wonderfully patient about it. Probably their guests change once a week ; some of them can speak French and some not ; some understand how to show them proper consideration, and some, I fear, do not. Our own experience is that at first they are careful not to do too much for us, but after we have been with them a day or so, and they have found that we are civil and careful to do no damage, they will do anything in reason to oblige us. But I fear that the British Army will leave behind it in France a reputation for wastefulness and extravagance. Tommy Atkins will pull down a barn to light fires if he is not watched, and spends his pay with both hands. He is, of course, popular in consequence of the latter characteristic, with the keepers of the little village shops and cafés invaded by this army of reckless millionaires. To set against our faults I think our Allies will record our amazing passion for cleanliness and strange interest in sanitation. Our men are better turned out than the French, drill better and march better. Many a farmhouse has never been so clean within the memory of the oldest inhabitant as after a good, well-officered British company has been there a week. *Quieta non movere* seems to be the farmer's motto ; but, on the arrival of our men, out comes the dirty straw, perhaps two feet deep, from the old barn and the combined cesspool, manure heap and chicken run round which the house is built, is drained and cleaned. There is even a trained party turned on to repair the holes in the lath and mud-plaster walls of the said barn."

During the whole stay at Sailly Laurette the weather was amazingly mild and there were some fine clear mornings which made training on the high ground quite enjoyable. The casualties for the month were only three slightly wounded, while drafts of 114 O.R. from the 9th Entrenching Battalion and 9 officers joined up. Among the latter were Major Sampson and Lieuts. Brown, G. Nathan. F. G. Garside, R. P. Goddard and—Davis.

One of the athletic events arranged was a " Cross-country Race," for the organisation of which Major Sampson was responsible. The object was to get as large a number of men as possible to run. The course was about three and a half miles and marks ranging from seven for the winner to 2 marks for the tenth, and one mark for each man finishing within ten minutes of the winner. The result was a field of about 120 or 130, of whom no less than 80 earned their 1 mark. Seeing that not more than some 500 men were available to run this was considered distinctly satisfactory. Another gratifying feature was that a subaltern gained the second place.

K

CHAPTER XVII

A Change of Divisions

From the 5th to the 56th
A Welcome Rest

AT nine o'clock on the morning of January 30th the battalion marched from Sailly Laurette to billets in La Houssoye and from thence on the following day to Talmas. Here a halt was called for a full week, the men being exercised as before in company drill, open and close order, wood and village fighting, musketry and grenade practice, with a class of instruction for junior officers. In regard to "village fighting" one Q.V.R. writes : "We had a great fight in the streets yesterday. One company attacks and clears a corner of the village, opposed by another company who lie doggo in the houses and inflict heavy casualties with bombs and machine-guns. The bombs are represented by apples. For choice, a really rotten cider apple, of which there are plenty, as the effect of a mouldy brown one upon the face of an unsuspecting opponent who looks up at your window, is most satisfactory."

On February 8th a move was made to Cardonette, where for the next four days the same programme was gone through. Some good people of Cardonette had started a visitors' book in which all were implored to put their names and any sketch or "sentiment" they were disposed to add. At the top of one page was the Q.V.R. crest, cut from a sheet of note-paper, and below it two little rhymes and the signatures of a number of officers. On the opposite page was a caricature of a rifleman cigarette in mouth and pack on back. The rhymes, which were the contribution of Major Sampson, ran thus :

> Je voudrais faire une chansonette
> Sur bon acceuil de Cardonette.
>
> Some riflemen   Des " Boutons Noirs "
> And friends of France   Qui aiment la France
> Once turned up here   Se trouvent ici
> By great good chance.   Par très bon chance.

Our readers will remember the story of the " Black Buttons," told shortly after the arrival of the battalion in France. This Major Sampson immortalised as follows :

> Les " Boutons Noirs "
> Sont bon soldats.

A march of fourteen miles on February 12th brought the Q.V.R. to Picquigny and another of twenty miles on the 13th to billets at Vaux-Marquenneville and Fresnes, where from the 14th to the 26th they stayed in billets, the Head-quarters and " C " and " D " Companies at Fresnes and the remaining two companies at Vaux-Marquenneville. There were no casualties of any kind recorded during February, while on the 17th a welcome draft of 99 O.R. arrived.

On the 12th February, 1916, the Q.V.R. left the 13th Infantry Brigade, 5th Division, and were posted to the 16th Infantry Brigade, 56th Division. It is needless to say that genuine regret at this severance of a fifteen-months' comradeship was felt by all. Many references are made in letters and diaries to the parting. " We took with us," says Major Sampson, " many messages of thanks and of regret from Brigadier, Divisional-General and our many friends in the division. It is no small thing to have earned the high opinion of this division, perhaps the most famous in the Army, with Mons, Le Cateau, both battles of Ypres and other engagements on its list, and to have so shared them from the early days when the British Army had in the field only one soldier for every ten it has now. But these things have now passed imperishably into history and nothing can deprive us of them." A familiar figure among both officers and men was the Brigade Chaplain, the Rev. Pym. Lieut. Tabberer writes : " I was immensely sorry to have to lose touch with Pym, the padré. He had such a delightful way with him, he was almost Franciscan in character, with a quiet sense of humour and a capacity for the enjoyment of the simple and natural things of life. Instinctively we were on our best behaviour in his presence without feeling this to be at all a strain. Pym will long be remembered and loved by Q.V.R."

In bidding the Q.V.R. " good-bye " Major-Gen. Kavanagh, G.O.C., 5th Division, wrote Col. Dickins under date of Feb. 1st:

"MY DEAR DICKINS,—

"I am very sorry that I hear an order is coming for your battalion to leave the division.—I know I am expressing the feeling of the whole division when I tell you how sorry we shall be at the departure of the Battalion, and I personally wish to thank you and all those under you, both officers, N.C.O.'s and men for the good work you have done since I have been in command of the division. All the 5th Division will watch the future career of the Q.V.R. with the greatest interest and will feel that the future successes you are sure to have during the war will add to the credit of your old division. Wishing you and all those under you the best of luck in the future.
Yours sincerely,
(Signed) C. M. KAVANAGH.

"P.S.—I hope you will let Forsyth and the other four members of the Whizzbangs remain on as at present, at any rate for some time, as they could not carry on without them. Though I am writing this I shall try and come over to Talmas to see you before you leave."

The new division was composed as follows :—

167*th Brigade.*
7th Middlesex.
8th   ,,
1st London R.F.
3rd   ,,   ,,

168*th Brigade.*
4th London R.F.
12th   ,,   (Rangers).
13th   ,,   (Kensingtons).
14th   ,,   (L. Scottish).

169*th Brigade.*
2nd London R.F.   9th London (Q.V.R.).
5th   ,,   (L.R.B.).   16th   ,,   (Q.W.R.).

All London Territorials except the 7th and 8th Middlesex.

The commanders were respectively Brig.-Gens. F. H. Burnell-Nugent, G. G. Loch and E. S. Coke.

The Queen Victorias saluted their new Brigadier, Gen. Coke,

A CHANGE OF DIVISIONS

C.O. of their old friends the K.O.S.B. in the 13th Brigade, for the first time on their arrival at Ailly-Le-Haut-Clocher, into which they marched on the afternoon of February 27th. During the march a heavy snowstorm was encountered. From 28th February to 11th March the battalion remained at Ailly, the routine being much the same as that of the two preceding months, except that we find " training snipers " introduced into it. On one day there was a special exhibition attack in the presence of the new brigadier. By this time the weather had become extremely cold and snow fell on several days. Still it was not too cold for football and several matches were played with neighbouring battalions. The Q.V.R. now appeared in rifle-green jerseys, which had been sent out from England and emblazoned with a red Maltese cross on the left breast. This was cut out of red flannel bought locally and sewn on by the regimental tailor and made a most distinctive turn-out. Four matches were played with other teams, in three there was no score, the fourth was won by the Q.V.R. by two tries to a goal. If was about this time that an unfortunate accident occurred. In some way a live cartridge had got into a clip of dummy ones and while a squad was at practice one of the men got shot in the leg. It was some time before he could be conveyed to hospital; the Field Ambulance had only arrived that day from England and the snow-bound roads and the rawness of the ambulance men were no doubt responsible for the delay. The man subsequently lost his leg and the N.C.O. in command of the section was severely reprimanded. By the irony of fate this corporal later lost his leg in battle.

From Ailly the brigade moved to Fienvillers in the Doullens area, a distance of twelve miles, on March 12th, but only stayed there a couple of nights. On one of them, the 14th, the " fire alarm " was sounded. " I ran out of my company ('D') Mess," relates its commander, Capt. Lindsey-Renton, " and found that a large barn in which some of my company were billeted was blazing furiously. It was full of every kind of hay, straw, etc., along which the flames ran quickly. It was impossible to save it and all attempts were concentrated on limiting the range of the fire. The only fire-fighting appliance at hand was an antiquated hand-pump attached to a small tank on wheels, and this was wheeled up to the barn and a long double row of men formed between it and an evil-smelling pond some distance away. Empty buckets were passed down one row, filled out of the pond, and then passed up and emptied into the tank. People familiar with the nature of the usual French village pond will appreciate how unpleasant was the job of those filling the buckets, especially in the case of one unfortunate man who fell in. The transport officer, Lieut. Mackenzie, thoroughly enjoyed himself with the hose pipe, though nearly as much water went on the spectators as on the fire. Col. Dickins narrowly missed being soaked by an ill-directed aim of the hose. The barn was absolutely gutted and some time after midnight the fire was got under, but as it was still smouldering one platoon of 'D' Company was kept on it all night. Next morning the battalion marched to Doullens. A Court of Enquiry was, however, assembled at Fienvillers presided over by Col. Shoolbred, Queen's Westminster Rifles. One platoon of 'D' Company was also left behind to see that the fire was really extinguished. This was the platoon in whose billet the fire arose. This platoon had a great portion of its equipment and a lot of clothing, etc., destroyed. They marched to Doullens under Lieut. Hodgson, who had been the orderly officer at the time of the fire, and a motley crew they looked, some without caps, some minus puttees, and others having had their packs burnt, carrying their personal belongings in bundles, half the party with rifles and half without!"

Leaving Doullens on the morning of March 16th the brigade marched into the Le Couroy area, the Q.V.R. to a small village named Houvin-Houvigneul, where it was destined to remain until May 7th. The village straggles over about a mile of the main road and spreads down the side roads for about 100 yards on each side. It is surrounded by the usual orchards and boasts two churches, both very ugly, and a large but dilapidated château, once evidently the residence of a man of means but now to be used as Brigade Head-quarters. The country round about is rather dull, a succession of rolling uplands, all of it arable and so affording few places for training troops. Nevertheless the eternal training went on, company and battalion, time marches, musketry and bayonet fighting, and what not. On 18th March a demonstration of the German flammenwerfer apparatus was given before a group of 40 officers, and N.C.O.'s from local units attended, and selected victims were put into a trench which was then squirted with the liquid fire. Sergt. Sim, one of these victims, writes : " Lieut. Fleetwood and I got in the trench. Effect very terrifying at first, but otherwise harmless." Major Sampson adds : " It is all bark and little bite as the occupants of the trenches, 20 yards from the apparatus, felt nothing beyond a scorching heat passing over their heads, while spectators 40 yards away, of whom I was one, stood calmly in the open without feeling any discomfort. Thus is another German bogey laid." Returning to the Mess he is a witness of a demonstration of another kind of frightfulness. " I find," says he, " the transport officer has been having a ' strafe ' with a very young subaltern of the A.S.C., who objects to an official complaint which we have made as to the quality of the hay issued by his distinguished branch of the service. This young man has only just come out from England, while our T.O. is (comparatively) a veteran soldier and a past-master of the art of vituperation. His opinion of the boy was clearly and lucidly expressed, but the climax was reached when he called him a ' war-baby.' "

The day following these little divertisements a draft of five officers arrived from England followed on the 23rd by thirty-eight Other Ranks. On April 4th the new shrapnel helmet—the subsequently famous Tin Hat—was issued to the whole battalion. On 7th of April Lieut.-Col. Dickins went home for a month's leave, in the course of which he attended an Investiture at Buckingham Palace and received the D.S.O. from His Majesty. During his absence the battalion was under the command of Major S. J. M. Sampson, M.C. A great improvement in weather conditions is noted by Major Sampson, who, writing about this time, says : " The only matter worthy of record is the sudden and entirely delightful change in the weather. Last Sunday we had snow. To-day I am sitting in the orchard, basking in the sun and writing. The air is still and fresh, the sun warm and not a cloud in the sky. The hedges are beginning to get green. The little birds are asking one another where the best nesting-places are, and the discussion of this interesting subject is evidently productive of a variety of opinion—a ceaseless rumble fills the air. It is a sound of which I am heartily tired, the sound of artillery." The fine weather did not last long; on the 28th it is described as "appalling." In notifying his friends of his taking over the command the new O.C. says: "Whether my period of command be long or short it will always be a time to be looked back upon with pride, for I do not think there is a better battalion in Europe!" High praise indeed, but Major Sampson goes on to say: "This opinion I keep to myself for they have lots to learn and everyone wants keeping up to the mark." No excuse is offered for now making his opinion public. From his diary we learn that the period of his command expired on April 28th, on which day he left to go home on leave. Col. Dickins rejoined the battalion on May 6th.

During this year the "Conscientious Objector" made his presence felt in the Q.V.R. as in many another regiment. In spite of their protests a number of them were ordered to join up but in every way set the regimental authorities at defiance. There was one "Conchy" in particular who gave a great deal of trouble at Fovant where the 3rd Battalion was in training, and a whole string of questions concerning his treatment and whereabouts were addressed to the Secretary of State for the Home Department by an inquisitive member of the House of Commons.

Col. Dickins has a good story about one of the tribe who actually determined to "see it through." One day on his rounds in the trenches the Colonel was stopped by a rifleman who asked if he might speak to him for a minute. "Certainly," was the response, "What can I do for you?" "If you please, sir, I am a conscientious objector, and I feel that I cannot obey the orders given me." "But, how did you manage to get here in the firing line? This is the first time I have heard of it." "If you please, sir, I have a mortal terror of killing anything, but when I read of the terrible things the Germans had been doing to the men and women of France and Belgium, I thought it was my duty to come and help them, but now that I have been in the trenches I am more of a conscientious objector than ever, and my conscience will not let me shoot!" "Very well," said the Colonel, "hand over your rifle and bayonet; we will not ask you to shoot anyone. Instead of doing sentry-go we will give you another job, that of mending the wire in front of our trenches. As soon as it is dark you will ' go over the top ' and mend the wire that has been broken." "Thank you, sir," said the man, who appeared to be greatly relieved. When darkness fell he was given a pair of cutters and ordered to go into No Man's Land and mend any breaks he could discover in the wire. He had been gone but a few minutes when "whee-p" went a bullet close by his head and "phut, phut, phut," two or three more in the ground at his feet. He was back in the trench in no time calling out for the sergeant and on his coming shouted : " Give me my —— rifle, I'll teach the —— to shoot at me." His request was complied with and, says Col. Dickins, " I suppose he lived happy ever after, at any rate I heard no more of him or his objections."

"Those were halcyon days at Houvin," declares Lieut. Tabberer, "the spring season was at its best and daffodils covered the woods. Easter Day came round while we were there, and I can remember the very wonderful Holy Communion service that early morning. The chapel was a barn next to Mo. 7 Platoon billet. So crowded were we that we had to stand throughout the service. I can remember some of the many who were there—Basil Clarke, Mack, Rumsey, Garside, Kingly Cunningham and, in fact, most of the officers then with the regiment and very many of the boys. One realised then that the Holy Communion is *par excellence* a Society of Friends."

The merry month of May found the Q.V.R. moving about the country again after making the longest stay in one place since their arrival in France seventeen months previously. On the 1st Houvin was left at 9.30 a.m. and Dainville reached about 7.30 p.m. On the 4th they returned to their original billets at Houvin, only to leave them three days later when the whole brigade went to Halloy in the Henu area. The succeeding twelve days were passed in the usual training, our old friend, " Night Ops," reappearing in the programme. The men, we are told, were all together in huts, as were also the company officers and the H.Q. in billets. Halloy was quitted on May 20th, the Q.V.R. marching to billets for the night at St. Amand, and next day to Sailly-au-Bois, where H.Q. and " A " and " C " Companys were stationed while the two remaining companies went up to the Keep at Hebuterne, relieving the 1st Battalion London Regiment.

CHAPTER XVIII

PREPARATIONS FOR "THE GREAT PUSH"

FROM the 22nd to the 25th May the battalion was in reserve, two companies at the Keep in Hebuterne and two companies and H.Q. in Sailly-au-Bois. On the 26th the whole of 167th Brigade left their rest billets and marched through Sailly towards the line for the purpose of starting Assembly Trenches. It was a fine day and the Germans had a couple of observation balloons up which spotted the movement and when the troops arrived in the neighbourhood of Sailly a heavy barrage was put upon the village. In the course of this the Q.V.R. Head-quarters Staff had the narrowest escape from extinction. Col. Dickins Major Sampson, Capt. Andrews, the Adjutant and Capt. Clarke, the M.O., occupied a cottage owned by a couple of ancients, man and wife. They had just finished lunch and were enjoying a smoke or writing letters home when suddenly a flight of shells burst all around the cottage; three fell in the front garden and four others in the back, none of them many yards away. One shell fell about four yards only from the open front door, causing a lot of damage to the cottage bringing down most of the tiles and chipping the walls with flying fragments, and doing considerable harm to the walls ceilings, and appointments inside. The dust was so thick that for some time it was impossible to see what had really happened but when it had settled down a bit it was found that none of the inmates was harmed. This was remarkable, considering the number of pieces of shell and splinters that were flying in all directions. In the village one shell burst by "D" Company's Sergeants' Mess, killing or wounding four of its members. Sergt. Redgell, the sergeant cook, was later found killed in the village.

Sergt. Frank Hubert Stone, aged twenty-three, one of the two sergeants killed, was the son of Mr. F. R. Stone, of 33 Vestry Road, Camberwell, and was educated at Alleyn's School. Dulwich, where he established a reputation on the sports side, He was captain of the Old Silverdalians F.C. He joined the Q.V.R. on the outbreak of war and went to France with the battalion in November, 1914. In apprising his father of his death Capt. Lindsey-Renton wrote : " No cheerier soul could have been found in the British Army. No matter what discomforts or what dangers surrounded him, he was always cheerful, always had a bright smile and a cheerful word for everybody." The other was Lce.-Sergt. Harold Wilton Stephenson.

On the night of May 26th/27th the 167th Brigade had been digging a new trench 500 yards to the front of the existing front line on a frontage of 3000 yards. On the night of the 27th the L.R.B., who were in the line, occupied portions of this new trench by detached posts. On the evening of the 28th two companies of the Q.V.R., of which " D " was one, relieved the L.R.B. As soon as it got dark the guide started off with " D " Company's garrison for the three posts. One post, under Lieut. Ogilvie, was to be at the left of " Z " hedge, so named from its shape ; the centre post on the right of " Z " hedge, under Lieut. A. C. Rumsey, and the right post, under Lieut. Hodgson, at a place called the Maybush. Soon afterwards Capt. Lindsey-Renton visited the posts to see if they were all correct, but found that the guide had taken both the centre and right posts to the Maybush. Having directed them to their proper positions, Capt. Lindsey-Renton was returning at 10.15 to the front line when the Germans put down a very heavy barrage, concentrated on the line. He managed to get into a trench and take cover behind a traverse which soon became crowded by others trying to squeeze in at either end. During this barrage " D " Company suffered several casualties, including Rfn. Cade, who was killed. Later in the evening Capt. Lindsey-Renton paid a second visit to the posts and found them all correct and with very few casualties except the party at the Maybush. On his way back he encountered a similar fierce barrage and he experienced some difficulty in getting through the wire and taking refuge in a shallow trench, where he found Capt. Leys Cox. They lay low for some five or ten minutes with the shells bursting all around them and lighting up the whole place. These barrages were doubtless put down to catch the working parties which the Germans expected would be there, but luckily the brigade was not out that night, having worked on the 26th and 27th practically undisturbed.

The digging of the above-mentioned trench is described by Major Dudley Ward in his History of the 56th Division as " a task of appalling magnitude." The task was allotted to Brig.-Gen. Nugent and the 167th Brigade, and although the trench was dug in one night the whole operation required three nights to complete ; the first was utilised in marking out the line with string and pegs ; the next in digging the trench, when there were 3000 men out in No Man's Land. " By 2.30 a.m.," says Major Dudley Ward, " the trench had been made and was held by posts, found from the covering parties, reinforced with Lewis guns ; they had rations, water and shovels to improve their positions, and were in telephonic communication with the old trench, and all the working parties had filed away as silently as they had come. . . . On the night of 27th/28th the same number of men were out working again, improving the front-line trench and wire, digging support lines and two other communication trenches. The new work had been pegged out the previous night by the Engineers. The 56th Division had then started its career with the astounding feat of having in the space of forty-eight hours constructed and wired a new system of trenches, comprising 2900 yards of fire trench and 1500 yards of communication trenches, in No Man's Land and within 250 yards of the enemy. Casualties were 8 killed and 55 wounded. A little luck had waited on audacity, but the success of the whole operation was undoubtedly due to the intelligence and keenness of the men. . . . It only required one foolish man to lose his head and disaster would have descended on the whole brigade."

On that and the following night, when working parties were continually under, fire some splendid work was done by various N.C.O.'s. Sergt. H. C. Munnings, who rose later to be a R.S.M., gained the Military Medal for his handling of the men under heavy shell-fire when out on wiring and covering parties.

1916] PREPARATIONS FOR "THE GREAT PUSH" 141

Sergt. A. J. Wilson also won the M.M. for his work on the night of May 30th/31st, when out with a covering party which was heavily shelled and suffered a number of casualties. As these occurred he so distributed the men that they still covered all the men at work; he also brought in all his casualties. It was owing to the example he showed that the covering parties carried on, thus allowing the working parties to continue their important work. The total casualties in May were 14 killed and 59 wounded. The first days of June proved unlucky ones for the Q.V.R. While still at Hebuterne on June 1st two companies in the trenches were heavily shelled, with the result that one man was killed and 16 wounded; on the following day 2 men were wounded; on June 3rd 1 killed and 2 wounded, and on the 4th 1 officer wounded. On the 3rd Lieut.-Col. Dickins was " Mentioned in Dispatches," for the second time. On this day the battalion was relieved by the 2nd London Regiment. "We came out of the trenches last night," says Major Sampson, "and were very glad to do so. We have only moved into dug-outs a short distance back, and the men are doing various jobs, but it is easier work as it is done in daylight and with very few, if any, casualties. The thing we all want is a good night's rest and that we hope for to-night. I think I said," he goes on, "we had been digging a new trench which had annoyed the Hun. I don't think there is now any harm in my saying that what we have done is to go forward into No Man's Land and help ourselves to a piece of it, 1400 yards long and 500 in depth. The result has been great artillery activity on both sides and our men have had to dig under shell-fire at night, in the open, which is very trying. Most of them are rather shaken, as they have been shelled off and on, and sometimes very heavily, for a week. Some of the men are rather jumpy, but on the whole it is distinctly a fine piece of work and we are by way of being the heroes of it, as, though other battalions have been engaged, we have had the dirty end of the stick. However, the Hun has had a worse time in many ways as he is thoroughly frightened; and our gunners have sent him some tokens of their esteem and affection."

As was widely known throughout the whole of the army on the Western Front, the Q.V.R., in the person of Lieut.-Col.

"Tim" O'Shea, possessed a Grand Old Man of their own beloved by all from the Commanding Officer to the latest joined rifleman who wanted something—he always got something if not the precise thing he was seeking to draw from the Q.M. stores. No one was sent away empty-handed, when breeches were not forthcoming he received a mess tin. Major Sampson concludes the letter we have just quoted with "Our Quartermaster has just got a D.S.O., which pleases us all as it is rarely given to a quartermaster. He is a splendid old man, sixty years old, but full of buck. He was over twenty in the K.R.R.C."

Lieut.-Col. T. O'Shea died on the 7th July, 1921, aged sixty-five. He was buried at East Finchley Cemetery, his comrades of the Q.V.R. forming an escort.

A writer in *The Times*, calling attention to his passing says : " Riflemen throughout the empire will learn with deep regret of the death of Lieut.-Col. Timothy O'Shea, D.S.O ('Tim'). For many years he served with the 60th Rifles being with them in campaigns in India, Burmah and South Africa. Later he did invaluable work with Queen Victoria's Rifles. With this battalion he went to France on November 4th, 1914, and stayed with them until illness forced him to duty in England in September, 1918. With his death a most popular figure disappears, and the 'Greenjackets,' the 'Celer et Audax ' Club, and the Rifles Veteran Association loses an indefatigable worker."

The same gazette which brought the news of "Tim's" D.S.O. also recorded that the Military Cross had been awarded to Lieut. Eccles for his gallantry in carrying back a wounded man in connection with the raid on the enemy's trenches in December, 1915. He was wounded on that occasion, but rejoined the battalion in April, 1916.

From the 4th to the 8th June, on which day the battalion was relieved by the London Scottish, it was in reserve in Hebuterne Keep. On the last-mentioned date it returned to Halloy where it was employed in "Attack Practice" until June 13th when two companies went to Sailly-au-bois and the other two to Hebuterne. Sergeant Sim in his diary says the attack was practised on a system of trenches similar to that of the Germans at Gommecourt ; the Q.V.R. and the L.R.B. led

"TIM." AND "THE DOC."
LT.-COL. T. O'SHEA, D.S.O., AND LT.-COL. F. W. ROE, D.S.O.

1916] PREPARATIONS FOR "THE GREAT PUSH." 143

the attack. His platoon led for "C" Company and had to capture three lines of German trenches. "Got wet through during this affair and again in the afternoon while on digging fatigue." He further mentions that Sergt. F. H. C. Hickman had been awarded the Military Medal and Lce.-Cpl. E. E. Eames the D.C.M. From the 14th to the 20th the battalion was engaged in digging "Boyaux de services" and other assembly trenches. On the 18th, according to Sergt. Sim, a new short rifle and "dulled" sword were issued. On the 26th it was announced in orders that he also had been awarded the M.M. Five additional casualties occurred during the period June 18th/30th, bringing the total for the month up to 2 killed and 25 wounded.

"Summer Time" was adopted on June 14th, the clock being advanced from 11 p.m. to 12.0.

A memorable dinner took place at Halloy while the battalion was training there. About forty officers assembled in a big hut on the evening of June 23rd. It was a sort of "send off" for the "Great Push" which it was expected would take place within a day or two. Menu cards were passed round and autographed by all present. Contrary to Mess custom a few speeches were made wishing success to the battalion in the approaching battle and altogether a very pleasant evening was spent. Sixteen of the signatories of the menus figured in the casualty list for July 1st, and the cards are now highly prized by the fortunate survivors as a melancholy souvenir of their former companions.

Between June 9th and 14th and June 22nd to 27th the brigade was billeted at Halloy, and during both those periods the attack was practised over and over again. A copy of the German trenches which were to be attacked had been constructed on a large scale, also the system of trenches in which the assaulting troops were to assemble. Everything was carefully gone through and rehearsed until each man knew exactly where he would start from, where he was to go, and what he had to do when he got there. The preparations for the attack were the best rehearsed of any that the Q.V.R. did. Instead of, as often occurred afterwards, hardly anyone knowing anything of the work to be done, every single man in the battalion knew all about the attack and what was expected of him. Everything possible was done to ensure success. To enable companies to be identified and to avoid confusion by men getting into the wrong trench, or staying in one when they should go forward, each company wore distinguishing colours on their shoulder-straps. Coloured boards on poles were issued to be waived to show the artillery and others in rear how far the troops had reached. Every trench in the system to be attacked was given a name, and maps with the names on were distributed widely; notice boards with these names painted on were carried, to be hoisted when the trench was captured, to facilitate men knowing where they were. Careful arrangements were made for the carriage of tools and stores in order that the assaulting waves should go forward only lightly burdened, the subsequent waves carrying most of the heavy stores.

The morale of the men at the time was perfectly wonderful. They all knew exactly what to do; they had seen the mass of artillery they had to support them and recognised that everything possible was being done to ensure success. A good example of their spirit was the attitude of the men of " D " Company, which had been selected as a reserve company and was not to go over the top with the assaulting wave, but to wait several hours before their time came. They considered it a slight that they had not been chosen to go with the first lot, and it had to be pointed out to them that somebody had to be kept in reserve and that as a matter of fact theirs would be the worst job, as by the time their turn came the enemy's barrage would certainly be down, whereas the first line *might* get across No Man's Land in comparative safety. As a matter of fact when their time did come it was apparent that no man could get across and live. A number of officers and N.C.O.'s had to be left behind as " Battle Surplus." They were all much upset about it and begged that they might be allowed to go over.

On June 26th the following warning (C.A. 104) to be " communicated verbally to all ranks before taking part in an assault " was issued by the General Staff :

" 1. All ranks must be on their guard against the various ruses at which the enemy has shown himself to be an adept, especially the use of British words of command, such as ' Retire,' etc.

2. The German machine-gun is carried on a sledge, and the Germans sometimes throw a blanket over the gun. This makes the sledge and gun resemble a stretcher.

3. It is the duty of all ranks to continue to use their weapons against the enemy's fighting troops, unless and until it is beyond all doubt that those have not only ceased all resistance, but that, whether through having voluntarily thrown down their weapons or otherwise, they have definitely and finally abandoned all hope or intention of resisting further. In the case of apparent surrender it lies with the enemy to prove his intention beyond the possibility of misunderstanding, before the surrender can be accepted as genuine."

CHAPTER XIX

"THE GREAT PUSH"—THE BATTLE OF GOMMECOURT
1ST JULY, 1916

A GOOD deal of stress has been laid upon the training of the regiment during the last three months under review. It was the same with every other unit both in France and England. Preparations had been going on for many months on a colossal scale. Never before had the world seen anything like it. Every battalion was brought up to its full strength, and new ones formed, and the British Army grew and grew till it vied in numbers and equipment with these of France and Germany; guns and projectiles of all sorts and sizes had been hurried to the front until the huge machine was ready to be launched with every prospect of success on the great enterprise that everyone, including the enemy, had so long expected. Originally fixed for June 29th it was on that day postponed for forty-eight hours, at least so it was whispered in the British trenches and billets. On Saturday, June 24th, began the tremendous artillery bombardment along a line of eighty miles from the Yser to the Somme. Although insignificant compared with some of the later concentrations of gunfire it was one of the most wonderful seen until that time. Whilst the Q.V.R. were at Halloy it was a wonderful sight to watch at night-time the sky being made brilliant by the unending bursting of shells. Even in those times the troops held their concerts and " between the turns " men would go outside and watch the shelling from a point of vantage. For the last few days of June the battalion was at St. Amand, where a number of heavy guns were gathered. Amongst others was a battery of 9·2 howitzers, round which a large crowd of spectators was always assembled. There was also one enormous howitzer, either 12 or 15 inch, which was a special attraction.

On the afternoon and evening of June 30th the Q.V.R. left St. Amand and marched to Hebuterne to take up their position in the Assembly Trenches. Each man carried 200 rounds small arms ammunition, 3 Mills' grenades, 3 sandbags, 2 tube helmets, waterproof sheet, haversack, current day's ration and an iron ration; picks, shovels and other tools and notice boards were also carried. Everyone felt that they were in for a big success ; all were cheerful and full of spirit and no one who saw the departure of the Q.V.R. from St. Amand will ever forget that wonderful scene. They took over the front line assembly trenches and stood by in readiness for the great morning offensive. They were heavily shelled during the night. Hot pea-soup was issued at 4 a.m.

The VIIth Army Corps comprised the 37th, 46th and 56th Divisions, in the last-named being the Q.V.R., who with the 2nd London Regiment, the London Rifle Brigade, the Queen's Westminsters, a Trench Mortar Battery, some 5th Cheshire Pioneers and a few 2/1st London R.E., made up the 169th Brigade. Their immediate task was to establish themselves on " a line N.E. of 16 Poplars—E. of Nameless Farm " involving the taking of three lines of German trenches and the subsequent clearing up and consolidating of the Park and village of Gommecourt. The L.R.B. and the Q.V.R. were to lead, followed by the Westminsters with the 2nd London in reserve. The password was " London."

How the brigade fared let two graphic war correspondents tell :

" THE WORST CORNER "

The late John D. Irvine, a well-known London Journalist, who at the time was the special correspondent of the *Daily Express*, wrote : " I am able to give first-hand information concerning the part which has been played by certain of our famous London regiments. These regiments, which include the Rangers, the Queen Victoria's Rifles, the London Rifle Brigade, the London Scottish and the Queen's Westminsters, were assigned certain objectives near Gommecourt, towards the northern end of our original line of advance, where, owing to the extraordinary preparations made by the enemy, we did not fare so well as we have done and continue to do further south. The London regiments, who fought with magnificent gallantry and tenacity, did in fact, accomplish their primary objects, but owing to circumstances beyond their control they subsequently had to retire to a line which nearly corresponded to that they occupied before the battle began. It certainly represents no surrender of territory; the enemy is fully contained and is kept busy night and day, with the result that he can send neither guns nor men to assist his hard-pressed troops within the zone of our continuous penetration of his lines. When the regiments received the order to leave their trenches at 7.30 on the morning of July 1st, a gap of from 250 to 300 yards in a valley separated them from the first line trenches of the enemy. At the given signal they leapt across their parapets, and with magnificent steadiness, advanced in the open under cover of smoke which had been sent up with the object of screening their movements from the enemy. Within half an hour they were in possession of the main objective. Immediately afterwards the enemy started to set up a terrific barrage fire, which almost pulverised the front line trenches from which our men originally started, and, what was of graver consequence, stopped all efforts to send up supports and carrying parties bearing munitions essential to the continuance of our advance. The most gallant attempts were made to establish communication, and a series of enterprises characterised by desperate bravery involved us in heavy losses. Out of one party of fifty-nine which started across the shell-swept valley, one only reached his comrades and but three returned to our lines. Reports sent back shortly before this showed that our artillery had succeeding in smashing up the German parapets and barbed wire entanglements, but had failed—as has been the experience everywhere—to crumple up the deep dug-outs in which it is the habit of the Boches to sit down and bide their opportunity. So when our men entered the enemy trenches, they were confronted by crowds of these cave-dwellers armed with bombs, and a series of hand-to-hand conflicts, in which we succeeded in killing many and capturing some Germans, ensued. A certain number of the Boches showed a readiness to surrender, but they were influenced by more courageous comrades, who assured them that the English could not send up supplies, and that very soon they would have to go back to their own territory. The Londoners did succeed in capturing about 200 unwounded or slightly wounded Germans, but as these hapless individuals were being sent across to our lines they came under the fire of their own artillery. In bombing, during the time they were in the trenches, the Londoners easily outthrew the Germans, and all along they were getting the best of the fight when the enemy succeeded in working partially round our flanks, cutting off communication with the units of another division. The London Scottish on the right flank put up a great fight, and further towards the left, superb gallantry was displayed by the Queen's Westminsters, the L.R.B. and the 'Vics.' Owing, however, to the fact that our supply of bombs and other ammunition had now reached the point of exhaustion, and that it was impossible to send up fresh supplies, our men had no option but to fall back, which they did with extreme reluctance, though in perfect order. A chapter of accidents robbed them of what would have been a fruitful victory."

According to Col. V. W. F. Dickins, D.S.O., V.D., the German troops against which the Londoners fought were the 56th Division and a Guards Reserve Division.

Another interesting version of the advance of the Londoners is given by Mr. Phillip Gibbs, the *Daily Telegraph* correspondent who says: " When the four leading battalions left their trenches near Gommecourt at 7.30 after the great bombardment of the German positions, they had a long way to go before they reached the enemy's front lines. No Man's Land was a broad stretch of ground, 400 yards across in some parts, and not less than 200 yards at the narrowest part. It was a long, long journey in the open, for fifty yards, or twenty, are long enough to become a great graveyard if the enemy's machine-guns get to work. But they advanced behind dense smoke-like clouds, which rolled steadily towards the German trenches and kept down the machine-gun fire, and their chief risk was from the barrage of shell-fire which the enemy flung across No Man's Land with some intensity. But the Londoners started forward to this line of high explosives, and went on, and through, at a quick pace, in open order. On the left was the London Rifle Brigade, in the centre came the 'Vics.' and Rangers, on the right the London Scottish, and behind the Queen's Westminsters and Kensingtons, who were to advance through the others. Men fell across the open ground, caught by flying bits of shell or buried by the great bursts of high explosives which opened up the earth. But the others did not look back, afraid to weaken themselves by the sight of their stricken comrades, and at a great pace, half walking and half running, they reached the German line. It was no longer a system of trenches. It was a sea of earth with solid waves. Our heavy guns had annihilated parapet and parados, smashed the timbers into matchwood, strewed sandbags into rubbish heaps and made a great wreckage. But German industry below ground was proof against all this shell-fire, and many of the dug-outs still stood. They were full of Germans, for the line was strongly held, and many of these men came up with their machine-guns and bombs to resist the attack. But the Londoners sprang upon them, swept over them, and captured the front network of trenches with amazing speed. It was not a steady-going business, slow and deliberate. The quick mind of the London man spurred him to quick action. He did not linger to collect souvenirs or to chat with English-speaking Germans. 'London leads!' was the shout of Victorias and Westminsters. The London Scottish were racing forward on the right with their brown kilts swinging across the broken ground. But the officers kept their heads and as much order as possible at such a time. They held back enough men to clear the dug-outs and collect prisoners—the best kind of souvenirs. Two hundred of them were captured in the dug-outs and brought up and sent back over the place that had been No Man's Land and now, for a time, was ours. At least 200 came back, but there were many more who never got back, though they started on the journey under armed guard. The enemy's artillery was increasing the density of the barrage upon our old front-line trenches and the ground in front of it. He made a wall of high explosives through which no living thing could pass. The escorts and their prisoners tried to pass—and failed. The German gunners must have seen their grey-clad men going back, but they obeyed the laws of war and did not give them a chance, because if they passed back other British soldiers could pass forward,

and it was for the guns to stop them. At the time the London
men fighting forward did not think of the barrage behind them.
They were eager to get on, to be quick over the first part of
their business before taking breath for the next. And they
got on with astonishing speed. In less than the time it has
taken me to write this narrative No Man's Land had been
crossed, the trenches had been taken, the prisoners collected
and sent back on their way, and German strongholds and
redoubts behind the first system of trench work had been
seized by London regiments. It would have taken them longer
to walk from Charing-cross to St. Paul's Churchyard with no
Germans in the way. It was the quickest bit of work that has
been done by any freemen of the City. The riflemen had
swarmed into a strong point on the left, knocking out the
machine-guns, and on the right the London Scots were holding
a strong redoubt in a very ugly corner of ground. Everything
had been won that London had been asked to win. Before
some hours had passed these London soldiers knew that they
were in a death-trap, and cut off from escape, owing to the
great strength of the enemy to the right and left of the position,
where they had concentrated masses of guns, and where the
ground was more difficult to carry. The troops on either side
of the Londoners, in spite of heroic courage and complete
self-sacrifice, had (not ?) advanced so far. The London men
had therefore thrust forward a salient into the German lines,
and were enclosed by the enemy. Behind them, on the way
to their own lines, the enemy's barrage was steadily becoming
more violent. Having stopped the other attacks to the north
and south, he was now able to concentrate the fire of his guns
upon the ground of the London area, and by the early afternoon he had smashed our trenches and communication trenches
while still flinging out a line of high explosives to prevent
supports coming up to the men who were in the captured
salient. They were cut off, and had no other means of rescue
but their own courage. Desperate efforts were made by the
comrades behind to send up supplies of ammunition and other
means of defence. The carrying parties attempted again and
again to cross No Man's Land, but suffered heavy casualties.
One party of sixty men with supplies of hand-grenades, set
out [on this journey, but only three came back. **Single men**

went on with a few grenades, determined to carry some kind of support to the men in front, but fell dead or wounded before they reached their goal. In the meantime, as the day lengthened, the enemy organised a series of counter-attacks. Their grenadiers showed a great courage and daring, working down their communication trenches under heavy fire from our artillery and even crossing on top of the trenches in small groups until they were close enough for bomb throwing. Other parties came down on the left of the Londoners from the northern position, and from this direction also very heavy machine-gun fire began to enfilade our riflemen. . . . It is a tragic narrative " the dispatch concludes, " but the London battalions who went out there beyond No Man's Land, did as well as any soldiers could, and the brave hearts which beat once to the pulse of London's great tide of life should be remembered on the long roll-call of honour which stretches back through the history of our great old town. ' London leads ! ' was the cry of these men."

The Attack Order No. 1 for the operations was as follows :

Q.V.R. ATTACK ORDER No. 1

Reference, H1/10,000 Hebuterne Fonquevillers.

1. The VIIth Corps' intention is to establish itself on a line which runs approximately from our present front line—25 yards N.E. of 16 Poplars—E. of Nameless Fm.—along ridge in K.5a and E.29c—Little Z, and thence back to our line.

46th Division attacks from the N.W. and 56th Division from S.W., the two Divisions to meet about E.29c 6.0.

The 168th Brigade will attack on the right of the 169th. The left of the 168th Brigade will rest on a point in Fell 50 yards N.W. of trench junction K.5c.52. They will establish a strong point about cross trenches of Fell and Felon with Epte.

2. The task of the 169th Brigade will be carried out in 4 Phases.

1ST PHASE. To capture from left of 168th Brigade along Fell, Fellow, Feud, Cemetery, Eck, Maze, Eel and Fir, and establish three strong points, viz :

(1) Near Cemetery,
(2) At the Maze.
(3) At the S.E. corner of Gommecourt Park.

2nd Phase (immediately after 1st). To clear Ems, Etch and capture the quadrilateral.

3rd Phase (immediately after 2nd). To secure cross trenches at K.5a.78, where Indus crosses Fell and Fillet to join hands with 46th Division along Fill and consolidate Fillet, facing E.

4th Phase (to commence three hours after Zero). To clear both Gommecourt Village and Park in a N.W. direction from line Fir-Eel-Maze-Eck-Cemetery.

46th Division will clear the village in a S.E. direction. Further details later.

3. Assembly of Battalion. "A" and "C" in Y.47 and Boyau. 1 platoon 5th Cheshires and 8 R.E. (attached "C" Company) Boyau.

"B" in Y.47.L. Left and right of Yankee Street.

"D" in Y.47.R. In reserve.

4. Advance Formation
1st Wave—
   "A" 1 platoon from right to left at 4 paces interval.
   "C" 1   ,,   ,,   ,,   ,, 4 ,,   ,,
2nd Wave—
   "A" 2 platoons ,,   ,,   ,, 2 ,,   ,,
   "C" 2   ,,   ,,   ,, 2 ..   ,
3rd Wave—
   "A" 1 platoon   ,,   ,,   ,, 4 ,,   ,,
   "C" 1   ,,   ,,   ,,   ,, 4 ,,   ,,
4th Wave—
   3 Sections Battn. Bombers ,,   ,, 2 ,,   ,,
   1 platoon Cheshires   ,,   ,, 2 ,   ,
   8 Sappers R.E.   ,,   ,, 2 ,,   ,,
Pioneers and Sappers will rmain in Feed until required.
5th Wave—
   "B" 4 platoons T.M.B., ½ Sect. Signallers, in line at 2 paces interval.
6th Wave—
   "D."

5. Objectives. "A" through Fever, Feint to Fell and Fellow.

"C" through Fern, Ems. (incl.) Feed, and Emden to Feud, Strong Point, Cemetery. As soon as Strong Point is established and Ems is clear, 1 platoon "C" in Feud will occupy Ems, getting in touch with Q.W.R. at Quadrilateral.

Platoons of "A" in Fellow and Fell will move to their left and be in support in Feud and Fellow.

"B" through Fever, Fern to Feint, Feed.

6. COMPANY BOMBERS. "A" clear Feint, Fell, Fellow, Etch above Fell until in touch with Q.W.R.

"C" clear Feed, Feud, Emden and Ems above Feud.

"B" clear Fever, Fern.

7. H.Q. BOMBERS. One group clear each of the C.T.s Etch, Ems, Emden from front line to third line.

8. LEWIS GUNS. 2 L.G. will be attached to each company and under the command of O.C. companies.

Lewis guns will not fire unless necessary, until the trenches are consolidated and position occupied, except in case of counter-attack.

9. CONTACT PATROLS. "A" and "C" will find contact patrols to keep in touch with 168th Brigade on our right (Left Battn.=Rangers) and L.R.B. on our left respectively.

10. STRETCHER BEARERS. 8 with 5th Wave, 8 at Dressing Station.

11. COMMUNICATIONS—
   (a) Telephonic.
   (b) Visual.
   (c) Runners.
   (d) C.Ts.

(a) *Telephonic.* A Report Centre (R.C.) is established at the junction of Yellow Street and front line, connected to Battn. H.Q. by D 5 cable (2 lines).

ASSAULT—

(1) 4 Signallers will carry across wires in duplicate to establish an Advanced Report Centre (A.R.C.) at the junction of Ems and Feed. Similarly

    L.R.B. establish A.R.C. up Exe.
    Q.W.R.   ,,   ,,   ,, Etch.

The calls for these, Etch on the right = R.
                  Ems centre   = C.
                  Exe on the left = L.

(2) 4 signallers will establish 'phone station in Feint 50 yards N.W. of junction of Feint and Epte.

(3) 4 signallers will lay line up Etch and laterally one along Feed to A.R.C.

One along Feint to Feint 'phone station.

(4) 8 signallers at R.C. for line work. Part of this personnel will also lay rabbit netting across No Man's Land.

Battn. Signallers will man R.C. from 11 a.m. Y day. At all trench junctions in German 2nd line notice boards will be fixed denoting direction of A.R.C. and 'phone station.

All signallers advancing, advance with the 5th Wave = " B " Company. Lieut. Meeking will be i/c A.R.C.

(b) *Visual.* 4 Signallers will establish a Visual Station at Cemetery, working back to Battn. H.Q.

Brigade Visual Station near junction of Yiddish Street and Y.48.R. Each message will be sent twice.

(c) *Runners* 4 per company with O.C. companies.
    2 ,, ,, of " A," " B," " C " at A.R.C.
    2 ,, ,, at Battn. H.Q.

Should telephonic communication break down between R.C. and A.R.C. the officer i/c latter will send runners to hand in messages at R.C. until the break can be repaired. R.C. will not be manned as a station, a clear line being left through from Battn. H.Q. to A.R.C.

Similarly when Battn. H.Q. advances a clear line must be left through from Brigade H.Q. to A.R.C.

(d) *C.Ts.* A new C.T. will be dug under divisional arrangements from Yellow Street to Ems. Yellow Street-Ems C.T. will be used for Up traffic only.

Q.W.R. are allotted exclusive use of Etch.

The first opportunity will be taken to remove one wire from the lines laid forward from R.C. and to place it in the new C.T.

Flares. Red flares will be placed on the objective trenches as soon as reached. O.C.'s companies will detail men to do this.

Boards. Companies will carry boards on which the names of their objective trenches are painted. These boards will be placed at centre of fire trenches and at W. end of C.Ts. on arrival.

12. DISTINGUISHING COLOURS—
"A" will wear Red tape on right shoulder strap.
"B" „ „ Blue „ „ „ „
"C" „ „ Black „ „ „ „
"D" „ „ Yellow „ „ „ „

All wire cutters will wear White on right shoulder strap in addition to company colours.

Signallers will wear Blue and White on right shoulder strap.
Right Company of L.R.B. wear Red on the left shoulder.
Other L.R.B. companies Blue, Yellow, Green on the left shoulder.

13. CONSOLIDATION AND WORK ON TRENCHES. As soon as objective trenches are reached by "A," "B," "C" no time must be wasted to commence work on consolidation. The first hour will no doubt be the quietest, and every man must do his utmost to make good and strengthen the trenches against counter-attack.

Frequent progress reports to be sent to C.O. via A.R.C.

14. CLEARING GOMMECOURT PARK AND VILLAGE. 3 hours after zero time Gommecourt Park and Village are to be cleared by L.R.B. and Q.V.R. respectively.

Small bombing parties will be formed from H.Q. "B," "D" Companies under Lieut. Caley. The village of Gommecourt will be systematically cleared from the Strong Point and Cemetery in a N.W. direction as far as the pond S. of Church and S.W. as far as Fibre and to get into touch with the L.R.B. clearing the Park. Progress to be reported to A.R.C.

15. TRENCH MORTARS. The ½ Section T.M.B. (2 mortars) will follow the 5th Wave and take up a suitable position about Emden to cover Cemetery and Strong Point.

O.C. "D," will detail 10 men to report to O.C. T.M.B. They will carry Stokes ammunition for the day.

16. S.A.A. AND GRENADES. Dumps as indicated in Administrative Instructions.

Every man will carry 120 rounds in equipment.
„ „ „ „ 100 „ „ 2 bandoliers.

Battn. Reserve S.A.A. will be situated at junction of Yankee Street and Y.47.L. This reserve will be sent forward to junction of Fern-Fever on application from A.R.C.

Every man with exceptions specified in Q.V. 368/a will carry 2 Mills.

O.C. Companies will arrange for dumps of these grenades to be made on arrival at their objectives.

17. DUMPS. Other than those mentioned in Administrative Instructions.

(1) ½ man loads (50–60 of wiring material) behind Y.47.L. right and left of Yankee Street.

(2) 25 ladders for carrying forward are in each of the portions of Y.47 occupied by "A" and "C": 25 per company.

(3) ½ man loads made up according to Johnsap is as under :

Screw pickets	2 per load.
Barbed wire	1 coil.
French wire	2 small coils and 6 staples.
X.P. metal	5 half sheets.
Planks 4'	4.
Pickets, wood 5'	3.
Sandbags	40.

The above is carried by " B."

18. BATTLE POLICE. 1 N.C.O. and 2 men with each section of company bombers. Battle Police will wear $4'' \times 2''$ round right forearm. Duties :

(a) The B.P. must know what trench they are in, and be able to direct any man who is lost or doubtful where he is.

(b) They must assist bombers in clearing trenches and take charge of any prisoners, disarm them, and see that they are escorted back.

(c) To see that no stragglers are left in the trenches behind those occupied by their companies ; any so found they must send up to their companies.

(d) To see that the C.T.'s are used correctly.

19. BRIDGES. 50 Bridges (light) for carrying forward are in Y.47. 23 for " A," 27 for " C."

" A " will bridge Fever, Feint, Fellow.

" C " will bridge Fern, Feed, Emden, Feud.

To be done as quickly as possible to enable Q.W.R. to pass over to the Quadrilateral.

20. SMOKE ARRANGEMENTS—

(1) Smoke will be freely used whatever the direction of the wind.

(2) Smoke will be propelled from (a) 4" Stokes mortars under arrangements by O.C. 5th Special Brigade R.E. (b) by hand, by 167th Brigade.

(3) On day of attack (a) Special Brigade will have 6 mortars for left smoke barrage on Fir, 12 mortars along front between Whiskey Street and Z hedge, to project smoke along the front. (b) Provided wind is favourable, smoke will be projected by hand along the whole Divisional front from Hebuterne-Puisieux road to the sap head at K.3.d.47.

The intention is that the assault should start as soon as possible after the commencement of the smoke, and that it should be kept up while the assaulting battalions are crossing No Man's Land, and that afterwards sufficient should be employed to screen parties working on C.Ts. across No Man's Land.

(4) Smoke will be used freely during the preliminary bombardment.

(5) Lines of chloride of lime will be laid at different points in the Southern parts of No Man's Land showing the true direction of advance. All ranks should look out for these lines and correct their direction by them.

Battalion H.Q. will be at junction of Yellow Street and Y.47.R., later at or near A.R.C.

J. C. ANDREWS,
27/6/16.   Captain and Adjutant, Q.V.R.

Battalion H.Q. was in a dug-out at the junction of the old front line and Yellow Street (on the main Communication Trench) and from just inside it a most extensive and close view of the ground could be obtained. "D" Company (under Capt. Lindsey-Renton) were disposed in the neighbourhood of Battalion H.Q. "A" (Cunningham), "B" (Houghton) and "C" (Leys Cox) were to assault. A nucleus of about 8 officers and 90 O.R., chiefly specialists as bombers and Lewis gunners, was left out of the battle with the transport ("Battle Surplus"). This was an innovation and was strictly carried out throughout the army. It was necessary, as it had often happened that battalions in battle had lost all their officers and a high proportion of N.C.O'.s and specialists. The nucleus was to serve as surplus round which reinforcements from the base could rally and be absorbed.

"For two hours," says Col. Dickins, "no news whatever was received from the front, all communication, visual and telephonic, having failed. Beyond answering constant appeals from the Brigade for information, we had leisure to observe what was going on. Meanwhile a steady shelling of our trenches was kept up and New Yellow Street (our up C.T. from the old front line) was filled up and destroyed for a great length of its course. Two companies of the 3rd Londons under Major Samuels attempted to dig a C.T. across No Man's Land, but heavy rifle and M.G. fire completely prevented them. Information was then received—more than an hour old—from both Cox and Houghton, that all their objectives had been quickly taken. This was brought by two plucky runners who returned to our line through the barrage. Thenceforward the day went ill. The stubborn resistance of the enemy, the shortage of bombs, and the impossibility of getting more across to our men on the far side, and lastly the complete failure of the 46th Division's assault on the left and the repulse of the 31st Division on our right, were the causes of our disastrous reverse at Gommecourt."

CHAPTER XX

THE BATTLE OF GOMMECOURT—*Continued*

PERSONAL REMINISCENCES

"THE sector for which our division was responsible," says Lieut. S. J. Holloway, "was a line originally held by the French in front of Hebuterne Village. Hebuterne, insignificant in times of peace, comprised a number of small farmsteads, owned before their desolation by industrious farmers in comfortable circumstances. At the rear of the village was the 'Keep,' a system of trenches protected with barbed wire, commanding the front, flanks and rear. Along the main street at intervals of about 100 yards were the entrances to communication trenches bearing such names as Yankee Street, Yellow Street, Yiddish Street, York Street and Yule Street, in alphabetical order of the vowels. A tortuous journey of ten minutes along these trenches brought one to the fire trench. Across No Man's Land about 1000 yards distance, where the German line stretched out, was Gommecourt Wood, behind which was Gommecourt Park. For many months, after unsuccessful and sanguinary battles for the possession of the wood and the ridge beyond, the French and the Huns had sat and watched. One serene Sunday night at the end of May found our Division digging a new line of trenches in No Man's Land, 500 yards in front of the old trench. The men worked with that energy which only the primitive instinct for personal safety can make possible. Parallel to the front line, several lines of trenches were dug for jumping off. These we had to protect from the enemy, which was done by small posts of half a platoon strength at intervals of 80 to 100 yards."

Lt.-Col. Dickins (O.C.), in notes taken down at the time the fighting was in progress, thus tells the story : " As soon as the assault commenced, the German barrage was opened on to our trenches; though not severe at first, it increased in intensity later. By 9.48 the assaulting companies had reached their objective and occupied it after heavy fighting. They did not, however, get in touch with the battalion on the right. At the same time the third company was consolidating the German second line. The Germans were pressing hard at this time and the shortage of bombs began to be felt. In accordance with the order as to the fourth phase of the battle, three sections of bombers with battle police from the reserve company were ordered at 9.30 a.m. to join the companies in the German line. Owing, however, to congestion in the communication trenches, this party did not leave until after 10.30. As soon as they had left the trench they came under heavy machine-gun fire and half the party became casualties immediately. This party was unable to get across No Man's Land, the enemy's barrage by this time being intense. At eleven o'clock the shortage of bombs became critical. From 12.30 to 1.30 the German counter-attack increased in force, and the companies were driven back from the third line to the second line. At 2 o'clock the companies were driven back to the German first line. About this time a few wounded men began to reach our lines. At 4.30 orders were given to collect all stragglers in our lines, and hold the assembly trench strongly. From this time until about 7 p.m. survivors in German trenches kept up their resistance in the first line, but at 7 o'clock they were finally driven out, and those who got across No Man's Land began to return to our trenches. After dark the battalion took up the position from which it started and remained there for the night and until the afternoon of the next day, when it was relieved and then withdrew to Bayencourt."

Writing a day or two after the battle to Lieut.-Col. Shipley, whom it will be remembered he succeeded in the command of the regiment, Lieut.-Col. Dickins says: " I must say that all officers, N.C.O.'s and men did behave and act in a most mangificent manner when they advanced and during the assault last Saturday week, the 1st July—a day never to be forgotten in the regiment. No battalion could have advanced better or been more steady than our lads were and I feel awfully proud of them all; they went straight at it in a most determined and deliberate way and gained their objective, i.e. three lines of German trenches in half an hour. Here they set to work to consolidate the trenches and make good, and held on from the early morning until about 2.30 p.m., when from want of support on both flanks, and the supply of bombs, etc., giving out, they were obliged to withdraw slowly, holding each line back as long as possible. If we could only have got bombs over to them I think they might have managed to hold on until dark, but the artillery barrage and machine-gun fire put up in No Man's Land was so heavy that it was impossible for anyone to get across or live there. I ordered the reserve company, "D," to try to get parties across. They made three attempts, but each time all who started became casualties. It was a great disappointment to everyone; especially the men feel it, that they had to give up what they had so gloriously gained, but the powers that be say we did our job and held the enemy, or great numbers of them, in front of us and so helped the push in other places. Out of the three companies, "A," "B" and "C," that went over to the assault, only sixty-four got back that evening; a few have turned up since. All the officers of those companies, in all fifteen, were put out of action and also E. A. J. A. Lane, who was attached to the Trench Mortar Company. I deplore the loss of these brave lads, but I feel they one and all fought and died like true British soldiers."

This letter was issued as a Special Order of the Day and read to the 2nd and 3rd Battalions of the Q.V.R. on parade at Ipswich and Fovant respectively.

In a letter composed at a time when he had more leisure, namely, on July 11th, Col. Dickins wrote: "I am sure you will be glad to hear that a few of us are still alive. We were in a most terrific battle, as no doubt you have by this time heard. The L.R.B. and ourselves had the place of honour to lead the attack and assault of the brigade. We had a task given us to assault three lines of German trenches and take them. This we did in half an hour, and captured all our objectives in the most brilliant manner and held them from early morning until 2.30 p.m., when our three companies were obliged to withdraw, one line at a time, on account of our bombs giving out and not having the support on our flanks as we should have had, and expected, also we were so reduced in numbers. The enemy put up such a terrific artillery barrage and machine-gun fire that it was quite impossible to get any supply of bombs over No Man's Land. I tried to get three parties in turn to carry bombs over, but as soon as they appeared in the open they were wiped out. Of the three companies, " A," " B " and " C," that advanced to the assault with 15 officers, 5 each, only 64 got back and all the officers were put out of action. Poor Leys Cox, Meeking, Cary and Bennett are missing, but there is just the chance they may be wounded and are prisoners. All the others are killed or wounded. I feel awfully proud and full of admiration of the magnificent way the whole battalion went up and advanced to the assault and the determined way in which they all fought like cats. I deplore the heavy losses that we have had and I feel that I have lost all my old friends and pals ; on this day our casualty list was 16 officers and 518 men, and the day before that 108. So we have had a very hard knock, but are doing our best with what remains to keep cheery and carry on."

A similar story but with interesting additions is told by Capt. Lindsey-Renton, " D " (Reserve) Company :—

" At 6.25 the final intensive bombardment started, and a most wonderful sight it was. Our shells appeared to be falling everywhere, and the German trenches were enveloped in clouds of smoke, with earth, bricks, and trees shooting up into the air whenever a big shell burst. All the troops in the old front line were standing on the firestep gleefully surveying the scene. At 7.20 the smoke barrage began and five minutes later had extended all along the line. At 7.30 the attack commenced, the front line men advancing over the top just as though they were on parade, calmly and slowly while the reserve men stood up on the parapet cheering them on. It was truly a weird sight as the troops gradually disappeared in the smoke. For some time nothing could be seen, but as the smoke began to clear away the advance could be followed. At one point the attacking party appeared to be held up and could be seen lining a bank, or the edge of a road, but after a time they got up and pushed forward. Then the enemy's barrage came. It was terrific and rendered it impossible for any further body of men to get across. At 9.30 instructions were given to 2nd Lieut. Ord MacKenzie to take the company bombers with him, but owing to congestion in the trenches they did not get away until 10.30, and then had to start from the old front line. No sooner were they over than they came under heavy machine-gun fire which made half of them casualties. They were greatly handicapped from the fact that as the assaulting troops had started in front of that line the wire there had not been cut. Splendid work was here done by Lce.-Cpl. Appleyard, who, though himself wounded in two places, went out again, despite the firing, to search for any wounded who had been unable to get back. Then Lieut. Hodgson was detailed to take his platoon over via the new front line. Presently a message came back saying that the barrage was very heavy and that some of the Q.V.R. were unable to get across. It being essential that reinforcements of men and bombs should be kept up, a second urgent message was sent to Lieut. Hodgson to try and push across. For some reason or other the runner who took the message failed to deliver it, probably he got lost or knocked over, and then orders came that no more reinforcements were to be sent, as owing to the intensity of the German barrage it was impossible for men to get across alive. About 2 p.m. the first news arrived from the front. Things, we were informed, were not going well; the attackers were being heavily counter-attacked and were being driven back. Captain Leys Cox, the senior officer who went forward, it transpired, had tried to send several messages to the reserve but the runners had all been knocked out. Eventually his batman, Rfn. Armitage, volunteered to take a message, and though he was wounded on the way down, managed to get it delivered. For that exploit he afterwards received the Military Medal. Another runner, Rfn. Collins, " B " Company, displayed great gallantry and determintaion in getting his message through and succeeded in doing so. He was awarded the M.M. and, sometime afterwards, the Russian Cross of St. George, 4th Class.

" During the afternoon it became clear that the situation at the front was bad and orders were received that at night the old German front line should be consolidated, but even that was found to be impossible. It was feared that the enemy, counting on the disorganisation resulting from the failure of the attack, would make a counter-attack upon our original lines. Orders were accordingly issued to collect all available men, stragglers and anyone returning from the front, and occupy Y.47 L, one of the assembly trenches, but not the first one, which was to be held at all costs. The counter-attack, however, never developed. About six o'clock a runner reached Battalion H.Q. after a very difficult and trying journey. This was Rfn. Morris, quite a small youth. He arrived covered with mud and perspiration, delivered his message and then asked for some water. Having quenched his thirst he calmly sat down outside the H.Q. dug-out and thoroughly cleaned his rifle ! At dusk the survivors began to come in and a sad sight it was to see the remnant of the magnificent battalion that had gone forward that morning straggling back in twos and threes, tired to death, and completely overcome by the strain they had been through. All night stretcher bearers were out collecting the wounded.

"The following morning a remarkable thing occurred. A figure was observed standing up in the German trenches making friendly signals, which turned out to be an appeal for a truce. Eventually this was agreed to and both sides went out to collect their wounded. The Germans were very particular who went out, and fired at and wounded some men who started out still carrying their rifles. Both sides then proceeded to collect their wounded. There were many Germans who had been taken prisoners and sent back but got wounded or killed in crossing No Man's Land. The Higher Command had been rung up and asked to suspend all artillery fire, but unfortunately after a short cessation, whether through necessity or ignorance of the situation, the guns started firing over the area where the truce was, at some target on our right. The Germans thereupon intimated that they would give our men ten minutes to get back, when the truce would come to an end. Owing to this it was feared that many who might have been saved were missed. Later on the battalion, or rather all that remained of it, was withdrawn and sent to Bayencourt and thence to St. Amand, the place where it started from on June 30th. Although in the end a failure, the attack on July 1st was a wonderful piece of work ; the objective was reached in spite of the heavy fighting, but the divisions on both flanks failing to keep up both flanks became exposed. It was believed that the enemy anticipated the main British attack would develop in the locality where the Q.V.R. were, and had an enormous reserve of guns stationed in the neighbourhood for the purpose of smashing it."

Major Sampson, who took no part in the attack, gives the following impression of it : " In the evening a message came that I was to go up, and after dinner I set off and walked about five miles up to the trenches. I found that the battalion, and in fact the whole division, had had to come back to its original trenches, or rather that practically all those who had gone forward were wiped out. I will not go into technical details. It is enough to say, first, that the battalion has fought absolutely splendidly, earning the thanks of Sir Douglas Haig and everyone else, and second, that the casualties have been very heavy indeed. The trying thing is that many of them are left, wounded or killed, in the German trenches, and whether they are alive or dead we do not know. We are filled with pride for all that has been done, bitterness for the little there is to show for it, and sorrow for those we shall never see again. We are told we have, in fact, helped in the general scheme, and done our job, but the battalion is sadly mauled about. I feel that our job is done as regards actual fighting for many months and for, perhaps, the rest of the war. Another feeling is unexpected : it is one of respect for the enemy. He fought well, and finally showed himself not unchivalrous. Most of the wounded were of course in front of his trenches, and in the afternoon of the following day he waved handkerchiefs, etc., and then his stretcher bearers came out. Ours followed, and soon an informal armistice started. I, myself, and many others stood on top of our trenches and saw the stretcher bearers of both sides collecting and bringing in the wounded men. Our doctor spoke to a German officer and got vague news of some of our wounded. I could write on and on about all that has happened these last two days, but this letter is long enough. The regiment has fought a fight which history will perhaps record, but probably forget, but which has been terrific. It has surpassed itself in deeds of gallantry and devotion." In a further letter Major Sampson adds: "The regiment has earned the thanks of the C.-in-C. and everyone else. But the divisions on our flanks were held up, and in the end we had to come back to our trenches, what was left of us. Casualties of course are heavy. Phil Houghton, I am afraid, is certainly killed. He was left in the German trenches, and was seen to be badly hit, and I fear there is no doubt. Leys Cox was also left there wounded, but it appears just possible he is only wounded and will recover in German hands." This letter concludes Major Sampson's interesting contributions to our chronicle. A week later he "got a chill of the feverish variety common out here" and was invalided home.

Sergt. C. K. Sim, from whose diary we have taken many extracts, writes against July 1st: "1 a.m. Our wire had to be cut, and at daylight when this was spotted the 'fun' began. The Germans shelled us heavily until our big bombardment commenced at 6.30 a.m. The shelling lasted for one hour and five minutes. Before it lifted on to the reserve trenches the smoke cloud was sent over and our boys began the advance. I was wounded in the left hand just as I had got on our parapet. Felt a bit dazed owing to a big 'crump' having burst unpleasantly close just before. Didn't twig much that happened, but had sense enough to hop off quickly to the dressing station in Wurzel Street where Doctor Clarke bandaged the wound and told me I should have to lose a finger. Walked to Sailly, got a private motor to clearing hospital at Couin and lorry from there to the railhead clearing hospital at Warlancourt." On July 3rd he lands at Southampton and concludes his diary with "Finis."

Another N.C.O., Cpl. Reggie Rose, who was subsequently given a commission in the 7th Manchesters and was killed in action in July, 1917, in a letter to his father at Deal says: "I am pleased to tell you all three of the Deal boys are safe and sound. We, as you know, made our attack last Saturday morning. It was a wonderful sight to see our boys going over, and one even playing a mouth-organ. The lines went over as straight as if we were on parade, despite the fact of the tremendous curtain of fire the Huns put up. We captured three lines of their trenches but unfortunately we had to give them up again just before nightfall. But we had attained our object—which was to kill Germans—and that we did right well. There were piles of dead in their trenches. They must have lost thousands of killed and wounded, and we took hundreds of prisoners. Of course the " Vics " lost a lot of men, but nothing like the number the enemy must have done. Our bombardment before we went over was simply marvellous. For over an hour every gun was working at top speed, and the noise of the firing was so intense that you could not hear yourself speak. We have been back since the attack for two or three days, and had reinforcements sent up from other regiments, so we are a mixed battalion now, but they are quite nice chaps and have been in some stiff fighting elsewhere for eighteen months, so they have some very interesting tales to relate."

In describing his experiences to a former platoon commander, Sergt. G. F. Telfer says : " As you no doubt know, the second as well as the first German line was taken with very little resistance, and it was getting to their third that we first caught it really badly. About 20 yards from our objective was a sunken road, about 6 feet deep, at which we were held up for some time, say ten minutes or a quarter of an hour, owing to the Boche fire being too heavy to climb up the bank and go forward. We were also subjected to a heavy cross-fire from our right flank as the Rangers had not come up. It was here that poor old Capt. Cunningham was bowled over and I am of opinion he was killed, but of course one did not have the chance of testing his pulse—this is only my opinion, and really I hold out very little hope for our poor skipper, for so many poor chaps were killed instantaneously with bullet wounds through the head when lying up on the bank pouring lead into the Hun. By this time we had suffered pretty seriously, the only officer remaining being Lieut. Simmonds and of the N.C.O.'s the C.S.M., Sergt. Wilson, Sergt. Lewis and myself. Lewis was knocked over shortly afterwards. Quite on his own initiative Lce.-Cpl. Packer, the bombing corporal of No. 1 Platoon, who led on our trek up to the trenches, although wounded in the ear, rushed forward and bombed the Germans, followed instantanously by several others, causing the occupants of the German third line to slacken their fire for a few seconds, and with the help of the Q.W.R. the third line was rushed and taken. Lieut.

Simmonds was doing splendidly and supervised the bombing of the communication trenches leading to the Quadrilateral, the objective of the Q.W.R. Whilst this was going on I took a small party to our right flank and lay out in the open, firing on the Huns who were causing us so much trouble with their cross-fire, and it was there that I was told by the C.S.M. later that Lieut. Simmonds had been killed. For several hours we held our own, getting into touch with ' C ' Company and the R.E. blowing up traverses, etc. The Rangers had not got up. The counter-attack then set in by means of bombing parties both from the front and on our right, and we held our own for quite a long time, but owing to a shortage of bombs and ammunition we found it necessary to fight our way down the communication trench leading to their original second line, where we made a stand for some time with the help of a machine-gun and German hand grenades. It was then found that the Boches had got in their second line trench between ourselves and ' C ' Company, who were also retiring, and it was not a long time before we were in their first line. By this time our numbers were very small, for reinforcements, bombs, etc., could not be obtained owing to the heavy curtain of fire put up between the old front lines, and after a consultation I had with the C.S.M. we decided it was a case for every man to do his best to get home, for there were not enough men to get to work with the bayonet in the open. Everybody hung on as long as possible, then small parties began to evacuate, but none got far before they were bowled over by machine-gun fire. It was when I tried to get home that I got one from the left through my thigh and, in getting up, one across my back from the right, just taking the skin off my spine and ripping a nice lump out of my left side in the small of the back. I was able to get up and rush into a shell-hole where I remained until about 11 p.m., having been there for about ten hours—it seemed ten weeks. I got down to the Canadian hospital at La Treport and eventually here (South National Red Cross Hospital, Glasgow). As far as No. 1 Platoon is concerned 3 men only returned unwounded, viz., Nightingale and Collins (runner) and one other. Whilst we were holding on the German prisoners were pretty good to our wounded and put them in their commodious dug-outs, and from what

I hear, Lieut. Meeking was in one of these and I understand wounded. You will therefore see I cannot speak at all definitely as to the actual fate of our splendid officers in 'A' Company. When we were in the sunken road I was with the Captain and Lieut. Simmonds, and I cannot express in words my admiration for their splendid work and coolness. As regards Buck and Newbold[1] I do not know what happened to them. I had often had anxious moments, wondering as to how the many new men would act in a scrap, and I assure you there was no reason for it at all, as everyone went forward without a hitch under terrific fire and fought splendidly. I get depressed if I think too much about the terrible day, and I try to console myself with the fact that it was inevitable. Speaking to the divisional commander at the railway base he said we had done splendidly and had obtained the object of our attack, i.e. held the enemy's reserve artillery and infantry on our front, thus enabling the army operating further south to break through. The C.S.M., who was slightly wounded, is in hospital at Rugby together with 30 other 'A' Company men. Packer is at Torquay."

A desperate dash for safety across the fire-swept battle zone is described by Lce.-Cpl. Cecil Dixon, of the signalling section, in apprising the parents of the death of a companion, Lce.-Cpl. L. W. Taylor : " I feel that I may be able to offer you some consolation if I tell you the splendid way in which he met his death. I was with him at the time and the shock has been so keen that I have not been able to bring myself to write about him till now (July 16th). On the morning of the attack I went up the line about ten o'clock, where I found Lionel. By that time the smoke had cleared away and the enemy had opened a heavy barrage and machine-gun fire across No Man's Land, making it impossible for messengers or reinforcements to reach the troops occupying their trenches. Nevertheless Lionel suggested, and I thoroughly agreed with him, that it was only fair that some attempt should be made to get across, and I gladly offered to accompany him for I knew him to be a brave, cool, and level-headed comrade. We had no sooner left our trench than a strong machine-gun and rifle fire opened on us,

[1] Killed.

but we managed to reach a shell-hole about 30 yards out, where we found an L.R.B. messenger whose comrade had just been killed. After a brief interval we all three decided to make another rush. We did so and fire was once more opened on us. Just as we reached the shell-hole we were making for, the L.R.B. man pitched into it dead, with a bullet through his head. We had but to show our heads above the hole to draw a hail of bullets, but as we were now near the German trenches Lionel suggested we should make a last dash for it, which we did. We had not gone 10 yards before Lionel pitched forward on his face. Thinking it was on account of the fire I dropped where I was, about 10 yards from him and called to him. To my horror I got no answer and observed he was lying absolutely still and that he had been shot right through the body. Twice I tried to crawl to him but both times the fire got so hot that I was forced to get what cover I could. The third time I tried to make a dash for him and drag his body into a shell-hole, but was hit before I could reach him and had to fall into a shell-hole with my left arm useless. About mid day part of our line broke back and, thinking there was a general retreat, I had to, much to my sorrow, get back as best I could and leave his body."

From the foregoing letters it may be surmised that the full casualty list was a heavy one. From the War Diary it appears that 6 officers were killed, 5 wounded and 5 missing. Other Ranks : 51 killed, 290 wounded and 188 missing.

The six officers killed were :

Lieut. E. J. A. Lane, " B " Company, attached T.M.B.
2nd Lieut. Simmonds, " A " ,,
,, Cary, " B " ,,
,, Mason, " B " ,,
,, Fielding, " C " ,,
,, Fleetwood, " C " ,,

Five wounded :

Lieut. W. Goodinge, " B " Company.
,, W. S. Stranack, " B " ,,
2nd Lieut. J. S. Hunter, " A " ,,
,, C. V. Davis, " B " ,,
,, F. G. Garside, " C " ,,

Five missing :
    Capt. R. W. Cunningham, " A " Company.
    ,,   H. E. L. Cox,   " C "   ,,
    ,,   R. Houghton,   " B "   ,,
    2nd Lieut. W. A. Meeking,   " B "   ,,
    ,,   R. Bennett,   " C "   ,,

Early intimation came to hand that Capts. Cunningham and Houghton and Lieut. Meeking had succumbed to their wounds ; also that Lieut. Bennett was wounded and in the hands of the enemy. Hope was entertained for a long time that Capt. Cox might be alive, but eventually it was officially announced that his death must be assumed to have occurred on the day of the battle. He was known to have been wounded, but nothing further has transpired concerning his end. The last message received from him was handed in at 12.20 and ran : " To O.C., Q.V.R. Reached third line German trenches. Cannot get in touch with Rangers. Q.W.R. still in third line German trench with us. Boches still very active. Barrage would help beyond third line. Bombs required urgent. Leys Cox." Known throughout the battalion as " The Bantam," Capt. Harold E. Leys Cox was most popular with all ranks and the men of his company were devoted to him. He was educated at St. George's School, Windsor Castle, and was presented with the Diamond Jubilee medal in 1897. Later he went to St. Paul's School. He joined the Q.V.R. in 1909 as 2nd Lieutenant, and got his Captaincy in August, 1914. His elder brother, Major R. H. Woodruff Cox, O.B.E., T.D., served with the Q.V.R. throughout the earlier part of the war. Their father, Mr. E. W. Cox of Ealing and Old Cavendish Street, was an old St. George's (6th Middlesex) Rifle Volunteer.

Capt. Philip Squarey Houghton was the only son of Mr. and Mrs. Philip A. Houghton, of Aldeburgh, Suffolk. He was born in 1895, educated at Brunswick, Haywards Heath, Charterhouse and University College, Oxford. He was gazetted in September, 1914, and went to the front in November of that year. He was promoted Lieutenant in July and Captain in May, 1916.

2nd Lieut. Francis Willoughby Fielding, known to everyone as " Jack," was the second son of Mrs. Harry Fielding of

Stoneleigh, Thame, Oxon. He was twenty-three years of age and was a member of the Victoria Rifles' Masonic Lodge, No. 822, in which he was initiated in January, 1916. He had gone to France in 1914 as a despatch rider with the Oxfordshire Hussars (Yeomanry), of which he was a member in pre-war days.

2nd Lieut. Cyril Percy Fleetwood was formerly Scoutmaster of the 57th North London Troop of Boy Scouts. He had only returned to the front a few days after being on leave. When war broke out he joined the Anti-Aircraft Corps, but after being with them for some time he considered he was not doing sufficient for his country and enrolled in the Inns of Court O.T.C., with which he trained for three months before obtaining his commission. He was a keen sportsman and a successful swimmer, and he took a great interest in the welfare and training of young lads. He was born and lived at Highgate and was thirty-three years of age.

Lieut. E. Aidan Lane, one of two soldier sons of the late Mr. Bernard Lane, for many years solo tenor and deputy conductor of the choir of the Church of the Sacred Heart, Edgehill, was educated at Wimbledon College, and when the war commenced joined the 1st Grenadier Guards as a private, but was soon given a commission in the Q.V.R. He had been at the front about fifteen months and was invalided home in July, 1915, through a shrapnel wound in his thigh. He was married and left a widow and a young child. He had just completed his thirtieth year.

The " Battle of the Somme " lasted for months, but for some weeks the poor shattered remnant of the Q.V.R. saw no more fighting. A few days after they were withdrawn and were stationed at St. Amand, the Army Corps Commander paid a visit and addressed the men. He said he could find no words to express his opinion of the splendid way they had fought, but the great accumulation of German forces on their particular front, an accumulation of nearly 100 German batteries and a reserve of Prussian Guards, had made their task a desperate one. They had seized all the points designated as their objectives and their achievements would stand out and compare favourably with any fighting in history, and had been " the foundation of the success further south and of the triumphant battle the sound of which was then dinning in their ears."

As a fitting conclusion to our account of "this desperate task" let us quote the graphic words of another eye-witness of it, Mr. Beach Thomas, the celebrated correspondent of the *Daily Mail*:

"*Our attack at Gommecourt, the northern end of the long-fronted battle, was as heroic as anything in the war. I know the trenches there well and happen to have intimate personal acquaintance with some of those engaged. I had played cricket with them, and football. The other day I was up in their trenches, and among other curious experiences put my head over the parapet—for all was dull and quiet—and stared at the silent and thorny German lines. But in spite of appearances the Germans (who held a sharp salient in Gommecourt Wood) were known to be both forewarned and forearmed.*

At 7.30 a.m., and earlier, on July 1st, their guns—closely concentrated and of full calibre—set up a triple barrage (fire curtain). Through all these three barrages of intense fire our men marched quite steadily, as if nothing was in the way, as if they were under review. At every step men fell ; and our trenches here are very far apart from the German. The gap was still wide, though a little while before the fighting we had built a completely new trench nearer the enemy in the course of a single night. When these steady, steadfast soldiers, true to the death, paraded in more than decimated numbers through and across the third barrage, the enemy—in their turn heroic—left their trenches, erected machine-guns on the parapets, and the two parties fought one another in the open.

I have not the hardihood to write more. Heroism could no further go. Our men died ; and in dying held in front of them enough German guns to have altered the fate of our principal and our most successful advance in the south.

THEY DIED DEFEATED, BUT WON AS GREAT A VICTORY IN SPIRIT AND IN FACT AS ENGLISH HISTORY OR ANY HISTORY WILL EVER CHRONICLE."

The character of these operations is thus described by Major C. H. Dudley Ward, D.S.O., M.C., in his history of "The 56th Division": "There is no doubt that the main object of the attack had been fulfilled. Unpleasant as it may seem, the rôle of the 56th Division was to induce the enemy to shoot at them with as many guns as could be gathered together and also to prevent him from moving troops."

One of those who were taken prisoners on that memorable day in a letter to his people says :

July 30th, 1916.

"Sunday, and we have just had our dinner, or so called. Am still in bed and getting on well—only flesh wounds, but you know what I am, things never will heal up quickly on me—all in my legs too and such lovely weather too !

Now to come to the food question. Whilst we are in hospital we manage just to exist, that's all. Outside fellows have to live solely on parcels sent from England. Do send some milk.

My back is so horribly sore with being on it so long, but hope to be about soon. Do you think you could write Headquarters and tell them I have not any clothes, and you might inquire if they send out any food to prisoners of war.

I do hope I am not worrying you telling you all my troubles, but everyone is writing home in the same strain. And I tell you it is really necessary. If I could manage I would, as you know, but we've had no solid food for a month—every meal is a stew made of barley, macaroni or potatoes and greens. Meat once or twice a week, a very small piece, and the old coffee and black bread of which I am just going to eat some now, two o'clock."

All that was left of the battalion spent the night in the trenches they had started from on that fateful morn, and on the afternoon of July 2nd was relieved by the 2nd London Regiment (Fusiliers). A halt was made at Bayencourt for the night, and at 3 p.m. on the following day, after an hour's march, St. Amand was reached once more. On the way the battalion passed General Hull, the Divisional Commander, who said to Col. Dickins, "Well done, Q.V.R.; you have done wonders." Again on the 4th, he visited and inspected the men and once more highly complimented all ranks on their splendid behaviour.

The work of building up the battalion was at once begun.

No time was lost in waiting for drafts from either of the Q.V.R. battalions in England, but men on the spot were posted to it. For the first time the Q.V.R. had to welcome men who were not of their own regiment. On July 4th two drafts of 80 men each arrived from the 7th and 8th Middlesex ; on the 12th, 82 men joined from the 20th Londons, and on the 16th,

6 men from the 1st London Regt.				
15	,,	3rd	,,	,,
8	,,	4th	,,	,,
189	,,	8th	,,	,,
10	,,	10th	,,	,,
24	,,	14th	,,	,,

Disappointment was mutual for the new arrivals had anticipated joining their first line battalions, while the Q.V.R. had been expecting a draft of their own men. The contingents from the 1st, 3rd, 4th, 10th and 14th, only stayed with the Q.V.R. until July 26th, when they were transferred to their own units. The men from the Middlesex Regiments had been looking forward to joining their first line battalion in the 167th Brigade. However, they soon turned into fine Riflemen and with their hard training gained in Egypt proved most valuable soldiers. During the process of making up, Col. Dickins in conversation with the Divisional Commander once facetiously claimed that he was commanding 17 regiments.

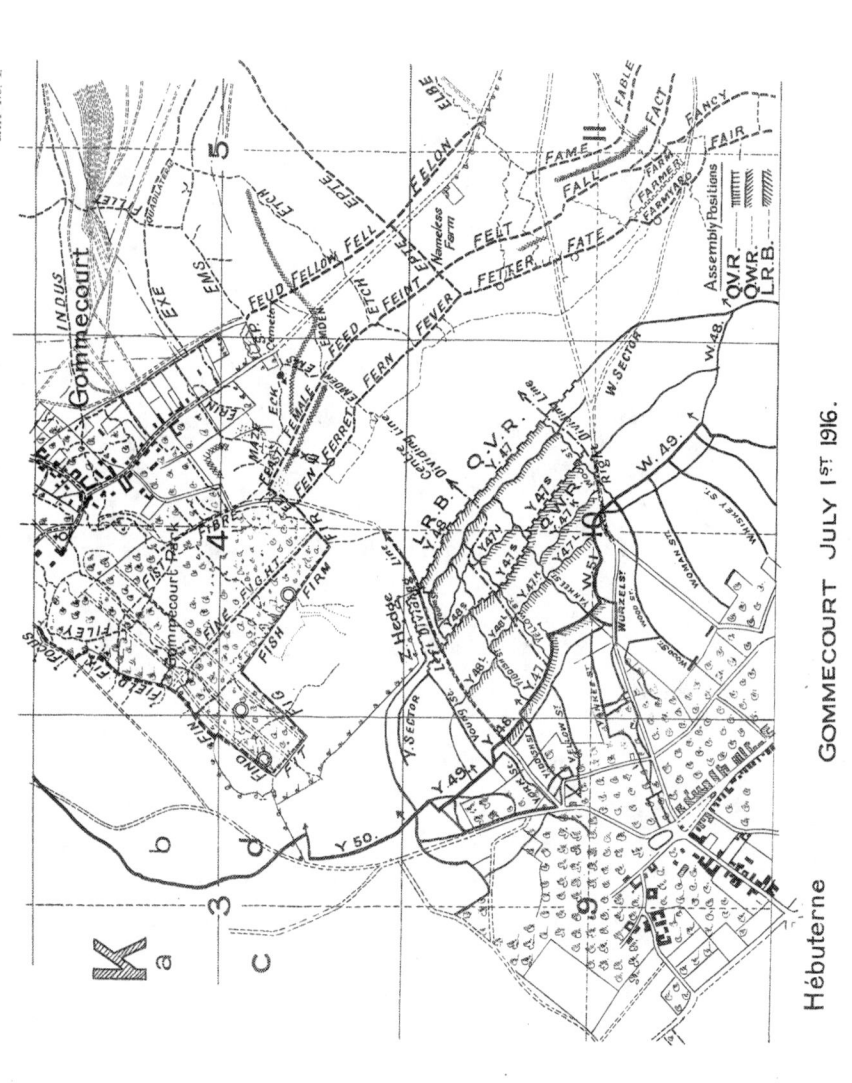

CHAPTER XXI

THE BATTLES OF THE SOMME—LEUZE WOOD

DURING July, the battalion was mostly employed in trenches and reserve dug-outs in the neighbourhood of St. Amand, Fonquevillers, Hannescamp and Bienvillers. While at the latter place on the 20th, a working party doing R.E. fatigues, digging and clearing communication trenches, was heavily shelled, losing 5 killed and 11 wounded; a similar accident occurred the next morning, the casualties on this occasion amounting to 4 killed and 1 wounded. Bienvillers seems to have been rather an unhealthy place, for on the 24th one man was killed and 4 wounded; on the 25th, 4 killed and 8 wounded, and on the 26th, 1 wounded.

Regarding the shelling on July 21st, Capt. Lindsey-Renton says: "Just before 8 a.m. I had got out of bed and was putting on my slippers when I heard a noise and went to the front door to listen. Suddenly there was a tremendous 'swish' in the air and a flight of shells came and burst all over the village. I at once ran to a narrow trench behind H.Q., provided for the purpose, and waited for the shelling to finish. A large number of shells came over and caused several casualties in the battalion. Col. Dickins jumped out of bed, but could not find his boots, so had to go in his stockinged feet into the cellar of the house, and on his arrival there found his batman, who had also taken refuge there, with the Colonel's boots in his hands. Capt. Andrews and Capt. Clarke, the M.O., were caught while in their baths and had to stay and take their chance. Later on we were going round the village seeing what damage had been done, etc., when, at 10 o'clock, another barrage came down. The only place of safety I could think of was the trench behind Battalion H.Q.

I therefore ran as hard as I could down the road and jus
before I got to H.Q. nearly ran into Col. Dickins, who wa
doing likewise, and together we dashed into our little trench
I remember noticing that the Colonel had still got his pipe i
his mouth. That afternoon I had to walk over to Fonque
villers and walked into a nice steady bombardment of tha
village. Three times in one day was too much of a goo
thing."

August was passed in similar circumstances on the sam
training grounds. One grateful rifleman records that o
August 2nd " C " Company officers bought 55 bottles of re
wine for their men. On the 4th the battalion was inspecte
by Brig.-Gen. E. S. Coke, C.M.G., Commanding 169th Infantr
Brigade, who presented Divisional Cards to seven men fo
meritorious service on July 1st. On the 6th, Capt. R. fF
Davies (an N.R.A. Gold Medalist), an old and well-know
member of the regiment, came out from England and joine
up at St. Amand. On the 7th two men were wounded whil
in the trenches at Fonquevillers, which had been taken ove
that morning from the Q.W.R. ; another man was wounde
just a week later. On the 18th the battalion was relieved b
the Staffordshire Regiment, and marched at 7 p.m. by half
companies to St. Amand, and thence by companies to Gau
diempre, and thence as a battalion to Beaudricourt, whicl
was reached at 1.30 a.m. At the end of three days spen
in company training another move was made to Viller
l'Hôpital, and a third on August 23rd to Argenvillers, wher
a comprehensive training for companies and all details wa
carried out, including battalion attack practice and experi
mental attacks with tanks. In the evenings some interestin
lectures on "The Spirit of the Bayonet" were given b
Major Ronnie Campbell. On others the divisional ban
played on the village green, when the Brigadier would si
with the troops and listen to the music. Also the famou
" Bow Bells " Concert troop gave nightly entertainments
Everyone turned out to watch the practice of the tank attack
H.R.H. the Prince of Wales was there laughing and chattin
with the troops. " As a spectacular affair " wrote Capt
Nichols, who had succeeded Capt. Andrews as regimenta
Adjutant on September 3rd, " it was a disappointment.

On that date the Q.V.R.'s left Argenvillers at 5.55 a.m., marched to St. Requier, where they entrained with the rest of the 169th Brigade for Corbie.

"As the train neared Corbie," says Capt. J. Nichols, "the long, almost continual roll of gunfire became audible. We were getting nearer, nearer to the next big gamble of Life. We got into the billets about 2 p.m. Corbie was very crowded; wounded British soldiers and German prisoners kept on arriving all day. In the evening some of the men bathed in the ponds. Capt. Eccles even took some of his company bathing before breakfast on September 4th. About 1 p.m. on that afternoon an urgent operation order arrived, ordering the 169th Brigade to move and saying the head of the column would pass the starting point about a mile along the Corbie-Bray road at 2 p.m. The troops hurriedly put their lunch in their pockets and fell in. Up the dusty hill marched the brigade, past the brickworks, midst lines of scowling Prussian prisoners breaking stones; no time to think or worry; ' on, on, little Cockneys. Nous les aurons.' Through Morlancourt, where the Brigade of Guards were at rest, along the rough tracks and newly made roads, toiled the long column of the 169th Infantry Brigade. Lewis Gun hand carts, stuck deep in the mud, were surrounded by little knots of swearing men. ' Our Lewis Guns have all fallen out, Sir,' reported the Adjutant to the Colonel, who merely nodded and smiled, observing, ' Drop a man at each cross-road to guide them. They will soon catch us up.' At seven the Happy Valley (near Bray) was reached. It was a very wet night and there were not nearly enough tents to go round, and so throughout the night sodden little groups of Q.V.R.'s and Q.W.R.'s sat huddled together and sang ' The long Trail,' wondering, perhaps, when their turn would come to pass along it into the Great Beyond, where former friends gazed down ' still believing the God who gave the cannon gave the Cross.' More tents arrived on September 5th, and the men were also able to sit out in the sun and get dry. The Q.V.R. remained in camp all day, ready to move at a moment's notice. But no order arrived and the troops lay down to sleep, thankful for another night's rest. The late night communiqué announced the capture of an important position known as the ' Bois de Leuze.' On the morning of the 6th the air was full of rumours, but there being nothing definite, a game of Rugby was arranged for the afternoon. However, at three o'clock orders were received for the battalion and transport to move at once to Billon Farm, just south of the Albert–Peronne road. By six the whole of of the 169th Brigade were massed round Bronfay and Billon Farms. No information was available as to whether a further move was intended or not. At eight a further order was received for the move to be continued, the Q.V.R. to take over a system known as Casement Trenches, astride the Maricourt–Longueval road, about half a mile south of Bernafay Wood. This move was completed with difficulty as the night was dark and the traffic and gun-fire very considerable. There was little protection from either rain or shell-fire in the trenches, but the German artillery mainly concerned itself with the forward areas. The transport moved back to the Happy Valley. These trenches were 4000 yards from the front line, which ran : Delville Wood–Leuze Wood—west of Combles.

The morning of September 7th was quiet for the Q.V.R., but the Q.W.R., immediately south of Bernafay Wood, were heavily shelled and suffered a number of casualties. At 1 p.m., Lieut.-Col. V. W. F. Dickins, D.S.O., V.D., and the Adjutant, Capt. J. Nichols, were summoned to Brigade H.Q. in the Valley of Death (between Trones Wood and Faviere Wood). Lieut.-Col. R. R. Husey, M.C., commanding the L.R.B., Col. R. Shoolbred, C.M.G., Queen's Westminsters, and Lieut.-Col. J. Attenborough, C.M.G., 2nd London Regiment, also attended the conference. Orders were given for the Q.V.R. to relieve the London Scottish in Leuze Wood that night, and for all C.O.'s to reconnoitre the vicinity of Leuze Wood from the O.P. on Hardecourt Ridge. Brig.-Gen. E. S. D. E. Coke, C.M.G., warned all C.O.'s that the 169th Infantry Brigade would attack from Leuze Wood at an early date, probably on September 9th. Observation from Hardecourt O.P. revealed an intense bombardment of the line going on between Falfemont Farm and Leuze Wood."

"After the conference of C.O.'s," observes Col. Dickins, "the Adjutant and I accompanied the Brigadier to the O.P. on Hardecourt Ridge, where he pointed out in the distance the approximate lines of trenches that should be occupied by the Q.V.R. when they relieved the London Scottish, also suggesting that the Battalion H.Q. should be established at Wedge Wood Farm or in the immediate vicinity."

"Returning to Capt. Nichols' narrative we are told: "At 8 p.m. the Q.V.R. moved off from Casement Trenches to the Valley of Death, where they were met by guides from the London Scottish. While drawing tools at the rendezvous the Germans started shelling with 8-inch, a direct hit being scored on an artillery limber, while several shells fell close to the Q.V.R. Shortly after nine the last company was clear of the Valley of Death.

"The companies were commanded as follows :—

"A" Company . . Capt. G. Woods
"B" Company . . Capt. J. D. Eccles
"C" Company . . Capt. E. D. Symes
"D" Company . . Capt. R. fF. Davies.

"The relief was carried out with the greatest difficulty. The Germans continuously shelled the greater part of the ground between Hardecourt and the front line. The route for the relieving troops was: Hardecourt–Angle Wood—thence north up the re-entrant to Wedge Wood–Leuze Wood. The men were heavily laden and the guides had only traversed the ground once before. Trenches had been obliterated, villages pounded to dust, a few stark, broken trees were all that remained of the luxuriant woods. The ground was pitted with shell-holes, from the depths of which gazed fearsome black faces with shining white teeth, whose swollen bodies had long ceased to struggle. Groups of German machine-gunners caught in the last act of fighting their guns were lying near the blown-in mine shafts; stiff and cold against the parapet lay the bomber, the stick grenade still grasped tightly in his hand. Through scenes such as these the struggling columns followed the figures in the grey kilts."

Col. Dickins taking up the running here explains: "About 11.30 p.m. the Battalion H.Q. after a very difficult journey in the dark over the heavily shelled area arrived in the neighbourhood of Wedge Wood Farm, or where it was supposed to be. After walking about in the dark for a considerable time, with many enemy shells flying overhead which did not particularly add to the pleasantness of the situation, no trace whatever could be found of the farm or of its buildings. At this time I lighted upon two R.E. officers and asked them if they could point out to me the whereabouts of Wedge Wood Farm as I had to form our H.Q. there. They replied that we were standing in the very middle of the ground where Wedge Wood Farm once stood, but that it had been utterly razed to the ground by the intense bombardment, and not a vestige of any farm or building remained. So this spot had to be abandoned as a 'suitable place' for H.Q., and eventually they were established in shell-holes in the low ground south-west of Leuze Wood. A most uncomfortable night was spent in a partly made trench dug out in the chalk. We had no head cover and a drizzling rain during the night made it very unpleasant.

"We were about half-way between Falfemont Farm and Wedge Wood," continues Capt. Nichols. "There was no cover from fire or weather or even view, and the use of torches for leading purposes soon drew machine-gun and rifle fire from the direction of Guillemont. In these circumstances it was not until 4.30 a.m. that 'relief complete' was finally reported. German artillery was intermittently active throughout the night on Leuze Wood and drove a company of 5th Cheshire Pioneers, who were working on a communication trench, to the south-west corner of the Wood. The morning of September 8th was fairly quiet. Shortly after 1 p.m. an operation order for the attacks to be resumed by the 169th Brigade was received. At the same time the enemy appeared to have spotted the Q.V.R. Battalion H.Q., which was henceforth systematically shelled.

"Zero hour for the assault was fixed at 4.45 p.m. on September 9th. The Q.V.R. objective was a trench running through Bouleaux Wood, 300 yards east of Leuze Wood, and the southwest corner of Bouleaux Wood. The L.R.B. to co-operate with the Q.V.R. on the right and the 167th Infantry Brigade on the left. A conference was held in a partially completed mineshaft, which Lieut.-Col. Husey (L.R.B.) also attended. The accuracy of the German artillery considerably hampered the progress of the conference. The D.A.D.M.S. of the 56th Division had his leg blown off by an 8-inch howitzer about

4 p.m. After much deliberation plans for the attack were made. As a result of the constant moving for the last forty-eight hours all ranks of the Q.V.R. were by this time suffering from fatigue. There had been no time for washing or shaving, little opportunity for eating, no hot food and no sleep. Confronted by these adverse circumstances the task of arranging for an attack was extremely difficult. However, the assault was to be carried out by 'A' and 'D' Companies in front with 'B' in support and 'C' in reserve. Under the cover of a creeping barrage the attack was to be pushed through to the final objective in Bouleaux Wood by 'A' and 'D' Companies without any halt except to kill those who remained in the way and showed fight.

"Throughout the night of the 8th/9th September, Lieut.-Col. Dickins, Major Lindsey-Renton and Capt. Nichols continued to work out the many details for the assault. On several occasions sleep gained a momentary victory, the tired eyes closed and the head sank forward on the breast. Regardless of the arduous duties of the morrow, of the incessant shelling going on outside the trench, sleep again and again attempted to stop the working of the weary brain. But there is no time for sleep. There is yet work to be done, and after that the attack. In the trenches the men sprawled in every imaginable attitude of sheer exhaustion. Relieved sentries lay on their backs with arms outstretched, or face downwards, their heads pressed hard against the white chalk. By four o'clock the written orders were completed and the weary H.Q. sank down on the steps of the shaft for a short half hour's sleep. About 5 a.m. Battalion H.Q. was moved forward to the western point of Leuze Wood, where a joint H.Q. was established with Capt. Eccles, who commanded the support company of the Q.V.R., the Regimental Aid Post being close at hand alongside some German concrete shelters. From 6 till 11 German 'whizz-bangs' were very active in the vicinity of Battalion H.Q. and the Regimental Aid Post. The vicious hiss of an arriving shell was constantly followed by the shriek of agony from some poor fellow sent suddenly to his doom. At eight a final conference was held with the four company commanders. Everyone looked tired from want of sleep."

It may be as well here to give a short description of what

was then so graphically termed " Lousy Wood." About 900 yards in length from north to south and 500 yards in width the wood stood on the summit of the spur commanding practically the whole of the ground from Hardecourt to Guillemont " Tall trees, broken and splintered," says Capt. Nichols " lay scattered in the undergrowth ; a few concrete emplacements lined the western side ; vast shell-holes, reeking of ' H.E.'—and worse things—and here and there limp, shapeless forms covered with blue-bottles and flies, pinned beneath the trees. Throughout the morning the British heavy artillery continuously dropped short on ' A ' and ' D ' Companies of the Q.V.R. 2nd Lieut. R. B. Scott was killed and 2nd Lieut W. F. Ogilvie blinded by our own shells and many Other Ranks killed or wounded. The intensity of the German artillery rendered useless all telephonic means of communication, and it was impossible to warn the gunners of their range. Two forward gunner officers were lying dead outside Battalion H.Q. ' C ' Company under Capt. Symes provided large carrying parties for ammunition and rations throughout the morning and did excellent work. The journeys to the dumps were as far back as Hardecourt, under continual shell-fire and over the roughest ground. Comparative quiet reigned till about 4 p.m. when the Germans put down an intense concentrated fire on the south-west corner of the wood amongst the asembling troops. This was no affair of whizz-bangs, but of 5·9's and 8-inch shells. Despite the shelling the company commanders managed to get their men in their battle position when the British barrage came down at 4.45 p.m.

" The dispositions of the 169th Infantry Brigade at that time were as follows : The Q.V.R. and the L.R.B. were in assembly positions in Leuze Wood and south of it. ; 2nd London Regiment in support at Falfemont Farm and the Falfemont Farm Line. The Q.W.R. were in reserve in some trenches immediately east of the Valley of Death ; Brigade H.Q. in the valley. Following the creeping barrage the Q.V.R. companies, tired of waiting, assaulted with an irresistible fury. The Germans, caught at their tea, rushed to their guns and offered the usual stubborn resistance. At the same time the Germans put down a barrage on the south-west edge of Leuze Wood and the Falfemont Farm Line. Capts. G. Wood and R. fF. Davies, gallantly leading the attacking companies, were killed in the first few minutes, and Capt. J. D. Eccles of ' B ' Company fell mortally wounded shortly afterwards.

"Back in the small shelter at Battalion H.Q. Col. Dickins sat waiting for news, heavy shells bursting all around, some just over and some short, while the Regimental Aid Post was one huge cloud of smoke and bursting shell. Wounded men, with dirty, sweating faces, their garments drenched with blood, sat round the smiling young doctor, ducking their heads as some pretty hot shot passed. The M.O. in shirt sleeves with an old tin hat on the back of his curly head, calmly passed from case to case, hardly appearing to notice the terrific explosions which from time to time snatched one of the casualties from any help that he could give. About five o'clock, Capt. Symes, who had moved up behind "B" Company, reported that the objective had been gained, and a little later a message was received from Sergt. W. Brawn that the final objective had been captured and was being consolidated. The message added that the casualties had been very heavy and that there were no officers left with the two attacking companies. Capt. Symes was therefore directed to go forward and reorganise the situation. It was confirmed that very few, if any, officers were left. Lieut. N. Y. Sim of ' B ' Company had been killed while lying down and using his body as a parapet for a Lewis Gun. Lieuts. A. A. Taylor and D. Rollitt had both been wounded. No information was forthcoming of the progress of the L.R.B. on the right. About 150 German prisoners were sent down to 169th Infantry Brigade H.Q. at Hardecourt. At 6.30 p.m. Sergt. Brawn came back to Battalion H.Q. and asked for more officers, and at the same time wounded men coming back brought news that the Germans were counter-attacking on the right, but these reports were not confirmed by Capt. Symes, who reported that the situation was well in hand. About seven o'clock, however, he sent word that the Germans were moving round on the right. At the same time their artillery barrage increased to a very heavy rate of fire, and although no signs of their presence could be detected, it was obvious that the right of the position was unprotected owing to the small progress made by the L.R.B. Presently reports came in that the Germans were surrounding the Wood and a

S.O.S. pigeon message was sent to 169th Infantry Brigade asking for immediate reinforcements. A runner was also sent to Lieut.-Col. Attenborough, commanding 2nd Londons at Falfemont Farm, asking for two companies. The request was immediately complied with and the two companies were placed in position along the south-eastern edge of Leuze Wood to connect up with the L.R.B. Further reports from Capt. Symes proved reassuring, and with the arrival of the remainder of the 2nd London Regiment any successful attack by the Germans appeared improbable. The German artillery fire continued with unabated fury, and at 11 p.m., amidst a deluge of heavy shells, the whole battalion of the Q.W.R. entered the south-west corner of Leuze Wood, taking up a position along its edge. Lieut.-Col. Shoolbred, in command, established his H.Q. at the western corner of the wood with the Q.V.R. H.Q.

"Throughout the night of September 9th/10th the Q.V.R. continued to dig themselves in and consolidate their newly gained position which was first named Victoria Trench, but afterwards renamed by the Division Bully Trench. Shortly after dawn on the 10th the Q.W.R. tried to push forward on the right so as to conform with the Q.V.R. This attempt, however, did not succeed owing to the accurate German machine-gun fire and the activities of their rifle grenadiers. About 1 p.m. the Q.W.R. again attacked, but were once more driven back with heavy losses. By this time the casualties of the Q.V.R. were very numerous and Capt. Basil Clarke, their M.O., had not a moment's rest. Throughout the afternoon of September 9th and the long night which followed he had been continuously exposed to the incessant fire of the German artillery, attending the wounded for thirty hours on end. He was afterwards awarded the M.C. for his good work.

"The remainder of the afternoon of September 10th was quiet except for intermittent shelling. About 5 a.m. a warning order was received from H.Q. that the Brigade would be relieved that night by the 13th Infantry Brigade, 5th Division. Major Lindsey-Renton thereupon proceeded to Brigade H.Q. to make the necessary arrangements as to guides, etc. But as luck would have it, from 6 to 8 p.m. the Germans renewed their bombardment of the whole wood. Every man was tired out and there had been but little to eat or drink for the whole three days. The shelling continued with undiminished vigour, and the S.O.S. was sent up from the Q.V.R. Visual Station at the western edge of the wood. The place resounded with the crash of the Hun salvos and the fumes from their shells became intense. Towards nine o'clock the fire slackened off a bit and a couple of hours later the 1st R.W. Kents arrived under the command of Lieut.-Col. Buchanan Dunlop, D.S.O. By one o'clock the last company of the Q.V.R. was on its way to the Citadel, west of Fricourt, for a rest. Thanks to the magnificent work of Capt. Clarke all the wounded were cleared at the same time. The two days' operations had cost the battalion 350 of all ranks. By 5 a.m. what was left of it were sound asleep in their tents in the Citadel."

Capt. Robert fFinden Davies, who fell on September 9th, was the elder son of Mr. F. Herbert Davies, of 46 Hamilton Terrace, N.W., and was born on 10th December, 1876. He was educated at Marlborough, where he was Captain of the School Cadet Corps. Soon after leaving school he joined the Victoria and St. George's R.V.C. and became one of their most noted shots. He was four times in the final for the King's Prize at Bisley, and won it in 1906 with a record score of 324 out of a possible 355. He transferred to the Territorial Force Reserve in 1908, but maintained a strong interest in shooting, being Honorary Secretary of the North London Rifle Club. He served in South Africa with the Victoria Rifles Service Company of the K.R.R.C. and was awarded the Queen's medal with three clasps. On the outbreak of war he immediately rejoined the Q.V.R. and, as before mentioned, he only joined the 1st Battalion in France on August 6th. He was an honorary captain in the regular army. He was Master of the Victoria Rifles Masonic Lodge, No. 822, in 1910–1911.

Capt. John Dennison Eccles, M.C., was the eldest son of Major McAdam Eccles, R.A.M.C., and Mrs. Eccles, of 124 Harley Street, W., and had not entered on his twenty-first year. He was educated at Fretherne House and Winchester College, where he was President of the Boat Club in 1913–1914. On the outbreak of war he obtained a commission in the Q.V.R. and went to France in 1915. As already chronicled, he was wounded in December of that year. For conspicuous bravery and bringing in a wounded man on that occasion he was awarded the Military Cross. He rejoined the regiment in April, 1916, and was wounded on September 9th, succumbing to his injuries on September 27th.

Capt. George Woods was in command of " A " Company and was only twenty-two years of age.

Another very gallant young officer who fell in this action was 2nd Lieut. Norman Young Sim. An account of his heroic end has been preserved :

"For outstanding bravery and devotion to duty," writes Rfn. Surtees, " I think the following incident should be featured in any records of the Q.V.R. The regiment were attacking in Leuze Wood on September 9th and were ordered to advance through the wood. They were successful in gaining and holding their objective, but while consolidating it, came under very heavy shell-fire. Lce.-Cpl. Boismaison was in charge of a Lewis Gun and occupied a smashed-up trench which offered but little cover and small hope of a good gun position. In the same portion of the trench system was a young officer, 2nd Lieut. Sim, who had only joined us a few days previous to ' going up.' After the position had been carried we were facing a slight crest and to reach us the enemy had to come into full view, thus affording an excellent target. Seeing no chance of securing a good position for the gun this young officer stood with it on his shoulder whilst Lce.-Cpl. Boismaison brought it into action with good results, but it was not long before this gallant officer was shot. Nothing daunted and aware of his danger young Boismaison immediately placed the gun over his own shoulder and called upon No. 2 to ' carry on.' He obeyed and continued until the cylinder was pierced by a stray piece of shrapnel and the gun rendered useless. Seeing that he could be of no further use as a gunner Boismaison attached himself to H.Q. bombers, who were on the left, and remained with them until killed."

Sergt. W. Brawn was afterwards awarded the D.C.M. for his gallant conduct in keeping his company together, organising and consolidating the objective gained after his company officers had become casualties ; also for sending in the most valuable information regarding the general situation. During

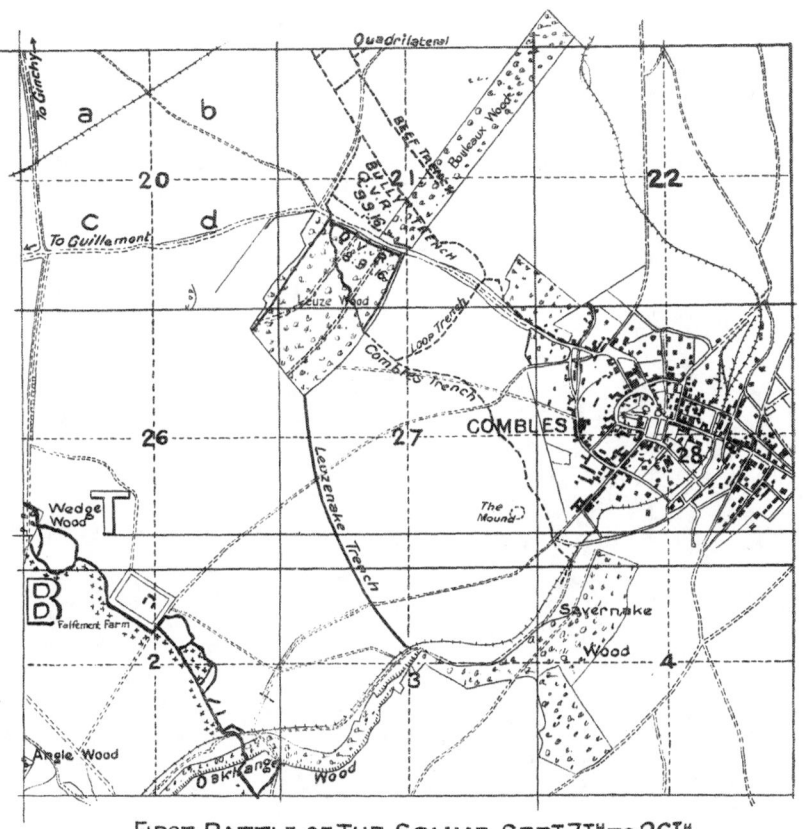

MAP No. 5.

FIRST BATTLE OF THE SOMME. SEPT 7TH TO 26TH 1916.

the whole time he was exposed to the most terrific shell and machine-gun fire.

Capt. J. C. Andrews, who had been acting as Adjutant of the battalion from shortly after the Hill 60 affair, and was ordered to join Divisional H.Q. on September 6th, having previously handed over the duties to Capt. Nichols says : " The battle went on unceasingly, brigades being withdrawn for a few days to the uncomfortable camp around the Citadel and then sent back to the fighting line with depleted ranks hardly filled with inexperienced officers and men. The 56th Division was kept at it for six weeks, a very much longer period than other Divisions, with a consequent loss of efficiency. In many instances drafts, after one night at the transport lines were sent up into the line, assaulted the following morning, and became casualties before their names were known to the C.O. and their company commanders. I cannot recall the casualties of the Division in this phase of the Somme battle, but they were very heavy and it was a long time before recovery took place."

CHAPTER XXII

A Tale of the Tanks

AFTER a welcome two days' rest the Q.V.R. left Citadel Camp and marched to Billon Wood, where they bivouacked for the night of September 12th. The next day they relieved the 13th Composite Brigade and took over Leuzenake Trenches, south of Leuze Wood. On the 15th the offensive was resumed, a general attack being made all along the line at 6.30 a.m. The Q.V.R. were on the extreme right of the British line and formed the pivot and defensive flank for the XIVth Corps operations. In this action " tanks " were used for the first time. Rfn. W. J. Gray supplies the following account of their being led into position : " On September 14th, 1916, an officer in charge of four tanks reported at Brigade H.Q., and after a consultation with the Brigadier left at eight o'clock with the tanks to take up his position a few yards behind the front line before going over the top the following day. I was a runner on brigade at the time and it was my turn for duty and it fell to me to act as guide to them. The run between Brigade H.Q. and Battalion H.Q. would usually take something like twenty minutes, but owing to unsuitable ground a longer route had to be taken which should have been covered in about thirty minutes, but the tanks' capabilities in those days were not so good as they subsequently became, and after a struggle of three hours and twenty minutes the first tank got into position a few yards behind our section of the line and was shortly followed by the others. Leaving Brigade H.Q. at eight o'clock we followed a track marked with tape for some little distance, the tanks following one behind the other. The ground over which they had to go was very soft and nothing but a mass of shell-holes, some of them very large indeed, and as it was dark the drivers could not see where they were going. Before long they were in difficulties, as one caterpillar might go well down in a shell-hole and the other remain on the level, but owing to its capabilities it would not capsize although it required extra power to get it into position, when after a struggle it would be ready to move off again. There being but one guide, if one tank got into difficulties the remainder had to wait until it was able to move on again. This sort of thing kept on occurring till at last the officer in charge, who was in the leading tank, got out and said : ' I think we should get on much better if you had my torch and walked 5 or 6 yards in front of the leading tank, picking out the most suitable ground for the tanks to take, throwing the light on the track so that the driver may follow.' One of the four tanks had broken down and had to be left behind on account of one of its caterpillars having gone wrong. With the aid of the torch we were able to get along much better though the pace was still very slow. At this time our battalion was on the right of the British line and linked up with the French, and the ground we were going over was where the French supports were. The track was still bad and the tanks were spitting fire, making no end of a row with their engines, which attracted the Poilus' attention. They poured out of their dug-outs to see what was going on, and soon there was quite a large number gazing in amazement at the new instrument of war, the like of which they had never seen. One of the tanks here got into difficulties and gave the Poilus a good chance of examining it, but as it had only two small holes for the driver to peer through little or nothing could be seen of the inside or the occupants. Being anxious to get a glimpse of the interior they clambered all over the tank but could see nothing beyond the muzzles of the machine-guns and 2-pounders. As I, of course, was flashing the torch about quite a crowd collected round me to get a good view of them, and from what little French I knew they seemed to think that ' les diables,' as they called them, would drive Jerry miles back the following day. I am afraid they did not realise all that was expected of them, but I guess the Poilus followed them as they went over the top with the greatest attention. The tank having got over its difficulty we continued our journey, the Poilus following for some little distance. We were now not far from Battalion H.Q. and naturally I did not like the idea of continuously showing a light to guide the tanks, so only gave a flash now and again, whereupon the officer alighted and wanted to know what was the matter. I explained that we were getting close to the line and the light would no doubt attract attention and bring over some whizz bangs, which were pretty common in this part of the world but he replied that we were very late and as they must get the tanks up at any cost they must take the risk. Shortly after we arrived at Battalion H.Q., and considering all things and especially the flashings of the torch I think we were lucky to have done so without mishap. I reported at H.Q. and was told the exact position to lead the first tank on, the remaining two having to go a little further. I left H.Q. with plenty of wind up as the tank I had now to lead had to be taken practically up to the front line with myself leading and flashing the light which I was anxious to get rid of, you bet ! The tank once more got into difficulties half-way to its position, and the torch had to be brought into use more than ever. A strafe took place while we were trying to get a move on. It may have been only the usual strafe or it may have been brought about by the use of the torch, but whatever was the cause it was none too healthy and I didn't enjoy it a bit. After a kick and a splutter Tank was ready to move and we were off again. The ground was still very bad and sloshy and Tank pursued its noisy way. The strafe was over and things were now pretty quiet for that part of the line, but Jerry may possibly have heard the noise of the engine, which would travel far. Anyhow, he showed all sorts of lights, and a searchlight was also put up seeking for aeroplanes, though none were up. Shortly after the tank found its position and my job was over for which I was profoundly thankful. The time was now 11.19 and I alleyed back as quick as I could to report all correct. The following day the tanks went over, but of their progress I can give no particulars as I remained at Brigade H.Q., which was the best place, I can assure you."

Major Lindsey-Renton, referring to Rfn. Gray's story, says " I am nearly certain, as certain as one can be after an interval of four years, that aeroplanes were used to drown the noise of the tanks taking up position, flying over the Boche line most of the night."

CHAPTER XXIII

LES BŒUFS (TRANSLOY RIDGE) AND NEUVE CHAPELLE

FROM 15th to 18th September the battalion occupied the Loop, Fusilier, Cheshire and Combles trenches. On 19th it was relieved by the 2nd Londons and went back to Falfemont Farm, occupying Falfemont trenches. On 23rd the Q.V.R. relieved the Q.W.R. in Q trenches. From a statement furnished by Col. Dickins it appears that, owing to the many casualties which had occurred in the fighting since the early part of September, the Q.V.R. now found themselves very weak in numbers, the total strength being about 350. On September 22nd the battalion was reinforced by a strong draft of 310 men, but of these some two-thirds were young soldiers sent straight from home without previous war service of any kind. On the night the draft arrived a drizzling rain was falling. The mud in the roads and over the whole Somme area made marching very difficult and tiring for men not accustomed to it, especially when accompanied with shell-fire for the first time. The C.O. inspected the draft as well as could be done in the trenches on its arrival and came to the conclusion that the men did not appear steady enough to be put into the firing line immediately, as the battalion was to resume the offensive in a day or two, so after carefully sifting out about a hundred who were mostly old soldiers and who had been wounded and returned fit, he sent the remainder back to the Transport lines under the charge of the transport officer, rather than run the risk, should the enemy attack unexpectedly, of the new men upsetting the steadiness of those seasoned by experience of fighting. On arrival at the transport lines the new draft were trained for a time under the supervision of Major Lindsey-Renton, who was taking a rest following an attack of " flu."

About this time the French on the right of the Q.V.R. were trying to outflank Combles from one side while the British were engaged in the same operation on the other. The Germans were holding a trench in front of Combles, known as Combles Trench. Rumours and reports were rife that the Germans were evacuating Combles, and on Sunday, September 24th a combined attack was arranged on the trench by the French at one end and the Q.V.R. from the other. There was a bombing block in the trench between the Q.V.R. and the Germans, none of whom could be seen. When, however, a rush was made over the barricade the Germans opened fire from concealed pits some little way behind the trench. Many of the Q.V.R. bombers were hit as they crossed the barricade, among them being 2nd Lieut. D. A. Ord Mackenzie, who led the attack. He was a very promising and conscientious officer and his death was a great loss to the battalion.

2nd Lieut. Arthur Charles Rumsey was wounded in the same attack and died of his wounds while being carried off the field. The son of Mr. Herbert Rumsey, 33 Lebanon Park, Twickenham, he was born in India, in 1888, educated at Hampton Grammar School and, on leaving there joined the staff of the London County and Westminster Bank. His body was taken to the cemetery at the Citadel, near Fricourt, and buried there.

Later on the same day the Q.V.R. were relieved by the L.R.B. and returned to Falfemont Farm trenches, where they went into Brigade Reserve. The XIVth Army Corps resumed the offensive on September 25th. Combles was evacuated by the Germans on 26th and was entered by the 2nd London Regiment, the L.R.B. and some French troops. The Q.V.R. stood by ready to enter in support. In the evening they were relieved by the 167th Brigade and withdrew to Casement trenches for the night.

The next day, September 27th, the welcome news came that the whole division was being relieved and that it was to move back into the neighbourhood of Ville sur Ancre and Meaulte, the Q.V.R. to be in billets in the last-named village. It was rumoured that they were to have at least six days' rest, which would not have been too much seeing that they had been continually in the front-line trenches since September 7th, except on the two days, September 11th and 12th, when they were in reserve in Casement trenches, and most of the time under heavy shell and machine-gun fire. During these twenty-one days little rest or sleep could be obtained, and neither officers nor riflemen could wash or clean themselves up as water was almost as rare as gold, every pint having to be carried up nightly in petrol cans on mule-back across the Somme Valley and generally under fire. The allowance for officer and man alike was two pints for twenty-four hours for all purposes. Not much for a tired and thirsty soldier on a hot September day.

The Q.V.R. arrived at Meaulte late on the afternoon of September 27th, pleased to be out of the fire zone at last, and actuated by only two thoughts—first to clean up, shave, have a good wash and change into clean under-clothing, the old it is needless to state being in a horrible condition after three weeks' use ; secondly, to have a good hot meal after subsisting on cold bully beef and damp biscuits washed down with a small modicum of chlorinated water. The 28th was spent in a thorough rest, but great was the disappointment on the receipt the same night of a warning order to be ready to move to the front again on the morrow. Gen. Hull commanding the 56th Division held a conference of all C.O.'s in the morning and informed them that the Division was to attack and capture the Green Line, i.e. the ridge in front of Le Transloy. The announcement caused a bit of a shock and gave rise to some anxiety, as owing to the heavy fighting the division had gone through some of the battalions were a bit worn-out and weak in numbers, especially as regards experienced officers, besides being depleted in bombers and Lewis gunners, so essential in trench warfare. However, it was no use pulling long faces, the best had to be made of a bad job, and at 2 p.m. the Q.V.R. marched away from Meaulte en route for the front line trenches.

The weather was atrocious, heavy showers of rain day after day had made the roads and tracks, in fact the whole country-side, in a terrible condition, impassable almost in places for transport or wheel traffic, but the old spirit of the Q.V.R. was there and the men plodded cheerfully along singing until they neared the front line. The night was spent in craters near German Wood. The next day, September 30th, the Q.V.R.

went up to Les Boeufs, relieving the 2nd Sherwood Foresters (6th Division) in Foggy, Shamrock and Fluffy trenches. It might be mentioned here that the 169th Brigade was for the second time on the extreme right of the British line and in touch with the French 71st Infantry Brigade. The situation was very obscure, as owing to the heavy rainfall no new maps or aeroplane photographs were available, while telephone wires from front-line trenches to supports and Battalion Headquarters were few and far between owing to most of them having been cut by shell-fire.

The exact position of the enemy was difficult to locate, so orders were given that battalions holding the front line should push out patrols at once and occupy a line of posts just over the crest of the ridge, keeping in touch with the troops on the right and left ; these posts were eventually to be joined up, but this, however, did not mature on the Q.V.R. front at least, owing to the heavy shelling. On October 1st the Q.V.R. were ordered to dig a trench known as 25 trench and also to extend Foggy Trench with the help of a company of the L.R.B. The Q.V.R. were also ordered to dig and improve a communication trench which had been started in the village of Les Boeufs. Owing to the shortage of picks and shovels this proved a long and difficult task ; small intrenching tools being the only implements available, while the hard ground and the still harder foundations of the ruined houses had to be penetrated. One young and inexperienced officer who had only just come out from home endeavoured to get his platoon to cut through a hard cobbled road but, though his intention was good, the result was small. Reporting upon these operations Capt. L. A. Newnham, Brigade Major 169th Infantry Brigade, says :

" (1) At 6.15 p.m. the situation was very obscure, but as far as could be ascertained the Q.W.R. party had run up against the enemy in some strength in trenches and had mostly returned, leaving several missing. The Q.V.R. left party had met with very heavy barrage and had not been able to go out from Foggy Trench. Q.V.R. right party had gone down the valley 400 yards and had not returned. Search parties were out several hours but could find no trace of the officer and several other ranks ; a few were brought in wounded.

"(2) Q.V.R. met with strong enemy barrage of H.E. for considerable time before Zero. Shelling on front line had been heavy during the whole morning and at 3.30 p.m. had increased to intense ; at 3.15 p.m. Foggy Trench was considerably damaged. Orders were very difficult to send owing to casualties to runners, touch between the various trenches was bad, no map showed the trenches accurately and the men were considerably shaken from the heavy bombardment.

"(3) The intention for the night's work was to dig a trench southwards to connect with a small dug-in post. This was found impracticable, as it was considered no starting-point could be fixed to work from the north, especially as the northern end of Foggy Trench was an isolated post and exact position unknown. I therefore arranged to work in a northerly or north-easterly direction from advanced post and arranged with Q.V.R. for a covering party of three platoons to extend due north-east from the dug-in advanced post.

"2/2nd R.E. moved off at 9.10 p.m. to work on making Foggy Trench really tenable to connect up the portions of trench and join up with detached post on left flank.

"(4) At about 10.5 p.m. party moved out to take trenches and allot tasks. At the same time orders were issued to the three working companies to move down to the main road and rendezvous. The country is extremely difficult to find one's way, few guides know the correct routes and owing to trenches not being named it is very difficult to reach intended destinations.

"Tasks were allotted as follows : 2nd Londons and L.R.B. to dig a communication trench.

"At about 1 a.m. I led the pioneer companies to their tasks and work progressed for twenty minutes. The enemy were sending up Very lights, and one fell on the northern covering party. One or two men being new and untrained fired at the point from whence the Very light was fired ; the enemy fired more lights into the covering party and opened rifle fire. Within ten minutes a machine-gun also opened, and I could observe plainly that the covering party was under accurate and observed fire, as the bullets were dropping round them. The enemy then sent up red-light signals and a heavy barrage, chiefly 4·2 was placed along the whole front. I ordered the northern covering party to withdraw man by man from the zone of Very lights and was also compelled to withdraw the platoons in the vicinity.

"(5) The barrage lasted to about half to three-quarters of an hour, causing considerable casualties.

"(6) About 4 a.m. a small party moving from New Trench to Foggy Trench again attracted attention, and as working parties were withdrawing at 4.15 a.m., a second barrage, lasting an hour, was placed over the whole area. Total estimated casualties : 1 officer, 35 Other Ranks.

"(7) The covering party of Q.V.R. remained particularly steadfast and all ranks, although mostly inexperienced, behaved well."

The right party referred to in Capt. Newnham's report (para. 1) was a strong patrol sent out on the afternoon of October 1st in charge of 2nd Lieut. Gutteridge under cover of a barrage fire. Its orders were to reconnoitre the enemy's position and form a strong point over the crest of the ridge in conjunction with other patrols of other battalions. The weather was thick and misty, the patrol became separated, lost touch with one another and met with no success. On its return its commander was reported missing (killed). On the following day the front and support lines were heavily shelled. At night the Q.V.R. were relieved by the L.R.B. and withdrew to Hog's Back Trenches in support. At 3 p.m. on 3rd they withdrew to the Citadel Camp, Fricourt, but their progress thither was considerably delayed by heavy hostile shelling and the bad state of the roads, and in consequence camp was not reached until midnight. While in Fricourt 12 new officers joined the battalion, none of them having had any war experience.

Col. Dickins reports : " I would like to mention here the remarkable pluck and determination of Sergt. Pickett, who was in command of his platoon at the time. Just after being relieved in the trenches by the L.R.B., Sergt. Pickett and his platoon were marching away when they came under heavy shell-fire. Sergt. Pickett ordered his platoon to go back and jump into the trench they had just vacated, but in jumping himself he fractured the small bone in his leg close to the ankle.

In a short time the fire abated and he marched his platoon back to the camp at Fricourt—a distance of some miles—where the battalion had been ordered to rest. It was not until the following morning that he asked his company commander if he might be excused from parade as his leg was so painful. This was reported to me and I asked the M.O. to examine the leg, which he did and found that the bone was broken. Capt. Clarke, the M.O., ordered him to hospital but he was very loth to go as he did not want to leave the battalion. The discomfort and pain that Sergt. Pickett must have suffered during his march from the trenches over muddy and rough roads, and carrying his full kit, must have been most severe, but it shows what stuff the men were made of and that a N.C.O. would not let his platoon down. Sergt. Pickett was sent home to England to recuperate and later returned to France. He was promoted and given a commission as 2nd Lieutenant, which he well deserved."

From 4th to 6th October the battalion remained in Citadel Camp, resting and cleaning arms and equipment. On 7th, at 7 a.m., it moved to the divisional reserve in trenches south-east of Ginchy. Late in the afternoon of the same day Col. Dickins was summoned to attend a conference at the 168th Brigade H.Q., to which brigade the Q.V.R. had been lent. He was then informed that the regiment would be under the orders of the 168th Brigade from that time and that the 167th and 168th Brigades were then attacking Spectrum, Rainbow and Hazy Trenches with the object of capturing the crest of the ridge in front of and overlooking Le Transloy, which place was to be taken at an early date. The assault took place at 1.45 p.m. on 7th; the left was fairly successful but the 168th fared badly on the right. After severe fighting it came under intense shell and heavy machine-gun fire from the Gun Pits and Dewdrop and Hazy trenches and was held up. The enemy had been reinforced in Hazy Trench and the North Gun Pits, and at 8.30 p.m. developed a strong counter-attack which forced the 168th Brigade back to their original line.

At 7.15 the Q.V.R. received orders to move up from Ginchy to support the 4th London Regiment in Hog's Back Trench. The weather was bad, a good deal of rain having fallen, and consequently the roads were in a terrible state of mud and full of shell-holes; the difficulties were increased by a great confusion of traffic and in addition the night was very dark. It was midnight before the Q.V.R. reached the Hog's Back, and it was well into the morning of October 9th before they were able to relieve the 4th Londons and the Rangers in the front line in Foggy, 25th, Burnaby and Thistle Trenches in the Les Bœufs sector. On arriving in the trenches the men were much fatigued, wet through and covered with mud, but found there was plenty of work to be done during the morning in carrying ammunition, bombs, tools and stores of all kinds. No sooner had they completed their task than a warning order was received that they were to attack that afternoon with the L.R.B. on the right and the 3rd Londons on the left. Shortly after midday orders were received that zero hour was 3.30 p.m. As a good deal of movement had taken place in daylight and in full view of the Boches it was feared that the enemy would be quite prepared for the attack when it came. The trenches, too, were so slippery from the mud that it was difficult for the men to get out of them quickly and over the top, especially as they were tired and their clothing wet.

The Q.V.R. had orders to attack the northern end of Hazy Trench and Dewdrop Trench. They advanced to the attack under a weak barrage with two companies in the firing line and two in support with the reserves in Thistle and part of Shamrock Trenches. The right company got as far as the gap between the North Gun Pits and the south end of Dewdrop Trench, where they were held up by severe machine-gun and rifle fire from Hazy Trench. They at once started to dig themselves in and consolidate the adjoining shell-holes, when the enemy in the Northern Gun Pits, who up to then had been silent, opened a terrific enfilade fire from their concealed positions. At the same time machine-gun and rifle fire from Dewdrop Trench on both flanks of the Q.V.R. right company practically wiped it out. The left company had been held up almost from the start in similar circumstances by the enemy holding Dewdrop Trench. The support and reserve companies also were unable to leave their trenches owing to a heavy artillery barrage that the Boches had put down upon them. Nearly all the officers in the two assaulting companies were either killed or wounded, but the depleted companies held on until dusk, when they were heavily counter-attacked and forced to withdraw between nine and ten o'clock to their original trenches.

The L.R.B. on the right fared somewhat better at the start, but were eventually compelled to fall back on their original position. Here great confusion ensued, men of all battalions getting mixed up in the dark while endeavouring to find their way back to their proper trenches, and it was almost impossible for Commanding Officers to forward to Brigade H.Q. definite information as to their positions.

The Divisional Commander then ordered that all Commanding Officers should reconnoitre personally their front line trenches and report to the Divisional H.Q. which trenches their battalions were holding. "This," says Col. Dickins, "was one of the most unpleasant duties and nights that I experienced whilst in France. Leaving Battn. H.Q. about 10.30 p.m. with a runner, Rfn. Howard, we made our way with difficulty over the open ground, which was pitted everywhere with shell-holes, to some old disused German gun pits in which Lieut. G. Foaden (our Lewis Gun and Intelligence Officer) had established himself and formed a forward Observation Post midway between our front-line trenches and Battn. H.Q. After some trouble, owing to the darkness, we found the O.P., and Lieut. Foaden then accompanied us to the front-line trenches. The Germans were sending over shells of all calibres, which continually lighted up the sky as they burst in the air. The noise of the guns, the bursting shells, the crackling of machine-gun and rifle fire from both sides was intense and highly trying to the nerves. On arriving at the trenches we had the greatest difficulty in proceeding along them owing to the number of dead and wounded men. In some parts the trenches were so full that it was impossible to step between or over their bodies. They were all lying about in heaps in a terrible state, dead and wounded together; at some points it was not possible to pass and we had to get out of the trench, when we were immediately shot at by Boches snipers, who were not far away and were watching every movement by the light of innumerable star shells. We found the men terribly mixed up, men of many regiments in each others' trenches, many so fatigued that they were unable

to keep awake, and were resting with their rifles in their hands
on the parapet or just where they happened to be; others lay
in heaps at the bottom of the trench overcome by sleep. It
was almost impossible to find out which trenches the different
battalions of the brigade were supposed to be holding, they
were so mixed up. It was not until after a search of five hours
that I was able to discover which lines of trenches the Q.V.R.
occupied. I then made my way back to Battn. H.Q. to make
my report. The shelling was very severe during the whole
night, with sniping going on everywhere. I am thankful to
say I reached the H.Q. safely about 3.30 a.m., very tired and
feeling depressed at what I had seen of the sad loss of life and
terrible sufferings of the many wounded, whom it was difficult
to get moved away owing to the shortage of stretcher bearers
and the continual shelling."

Consequent upon the following difficulties, this attack proved
a most costly affair:

(a) The enemy held a very strong position.

(b) The troops were tired on account of the fatiguing period
they had passed through for the last three weeks and the
exhausting march of the day and night before.

(c) The weather was atrocious.

(d) The roads and trenches were full of mud and shell-holes.

(e) Nearly all the junior officers had come straight out from
home and had had no previous fighting experience.

The Q.V.R. lost in this action, 6 officers killed and 7 wounded
and about 200 Other Ranks killed and wounded.

The officers killed in the Les Bœufs Sector were:

2nd Lieut. Richard Howard Gutteridge (2/10/16).
2nd Lieut. Owen Loftus Maddock (7/10/16).
2nd Lieut. Lionel Ludlow (8/10/16).
2nd Lieut. Alan Rowland Warren (8/10/16).
2nd Lieut. Charles Victor Dowswell (8/10/16).
2nd Lieut. Albert Jack Parslow (10/10/16), and
2nd Lieut. — Unwin (L.R.B. attached Q.V.R.).

On the night of the 9th October, the Q.V.R. were relieved
by the 1st Royal Irish Fusiliers and withdrawn to Bernafay
Wood. This closed the fighting the Q.V.R. had on the Somme
front in 1916.

MAP No. 6.

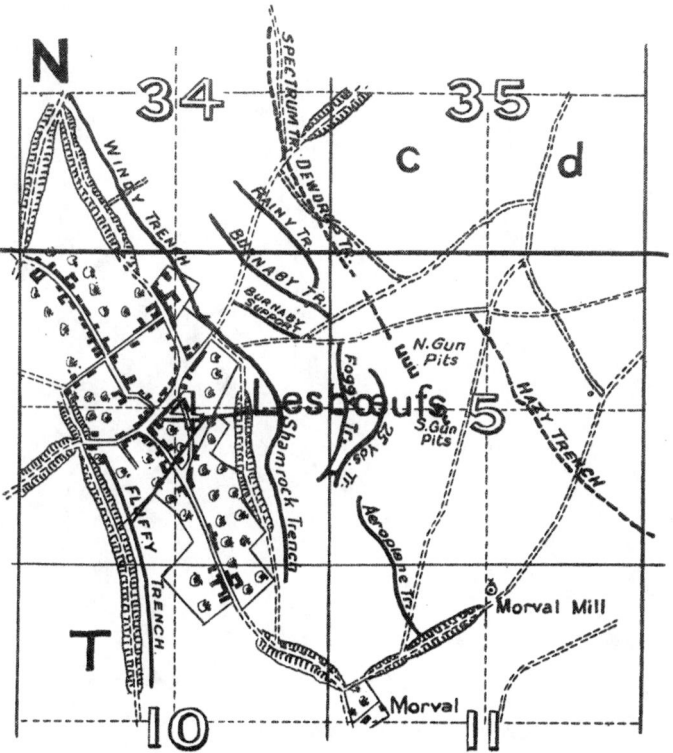

FIRST BATTLE OF THE SOMME SEPT 30TH-OCT 19TH
1916.

On 27th October the following Order was received by the 56th Division from G.O.C. Fourth Army (Lieut.-Gen. Sir H. Rawlinson), dated 27th October :

" I desire to place on record my appreciation of the work that was carried out by the 56th Division during the Battle of the Somme.

" The successful operations in the neighbourhood of Bouleaux Wood and Leuze Wood together with the capture of Combles between 9th and 27th September, were feats of arms deserving the highest praise, and I congratulate the Division on the gallantry, perseverance and endurance displayed by all ranks.

. . . .

" When after only two days rest the Division was again called upon to go into the line, they displayed a fine spirit of determination which deserved success.

. . . .

" The enterprise and hard work which the Division has shown in sapping forward and constructing trenches under fire has been a noticeable feature in the operations, and I specially congratulate the Infantry on the progress they made in this manner at Bouleaux Wood.

" It is a matter of regret to me that this fine Division has now left the Fourth Army, but I trust that at some future date I may find them under my command."

The following announcement was made in the *London Gazette* of 28th October, 1916 :

The undermentioned men have been awarded the Military Medal for services in the field :

    2361 Sergt. Telfer, G. F.
    1471 Sergt. Sim, C. K.
    1662 Cpl. Streather, W. A.
    2101 Rfn. Squires, A. W.

In the day's Orders the Commanding Officer congratulated the men and the regiment on these distinctions.

CHAPTER XXIV

NEUVE CHAPELLE AND THE MAUQUISSART CRATER

THE following day the battalion moved to Mansell Camp, Fricourt, where the Corp Commander invited all Commanding Officers to meet him at Corps H.Q., and congratulated them on the work of the past few months. Fricourt was left in its turn next morning, the battalion marching at 4.55 a.m. to Treux and proceeding from thence to Picquigny by motor buses. Here they remained until October 21st, the time being spent in the usual Company Training. The 169th Brigade moved into Huppy Area on Saturday, October 21st, the Q.V.R. leaving Picquigny at 7.50 a.m. and arriving at Limieux, after a march of 18 miles, at 4.30 p.m. Two days later they marched from Limieux to Pont Remy, where they entrained for Berguette. After detraining they marched to St. Venant, through pouring rain, for billets for the night. The next morning they were off once more in the everlasting rain, their destination being Lestrem, where they remained for three days, the rain continuing nearly all the time. Lestrem was left on October 27th, the battalion marching to Bout de Ville, where they relieved the 2/4th Gloucester Regiment, taking over the trenches from them the next morning in the left sector, Neuve Chapelle. The following three days were passed in the trenches, cleaning, draining and repairing.

On Friday, 3rd November, the Queen's Westminsters arrived and took over the trenches, and the Q.V.R. marched into billets at Bout de Ville, where they remained, carrying out Company Training, anti-gas measures, etc., until November 9th, when they took another turn of five days' duty in the trenches. They were relieved on 15th by the Q.W.R. and proceeded to Croix Barbée, three companies going into billets and one holding a defensive post. Six days later the Q.V.R. again took over the trenches from the Queen's Westminsters. The word " trench " is used for simplicity's sake, but actually, throughout the whole of the winter of 1916–1917, breastworks of sandbags formed the defensive works as, owing to the country being very flat and the water level only a few inches below the ground, it was impossible to dig trenches. Neuve Chapelle sector, says Major Lindsey-Renton, " was notorious for the unusual amount of trench-mortar and rifle-grenade activity (artillery was very quiet) as, owing to the proximity of the trenches and their being merely breastworks, it was an easy matter to inflict damage. This was increased in our case by the fact that although there was a breast work in front, there was little, if any, behind, so that any explosive falling behind the trench stood a good chance of doing damage to the garrison."

During their last visit to the trenches in November, lasting from 21st to 26th, a " Bangalore Torpedo " was successfully exploded under the enemy wire at 12.45 a.m. on 23rd. On 26th, two and a half companies were relieved by the 7th Battalion Middlesex Regiment. and withdrew to Riez Bailleul, and the remaining one and a half company on 27th, by the 16th Royal Warwicks, the whole battalion proceeding to billets in La Gorgue.

We now return to Major Lindsey-Renton's account of the winter of 1916–1917. Speaking of life in the trenches he says : " There were two very unpleasant points in our line, ' The Neb ' and ' Hell Corner.' These points, especially Hell Corner, seemed to attract a great deal of the enemy's attention, as day and night a steady stream of trench-mortars and rifle grenades were fired at them. It was necessary to have parties at all times ready to rebuild any part of the breastwork which might be blown down. It was almost impossible to avoid these points when going round the line and no one ever tarried in their neighbourhood. It must not, however, be thought from this that we did not give the Boche as much as and more than he gave us. Our ' Stokes ' and Medium (Mushroom) Trench Mortar kept up a pretty continual strafe, and numberless rifle grenades were fired by the infantry.

" The accommodation in the line was most inadequate and what there was could not, with one or two exceptions, keep out the smallest form of projectile. Opposite the right of the battalion's sector was the well-known 'Bois de Biez' or 'Mystery Wood,' as it was often called from the tradition that during the battle of Neuve Chapelle a large number of our troops entered it and were never seen or heard of again ! In this section of trenches the battalion for the first time found a light railway system, which was of great assistance in getting up rations and stores. While the Q.V.R. were there the line only went as far as 'Mogg's Hole,' a series of ruins and shelters, forming support companies, H.Q. and accommodation.

"Owing to alterations in the divisional frontage the battalion sector changed from time to time, being extended to the north until it included the 'Duck's Bill Crater.' This was a mine crater of considerable size, with a lake in the centre of unascertained depth, out in No Man's Land, which was connected with the front trench by a communication trench over 100 yards long. A number of fire bays had been cut into the lip of the crater, which were occupied by the garrison. It was not a pleasant place to be in as the enemy were in a neighbouring crater, and owing to its size and the strength of its garrison it could not be very strongly held. Before we got there the enemy had made an attempt to cut off the garrison by entering the trench connecting the crater with the front-line trench.

"A move still further north brought the 'Mauquissart Crater' into the battalion sector. This was another mine crater and one of the largest, if not the largest, in the area. The trenches here were in an appalling condition, so bad in places that it was quite impossible to occupy them. Deep mud of varying consistency, sandbags and revetting materials all jumbled up together made the place indescribably dreary and filthy. The appearance of the trenches was being continually altered by the damage done by mortar fire, which made the situation worse by blocking up such drainage as was made from time to time. This was a serious matter, as owing to the flat nature of the country it often depended upon an inch or two variation in the level as to whether the water flowed away. For miles behind it was necessary to have labour, in this case chiefly civilian, in cleaning all ditches, etc., as unless these

Col. Vernon W. F. Dickins, D.S.O., V.D.

were kept clear the water would not flow from the trenches. Further back it was necessary to keep pumping stations at work pumping the water which flowed back through the ditches."

At the end of November, Lieut.-Col. V. W. F. Dickins was granted thirty days' leave on account of ill-health, and left La Gorgue on 29th and crossed to England next day. Unfortunately for him, Colonel Dickins was unable to pass for foreign service again and was appointed Commanding Officer at a Divisional Training School for Officers at Colchester, where he remained until the end of the war. When the Territorial Forces were reorganised he was appointed to the command of the 9th London Regiment (Queen Victoria's Rifles), which he retained until January, 1921.

Major R. H. Lindsey-Renton was left in command of the battalion with Captain Symes, who was killed in the third battle of Ypres in the following August, as second in command.

Shortly before Christmas, Major Lindsey-Renton was called to Boulogne to attend a conference of Commanding Officers of the First Army. During his absence on the night of 23rd December, the Germans made a raid on a small post held by six men in the neighbourhood of the Mauquissart Crater. After shelling the post with " Minnies," etc., for two nights they entered that section of the front line trench at 12.30 a.m., took two prisoners and caused two other casualties. They stayed in the trench for a few minutes only and returned to their own lines under cover of a renewed bombardment. In describing the raid Rfn. J. C. Newman says: "In front of, and just touching, our front trenches was a huge mine crater called Mauquissart Crater which had to be held as a bombing post at night. On the night of 23rd December a section of the H.Q. bombers, of whom I was one, was ordered up to the front line for this duty. The section consisted of Lce.-Cpl. Earle, Rfn. Gaward, Hewlett, Green, Oakley, Selback, Burrell, Jaeger, myself and another man. We had the greatest difficulty in getting to our appointed post owing to the deep mud, which reached up to and above our knees and also to the awful state of the trenches where they had been smashed by Fritz's minnenwerfers. On arriving at the post we found it to be a fire bay and a sort of dug-out well in advance of our front line

—not a very enviable position, although patrols were supposed to visit it at stated intervals. Our trouble started by Hewlett being taken bad; he had not been well for several days and he had to be put in the dug-out to lie down. That reduced our strength to 7 men and 1 N.C.O. Having done extra sentry-go owing to Hewlett's illness I was told to go and take a rest in the dug-out. I had not been there very long before the Cpl. took two men to try and get in touch with our right flank company, and while he was gone it happened. All of a sudden there was a rush and automatic pistol bullets flying about and at the same time an intensive bombardment from the German trench artillery on either flank. Of course there was an immediate rush. Oakley never uttered a word—I think he must have been hit on the head and rendered senseless and I heard the man that was with him scream that he was hit through the arm. In the struggle I was knocked flying, and a stick-bomb landing near me at the same time I took no further interest in the proceedings for some time. I came to in a few minutes and could hear voices talking in German, but I lay still, seeing visions of Christmas Day spent in Germany and other things, and thinking of all the yarns I had heard about the Germans killing all bombers that fell into their hands. I lay still, however, and presently found myself being lifted up by a German who evidently thought I was dead, for he dropped me again and not very lightly at that. Apparently satisfied that they had done all the damage they could in the crater a whistle blew and they took themselves off as fast as they could, taking with them, as I afterwards learned, Oakley and the other man as prisoners, also Rfn. Burrell. He was, however, so badly wounded in both thighs that they dumped him in No Man's Land, from whence he was afterwards fetched and transferred safely to England. Poor old Hewlett was found nearly blown to pieces, but whether by a bomb or shell was never discovered. My own opinion is that he being wounded would not go with the Germans who had captured him so they simply slung a bomb at him and finished him off. After a time I heard someone call my name and asking if I was alive. I replied that I was but in a bad way, as my nose, ears and eyes were bleeding from the shock of the explosion. I then recognised the voice as that of Rfn. Selback, and together we crawled back to our own line to report. If the Germans had still been there we should have fared rather badly, for our sole arms were one Mills grenade and a bayonet, the latter being mine. On reaching the front line we found that all H.Q. had been blown in during the bombardment, but we managed to find someone in authority and reported the state of affairs, which of course resulted in a general 'stand to.' After that I was assisted down to Battalion H.Q., where I was seen by the M.O., and thus ended one of the most exciting times and the narrowest escape I ever had. A few days after the enemy tried to raid another crater, called Duckbill Crater, in another part of the sector, but he was unlucky, for everyone was on the watch, and he was wiped out with machine-gun and Lewis Gun fire before he got to the wire."

The battalion came out of the trenches on December 27th, when it was relieved by the Queen's Westminsters and proceeded to Pont Du Hem and Rouge Croix. The last days of the expiring year were spent in R.E. fatigue duties and sending working parties into the trenches. The men were in billets at Pont Du Hem.

CHAPTER XXV

1917—THE LAVENTIE POSTS

THE New Year opened with the battalion enjoying a welcome rest. On January 2nd the Q.V.R. were relieved by the Rangers (12th London Regiment) and moved into Divisional Reserve at Robermetz, where, until the 13th, they were engaged in company and specialist training in all branches and contributing working parties for various purposes. It was about this time that the brigade took over the northern sector of the divisional front known as the Laventie Sector. This, says Major Lindsey-Renton, " was an interesting sector from many points of view. In the first place the rest billets were in Laventie itself, rather less than a couple of miles behind the front-line trenches. Despite the proximity, civilians were still living in the village, and shops and estaminets carried on business as usual. Relief of the trenches was a very easy matter owing to the shortness of the march and the presence of a good road leading quite close to the line and to a good light railway system enabling rations and stores to be got up quickly and doing away with the necessity of large carrying parties. The Battalion H.Q. were in a house, known to all units who had been in that sector as " The Red House." Alone among the farms and other houses dotted round about it was practically untouched by shell-fire. Rumour had it that the owner had squared the enemy either in cash or by some nefarious agreement ! The more likely solution was the fact that owing to the lie of the land and some trees it was not under enemy observation. It was a curious but common experience to find an old lady from Laventie knocking at one's door with milk, eggs and the *Daily Mail* for sale. The Mess Room in the Red House was also famous among units which had visited the neighbourhood, for some of the visitors of an artistic temperament had left their marks, covering the walls with a number of topical paintings, humorous and otherwise. If the house survived the later stages of the war it should be quite a show-place. Close at hand was a sort of out-house which was used as a soup kitchen where hot soup could be had at any hour of the day or night, so that parties which had been working up in the line could always get a bowl of hot soup on their return from work. The light railway also commenced here, so that at night rations and stores found their way to H.Q. and were sorted out under the care of the R.S.M. and the trucks pushed up the line by parties told off for the purpose.

By means of patrols it had been discovered that owing to the flooded state of his trenches the enemy had abandoned a portion of his front line and retired to higher and drier ground in the rear. Two or three men were accordingly posted in the German line as observation posts and to keep a close watch on the enemy. After a time the post grew to a small party being there continuously, and eventually orders were issued that three strong posts should be permanently established in the old German front line. Not a cheerful idea at any time seeing that the Huns had abandoned the place owing to its water-logged condition. The Q.V.R. arrived at Laventie on January 14th, relieving the 3rd Londons, and on 20th took over the trenches from the 2nd Battalion London Regiment. On the night previous the posts held by that regiment had been raided by the Germans, losing one officer and a few men taken prisoners. The three posts taken over were known to us by the names " Irma, Bertha and Flame." Irma on the left (north), Bertha in the centre, and Flame on the right. " A " Company held " Irma " and " B " " Bertha " and " Flame." These posts were not actually in the German trenches but were situated on our side of what had originally been their parapet. Says Rfn. Frank Short : " The garrisoning of these positions called for extreme courage on the part of our men, as the enemy not only had the artillery range exactly but the advantage was in his favour for making surprise attacks at night. To the individual soldier it appeared folly to hold such positions, but the Brigade Commander had ordered the posts to be held at all costs and it is realised there must have been some special reason for this." What that special reason was, was never disclosed.

Just before the Q.V.R. went in the weather changed. A severe frost set in and lasted the whole time they were in the line, the temperature showing 20 to 25 degrees of frost. "This," says Major Lindsey-Renton, "had very important results which largely influenced the events which followed :

(i) "The ground and the trenches previously impassable were frozen hard making it easy for the Germans to approach the posts and raid them.

(ii) "Digging was practically impossible. A carefully organised plan for building a communication trench from our front line to the posts had to be abandoned.

(iii) "The garrisons suffered severely from exposure. During daylight all movement, however slight, brought shell-fire on the posts. At least one or two wounded men died from exposure.

(iv) "Snow also fell. This at once gave away to the Germans the exact position of the posts and the tracks across from our front line. (Our own aeroplanes photographed the area and I saw the result. As the enemy also photographed the position his photographs must have been of the greatest value to his artillery and raiding parties.)"

These posts were held by the Q.V.R. from the 20th to the 25th January inclusive.

The accounts we have of the raids are somewhat conflicting. The sole entry in the War Diary for January 21st to 25th is : "Battalion in trenches holding posts in old German front line. Posts heavily shelled and one post raided by enemy on two occasions. Considerable loss caused to our garrison." Lindsey-Renton says : "Our first night in the line was pretty quiet though parties of the enemy were seen moving about in front, but the second to the fifth night was practically one continuous period of raids successful, attempted raids and artillery duels. On the second night (Jan. 21st) an attempt was made to raid 'Irma,' but was beaten off. A party of Germans, however, succeeded in getting into 'Bertha' and driving out the garrison, but the party eventually went away and our patrols finding this out we reoccupied the post. As a result the posts were strengthened and a belt of wire put out in front. This was a difficult and dangerous matter as the ground was very hard and the slightest noise brought a salvo of shells, the German artillery having the place taped to an inch. The third night was practically one continuous battle either with Boche parties or artillery. A strong party again raided 'Bertha' and after severe fighting drove the garrison out. Patrols were at once sent out to see what the situation was and reported the Germans were still holding the posts and that there were two machine-guns which fired at the least sign of movement, and owing to the snow on the ground patrols were very easily seen. I reported all this to the brigade and received orders to counter-attack and retake 'Bertha.' I then pointed out that the Germans had no wish to occupy the post permanently as they had abandoned the trenches, and that if we waited until just before dawn they would have returned to their own lines and we could reoccupy the post. I received, however, definite orders to counter-attack, but was not given any definite time. I therefore decided to counter-attack just before dawn when the Germans would either have gone or be about to go. I felt certain that if I attacked at once I should have heavy casualties from machine-guns and quite unnecessarily. I proceeded to the front line to arrange for the counter-attack. Our artillery put down a barrage on the post, and when Capt. Brand with two platoons of "B" Company arrived there he found it empty. Whether the Germans had left previously or had been driven out by our barrage I do not know. We had, however, got back the post without further casualties, which was what I had hoped and anticipated. As a result of these two night experiences the Brigade issued orders for the strengthening of the garrison and having strong parties out in front wiring the front of the posts to prevent any further raids.

"On the following night these instructions were carried out. The Germans soon discovered, either by patrols or the noise made by the wiring parties, that there was a larger number of men out than usual and did not attempt a raid, but instead they suddenly put down a hurricane bombardment on the posts, chiefly 'Bertha,' with the result that there were 55 casualties incurred in a very short time and the remainder of the garrisons were severely shaken. On the following night parties of Germans were seen from time to time moving in the vicinity of the posts, but were unable to approach owing to our artillery firing along a line in front of the posts. Considerable excitement and anxiety was caused throughout the night by the presence of these patrols, as one was naturally led to expect further raids. The following night was quieter except for occasional bursts of fire on the posts ; it was very accurate and led to a number of casualties.

"The night after this the battalion was relieved, and on the next night the order was issued that the posts were to be evacuated and the garrisons were to bring back all the stores and return to our original line. On receipt of the order a great sigh of relief went up in the brigade, as everyone was heartily sick of the posts and the moral of the men was suffering badly under the stress of the weather and the continual strain of the posts."

Lieut. G. D. Mayer, writing of these posts, says : "They were merely converted shell-holes, with, in some cases, small shelters on our side of the parapet. There were three on our front being in the order named, 'Irma,' 'Bertha,' 'Flame,' the last two held by 'B' Company under Brand. No movement of any kind could be made during the day and very little by night. 'Flame's' position was, I think, never discovered. The posts were held in 12-hour shifts, the number being by day 1 officer and 12 men and by night 1 officer and about 24 men. Weather bitterly cold with thick frozen snow on ground. On this night (Jan. 21st) 2nd Lieut. Waghorne was in charge of 'Flame,' myself 'Bertha.' A quiet night.

"January 22nd, night. Intense whizz-bang bombardment put down on 'B' Company's front line, lasting about three-quarters of an hour. No casualties in trench. Immediately on cessation S.O.S. signal ; sound of heavy Lewis gun and rifle fire and bursting bombs, seen and heard from 'Bertha,' which was held by 2nd Lieut. Spaul. S.O.S. put through by wire and help sent out. I found Spaul some 500 yards from our trench dazed. It appeared that he had been thrown into the icy water and nearly drowned. The remainder of the garrison had been killed or wounded. The post was reoccupied.

"January 23rd. This night I was at 'Flame,' and 'Bertha' was again raided, though I cannot remember who was there. 2nd Lieut. Waghorne came to me and said that a patrol of ours had visited it and found all clear and that I was to reoccupy it whilst he remained at 'Flame.' He came with me as he knew the way. When about 50 yards from 'Bertha' two bombs were thrown at us, Very lights went up and machine-gun fire opened. We got down in time and only had, I think, 2 casualties. Waghorne wanted to attack the post at once and went on one side to collect some men, when machine-gun fire was again opened. Our party bunked, and I was left with Sergt. Brittain to make my way back to the front line. Waghorne was found to be missing but turned up later, having had a clout on the head with something or other which had knocked him insensible. I was sent out to 'Flame' again. Later on I had a message through the phone from Major Renton to find out if 'Bertha' was still occupied, so I reconnoitred with Sergts. Bevis and Chedgey—it was—I reported the news. It was then trench mortared, but as these put the wind up us in 'Flame' more than they would have done anything in 'Bertha' I managed to get them stopped. Later an 18-pounder barrage was put down and the post was attacked from two sides. The Boche had of course by then left.

"January 23rd. On this night 2n\l Lieut. Smith was at 'Bertha,' and in the early morning sounds of rifle fire, Lewis gun fire and the noise of bursting bombs suddenly broke out from the direction of the post. S.O.S. went up and the 18-pounder barrage came down. Unluckily the first three rounds burst on our parapet putting out two men of a Lewis gun team who had at once got into action directing flanking fire to the right of the post, also severely putting the wind up Major Renton, Capt. Brand, who dived head first into a pool of water, myself and Sergt. Chedgey, who was later on killed whilst in charge of a ration party on the Arras-Merville road. Wounded men began to come back from the post who said that the Germans were putting up a great fight. It appeared that the Boche had got hold of our password, which was changed every night—(I remember it being 'Blighty' and one night 'What 'opes'),—and had almost overwhelmed the post in the first rush, but were beaten off. They, however, formed up and charged again and again in the teeth of the barrage and heavy fire, practically all the garrison being casualties, including the greater part of a number of men who were rushed across to the post. 2nd Lieut. Smith ordered the few remaining to retire. One Lewis gunner behaved most gallantly. Though the only one left he remained firing his gun and literally had to be dragged away. The post was not held by the enemy and was reoccupied by a party under Lieut. Halifax.

"January 24th. This night was bright and clear. A wiring party of over 70 sent out to wire in 'Bertha' was spotted by the Boches and heavily shelled, suffering heavy casualties. Stretcher bearers brought up from the 2nd Londons, as well as some of our own, worked for hours bringing in the wounded. The Huns acted in a sporting manner and allowed them to carry on uninterrupted. 2nd Lieut. Waghorne was brought in from 'Flame' suffering from severe shell-shock. His place was filled by 2nd Lieut. Langley."

A few additional particulars are furnished by Lieut. D. F. Johnstone, who speaking of the night of the 22nd, says: "The night garrison went out to relieve the day garrison of 'Irma' post at dusk and had only just taken over when the Germans put down a barrage of trench mortar bombs upon it. Within two minutes one of the two men who had gone out to the left-hand shell-hole had to go back as he had been wounded. After a few minutes the barrage lifted and was put down between the post and our front line, and looking round we saw men moving about just behind a hummock in the parapet about 30 yards to the left of the post. They gave no reply to our challenge so one of our men threw a Mills' bomb. Unfortunately it fell short and a piece flew back and hit one of our own men in the hand. It served the purpose, however, of showing us roughly how many Huns were there, for in return they threw about four bombs. No one was wounded and the Lewis gun immediately opened fire. The signaller telephoned through the S.O.S. and within a very few moments our artillery put down a barrage in front of the post. The Huns fired a few shots and then ran back across the snow without attempting to get any nearer. For the rest of that night 'Irma' was left in peace. 'Bertha' post, however, was attacked by a raiding party about ten o'clock. The Germans made several attempts to capture the post and inflicted many casualties upon the garrison, but were eventually driven off. On the following night a party of the enemy approached ' Irma ' post, but they were heard walking over the ice and were driven back easily before they could get within bombing distance.

"At about seven o'clock that evening a heavy barrage was put down upon our front line and upon ' Bertha.' After half an hour it was lifted from the post, which was immediately attacked by a strong raiding party. Time after time the Huns were driven off and time after time they attacked again. They had somehow managed to get hold of our password, which for that night was ' Bully Beef,' and they advanced to the attack shouting ' Bully Biff, Bully Biff.' With each attack the garrison suffered many casualties until only the officer and 4 men were left and they were compelled to withdraw, leaving two wounded men in the post. At about five o'clock the next morning two parties were sent out to recapture the post, one approaching it from the front and the other from the right flank. The men went out and lay down in front of our own wire waiting for the shrapnel bombardment which was to be directed upon the post for three minutes. Unfortunately the guns fired short so that the majority of the shells burst over the heads of our own men. Four or five were wounded in this way. The remainder advanced to the post and found that the Germans had already evacuated it. By this time it was almost daylight, and we had great difficulty in getting the wounded back to our trenches in time. One man who had been only slightly wounded died from exposure before the stretcher bearers could reach him. Several other instances of the kind occurred during the week owing to the terribly severe cold.

"On each of the two remaining nights of our turn in the line ' Bertha ' was lost and retaken. When finally relieved the battalion had suffered 130 casualties."

Almost as soon as the Q.V.R. had taken over the posts Major Lindsey-Renton had a telephone line laid out to them so that he could be in direct touch from Battalion H.Q. with the garrison. This had not been done before. Reviewing the incidents Major Lindsey-Renton says : " The signallers were wonderful. Sitting in the open in a shell-hole without cover of any kind they kept me informed of what was happening despite everything. I especially remember Rfn. Newman and Rfn. Crook (afterwards killed). On one of the nights when the Germans were threatening to raid the posts no less than £40,000 worth of shells were fired to keep them off. On another occasion when the Germans got into 'Bertha,' I was up in the line and got the artillery to fire a salvo at the post, cautioning them to observe and check their fire previous to bombarding the Germans. The first salvo burst right on our trench, where I was at the telephone, and knocked out a Lewis gun team who were just in front of me. My indignation and reply to the artillery, when they inquired whether that was all right, had best be left to the imagination. Finally, I can only say that the behaviour of the men was wonderful. The strain on the nerves and endurance was tremendous, and yet at dawn and dusk the parties went out as a part of their normal routine to their posts, knowing the chances were greatly in favour of their being knocked out."

On January 25th Lieut.-Col. F. B. Follett (Royal Warwickshire Regiment) arrived and took over the command of the Q.V.R. The next day the battalion was relieved by the 2nd London Regiment and went into billets at Laventie, spending the remaining days of the month in training and inspection of companies and providing working parties. February 1st found them again in the trenches in the Fauquissart sector. The advanced posts had been abandoned and the original front line trenches strengthened with wire entanglements which had been ordered to be carried out with every possible speed. The Q.V.R. set to work with a will to strengthen the wiring. Each company had to make a return of the work done each night and the length of wire put out. Any company that was behindhand was told how much better the other companies had done until a spirit of intense rivalry arose, every available officer and man working for all they were worth on the wire. The result was that in their two turns in the line from February 1st to 7th, and 14th to 20th, the battalion put out no less than 1916 coils of wire! This was a remarkable feat, as there was, of course, other work to be done at the same time, keeping the trenches in repair, building

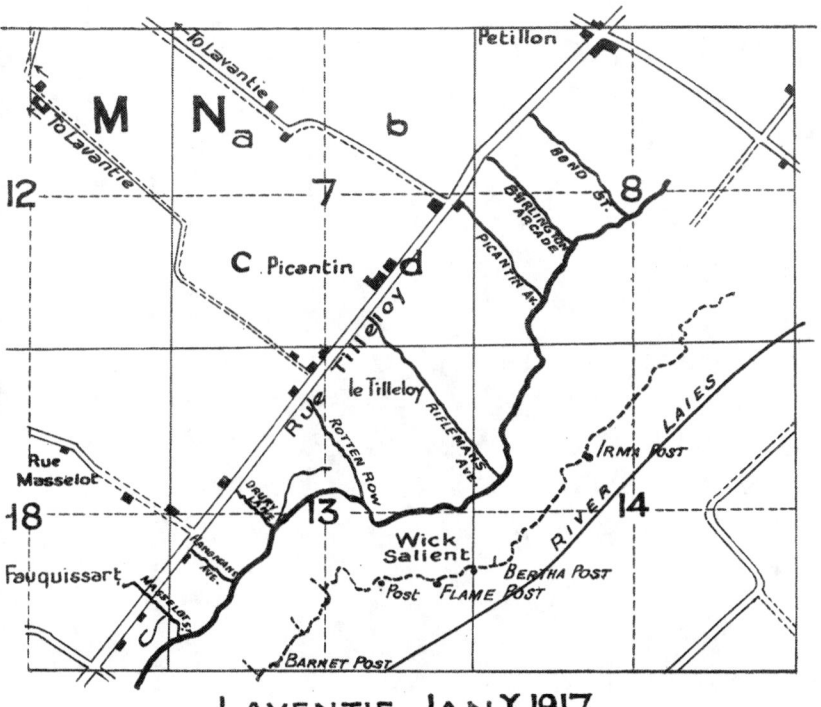

MAP No. 7.

LAVENTIE. JANY 1917.

shelters, etc. The rapidity with which the work was carried on was so unprecedented that at times it was delayed by the fact that all the dumps of barbed wire for miles around were used up and special arrangements had to be made to rush up supplies.

In their turns out of the line the battalion had experience of two different types of resting-places. One type was when other battalions in the same brigade were in the line and the Q.V.R. were in brigade reserve in villages close up to the line such as Laventie, Pont du Hem and Croix Barbée, when practically every man was engaged in working parties either by day or night up in the line and got but little rest beyond a fairly decent sleep in a dry place and proper meals. The other type was when the whole of the brigade was in divisional reserve and went back to the neighbourhood of such places as La Gorgue and Merville for about twelve days when the men could have quite a pleasant time. Of course a certain amount of training and smartening up had to be gone through, but the rest of the time was their own.

The advent of Col. Follett on January 25th marked a new departure on the part of the Army Council. Hitherto regiments of the Territorial Force had been commanded by one of their own officers, but dating from about the end of 1916 commands given to members of that Force were very few and far between, no matter how long they had served or how efficient they were in their duties. In practically every case a " Regular " Officer was appointed to the command of a regiment directly a vacancy occurred, and in some instances officers actually commanding a battalion in the field were on one pretext or another posted to a reserve battalion at home or found a job elsewhere. We have nothing to say against the new officers commanding, but the change caused considerable bitterness among those immediately concerned. No matter how brilliant their fighting record the professional soldier was ignorant of the traditions on which many Territorial regiments set great store, and never felt in full sympathy with the amateur, while the latter naturally resented his being passed over.

CHAPTER XXVI

The British Attack at Arras

ON March 1st the battalion was relieved in the Fauquissart sector by the 6th Battalion West Yorks Regiment and marched to billets at La Gorgue, looking forward to a much-needed rest. Leaving La Gorgue the next morning the Q.V.R. marched, by daily stages, via St. Floris, Sachin, Willeman, to Regnauville, which was to have been the training-ground. On arrival there, however, orders were received to proceed to the front in the Arras sector. They left Regnauville on the following day and marched via Ivergny and Gouy-en-Artois, being billeted for one night at each of the villages named. Five days, March 9th to 13th, were passed at Gouy for training in all branches ; on 14th a further move was made to Arras and the battalion at once began preparing for the battle of Arras, which was to take place in the following month. Arras at this time was a dismal place to be in. The Boches apparently were extremely anxious to know what was going on behind the British line, with the result that his aeroplanes were over and about the town off and on all day. In consequence no one was allowed out of billets during the day-time unless on duty, and when one did have to go out he had to stick close under the walls. Every evening the battalion was sent up to the ground in front of Achicourt, a suburb of Arras, to clear out old communication trenches and generally prepare for the push. On March 18th billets were taken over at Achicourt, and on the following day the Q.V.R. relieved their old friends, the 2nd Londons; in trenches at Beaurains which had been evacuated by the enemy a short time previously. These were consolidated and advance posts established.

In his *Memoirs* Hindenburg tells us that early in 1917 the

German High Command decided to withdraw their lines and transfer the line of defence which had been pushed in at one point to Peronne and bulged out to west of Bapaume, Roye and Noyon at others, to the chord position Arras-St. Quentin-Soissons. This new line was known to the Germans as the Siegfried Line and to the Allies as the Hindenburg Line. "So," he says, "it was a case of retreat on the Western Front instead of attack. It was a dreadful disappointment for the Army in the west, worse, perhaps, for the public at home, and worst, as we had good reason to fear, for our allies. Loud rejoicing among our enemies ! Could more suitable material for propaganda be imagined ? The brilliant, if somewhat belated, visible result of the bloody battle, the collapse of German resistance, the impetuous, unceasing pursuit, the paroxysms about our methods of warfare ! We could hear all the stops being drawn out beforehand. What a hail of propagandist literature would now descend on and behind our lines ! Our great retirement began on March 16th, 1917. The enemy followed us into the open, generally speaking with considerable caution. Where this caution was inclined to give place to greater haste our rearguards knew how to cool down the enemy zeal. The measures we took not only gave us more favourable local conditions on the Western Front, but improved our whole situation. The shortening of our lines in the west made it possible for us to build up strong reserves. . . . The situation which we created for ourselves by the spring of 1917 may perhaps be described as a great stage of strategic 'stand-to,' a stage in which we abandoned the initiative to the enemy for the time being, but from which we could emerge at any time to attack any of the enemy's weak points."

From March 19th to the end of the month the Q.V.R. were mostly occupied in digging communication and assembly trenches in readiness for the "Easter Affray." At the customary intervals they were relieved by either the 2nd Londons or the Q.W.R., and on April 1st by the "Rangers." On the latter date the regiment went into rest billets in Monchiet. The next five days were spent in training and preparing for the IIIrd Army offensive operations. On April 7th a move was made from Monchiet at 6 p.m. to C.1 area, south-west of Agny, the transport and Q.M. stores being established in Achicourt. Ordered to support the 167th Infantry Brigade in offensive operations on April 9th, the Q.V.R. moved up at 9 p.m. on 8th, Easter Sunday. During the day from 11 a.m. till 5 p.m. Achicourt was heavily shelled and the Quartermaster's stores considerably damaged. Several houses in the village caught fire. At the time the place was crowded with lorries laden with heavy-gun ammunition Major Campbell, of the Kensingtons, pluckily drove a number of these out of harm's way, their drivers having bolted Although the village was full of troops and details, by some good fortune the casualties were few. The Q.V.R. transport here sustained their first casualty, Rfn. Trew, a water-cart driver, being killed.

Punctually at 5.30 next morning, Easter Monday, the new British offensive commenced. At 7.45 the 56th, 14th and 30th Divisions of the VIIth Corps were launched for the attack, and at 9.30 the Q.V.R. moved forward to a system of trenches south of Beaurains ; at 2.30 they were placed under the orders of the B.G.C. 167th Infantry Brigade for tactical purposes and ordered to advance. This was done in " artillery formation ' under fierce fire of 4·2-calibre guns and gas shells. Lieut Halifax and some of his platoon were wounded in a sunken road.

The situation on the evening of the 9th was apparently that the Hindenburg Line had been captured as far south as Lion Lane. South of that the 30th Division were held up by uncut wire and machine-guns. Orders were therefore issued for the 167th Brigade with Queen Victoria's Rifles attached to clear the Hindenburg Line as far south as the Wancourt Line (Nepa Trench). "At 12.40 a.m.," records Capt. Bowditch, " a warning order was given that the battalion would attack from Lion Trench with the Wancourt Line as the objective at 12 noon, and the C.O. and the company commanders went forward to reconnoitre the position. Battalion H.Q. were established in Neuville Vitasse ; Lion Lane was the place of assembly for the Q.V.R.

" The Lane," continues Capt. W. G. Bowditch, M.C., D.C.M. " was one of the cross-sections between the two main lines of the Cojeul Switch, as that portion of the Hindenburg Line was called. From Lion Lane an attack was to be made along the main line with the Wancourt Line as the objective, all the intervening cross-sections being taken in our stride. This portion of the Hindenburg Line was rather like a ladder in formation running from Tilloy in the north to Bullecourt in the south, and consisting of two main lines with cross-sections forming, as it were, the steps of a ladder. At a point between Heninel-sur-Cojeul and Wancourt it was crossed at right angles by another main line, running north-east and south-west, called the Wancourt Line. This was to be our objective and Lion Lane, from which the attack was to be made, was one of the steps in the ladder and lay a short distance south-east of Neuville Vitasse. We learned incidentally that at the moment the orders for the attack were being discussed Lion Lane was in the hands of the enemy, but the 1st Londons were carrying out a night bombing raid on the position and it was assumed that by the morning of 10th it would be clear and ready for us to take over for jumping off from. It had been arranged that the C.O. and the four company commanders should go forward and reconnoitre the position before the attack took place, and for that purpose a guide had been provided by the 1st Londons to escort the reconnaissance party to that battalion's H.Q. at the ruins of the Sugar Factory in Neuville Vitasse. There a further guide would be provided to take them as near as possible to Lion Lane. The party consisted of the C.O., Col. Follett, D.S.O., Lieut. Wallace, the Battalion Intelligence Officer, Capts. Hamilton, Hadden, Blackwood and Bowditch, a runner from 'B' Company named Reynolds, and the guide. The Germans had been putting up an occasional show with gas shells during the night but, all things considered, it was pretty quiet and respirators had only been called into use for short periods. The short distance to Neuville Vitasse was soon covered, and we commenced to scramble through the ruins towards the Sugar Factory. Then by some mischance our guide lost his direction, a very easy thing to do in such a place, and we found ourselves in the middle of the village instead of being on the southern outskirts. Then it began to snow heavily; the Germans started shelling the village with H.E., and to complete our discomfort our guide reluctantly admitted he was lost. It was an awkward position and it was grimly humorous to see the C.O. and Lieut. Wallace crouching in the bottom of a huge crater trying, with the aid of an electric torch which they hardly dared to show, and with a map which it was almost impossible to set correctly, owing to the weather conditions, to find out where we were and the position of the 1st Londons H.Q. As a result of their deliberations we started off again in what ultimately proved to be the right direction. One of the party, tripping over some wire, scrambled down a bank and literally fell into their H.Q., a cellar beneath the factory. Here we were furnished with another guide and warned that the position had not yet been cleared and that too close an approach might lead to uncomfortable results. The first sign of dawn was beginning to appear when we reached a point beyond which, said our guide, it was unhealthy to proceed. It seemed a pity, however, that having come so far we should go back without seeing at least the entrance to Lion Lane, so leaving our guide behind we pushed along the trench, the C.O. leading the way. At this juncture it occurred to one of the party to inquire of a comrade if he had got his revolver with him. The answer he received was in the negative and similar inquiries elicited the fact that all were in the same plight; having been summoned in haste to the midnight meeting one and all had set out armed with nothing but their small box-respirators! The chapter of accidents was completed when it was ascertained that although 'B' Company runner had dutifully brought his rifle with him the 'pull-through' had that evening got jammed in the barrel! Undeterred, however, we proceeded, and in a few minutes reached the entrance to the Lane, and having made mental notes of the surroundings returned to Neuville Vitasse and our respective companies, which we joined about 7.0 a.m. A brief explanation of the position having been given and the different platoons having been allotted their several parts in the show, the battalion was soon under way by companies for Neuville Vitasse.

"On emerging into the open at the far side of the village there was some danger of being observed by the enemy from their position at Wancourt, but we entered the Hindenburg Line almost immediately, without anything untoward happening until two or three companies were safely in the trench. Then the Germans commenced to shell the outskirts of the village, but fortunately did not cause any casualties. Movement along the trench was fairly easy, as it was one of the latest that the Boches had constructed, being about 8 feet deep, 6 feet wide at ground level, with a 4-feet footway at the bottom. At regular intervals there were large concrete dug-outs which the enemy had not had time to destroy before retreating.

" On our way we passed a solitary German prisoner sitting at the side of the trench with his escort looking dolefully at our troops as they passed. He was a small man, but he had evidently put up some sort of a show during the previous night's operations and appeared to have been stopped suddenly by some Tommy's fist, for he had a most wonderful black eye that spread a colour scheme over half of one side of his face. The troops were in high spirits and chaffed him as they passed, bringing an occasional sickly smile to his picturesque face.

" Zero hour was 12 noon, and by 11.45 we were all in our positions ready for the barrage to open. ' C ' and ' D ' Companies were in Lion Lane and were to form the first wave. ' A ' Company was in a parallel trench a few yards in rear ready to act as a second wave, while ' B ' Company was in support in the main trench in rear of ' A.' At noon precisely the barrage began and the British attack started, and we (' A ' Company) stood ready to take our cue from the first wave, but, to our amazement no first wave appeared. At first we thought that they were a trifle slow in getting off the mark, but as the barrage crept forward to its full length, then halted and died away, and still no first wave appearing, it became pretty evident that all was not well with the leading companies. A patrol was accordingly sent down the main trench to Lion Lane to get information and returned soon after with the news that a German M.G. post still held the far end of the Lane and in consequence threatened the left flank of the leading wave. Capt. Hadden (' D ' Company) had set to work in the short time at his disposal to attempt to dislodge the Boches in time to allow his wave to go over. Up to twelve o'clock, however, all attempts had been unsuccessful, as had those of the 1st Londons during the preceding night, the Boche position being a very strong one. In the circumstances Capt. Hadden declined to let his company advance and the wave to be subjected to deadly enfilade fire from the enemy machine-guns. The news led to hurried consultations at H.Q. It was plain that no attack could be made across the open, and it was ultimately decided to resort to trench bombing tactics and to reach our objective by that method instead of attacking over the top.

"By 2.30 the companies had been formed into strong bombing parties"

In this connection Capt. Hamilton adds : " Communication from the front line was exceedingly difficult and it took a considerable time to get into touch with H.Q. This was exemplified by the fact that our message to the artillery about the Boche machine-gun which was holding us up took so long to reach them that they started a beautiful strafe on the exact spot about half an hour after the Boches had been driven out. Several men of 'D' Company were there at the moment, imagining they were going to have a few minutes rest and had to decamp with some speed."

"Within a short time," resumes Capt. Bowditch, " we had captured the nest of trenches known to us as 'The Egg' together with five Officers and 63 O.R. of the 31st German Regiment with 4 machine-guns. The enemy artillery had now got fully into action and had the range of our newly occupied positions to such a nicety as to make things decidedly unhealthy for both our troops and their prisoners. Here a German officer proved to be of some use. Among the stores lying about were supplies of 'Very' pistols and cartridges, and when the German artillery fire became so hot as to endanger the lives of both the captors and their captives it was suggested to one of the German officers that he should put up a signal to tell his artillery that they were firing on their own men. There was no fear of treachery from him as his interest at the moment was identical with ours. We therefore gave him a pistol and he fired the signal into the air, with the result after one or two more rounds the fire ceased altogether and allowed us to proceed along their trenches towards the Wancourt Line and to bomb the dug-outs in perfect comfort.

"We were now enabled to see the effect of our own artillery fire during the few days preceding our advance. The platoons detailed to clear up Zoo Trench soon after passing 'The Egg' lost sight of the main trench altogether and had to trace their route to the objective by the few remnants that were discoverable. The trench itself was reduced to a mass of shell-holes and was so much like the adjacent ground as to completely lose its identity as a trench. When it is remembered that before the bombardment it was about 6 feet deep and 6 feet across the top it will convey some idea of the intensity of a bombardment which had rendered it level with the surrounding ground. How many of the enemy were buried in the battered trench we never learned. The main line running parallel with it, up which the other platoons advanced had not fared so severely, but was badly knocked about in places as also were the shorter trenches connecting the two main lines."

"It was during the afternoon of this day," according to Capt. Hamilton, "while 'D' Company were in support in 'The Egg' that we saw a very rare incident in modern warfare. The plain to the N.E. of our position had now been cleared by the division on our left, and a cavalry division suddenly appeared on the scene, the horse gunners unlimbering and coming into action in the open. It reminded one very much of a big field-day at Aldershot in the old pre-war days." Capt. Hamilton relates another incident which rather amused those who were concerned in it. "Twice," he says, "during the evening the officers of 'D' Company, who were in 'The Egg,' received visits from officers of the division on our right flank to ask how near they were to 'The Egg' and Zoo Trench, as they had come up to reconnoitre these positions with a view to attacking them later in the evening. Their surprise was almost comical when they learned that they were actually in the trenches in question and had been in possession of the Q.V.R. for some five or six hours."

Returning to Capt. Bowditch's account that officer says : "It was early evening when we drew close to the Wancourt Line and where the enemy made a determined stand. A small force held a very strong position at the point which was to be our objective, and kept up a continuous fire of granatenwerfer, rifle grenades and machine-guns that made it necessary for us to pause and establish a position in a convenient trench, for to go forward in the open in the daylight was to court disaster. The short time that remained before darkness set in was spent in consolidating the position against the possibility of a counter attack, and in organising a further bombing attack which was to be launched as soon as it became dark enough to cover our movements.

"It had been a strenuous day. From dawn until dusk it had been spent in marching to our first position, there waiting on the qui vive for the attack and then bombing down the enemy's lines until the objective was almost reached, in spite of the fact that the attack, as originally planned, had been baulked at the outset. The men had worked as only British Tommies can work, scrambling over wire entanglements and battered trenches, searching dug-outs, deploying across the open when necessary, carrying forward fresh supplies of ammunition, and performing a host of other fatiguing duties inseparable from a great attack. Everything had been carried out with wonderful vigour and spirit, such as is known only to troops that are fighting and winning; still, there could be no thought of rest for anyone. The enemy might counter-attack at any moment and we must be ready to beat them off. And in any case our final objective must be gained before the dawn of the coming day. All the time we worked the enemy kept up an incessant fire, inflicting a number of casualties, but through it all we succeeded in putting the position into a state of defence.

"When darkness permitted, a patrol reconnoitred the enemy's position and a bombing party was sent forward to dislodge them. This attempt, however, proved abortive and the bombers were compelled to retire. Almost immediately another and stronger patrol, led by Lieut. Gibb, made the attempt, but again it was unsuccessful, the patrol being forced back over our barricade. The enemy had been reinforced by sufficient numbers to enable them to counter-attack in the open and to try to cut off our patrol. The Middlesex Regiment on our left had now reached a position from which they made an attack on the enemy's right flank, but it proved as unsuccessful as our own. It was then decided to make a concerted attack. A Stokes Trench Mortar was brought up and as much ammunition as was possible served out to the riflemen and Lewis gunners. Fresh supplies of bombs were hurried forward and Lieut. Spaul, the Q.V.R. Bombing Officer, came up to organise the parties for a supreme effort. It was nearly dawn when arrangements were completed, and although none of them had had half an hour's rest all went forward to the attack as vigorously as if following a good night's rest. At the first onslaught the enemy began to give way, though peppering the rear of the parties the whole time with rifle grenades and granatenwerfer. Additional bombs were rushed forward, everybody carrying loads that would have caused them to stagger at ordinary times. But we were winning. It is astonishing what a wonderful tonic that is. The men continued to press forward, and at 5.30, just as dawn was breaking, the position was won, with the enemy retreating by any meaus available, leaving their dead and wounded behind and the Q.V.R. masters of the field.

"A few minutes later there was light sufficient to enable us to perceive our late opponents scrambling away across the open, the trench affording too slow a means of escape from our attack. It was our turn now, and in a few seconds that portion of the Wancourt Line was manned and every rifle and Lewis gun turned on the fugitives. Unfortunately before any telling work could be put in they had gone to earth again in a shallow trench about 200 yards away. Whether it was their intention to dig in there and consolidate we did not know, but if such was their plan it was spoiled by an unexpected event which once more turned things in our favour.

"Almost simultaneous with our last bombing raid an infantry attack of fairly large proportions had been made under a barrage by troops on our right. The attack was supported by tanks, one of which seemed to be prowling about in search of more game. In our excitement we had paid scant attention to what was happening elsewhere and it came as a surprise to see the tank loom out of the semi-darkness and make for the spot where the last of our opponents had disappeared. It reached a point abreast of their cover and commenced to pump ammunition into them with such good effect that they once more came out of their holes and made off across the open. This gave another opportunity for rifle and Lewis gun and, as by this time the light was considerably stronger, we managed to pay off all the scores owing for the previous night's hold-up, and though some managed to escape a good number paid the toll."

From the high ground beyond larger German forces covered the retreat with rifle and machine-gun fire, causing a casualty here and there among those of our men who in the heat of victory exposed themselves too much. It was about this time that Lieut. D. F. Johnstone had to retire, after doing sterling work, with a bullet wound in his shoulder.

An examination of the captured position revealed the fact that the Germans were just about to have breakfast when they were disturbed, and "some sliced sausage, black bread of very good quality and, most welcome sight of all, boiled eggs neatly packed in paper boxes" rewarded the supperless and breakfastless, but victorious Vics. Plentiful stores of trench weapons were also found, including "Pineapple" bombs, with which the granatenwerfer had so liberally bespattered the attackers the night before, hand grenades, large quantities of S.A.A. and two or three machine-guns.

During the earlier operations Lieut. Ralls was wounded, and Riflemen Stancombe and Ireland killed.

Lieut. Smith, "B" Company, took over the first turn of duty following the capture of the position. The tank, which had rendered such valuable assistance and remained crawling about, and its commander paid a visit to Lieut. Smith in the trenches and arranged with him a series of signals by which information could be conveyed during a short reconnaisance it was proposed to make in the direction where the enemy was last seen. Unfortunately while standing in a rather exposed position to receive a signal from the tank Lieut. Smith was mortally wounded by a German sniper, a few of whom were still lurking under cover in the vicinity, and died before he could be carried to the rear. What might have been a very useful scheme cost the life of a very fine officer.

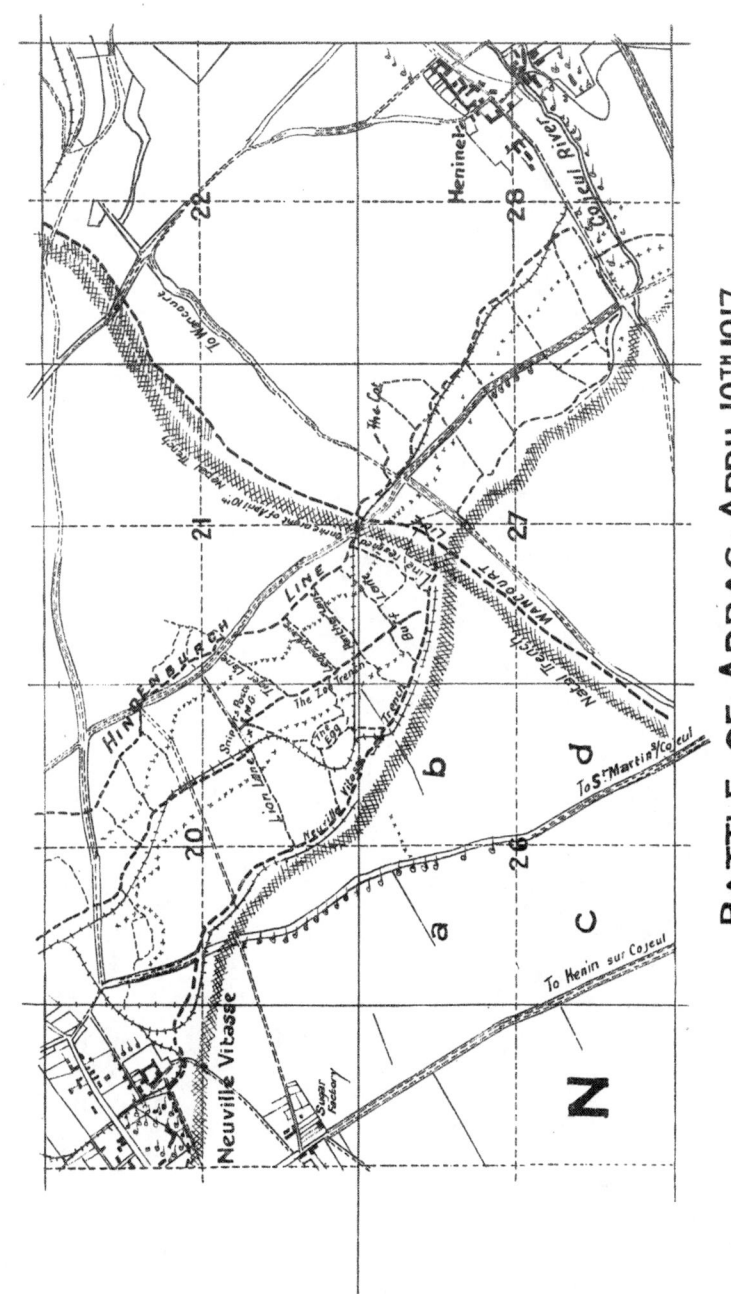

CHAPTER XXVII

IN THE COJEUL VALLEY AND THE ADVANCE ON CHERISY

"WE were not permitted to linger in our newly gained quarters," proceeds Capt. Bowditch, "for fresh troops were pushed forward to take over the Wancourt Line and we received orders to occupy all trenches down to the River Cojeul. Shortly before noon 'B' Company occupied 'the Cot' and pushing forward with 'A' Company and meeting with but slight resistance established posts in various trenches branching from the main line. Before evening fell the battalion was withdrawn to trenches in the neighbourhood of 'the Egg,' the lines we had lately occupied being taken over by troops that had moved up during the day. In the course of the night Lieut. Wallace (the Battalion I.O.) and one officer from each company went forward in the direction of Heninel studying the ground to be covered in the next day's operations. Before dawn on Thursday, April 12th, we were on the move in order to reach the cover of the Cojeul Valley before our advance could be detected. As it was, the enemy threw a few shells over the ground we had to traverse, fortunately without causing us any casualties. The four companies were distributed in the low ground just S.W. of Heninel, which had been taken during the attack on the morning of 11th, and a little beyond the Cojeul. There we spent a fairly quiet day, living for the most part in the open though there were plenty of dug-outs at hand for such as preferred to use them as sleeping quarters. Battalion H.Q. was established in 'the Cot' and for the first time during these operations visual signalling was possible between it and the companies, which seemed to herald the arrival of the long-looked-forward-to open warfare. Routine and reconnaissance work was carried on as usual, and while engaged on the latter a party from ' A ' Company discovered a deep German dug-out about 200 yards in length and having five or six entrances provided with wooden staircases. At one end we found some half a dozen wounded British soldiers who had been taken prisoners a few days previously and with them a couple of wounded Germans who had been left behind by their comrades when they retired. By means of signal flags stretcher parties were summoned and were soon on the spot to remove the wounded to a safer place in rear. A search revealed large stores of food and clothing, and once more our boys regaled themselves on German sausage, while those who needed them exchanged their old worn boots for new ones at the expense of Fritz. Orders had been issued warning all ranks against touching any food left behind by the enemy, but it is much easier to give such orders in the snug security of Divisional or Corps H.Q. than to have them obeyed in the van of an attack, and it was not unnatural that more palatable food should be welcomed when within easy reach, especially when ' Fray Bentos ' and biscuits had been the staple diet for more than a week.

" On active service the life of a pair of boots is not very long and during the last few days our boots had been worn-out and torn out at a very rapid rate, and although the efficiency of our ' Q ' department had kept most of our wants supplied it was an impossibility to meet the needs of a battalion advancing rapidly over such ground as we had covered. In these circumstances it did not take many minutes to empty the German store of everything worth having in the way of creature comforts.

"About 5 p.m. we received orders to support the 2nd Londons in an attack to be made on the following morning from the high ground beyond the Guemappe Road, where the Fusiliers had been preparing a jumping-off trench. The objective of the attack was the small town of Cherisy on the River Sensee. The necessary preparations having been made, the companies were moved at dawn to their supporting positions in readiness to go forward when the barrage opened, but for some reason there was no barrage, the premeditated attack was postponed and the day was spent in awaiting developments. In the evening orders were received for the Q.V.R.

to relieve the 2nd Londons in the front line. The relief was completed about 11 p.m., and just as sentries and patrols were being arranged, company commanders were summoned to Battalion H.Q. in a dug-out near the cemetery at Heninel. There we learned that the attack would take place at dawn on 14th.

"It was a decidedly sleepy set of officers that sat and listened to the C.O. as he read out the orders for the attack and detailed the duties allotted to companies. For the last six days few of them had enjoyed more than a couple of hours sleep in any twenty-four and the effect showed itself on every face in the small circle as we alternately nodded and jerked ourselves into wakefulness while we digested as well as we could the details of the scheme. The attack was to be made on a two-battalion front, each battalion moving on a two-company front and each company advancing in two lines. The leading battalions were the Q.V.R. on the right and Queen's Westminsters on the left. The 2nd Londons were in support of the Q.V.R., and the L.R.B. of the Q.W.R. To the Westminsters was allotted the actual taking of Cherisy and to the Q.V.R. the capture of the enemy positions running south from the end of the village to a small wood, a little to the north of Fontaine-les-Croisilles. The completion of our task after assaulting these positions lay in the establishment of a number of strong points on the road running through Cherisy and on the bank of the River Sensee, which at that point ran almost north and south about 400 yards beyond. The most minute details having been given and received the officers returned to their companies to go through them again with the platoon commanders and N.C.O.'s. It was close upon four o'clock when that had been done, and as the barrage was to open at five little, if any, time remained for sleep.

"To most of us the enterprise appeared to be over rash. In front of the Q.V.R. at a distance of about 1800 yards from the starting-point and about 1000 yards short of the final objective was an enemy trench about 800 yards in length which had only recently been dug and manned. Part of our job was to take this trench in our stride and dropping 'A' and 'B' Companies there to consolidate the position; the second wave consisting of 'C' and 'D' Companies would pass over 'A' and 'B,' and follow a creeping barrage to the final objective. Those of us who had seen on the previous day the ground to be traversed and formed a fairly shrewd idea of the positions of the enemy's M.Gs. realised the difficulties of the task that lay before us. There was, however, no time to discuss the chances of the show.

"Promptly at 5.0 a.m. the barrage opened and the ill-fated attack commenced. The men were as splendid as ever. In spite of the fatigues they had experienced, nearly everyone went over with a laugh and a joke, and the front lines of 'A' and 'B' Companies as they went forward were almost as regular as if they had been 'dressed by the right' before advancing. Our barrage was as fierce as could be desired, but it was only a shrapnel barrage and could only protect us from infantry retaliation. Within a few seconds, or so it seemed, the German heavy guns opened a counter-barrage on the advancing lines and played havoc among our men. Still they pushed on to their objective, their numbers sadly depleted. The enemy H.E., however, had checked their attempt to keep close up to our barrage, which gradually crept further and further away, with the result that before the first objective was reached our guns firing to the time-table had lifted beyond and our men as they advanced were at the mercy of the German infantry and machine gunners who could now come up and open a decimating fire. To add to our discomfort a deadly enfilade fire was opened on our left from a trench hidden from our view at the starting-point by a steep bank, and as we pushed on this became almost a reverse fire. Thus we had machine-guns and rifles pumping lead into our ranks from both front and rear with the heavy guns to complete what they left undone. About twenty of each of the leading companies succeeded in reaching a point some 60 yards short of the first objective, and there, taking cover behind a shallow bank or any mound that seemed to offer safety, they returned the enemy's fire as fast as they were able. For a quarter of an hour there was a desperate short range rifle duel between the remnants of 'A' and 'B' Companies and the German infantry in front. Then the guns gradually ceased fire and the battle fizzled out, leaving a small body of our men isolated in front of the enemy's position, unable to move either backward or forward, as for anyone to stand up or even to show any part of his body, drew an instant hail of bullets in his direction. There they were constrained to lie, the majority of them wounded, but all ready to put up a fight if any attempt was made on the part of the enemy to take them prisoners. Why the attempt was not made was a source of wonder, since we were over a mile from the nearest British line and dead ground between the two prevented any chance of their being seen. The only conclusion we could come to was that the Boches, even though they had beaten off the attack, had not the courage to exploit their success.

"The little remnant of the Q.V.R. had no choice but to hang on where they were in the hope that darkness would find them still alive and able to crawl back to the trench they had started from. There was a long time to wait, and the chances against their ever getting back were many. They had reached their present position about 5.30 a.m. and it would not be dark enough to make the attempt until about half-past eight or nine at night! Fortunately the weather was fine, and though they were denied the consolation of a cigarette, as the ascending wreath of smoke would have given their position away to German sentries only 60 yards distant, they preserved their spirits to the end. The day, however, did not pass without its thrills. Quite early in the morning a sound of vigorous bombing not far off on their right front attracted their attention. This they afterwards learned was due to a determined but unsuccessful attempt by some of the men of the front and support companies to bomb their way into the objective by way of a flanking trench on which they had stumbled during the attack. At another time an unpleasant quarter of an hour was occasioned by shells from our own artillery, who were unaware of their wherabouts, bursting over them.

"Certain men had been provided with red ground flares, which were to have been lit on our obtaining the objective to acquaint the artillery of the position of the foremost troops. These flares when lit after a successful engagement always had the disadvantage of disclosing our positions to the enemy's artillery as well as our own, and in the present circumstances it would have been suicidal to attempt to use one. Meanwhile a British aeroplane hovered around giving the signal on a klaxon horn for the flares to be lit to show where our foremost line lay. The plane flew so low, despite the German fire aimed at it, that the pilot could be distinctly seen by those on the ground, and it was highly exasperating to them to be unable to give the signal which would save them from their own artillery fire. This object, however, was ultimately achieved by a man in 'A' Company (Rfn. Hawtin) who possessed a red handkerchief. It being impossible to wave it he attached it to the back of his haversack and moved it backwards and forwards over a few feet of ground. This fortunately produced the desired effect, for the pilot flew back and our guns shortly after lifted their range.

"At one time during the morning a large stack of German shells which stood right in the midst of our men was partially ignited by gunfire and the fuses commenced to send out spurts of fire in all directions, causing those nearest to it to crawl to a safer distance as quickly as they were able. Fortunately nothing further resulted from this. Had the whole stack exploded it must have killed nearly all who remained after the attack had failed. During the afternoon a relief took place in the concealed German line from which the enfilade fire had been directed in the morning. This gave rise to increased anxiety as it looked at one time as if a large German force was going to move across the ground where our men were lying. Everyone prepared to put up as good a fight as possible but their relief was great when they saw the Boches move off in a different direction. During quiet intervals those who were unwounded or only slightly hurt did the best they could to lighten their comrades' sufferings by crawling among them and bandaging their wounds. Some, alas, were beyond all aid and died before the close of day, others were killed even while this work of mercy was going on.

"At long last evening began to fall and all who could do so commenced the journey back to the British lines as soon as it was sufficiently dark to cover their movements. Only the dead and the dying were left behind. The badly hurt were assisted by their more fortunate comrades. Thus every man who was conscious was by one means and another brought into our lines, whence stretcher bearers were sent out to scour the ground for further survivors. The Germans, evidently suspect ing what was happening, put a heavy bombardment all over the scene of the morning's advance, inflicting a few additional casualties among those who were making their way back, having survived the dangers of the day only to fall when almost within reach of safety."

The total casualties for the day were returned approximately at 11 officers and 350 Other Ranks killed and wounded. Among the wounded officers was Capt. Bowditch, from whose notes the foregoing account of the battle has been chiefly compiled. Included in the officers killed were Lieut. How in command of " B " Company ; Lieut. Blackwood, also " B " Company ; and Lieut. Gibb, " A " Company ; and Lieuts. Bartman and Saxby, all of whom died of wounds.

In addition to the difficulties besetting the advance mentioned by Capt. Bowditch, Capt. Hamilton of " D " Company, which with " C " were to constitute the second wave, says : " We were badly handicapped by some Boche Sausage balloons which spent a large part of the day in watching our every movement. The result was that the German barrage opened on our front line almost as soon as ' A ' and ' B ' Companies left it, and made it quite hopeless for the subsequent waves to get through. Certainly in ' D ' Company I don't think anyone succeeded. I was wounded right in the barrage myself, and there were very few of the company advancing then. When I got back to Heninel Cemetery the remnant of the company, consisting of a sergeant and a handful of men, had already returned to Battalion H.Q. for further instructions."

At eleven at night the battalion was relieved by the 4th London Regiment and returned to " the Egg," and on the afternoon of 15th it went to Beaurains into dug-outs. There it stayed until 19th, when it was conveyed by motor-bus to Souastre, where it remained until 23rd of April.

CHAPTER XXVIII

MORE CONCERNING "THE GREAT CRISIS AT ARRAS"
(HINDENBURG)

WRITING on May 12th Mr. Philip Gibbs (*Daily Telegraph* Correspondent) says : " In all the battles of this war London men have fought as well as any of our fighting men, from whatever part of the Empire they have come. As well, and that is good enough. From one end of the front to the other, from Ypres Salient to the Somme, and later, the Royal Fusiliers and the Queen Victoria Rifles and the Middlesex Regiment and the Rangers and the Post Office Rifles and the Kensingtons and the City of London Regiment have held the lines and gone over the bags and struggled forward through shell-slashed woods, and proved themselves every time worthy sons of the great old city which is London.

ATTACK AT DAWN

" On April 9th the Londoners' attack at dawn was one of the splendid episodes of the battle. They went through the German lines in long waves, and streamed forward like a living tide, very quick and very far, taking a thousand prisoners on their way. Later in the day they were held up on their right flank by enfilade fire, as the troops on their right were in difficulties against the uncut wire and machine-guns, and from that time onwards the London men had perilous hours and hard and costly fighting. They were forced to extend beyond their line on the left to join up a gap between themselves and the troops to their north, and to work down with bombing parties on the right to gain ground in which the Germans were holding out desperately and inflicting many casualties on our men. In the centre London men were ordered to attack fortified villages from which machine-gun bullets swept the ground, and where our assault was checked by stout belts of wire with unbroken strands. It was in those hours on April 9th and 10th that many young London men showed the highest qualities of spirit, risking death and worse than death with most careless gallantry and steeling their hearts against any creeping fear. A young subaltern saw those wire traps in the centre of a village and led the way to them with a party of bombers and Lewis gunners, and smashed them up and jumped on the machine-guns beyond. It opened the gate to all the other Londoners, who swept through this village and beyond. Many officers fell, but there was always someone to take command and lead the men, a sergeant with a cool head, a 2nd lieutenant with a flame in his eye. It was a boy of nineteen who took command of one company when he was the only one to lead. He had never been under fire before, and had never seen all this blood and horror. He was a slip of a fellow who had been spelling out fairy tales ten years ago, which is not far back in history. Now he led a company of fighting men, who followed him as a great captain all through that day's battle, and from one German line to another, and from one village to another, until all the ground had been gained according to the first plan.

Gallant Young Officers

"It was a battle of second lieutenants of London, owing to the heavy casualties of commanding officers. One of them was wounded in the head early in the day, but led his men until hours later he fell and fainted. Another young officer went out with three men in the darkness when the infantry was held up by serious obstacles, and, under heavy fire, brought back information which saved many lives, and enabled the whole line to advance. There was a second lieutenant who behaved with a quick decision and daring which seemed inspired by something more than sound judgment. The enemy was holding out in a trench and sweeping men down with that death-rattle of bullets which is the worst thing in all this fighting. In front of them was uncut wire, which is always a trap. Our London lieutenant did not go straight ahead. He flung his platoon round to the flank, smashed through the wire here, and sprang at the German gun team with a revolver in one hand and a bomb in the other. The whole team was destroyed except one man, who fell wounded, and above those dead bodies the second lieutenant waved his revolver to his men, and said, ' Let's get on.' The London men went on for nine days, which is like ninety years on such a battle-field. They went on until they were checked and held by the enemy, who had time to rush up strong reserves and bring up new weight of guns. The shell-fire increased hour by hour. From many hidden places machine-guns poured bullets across the ground. German snipers lay out in shell-holes picking off our men. This sniping was intolerable, and a second lieutenant and a sergeant crawled out into No Man's Land to deal with it. They dragged three snipers out of one hole, and searched others, and helped to check this hidden fire. One London rifleman went forward to kill a machine-gun with its hideous tat-tat-tat. It was a bolder thing than St. George's attack on the dragon, which was a harmless beast compared with this spit-fire devil. The rifle man armed himself with a Lewis gun, carried at the hip, and fired so coolly that he scattered the German team and captured the gun.

London Pride

" All through those nine days, and afterwards in a second spell worse than those, the London men lived under a great fire, those that had the luck to live. And though their nerves were all frayed with the strain of it, and they suffered agonies, they never lost courage, and kept their pride—London pride. It is absurd to tell single instances, except as examples. Every hour of those frightful hours was filled with brave acts by great numbers of men in this comradeship of terror, the living terror which is war. . . . A London private remained out to look after the wounded in an exposed place, and in his spare time saved other men attacked by small parties of Germans by killing nine of them and taking one man prisoner. Another second lieutenant, one of those boys who have poured out the blood of youth upon these battlefields, took two Vickers guns with their teams through two barrages—only those who have seen a barrage can know the meaning of that—and, by great skill and cunning, carried his men through without a single casualty, so that the infantry followed with high hearts. Out of a burning billet, and out of an exploding ammunition dump a transport driver brought some charges urgently needed for battle. A man who entered a cage of tigers to draw their teeth would not want greater nerve than this. But why go on ? Those London men on the Arras battlefield went about their business, a grim and ugly business, not at all to their liking, with a fine pride and spirit, fine and beautiful in spite of filthy sights and sounds, abominable agonies, and most damnable strife of men."

How near we were to success on that eventful Easter Monday Hindenburg himself testifies. "The attack was prepared for days with the whole fury of masses of enemy artillery and trench mortars. There was nothing of the surprise tactics which Nivelle had employed in the October of the previous year. Did not the English believe in these tactics, or did they feel themselves too inexperienced to adopt them ? For the moment the reason was immaterial. The fact alone was sufficient and spoke a fearful language. The English attack swept over our first, second and third lines. Groups of strong points were overwhelmed or silenced after a heroic resistance. Masses of artillery were lost. Our defensive system had apparently failed !

"A serious crisis was supervened, one of those situations in which everything appears to be beyond control. . . . The evening report of this April 9th revealed rather a dark picture. Many shadows—little light. In such cases more light must be sought. A ray appeared, though a tiny flickering ray. The English did not seem to have known how to exploit the success they had gained to the full. This was a piece of luck for us, as so often before. After the report I pressed the hand of my first Quartermaster-General with the words : ' We have lived through more critical times than to-day together.' To-day ! It was his birthday ! My confidence was unshaken. I knew that reinforcements were marching to the battlefield and that trains were hastening that way. The crisis was over. Within me it was certainly over. But the battle raged on."

In reference to these operations the following congratulatory testimonials to the courage, ability and endurance displayed by all ranks appeared in orders :

169th Infantry Brigade.

May I be allowed to express my thanks and that of my Brigade for the splendid work of your men, especially the Queen Victoria Rifles, did on the 11th April.

Our men were absolutely held up by uncut wire and machine-guns, but the Queen Victoria Rifles bombed down my front and allowed us to get in, after which, I am glad to say, we were able to do exactly the same thing that night and clear the front of the 21st Division, and gain the high ground south of the River Cojeul.

It was entirely owing to the grand work you did that we were enabled to do this.

May our appreciation of what they did be communicated to the troops concerned.

(Sgd.) H. STANLEY, Brig.-Gen.,
13/4/1917.   89th Infantry Brigade.

Brigadier-General-Commanding, 169th Infantry Brigade.
G/931.

In forwarding the attached message from the B.G.C., 89th Infantry Brigade, may I be permitted to add my appreciation of the fine work done by the Officers, N.C.O.'s and Men of the Queen Victoria's Rifles.

In particular, I would refer to the great assistance rendered by Lieut.-Col. Follett, who, by his clear reports, grasp of the situation, and handling of his battalion, was of the greatest value to me.

(Sgd.) G. FREETH, Brig.-Gen.,
Commanding 167th Brigade.

O.C., Q.V.R.   B.M./843.

Forwarded for communication to all ranks. The Brigadier is very proud to hear that your battalion did such excellent work in addition to that which it performed while under his command.

(Sgd.) L. A. NEWNHAM, Capt.,
Brig.-Major,
16/4/1917.   169th Infantry Brigade.

"THE GREAT CRISIS AT ARRAS"

169*th Infantry Brigade.*

The G.O.C. has received with great pleasure a report from the officer commanding the 513th Field Company, R.E., on the gallant conduct of your Brigade Pioneers belonging to the L.R.B. and Q.V.R., attached 513th Field Company, during and after the bombardment of Achicourt which occurred on April 8th, 1917.

He wishes to convey to them, through you, his warm appreciation of their good work.

(Sgd.) H. W. GRUBB, Lieut.-Col.,
16/4/1917.   A.A. & Q.M.G., 56th Division.

O.C., L.R.B.   S.C./243k.
Q.V.R.

In forwarding the attached the G.O.C. wishes to add his congratulations of the gallant conduct displayed by your Brigade Pioneers.

(Sgd.) E. R. BROADBENT, Capt.,
Staff Capt.,
16/4/1917.   169th Infantry Brigade.

To O.C. Companies, Q.V.R.

Will you please read this out in conjunction with the attached reports on the Battalion to all the men of your company. High praise as they contain, it is no more than they deserve. Throughout the recent operations they have proved that in endurance, cheerfulness, and pluck they have no superiors, and have added to the fame of the regiment. My only regret is that so many of those who did so much towards the success of the Battalion are now no longer with us, especially 2nd Lieut. How, who was such a splendid example to all in courage and ability. I have no fear that in the future, whatever they are called upon to do, they will not fail to keep up the reputation they have earned.

(Sgd.) F. B. FOLLETT, Lieut.-Col,
O.C., 1st Bn., Q.V.R.

Capt. Henry Stear Blackwood ("C" Company), was educated at Eton and joined the Q.V.R. on the outbreak of war. He was severely wounded in the attack on Cherisy on April 14th and died of his wounds on May 1st. He was twenty-three years of age, and was the only son of the late Hans Stevenson Blackwood, of Meath Court, Goring, Oxfordshire, and grandson of the late Rev. the Hon. William Stear Blackwood, of Ballinderry, Co. Meath.

Lieut. H. J. How served as a Territorial in the Q.V.R. previous to the war from 1909 to March 1914. On the outbreak of the war he once more joined as a Rifleman (No. 2375), and went out to France with the battalion on November 4th. He speedily worked his way up through the ranks to Company Sergeant-Major and was eventually given a Commission in the field, in December, 1916. On April 12th he was placed in command of his company by Lieut.-Col. Follett, O.C., owing to his great courage and ability, and two days later was mortally wounded while leading his men to the attack. In a letter to his father Col. Follett wrote : " Had he lived I should have made him a Company Commander on the first opportunity." Lieut. How was three times mentioned in dispatches. He took part in the severe fighting for the possession of Hill 60 under Lieut. H. G. Woolley, V.C., and his name appeared in the special order issued by Col. R. B. Shipley, following the battle.

Lieut. Gibb was attached to the Q.V.R. from the 11th London Regiment.

The following awards for valuable services were made in connection with these operations :—

Lieut.-Col. F. B. Follett, M.C., was awarded the D.S.O.

For great bravery and fine leadership as a company commander throughout the operations on April 10th and by his initiative, perseverance and courage, 2nd Lieut. George William Bowditch was largely responsible for the successful attack on Wancourt Line, thereby attaining the final objective and capturing three machine-guns. On April 14th Lieut. Bowditch led his company as far as the first objective, where he was compelled to lie out in front of the enemy wire. In the evening although wounded he directed the withdrawal of the few remaining men. He then reported to Battn. H.Q., giving a valuable detailed account of the enemy movement throughout the day. During the whole of the operations his cheerfulness and courage permeated, and he dealt with the many difficult situations which confronted him with the greatest ability. On 15th May following he was awarded the Military Cross.

2nd Lieut. G. D. Mayer with great bravery led the attack as far as the Cojeul River, and was thereby responsible for the capture of the system of trenches from the Wancourt Line to the river. By his untiring energy and dash he succeeded in expelling the enemy from many blocks and posts, and he never failed to press them when he saw their hold was weakening. He set his men a fine example until he fell wounded in the advance on Cherisy on April 14th. Lieut. Mayer was awarded the M.C. for these services.

When the advance from Lion Trench was held up by machine-gun fire from an established post, Sergt. Herbert Tuckley made two attempts to get within bombing distance of the position. Later he was instrumental in the clearing of this post, and by his good leadership and dash enabled the advance to proceed. The obtaining of this objective by this company was due in great measure to the fine example of courage shown by this N.C.O. For this service he was granted the Military Medal.

On April 14th, during the attack at dawn, Sergt. Harry Ingis Spiller led his platoon through a heavy barrage as far as the enemy wire. By his splendid courage and fine leadership he compelled others who might have taken cover to follow him to the objective. He remained under the wire throughout the day and superintended the withdrawal of his men under cover of darkness. He never neglected an opportunity to inflict casualties upon the enemy and imparted a similar spirit to all under his command. He was one of seven N.C.O.'s that won the Military Medal during these operations.

Sergt. Wilfrid Horace Pearson with a few men was cut off from the rest of his company at the top of a communicaton trench leading into the first objective, which was strongly held by the enemy. He organised several bombing attacks, but they all failed owing to lack of numbers, whereupon he established a block in the trench and prevented any hostile advance. In this he was assisted by Sergt. Percy George Rowe, who then reported to Battn. H.Q., giving the exact position of the post and other valuable information. He returned to the post in daylight although continually shot at by snipers. At nightfall he assisted in the withdrawal of the wounded and displayed fine courage in face of very adverse conditions. Both these sergeants were recipients of the M.M.

During the assault on the German trenches at Heninel, Capt. Austin Basil Clark, R.A.M.C., and attached as M.O. to the Q.V.R., showed the greatest energy and courage under continuous shell and machine-gun fire, attending to the wounded in the open. After dark he went out and searched the ground over which the unsuccessful attack had taken place and was responsible for a very large number of wounded being brought back into the lines, despite continuous machine-gun fire from the enemy. He was recommended for a bar to the M.C. he had previously been awarded.

On the morning of 14th Rfn. A. W. Tolliday, a company signaller, went forward to the most advanced post established. At one point there was a bridge across a C.T. which the enemy had rendered very difficult to pass beneath. Rfn. Tolliday managed to crawl under and deepened the aperture so that wounded men could pass through. All the time he was working on this part of the trench he was under persistent rifle fire, and without his assistance the traffic in the trench would undoubtedly have been blocked.

During the attack on 14th inst. Rfn. W. H. Riddle climbed out of a communication trench and while fully exposed to the enemy's fire kept down several snipers who were inflicting casualties on the men in the trench. Despite the fact that men who had previously made the attempt had been shot he remained in the same position for about five hours, and it was entirely due to the resourcefulness and courage of Rfn. Riddle that many more casualties did not occur. For this he received the Military Medal.

Rfn. Robert James Hawtin (4703) went with one of the assaulting companies that was compelled to lie out under the enemy's fire throughout the day. In order to draw the attention of a contact control aeroplane to the position of his company he waved a red handkerchief, and although he immediately drew the enemy's fire on himself he continued his signals for some time. For this he was awarded the Croix de Guerre.

BATTLE OF ARRAS APRIL 14TH 1917.

Another recipient of the Military Medal was a young headquarter's runner, Rfn. George Thomas Phillips. On two occasions when volunteers were asked for he went forward through a very heavy artillery barrage and machine-gun fire to get touch with the assaulting companies. His information was always accurate and of the greatest value, and he was at all times entirely regardless of personal risk. On his own initiative he organised leaderless men into groups, and by his coolness and self-confidence in the face of great danger was a splendid example to all.

CHAPTER XXIX

THE THIRD BATTLE OF YPRES—THE FIGHT IN GLENCORSE
WOOD AND INVERNESS COPSE

ON April 24th the battalion moved to new billets in Wanquetin, on the 26th to Berneville, and on the 28th to trenches near "Airy Corner," taking over on the following day the front line East of Guemappe from the 3rd and 1st London Regiments.

On May 1st the battalion was relieved in the line by the 2nd Londons. On 2nd it rested during the day and moved up at midnight to the Assembly Area W. of Guemappe, the move being made through a heavy gas shell bombardment. At 3.45 a.m.—Zero hour for the Ist, IIIrd and Vth Armies' offensive—the battalion moved to assembly trenches vacated by 2nd Londons, who with the L.R.B. made an assault on Cavalry Farm. There was a very heavy artillery fire on both sides, in the course of which 2nd Lieut. D. G. Davies was wounded. At seven o'clock "D" Company made a bombing attack on Cavalry Farm, which they reported to have been evacuated, and it was taken over by the 2nd Londons, the L.R.B. occupying Pit Trench. At eight o'clock "A" Company of the Q.V.R. were in Tank Trench and "B," "C" and "D" Companies in Gordon Support Trench. Both positions were heavily bombarded and several casualties occurred in all companies. At five in the evening the Q.V.R. were ordered to relieve the 2nd Londons and the L.R.B. in Cavalry Farm Trench, but this was prevented by a heavy hostile barrage, and the relief was not carried out until 11.30. In the meantime the Germans had made a successful counter-attack on Cherisy. The two battalions relieved were withdrawn to trenches west of Wancourt Line. On 4th May 2 Officers and 15 O.R. of the 41st German Infantry Regiment surrendered to "B" and "D" Companies in Cavalry Farm. A sergeant of the 2nd Londons, who had previously been the prisoner of the party, was found with them and was released. The Q.V.R. casualties from May 1st to 4th were estimated at 100. The attack was unsuccessful, and the 168th Brigade relieved the 169th in the course of the night of May 4th.

From 5th to 9th of May the battalion was in trenches in the Tilloy area. The next day they relieved the Q.W.R. in the Wancourt line and came under the orders of the 168th Brigade, remaining in the command until 12th. On 11th a most successful minor enterprise was carried out by the London Scottish and 4th Londons, who attacked and captured several hundred yards of Tool Trench. This was taken in the late afternoon without any preliminary bombardment. A couple of days were spent in trenches in Bois des Bœufs, and on 14th the battalion relieved the 7th Middlesex Regiment in the Wancourt Line and became the right reserve battalion of the 167th Infantry Brigade until 19th. A large portion of this time was occupied in providing burial parties at night to clear the forward area, where many bodies were lying. On May 20th the battalion was relieved by the 11th Royal Warwicks and marched to huts in Duisans, doing three days' company training there and proceeding on 24th to Agnez les Duisans where a stay was made until June 9th. While there they were inspected by the G.O.C. 56th Division on May 28th, when a number of men were presented with medal ribands. The whole period was devoted to training in all branches.

June was a very uneventful month for the Q.V.R.

On 9th, the day of the British victory at Messines Ridge, the 169th Infantry Brigade moved to Telegraph Hill area and the battalion relieved the 8th Battalion K.R.R.C. Next day the 56th Division took over the line in Wancourt Sector, the Q.V.R. remaining in support trenches until 15th, when they relieved the Q.W.R. in the front-line trenches. Next day two advanced posts were occupied during the night and two others on the following night, the whole front being wired by the 5th Cheshire Regiment. The enemy tried to rush one of the new posts, but were driven off with Lewis gun and rifle fire. On the night of June 20th/21st the battalion was relieved

in the line by the 12th Londons—Rangers—and marched t
camp west of Beaurains. June 26th, 1917, it may be remem
bered, witnessed the arrival of the first American troops in
France. The battalion remained in billets in Beaurain
until July 2nd, the usual training being pursued. On
2nd a move was made to Gouy-en-Artois, and another nex
day to Sus-St.-Leger. Here a further long spell in more or les
comfortable billets was enjoyed, the intervening period being
taken up with training of all sorts, including both battalion
and brigade sports, all this preparatory for the third battle
of Ypres. This welcome "holiday" came to an end on July
24th when the battalion left Sus-St.-Leger at 7.30 a.m. and
marched to Bouquemaison Station, where it entrained for
Wizernes, marching from thence to billets in Nortleulingham
Here it left the VIIth Corps and came under the command of
the Vth Corps, 5th Army.

From July 25th to August 5th the Q.V.R. remained in
billets and continued their training, attention being particu
larly directed to open warfare, attack practice and outpost
schemes. On August 6th the battalion entrained at Watten
and proceeded to the Wippenhœk area, detraining at Abeele
three miles S.W. of Poperinghe. It was now transferred to
the 2nd Army Corps and remained in billets in the neighbourhood of Abeele until 11th, when it moved by rail to Ouderdom and marched thence to Chateau Segard.

On July 31st had commenced the great Allied attack round
Ypres. Up to August 12th the Q.V.R. had taken no active
part in it, but on that day they relieved the 8th Norfolk Regiment in the front line, north of the Ypres-Menin Road, with
the Q.W.R. on the left and the 8th Suffolks on their right
Orders had been given for 167th and 169th Brigades to attack
in conjunction with the brigades of the XVIIIth Corps on a
front due E. of Zillebeeke, 168th Brigade being held in Divisional Reserve. Early on the morning of 12th 2nd Lieut.
A. G. H. Long was mortally wounded on the banks of the
Yser Canal.

During the night "D" Company in No. 9 Strong Point
between Glencorse Wood and Inverness Copse were heavily
shelled. A reconnoitring patrol consisting of Capt. Ralls and
C.S.M. Gander went out several times to the right, and although

they went as far as 200 yards they failed to discover any troops on that flank. Patrols were also sent out and discovered that there were some dug-outs containing Germans in Glencorse Wood, these dug-outs being well concealed by natural undergrowth. Inverness Copse was found to be full of trenches similarly hidden. On August 13th heavy shelling took place all day, 2nd Lieut. M. C. T. Bate being killed at 9.30 a.m. An hour later an endeavour was made to establish a line of posts in Glencorse Wood, in the course of which Capt. E. D. Symes, M.C., was killed and 2nd Lieut. Pelham Russell Caley mortally wounded. He died four days later. On 14th the battalion was relieved by the 1st L.R.B. and withdrew to "Half-Way House." Shell-fire continued throughout the day, 2nd Lieut. N. Haynes being wounded.

"Half Way House," says Capt. Collingwood Andrews, "figures on all the maps as a house of considerable size, but not a vestige of a house was to be seen. It was a large dug-out with several entrances, a veritable warren of galleries and chambers. In it were brigaded 3 Brigade H.Q., a battalion and 2 machine-gun corps, to say nothing of oddments such as sappers and gunners, etc., who sought temporary refuge in what was the only spot with any pretentions to safety on the ridge. Below, the atmosphere was appalling, and conditions were not improved by the constant drip of moisture and the presence of 2 inches of slimy mud on the floor. An engine used to pump day and night to keep the water down; it also lit some of the chambers with electric light. The dug-out was so crammed that men were sleeping in the passages and communication was difficult. It was a perfect maze, but I had a rough plan made and always carried it with me."

On August 15th orders were received for general offensive operations on the following morning. At 6 p.m. 2nd Lieut. Alfred Lewis Arnold, who was in command of a company, was killed instantaneously by a shell. He was a solicitor in London and left a widow and two baby boys. His death was communicated to his family by Col. Follett, who wrote: "He had proved himself to be a most capable and brave officer and his death is a very great loss to me. Had he lived there is no doubt his promotion would have been rapid. I feel his death very keenly, he had such a splendid character." He was twenty-eight years old. At 8 p.m. the Q.V.R. moved forward to an assembly area round " Surbiton Villas," and on the way were heavily shelled, particularly in the neighbourhood of Sanctuary Wood.

At 4.30 on the morning of 16th of August the Fifth Army offensive operations were resumed. The 169th Brigade was in front, the L.R.B. on the right, and the 2nd London on the left, with the Q.V.R. as right support and the Q.W.R. left support. Their objective was to seize a line 500 yards inside Polygon Wood, the distribution being the L.R.B. and 2nd London as the assaulting wave and the Q.V.R. and the Q.W.R. the second wave. At 1 a.m. " B " Company of the Queen Victoria's had moved forward and endeavoured to take up their position ready for the attack. They found the task very difficult as the ground in that particular area was very muddy and it was almost impossible to find any firm ground. Owing to heavy casualties the companies, too, were very short of men. " A " and " C " Companies were told off to make strong posts along the right of Glencorse Wood to protect the flank of attacking troops. They were subjected to machine-gun fire and there was considerable enemy air-craft activity. " D " Company supported in rear and were ordered to hold the original front line, which they did, while " C " Company collected many men who had fallen out from attacking waves and used them in consolidating strong posts. Prior to the attack the troops were informed that our barrage was to be the heaviest ever known, and although it turned out to be so it was far too slow and consequently the front waves were caught up by the rear waves and became inextricably mixed, leaving no one to mop up sufficiently.

" B " Company were told that their objective was the racecourse about two and a half miles distant and on the far side of Polygon Wood. They advanced with roughly the fourth or fifth wave, but owing to the slowness of the barrage a good many of the men got mixed up with the waves in front. Having reached a position in rear and to the right of Glencorse Wood the company found eight large dug-outs, each occupied by strong parties of the enemy. The strength of " B " Company at this point was only twelve, nevertheless they proceeded to " mop up." They had cleared three or four of

THE THIRD BATTLE OF YPRES

the dug-outs when the supply of bombs ran out. Meanwhile their strength had diminished until they barely mustered half a dozen. Cleared dug-outs were ransacked for German bombs and fortunately a good supply was found. When the last dug-out was reached but three men remained, and these were held up by a machine-gun which could not be reached by bombs. Suddenly it was discovered that several waves of German infantry were advancing on the right flank from east of Inverness Copse and the three survivors, realising that they were cut off in all directions, sought shelter in one of the cleared dug-outs and were subsequently taken prisoners. The advancing German troops appear to have gone behind Glencorse Wood and to have attacked from the north of the wood, but were held up by overhead machine-gun fire from the rear of the British position.

It was unfortunate that on the morning of 16th the battalion was only in the possession of one Lewis gun, which was with "D" Company, the remainder with the personnel having been put out of action in previous days' fighting. Eventually the original front line was consolidated by "D" Company and the men collected from the first attacking waves. The whole of the 169th Brigade was also compelled to withdraw to its original front line position. As may be gathered from the fate that befell "B" Company the casualties in the Q.V.R. were severe.

Many doughty deeds were performed that day. 2nd Lieut. (acting captain) Frederic Hamilton Ralls (awarded Military Cross) reorganised his men after the German counter-attack, and by his grasp of the situation prevented the enemy making further progress. 2nd Lieut. Reginald Lucas Jones (Military Cross) displayed great courage and gallantry in the hand-to-hand fighting both in the open and in dug-outs in Glencorse Wood. He cleared a tunnel dug-out with a Lewis gun and inflicted a large number of casualties on the enemy. 2nd Lieut. Benjamin George Wagstaff (M.C.) showed an utter disregard of danger and led his men successfully against strong points and emplacements in the wood. His example was magnificent. He personally bombed dug-outs and killed many of the enemy. Sergt. H. C. Hawkins (Military Medal) led a patrol through the wood under machine-gun and rifle fire to ascertain the whereabouts of the battalion on the left. His success was due to his fine leadership. Sergt. A. W. Madge (Military Medal), at a critical phase in the attack when his platoon was held up by a party of Germans in a shell-hole, went forward, bayoneted the lot and enabled his men to push forward. Sergt. C. J. Withers (M.M.) handled his men with an utter disregard for personal danger when directing the consolidation of some shell-holes. Although snipers were very active he walked about in the open and cheered on his men until he was badly wounded. Sergt. A. E. Gander (M.M.) in spite of heavy artillery, machine-gun and rifle fire greatly assisted in the organisation of the front line against the German counter-attack. He was largely responsible for the establishment of an advanced post, and throughout the operations set a fine example to his men. Cpl. F. R. Gessy (M.M.) rendered great help in reorganising the men of his company after the counter-attack and later helped to establish a post. His handling of his men largely contributed to its consolidation. Lce.-Cpl. Moon (M.M.) rushed a party of Germans who were using an automatic rifle, and having bombed them he turned the abandoned automatic rifle on a line of the enemy advancing from the left and exterminated them. Lce.-Cpl. C. J. Mainwaring (M.M.) displayed great gallantry in carrying messages to and from the front line. During the three days previous to the attack he was constantly exposed to heavy fire, but he never failed to get his orders delivered and was largely responsible for the communication between Battalion H.Q. and the company commanders. He was awarded the M.M. on October 27th, 1916, and was now given a bar to it. Lce.-Cpl. P. H. Hornby (M.M.) was occupying a shell-hole with his Lewis gun when one of the panniers caught fire. Lce.-Cpl. Hornby at once seized it at imminent risk to himself and threw it clear of the shell-hole, thereby saving the lives of his team as the rounds in the magazine exploded when the pannier landed. Lce.-Cpl. G. Seymour (M.M.) bombed a German block-house in the wood, entered it and captured its garrison. Lce.-Cpl. T. Howell (M.M.) went alone into a German block-house, killed the entire machine-gun team there and destroyed the gun. Lce.-Cpl. A. W. Frost (M.M.) rushed a German position and bombed the gunners therein into the open, where they were taken prisoners. Rfn. W. A. Borrie (M.M.), oblivious of the risk he was running, attempted to establish visual communication from an advanced position although working under a very heavy barrage. Rfn. J. W. Pinner (M.M.), standing his ground, held up the enemy, who were attempting to cut off the retiring troops, and with rapid fire and good judgment enabled a large number of the troops to get clear. Eventually he fought his way back to the line under heavy fire. Rfn. T. A. Dutton (M.M.) successfully held up the enemy in similar circumstances. Rfn. A. H. Wooller collected a number of stragglers and organised them into parties. Later he brought up a ration party under shell-fire and the delivery of the rations was largely due to his pluck and determination. Rfn. E. W. Elkington (M.M.) repeatedly carried orders and guided ration parties and reliefs to the front line. On the night of 14th when parties of the relieving battalion were lost he guided them up to the front line. From 12th to 16th he had practically no rest and was always exposed to enemy fire. Rfn. C. T. Thomson (M.M.) entered several dug-outs in the wood seemingly quite unconscious of danger and killed many of the enemy. His splendd example inspired others to assist. Rfn. G. T. Joyce (M.M.) at great personal danger inflicted many casualties on the Germans as they emerged from Inverness Copse to counter-attack. The handling of his Lewis gun and his fine example were responsible for great losses inflicted on the enemy. Rfn. W. H. Darbey (M.M.) while guiding a platoon of the relieving battalion to the front line on August 17th was knocked down by a shell which burst at the head of the platoon. The officer was badly wounded, but Rfn. Darbey, although badly shocked, kept control of the party and finally brought them to the front line.

The transport section did wonders, too, behind the lines. Lieut. (acting captain) Kenneth Lucas Mackenzie by his splendid example during the whole of the operations from 12th to 17th was chiefly responsible for the transport of the rations and their subsequent issue at Battalion H.Q. Although under continual shell-fire from the moment they started out the transport never failed in delivering the rations. Lce.-Cpl. W. B. Hayne on one occasion was left in charge of the pack ponies on the Menin Road, while the T.O. was reconnoitring his way to the Battalion H.Q. The party came under heavy fire, but Lce.-Cpl. Hayne skilfully disposed of his ponies behind any cover available, thereby saving them and the men under him.

At 11 p.m. on August 16th the line was taken over by the 7th K.R.R.C. and 5th Oxford and Bucks L.I., and the Q.V.R. withdrew to Chateau Segard. At eleven next morning they proceeded by motor bus to the Wippenhoek area, where they went into billets until August 24th, on which day the battalion went by train from Abeele to Watten, marching thence to Serques. Only " company training " was done until the end of the month, when the 56th Division was transferred to the Third Army. On August 31st the Q.V.R. marched from Serques to Wizernes, where they entrained at 7.45 a.m. for Miraumont, arriving there at 4.45 p.m. and marching to camp near Bapaume, which was reached at ten o'clock.

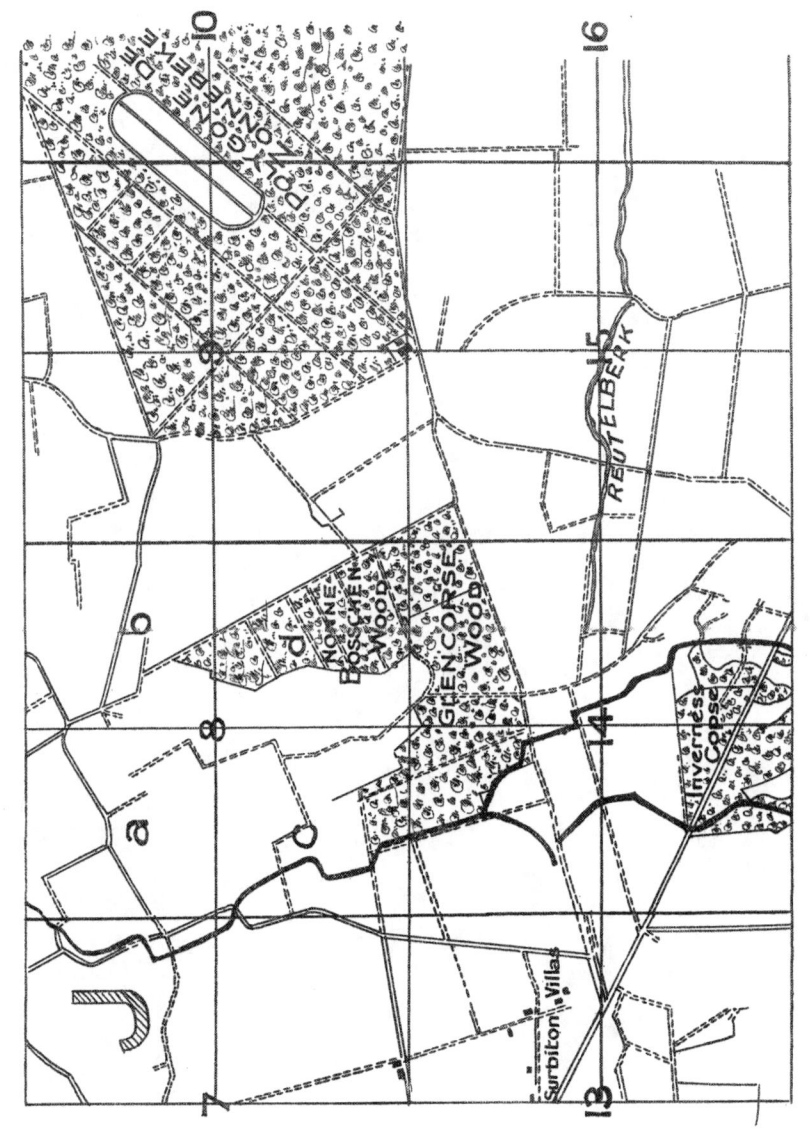

CHAPTER XXX

THE RAID AT DEMICOURT, 22RD OCTOBER, 1917

DURING September the battalion had a comparatively easy time, for the first four days in camp at Bapaume and for the remainder of the month at Lebucquiere, and in the trenches in the Louverval Sector. October was spent in similar manner. On 15th the Q.V.R. relieved the Q.W.R. in trenches in the Louverval right sub-sector and remained there until 22nd. On October 5th orders had been issued for a party of the Q.V.R. to make a raid on a portion of the enemy's line in front of Demicourt. The orders sufficiently indicate the aim and character of the enterprise :

1. (a) The object of the raid will be to kill the enemy.

(b) The point to be raided will be the two rifle pits immediately south of the dark clover crop in K.8.a at K.8.a.45.65 and K.8.a.45.70.

2. The raid will be carried out by a party of 2 Officers and 40 O.R. This party will be divided into

(a) An assaulting party of 1 Officer and 20 O.R.

(b) A covering party of 1 Officer and 20 O.R. The covering party will take 2 Lewis guns.

3. The raid will be in the nature of a surprise and without any previous artillery fire on the objective.

4. The wire in front of the objective will be cut by a Bangalore torpedo. For this purpose the assistance of 2 R.E. will be required.

The explosion of the Bangalore torpedo will be a signal to the artillery to open the box barrage detailed in my V.162.

5. The raiding party will leave the front line at a time to be arranged later and will move down the cart track running north-east towards the Dark Crop in K.8.a. for about 700

yards. At this point the party will turn east and move towards the objective. The assaulting party will be in the centre, and the covering party in two parties of 10 with a Lewis gun about 60 yards on either flank.

When the assaulting party is 75 yards distant from the belt of wire covering the centre of the 3 rifle pits immediately south of the Dark Crop, the whole party will halt.

The Bangalore torpedo party will then take out the Bangalore torpedo with a covering party of 2 on either flank and place it under the wire.

The covering party north of the assaulting party will lie out in extended order facing north; similarly the covering party south of the assaulting party will face south-east.

As soon as the Bangalore torpedo explodes the assaulting party will rush the centre rifle pit. Should this be empty a N.C.O. and 5 riflemen will be left in the centre rifle pit to keep off any enemy from trench running south-east and the remainder of the assaulting party will rush the northern pit.

The two covering parties will keep off any enemy patrols attempting to surround the assaulting party, and will not withdraw until the assaulting party are all reported back by their leader.

The raid came off on October 22nd, but alas for the carefully prepared plan! The enemy were found on the alert and the raiding party was driven off. Some casualties were claimed to have been inflicted on the enemy. The casualties to the raiding party were 1 Officer and 4 O.R. wounded. All were brought back in safety to the lines. Company Sergt.-Major Varney who took part in it thus tells the story of this unsuccessful adventure. " Whilst the battalion were holding the line at Demicourt, just in front of Cambrai, a certain officer (2nd Lieut. Amor) volunteered to do a big raid on a forward post occupied by Jerry, and Capt. Nichols, then Adjutant, arranged with the O.C. ' B ' Company and the higher authorities to plan out a good scheme for the raid. Then the picking out of good men commenced, 50 for the assaulting party and two Lewis gun teams for left and right covering parties. Now this is where the R.E's shine in making their famous torpedoes. We were kept out of the line for

8 days for special training and it was quite a good joke. We all had to have our faces, hands and all white parts blackened, which reminded me of the Mohawk Minstrels. I was nicknamed 'Masser Johnson,' why, I don't know, but I suppose it was because I was about the heaviest fellow of the lot—at that time nearly 14 stone. We rehearsed the raid over and over again before company commanders and brigadiers, with live Bangalore torpedoes, and everyone was so confident that it would be a wonderful success that they began to get impatient and itching for the night to come. At the end of our 8 days' training we all proceeded up the line looking forward to having a good time, which we did, for when we got to Battalion H.Q. we were regarded as precious men and were put into very deep dug-outs so that no harm could happen to us. Whilst in these dug-outs we were ordered to patrol the ground every night until the big night so that we should know it well. Capt. Brand, I believe, got arguing with two A.S.C. captains and told them they had never seen No Man's Land or barbed wire, which of course hurt their feelings. But I must say they were good sports and not at all windy and enjoyed the joke, in fact one of them joined the raiding party. We patrolled the ground and got all necessary requirements, such as the width of Jerry's wire, and if the post was strongly held, etc. It was a good thing we did, for we did not get much chance after, as the Boche patrols got stronger each night. After patrolling for about six nights, on four of which we were challenged, it was decided to do the dirty work, as I think by that time we had enticed a whole company of Boches to meet us. So off we started with two torpedoes, each 27 feet long. One was in three parts; the other was so frail that its own weight broke it and so we had to dump it. We next reached Jerry's wire and commenced to lay the tape out, which was done successfully, and we were just sliding the Bangalore under the wire when we were challenged. Down we all dropped, lying very low for some time. When we thought things were quiet 2nd Lieut. Amor got up and was immediately fired on and made our first casualty. Capt. Brand, who was forbidden to take part in the raid as he was proceeding on leave the following morning, was always out for sport and so of course could not resist the temptation and came out with us, for

which we were all pleased, for when Lieut. Amor was wounded the Captain took charge of the affair. By this time Jerry was letting us have it hot with rifle and machine-gun fire, but when we opened out I am certain he did not bargain for 2 Lewis guns and about 60 rifles. What damage we did we do not really know, but according to the number of rifle flashes from the enemy after we opened out they were very few. There was only a stray flash or two here and there. Anyhow, we withdrew, and collected our traps and casualties but forgot the Bangalore! On our return the roll was called and we went back to our dug-outs rather disappointed that the affair had not turned out as great a success as we expected. The battalion were very good to us, for they had managed to get round some responsible person of the S.R.D. department and got us a jar for ourselves. I might say it was very acceptable as we had been lying out for from two to three hours in the wet grass and were all perished with cold. After I had issued the rum round to all the boys some of them got very talkative and dissatisfied, while one or two wanted to do the job over again! Early next morning I received an order to go out and fetch in the Bangalore. I thought of the men who had wanted to go out again over night, but I won't say any more about that, or who did try to find the torpedo, but when they got out to Jerry's wire they found that he had been there before them! When the battalion was relieved and we had gone back for our 8 days' out a letter of congratulations was read to us from the Brigadier thanking us and the uninvited guests for our little stunt and the good work we had done."

Next day the battalion was relieved and moved into Divisional Reserve, where it remained until the end of the month.

For great gallantry whilst out on patrol east of Demicourt, in connection with this affair, on the night of 16th of October, Cpl. Henry James Hutchings was awarded the Military Medal. " Although under the observation of enemy patrols, he first measured the breadth of the enemy wire by running a tape through it and then proceeded into a rifle pit, supposed to be occupied by the enemy, which had been selected as the objective for the raid. Having carefully examined the pit, he passed back through the enemy wire and returned to the front line. Throughout the frequent previous reconnaissances this N.C.O. always displayed the greatest courage and resource and the information he obtained was of the greatest importance."

CHAPTER XXXI

Battle of Cambrai
Nov. 20th to Nov. 30th, 1917

THE first of November found the Q.V.R. back in the Louverval trenches once more. On 8th it was withdrawn to Brigade Reserve for a further 8 days and then went back to the trenches again. On 20th commenced the surprise attack on Cambrai. For many weeks very secret preparations for an offensive had been afoot. "The watchwords of these," writes Capt. J. C. Andrews, who was serving on the staff of the 168th Brigade, "may be said to have been 'Tanks and Surprise.' To prevent any possible leakage of our intentions all buzzers and instruments were removed from the front line for fear of Boche listening apparatus. Camouflage played a great part both in preparation and later in the offensive. Innumerable gun positions were constructed, the Bapaume-Cambrai road was put into condition by night, the Decauville light railways were extended in all directions and carefully covered. There was to be no increase in camp and hut accommodation in the back areas and all concentration of guns and troops were to be effected at the last minute. Meanwhile our 'gasmongers' became very offensive, employing light cylinders of gas fired electrically from mortars fixed in the ground. These attacks took place on our front and involved a great deal of heavy work for the men in carrying parties. As the result of complaints by the Special Brigade, R.E., who were responsible for the gas, that our men failed to carry all the cylinders to the appointed places, we determined that in future we should employ pack transport. So far as I know this was an innovation; it certainly was a somewhat bold experiment, and its complete success I attribute to the energy and efficiency of the Brigade T.O. and the transport of the division.

Clearly the available transport of our brigade was insufficient to carry 300 cylinders, which, with the mortars, represented 600 loads. Division were asked, therefore, to lend us the animals and pack ropes of the other two brigades (167th and 169th) whilst we supplied the men. The cylinders and mortars came up by light railway to Fremicourt, were roped up in daylight at the transport lines, and were transferred to lorries which arrived after dark in Lagnicourt. Here the pack animals were waiting and carried the loads up to the front line, passing over the rearward trenches by bridges. The result was most gratifying, all loads arriving safely, the only mishap being that one horse fell over a bridge into a trench."

The rôle assigned to the 56th Division in the coming offensive was to start after the Hindenburg line had been pierced. The 168th and 169th Brigades were to enter the breach in the line and bomb up it towards Queant, the 167th holding the whole of the Division's original front line. The 169th Brigade of Q.V.R., Q.W.R., L.R.B. and 2nd Londons was made responsible for the Demicourt-Boursies-Louverval sector, and for men who had been accustomed to close trench warfare for a considerable period, the new situation, says Capt. W. E. Bowler, M.C., "was extraordinarily novel. The enemy was occupying that wonderful trench system—the Hindenburg Line—a system which had been so well sited and protected by massive belts of wire that it was regarded as being more or less impregnable. Two important features—Tadpole Copse and Bourlon Wood—gave complete observation over our lines. Our own defences consisted of Platoon Posts, a number of which were unconnected. There was no support line, very little wire cut, and few communication trenches, whilst shelters were very few and inadequate. As may be imagined everyone had to work hard to improve this state of affairs before the winter set in, and by October the system had so improved that we began to receive visitors in the shape of Staff Officers, who complimented us on our model trenches. During September and October the front had been very quiet, the only fighting consisting of patrol encounters and an occasional raid. About 10th November we were suddenly ordered to widen the Bapaume-Cambrai road by digging up the broken macadam and laying a corduroy track of pit-props. This entailed very hard work on the part of all concerned, and as it had to be done during the period of rest, it was a most unwelcome job. We began to suspect, moreover, that this operation was not unconnected with our own front, and was the forerunner of other and more important events in which we would be directly interested—and we were right."

Major R. H. Lindsey-Renton, who was commanding the Q.V.R. at this time, also makes allusion to the preparations for the battle. "The attack in front of Cambrai," he says, "was organised as a surprise attack. The secret was very well kept as even troops involved did not know about it for long in advance. We knew something was afoot but had no idea as to what it really was. One current rumour was that a battalion raid was to take place on our right. When we did know we could appreciate the care that was being taken as to its secrecy. Although extra troops had to be brought up no extra accommodation was provided, but the existing accommodation made use of, e.g. one camp (called O'Shea Camp after the quartermaster of the Q.V.R. who had superintended the building thereof) built to take a battalion was made to house two battalions. Almost all of the transport work was done by night and similar precautions were taken in connection with everything. It came so suddenly on us that both the colonel and the adjutant were away on leave, so that I was in command with the assistant adjutant, 2nd Lieut. R. Johnson, acting as adjutant.

"It seemed as if the enemy had some idea that something was on just a few hours before the attack, as during the night of November 19th/20th his artillery was firing a great deal more than it had done since the battalion had been in the sector. During the early morning 2nd Lieut. May, who had only recently joined the battalion and showed promise of being a good officer, was killed by shell-fire."

"To complete the mystification of the enemy a number of dummy tanks," says Capt. Andrews, "and figures had been put out overnight in an old sector in front of Lagnicourt, and and we heard later that the Boches had spent several hours in pounding these dummies. Apparently it was not until the mist lifted that the flimsy nature of the target was discovered. The expression of the face of the Boche artillery observer when he saw one direct hit from a whizz-bang cause a life-sized tank to become a mass of splinters and canvas tatters must have been a study.

"At 5.30 on November 20th the guns of all calibres broke their silence," continues Capt. Andrews, "and within a minute the roar was like the incessant roll of gigantic drums. Day had not yet dawned and so the tanks got across in comparative comfort, and the much-vaunted Hindenburg Line was breached. The work of the low-flying, contact aeroplanes was much hampered by a ground mist, but during the morning news came through of the fall of Marcoing, Cantaing and other villages S.W. of Cambrai. Flequiers was stubbornly defended and only fell after many tanks had been put out of action by field guns at point-blank range."

Turning again to the work of the Q.V.R., Major Lindsey-Renton takes up the story: "Zero hour was rather a fine spectacle. In order that the dummy figures should be raised and the smoke bombs let off all together arrangements had been made to issue red Very lights to officers stationed at intervals along the line. At 6.20 a.m. these red lights were discharged along a considerable part (the whole Divisional front, I believe), and together with the ever-increasing cloud of smoke made a very pretty sight. I should state here that the main attack was to the east and south of where the battalion was. It was being made in a northerly direction with the Canal du Nord as the left flank. West of the canal the trenches, which on the east side ran east and west, ran north and south, and as the attack east of the canal progressed different units went over and bombed up the German trenches in a northerly direction. From the front line held by the Q.V.R. I got an excellent view of the main attack and could see the tanks moving forward closely followed by the infantry in file. Good use was made of the 56th Division's machine-guns on the morning of 20th. As our portion of the line faced east, whereas further south it was facing north, our guns could bring an enfilade fire at any Germans who were retiring or advancing in support. Sixteen machine-guns were placed in and near our trenches and put down a heavy M.G. barrage behind the enemy and also acted as a protective barrage for the advance of the main attack."

Continuing his narrative Capt. Bowler says : " I was commanding ' D ' Company, the strength of which was about 100. The platoon commanders were 2nd Lieuts. F. R. Wilson, S. B. Watson and S. C. Hall, whilst Sergt. Eames, D.C.M., was acting as C.S.M. My orders were briefly as follows : When the 36th (Irish) Division, on our right, had reached the Hindenburg Line they would turn north and bomb along the trenches until they reached the Bapaume-Cambrai road, when they would send up a couple of lights. This would be the signal for me to advance and occupy the outpost line, join up with the Irish, turn north and move towards Mœuvres, where I was to dig in. The remaining companies of the battalion would connect up with my left flank across No Man's Land, thus forming a new line north of the Baupaume-Cambrai road and facing Mœuvres. It will thus be seen that the battalion in the first stage of this battle had to make a tremendous left wheel, my company being on the outer flank and joining up with the Irish Division. The attack came off and proved a great and complete success, and the evening of 20th November found us in our allotted places digging in and wiring our new positions."

In his official notes the Officer Commanding Q.V.R. says : " November 20th, 6.20 a.m. The battalion participated in a dummy attack simultaneously with the main attack down south. Smoke was discharged all along the battalion front and dummy figures were raised and lowered for fifteen minutes in the neighbourhood of J.6.5 ; J.6.7.

" 3.0 p.m. The 109th Brigade having bombed up the Hindenburg Line as far as the Demicourt-Graincourt road a patrol ('B' Company) was sent along the road as far as the Three Craters in order to get in touch with them. The Craters were unoccupied and the patrol went along the outpost line as far as the Cambrai road.

" 6.0 p.m. (approximately).

" The 109th Brigade having reached the Cambrai road a patrol was sent along the road to get in touch with them at the Barricade. This was found to be unoccupied, but touch could not be got with the 109th Brigade. ' B ' and ' D ' Companies establish posts along Cambrai road facing north, with outposts about 150/200 yards in front.

"11.55 p.m.

"Touch got with 109th Brigade in Hindenburg Line north of Cambrai road."

November 21st (Capt. Bowler continued) : "The following day a determined attack was made on Mœuvres, which was captured by the Royal Irish Rifles, but was lost again during the afternoon. The Queen's Westminster then attacked Tadpole Copse and captured it with little loss. My own casualties were small, but I lost three N.C.O.'s, one of whom was Sergt. Cuthbert—wounded. I attached Hall and his platoon to the R.I.R. during the attack on Mœuvres and he kept me informed of the progress made by means of runners."

At 9 a.m. one platoon of "D" Company under 2nd Lieut. Hall was sent to accompany a battalion of the 109th Brigade in their progress up the Hindenburg Line to facilitate keeping touch. The touch was maintained until the 169th Brigade entered the Hindenburg Line and maintained touch there. This platoon was then withdrawn. At eleven o'clock "A" Company was ordered to clear the outpost line. Progress was delayed by the condition of the trenches and by the company working by mistake into the Hindenburg Line. "It was a pity," says Major Lindsey-Renton, "that 'A' Company lost its way, but it was quite excusable as I did the same in trying to find them. After a short distance along the outpost line there was a fork, one road leading into the Hindenburg Line, the other being the outpost line. The entrance to the continuation of the outpost line was a sharp left turn, whereas that into the Hindenburg Line was practically a straight continuation of the trench they had been proceeding along, and to add to the confusion the entrance to the continuation of the outpost line had been blocked by shell-fire and was invisible to people moving along the trench." At six the same evening two platoons of "C" Company took over from "A" Company and carried on along the outpost line, capturing seven prisoners and one light machine-gun. This party was held up by strong enemy resistance.

November 22nd was passed in holding on to the posts on the Cambrai road. On the 23rd the Division on the right was advanced and the posts withdrawn. The Q.V.R. were engaged in digging a communication trench. On the 25th the battalion relieved the 2nd Londons in the first and second line of the Hindenburg Line. "Here," says Major Lindsey-Renton "we had the first opportunity of really seeing the much talked-of Line. The trenches were very wide (presumably for protection against tanks) and the fire-bays were very long which made the trench very dangerous under shell-fire. This was made up for, however, by the splendid dug-outs which provided excellent shell-proof accommodation. One of the dug-outs we took over must have been a head-quarters. It was furnished and decorated more like a private house than a dug-out and must have been a very comfortable place except that it was very stuffy, possibly an advantage from the German point of view. There were several captured minenwerfers in position in the trench, with very elaborate entrenchments and plenty of ammunition. Unfortunately when the Germans captured, on November 30th, our first line (originally their second line) these had not been removed in time and they were able to make use of them."

During the whole battle Capt. Austin Basil Clarke, M.C. had been doing his usual wonderful work in patching up the wounded, on one occasion looking after a large number of wounded Railway Construction men who had been shelled while working on the Bapaume-Cambrai road. On the morning of November 23rd Capts. Clarke, Brand and Lloyd with a couple of runners, were walking round the old front line which was considered comparatively safe when a whizz bang burst just where they stood. Capt. Clarke was killed outright and Brand badly wounded, dying on his way down to the Casualty Clearing Station. Lloyd was only slightly wounded. Capts. Clarke and Brand were buried in the cemetery at Lebucquiere. The former was one of the most fearless doctors ever met and the men idolised him. Capt. William Douglas McLeod Brand also was a splendid soldier, beloved by all the men of his company, who would have followed him anywhere.

On November 27th there was considerable excitement in this sector as the Boches put down a heavy bombardment on the trenches and started bombing the battalion on the left near Tadpole Copse. "I was holding part of the Hindenburg Line," says Capt. Bowler, "when an enemy barrage was placed on the trench. At the same time (3.15 p.m.) an S.O.S. rocket was sent up by the Rangers on my left. I repeated the signal and stood to. I established communication with the front companies, who required no assistance. I sent Lieut. Watson to the Rangers, who returned with an urgent request for assistance and informed me that an attack was being made on their sector. I at once dispatched two platoons under 2nd Lieuts. Hall, and Malcolm and they carried between them sixty boxes of bombs and ten boxes S.A.A. to the scene of operations and the attack was beaten off. The ammunition had to be carried across the open for 400 yards and through the barrage and arrived at a critical time. The Commanding Officer of the Rangers was very grateful for the prompt assistance rendered and sent his thanks to the Company."

2nd Lieut. W. E. Richardson gives the following account of the disposition of " B " Company, of which he was in command, in the left sector of the Hindenburg Line : " On November 27th whilst occupying the sector, as right company, the enemy at 9.0 a.m. commenced a steady artillery fire, which continued throughout the day, and finally at 3.30 p.m. developed into a heavy barrage upon our support line, followed by an attack upon the right battalion (the Rangers) of the brigade on the left. During the attack, lasting about one and a half hours, the company 'stood to,' manning the parapet and holding the bombing block in the C.T. (E.19.a.8.5). Bombs, rifle grenades and S.A.A. were all held in readiness to supply the battalion on the left, but supplies were not called for. Communication between the right flank of the left company and the left flank of the battalion on the right was maintained throughout the attack."

November 28th passed quietly and during the night of the 29th the battalion was relieved by the 2nd London Regiment and moved back to the old front line at Boursies early on the morning of 30th. This was the day of the great German counter-attack. The day on which the 56th (London) Division, the 2nd Division and the 47th (London) Division earned such high praise for preventing the Germans breaking through or gaining much ground, while on the southern portion of the attack they did get through and were only stopped by the Guards' attack. The enemy had taken a leaf out of our book ;

they advanced without the customary long preparatory artillery bombardment but attacked with surprising rapidity. "About 11 a.m.," says Capt. Bowler, "I was ordered to reinforce the 2nd Londons who were being heavily attacked, from Bourlon Wood to Tadpole Copse. I proceeded along the Inchy road to the Hindenburg Line in artillery formation—owing to the heavy shell-fire and bombing from low-flying machines. I found the front line had been lost but that the C.T.s leading to the lost trench were being held by bombing groups of 2nd Londons. Each of these blocks was taken over by platoons of my company and the bombing continued successfully until the company was relieved by the 3rd London Regiment the following morning. Eighteen casualties were sustained during these operations and I lost another sergeant—Sanger—killed. My three Platoon commanders during this period were 2nd Lieuts. Watson, Hall and Malcolm. The commanding officer of the 2nd London Regiment was very grateful for the help we had given and asked me to thank the company."

"A" Company was sent to reinforce the Q.W.R. and also carried up a supply of bombs and S.A.A. On arrival it took over all bombing blocks in the communication trench. "C" Company was ordered to report to the O.C. Q.W.R., but on arrival was diverted to the 2nd Londons, where it was ordered to dig in in the enemy's old outpost line.

"The enemy's barrage that came down on the morning of the 30th," recounts Major Lindsey-Renton, "was very heavy. My first intimation of it was hearing some shell burst near by. I went out to see what was up when a shell burst on the opposite side of the road and flung a man who was passing by on to me and both of us into the rough shelter which formed Battalion H.Q. After a time I went out to see what was going on and found the whole front line as far as we could see concealed by a cloud of smoke from the bursting shells. Shortly afterwards I was speaking to the brigadier on the 'phone and heard an artillery officer saying 'huge masses of the enemy entering Mœuvres.' I therefore sent out messages to all the companies to 'stand to' and be in readiness to move off at short notice. In due course we received orders to send up two companies to support the front line, and later on a third and then a fourth. The advance of all these companies had to be carried out in the open, across the old No Man's Land between the old British front line and the Hindenburg Line, from 1,500 to 2,000 yards away, under heavy shell and machine-gun fire. We were lucky to get off with the casualties we did. These companies had to collect their bombs, etc., from 'Hound Dump,' a dump of all sorts of ammunition, grenades, etc. It was being heavily shelled and several explosions occurred in the stores, which made it rather a ticklish job to carry out. As soon as the companies got up they took over the bombing blocks in the communication trenches between the line held by the troops in the line and the trench captured by the Germans. From the position I was in at Battalion H.Q. I had a very good view of the fighting between Mœuvres and Bourlon Wood and could see the waves of Germans advancing to the attack and their field guns in position."

On the night of the 30th the Q.V.R. were relieved and went back, two companies to the old British front line and Battalion H.Q. and the remaining two companies to the neighbourhood of Louverval. The area in which Battalion H.Q. was situated was heavily shelled with gas shells during the night, but luckily they were in a gas-proof dug-out, for next morning the ground all round was pitted with shell-holes while one shell fell in the next shelter gassing several men of the T.M. Battery. The night of December 2nd was spent in " O'Shea Camp " and next day the Q.V.R. marched to Fremicourt, where they entrained at 10.30 a.m. for Beaumetz, marching thence to Berneville. A couple of days were passed here and two more in camp at St. Catherine. On 7th Battalion H.Q. and two companies moved to Roundhay Camp and the two remaining companies to Red Line. Alternative spells in the trenches, in fatigues and working parties filled up the time to December 24th, on which day the Q.V.R. moved into divisional reserve at Aubrey Camp, Roclincourt, where Christmas was passed.

In telling the " Story of a Great Fight " the Special Correspondent of *The Times* commences by quoting the following telegram from Sir D. Haig : " November 30th.—At 8 a.m. this morning, after a violent bombardment, the enemy attacked with strong forces on a wide front south of Cambrai between Vendhuile and Crevecœur-sur-l'Escaut. Shortly afterwards heavy attacks also developed against our positions west of Cambrai in the neighbourhood of Bourlon Wood and Mœuvres.

" From Masnieres to Mœuvres all the enemy's attacks have been repulsed after many hours of fierce fighting, in which great loss was inflicted on the attacking German infantry by our artillery, rifle and machine-gun fire.

" On the morning of November 30th, 1917, the 47th (London) Territorial Division, the 2nd Division and the right brigade of the 56th (London) Territorial Division were holding a front of about five miles extending from the eastern ridge of Bourlon Wood to Tadpole Copse, in the Hindenburg Line, west of Mœuvres. From Tadpole Copse the left brigade of the 56th Division formed a defensive flank across No Man's Land to our old front line. The 56th Division had been in line before the British attack of November 20th, in which its right brigade had taken part, and since that date had captured and held about a mile of the Hindenburg Line west of Mœuvres, including Tadpole Copse. Almost constant fighting had taken place in this area since our attack, and the division which at one time had been holding a front of 11,000 yards, had already been subjected to a very severe strain. On the night of November 26th/27th the 2nd Division had taken over from the troops engaged in the original advance the portion of our front lying between Bourlon Wood and Mœuvres. The division had recently completed a short period of progressive training, the great value of which at once became apparent. . . .

" At 9.20 a.m. the enemy had been seen advancing from the north towards the Canal Du Nord, and subsequently attack after attack was delivered by him on both sides of the canal against the 6th and 169th Infantry Brigades. . . . From Mœuvres westward to Tadpole Copse, a desperate struggle was taking place for the possession of the Hindenburg Line, in the course of which the enemy at one time reached the Battalion Head-quarters of the 8th Battalion Middlesex Regiment, attached to the 168th Brigade, 56th Division. Here the German infantry were stopped by the gallant defence of the officer commanding the battalion, who, with the assistance of his head-quarters staff, held off the enemy with bombs until further help was organised and the trench regained. Though much reduced in strength by the fighting of the preceding days,

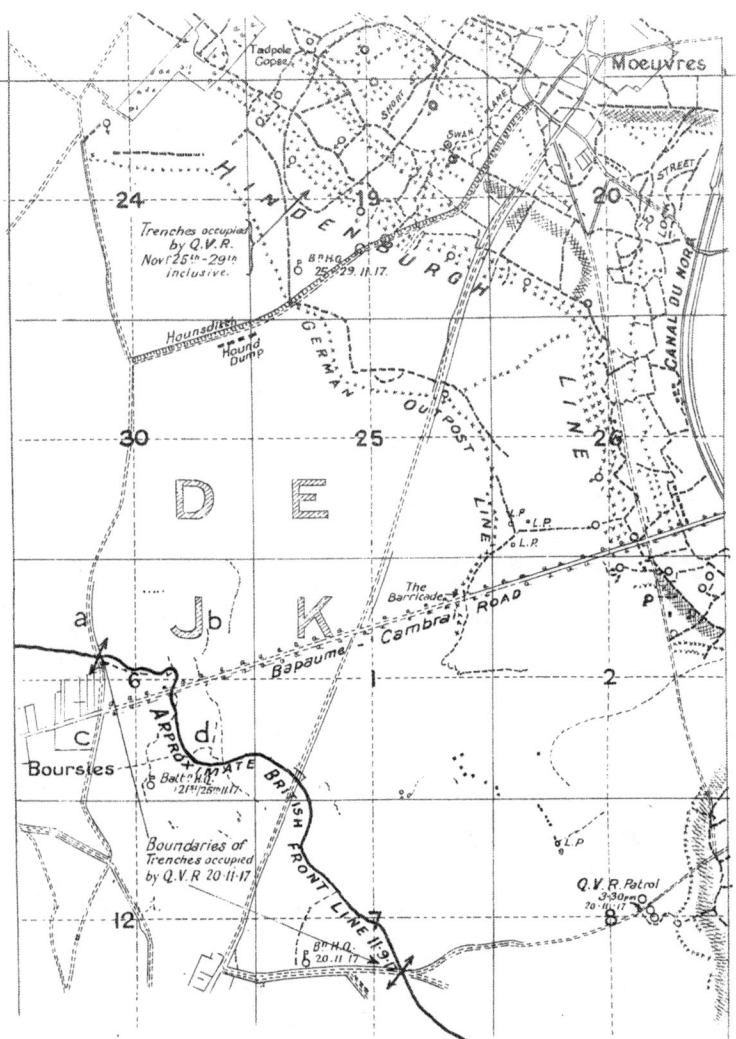

BATTLE OF CAMBRAI NOV^R 20TH 30TH 1917.

and hard pressed by superior forces, the troops of the 168th and 169th Brigades beat off all attacks. Queen's Westminsters, London Scottish and men of the 1st/2nd Battalion London Regiment and 1st/8th Battalion Middlesex Regiment vied with one another in the valour of their resistance.

"At the end of this day of high courage and glorious achievement, except for a few advanced positions, some of which were afterwards regained, our line had been maintained intact. The men who had come triumphantly through this mighty contest felt, and rightly felt, that they had won a great victory, in which the enemy had come against them in his full strength and had been defeated with losses at which even the victors stood aghast."

PART II
THE SECOND BATTALION

CHAPTER I

IN THE MAKING

THE 1st Battalion Q.V.R. had filled up to war strength within forty-eight hours of the declaration of war. It is claimed that the 2nd was recruited to similar numbers only four days later. At any rate, it is certain that it received official recognition somewhere about the middle of August. Lieut.-Col. P. E. Langworthy Parry, D.S.O., O.B.E., T.D., who subsequently commanded the battalion, writing of its earliest days, says: " One morning late in August, 1914, the commanding officer rang me up on the 'phone at my office and asked me if I could come up at once to Head-quarters as he had ordered the thousand or so recruits to parade in Hyde Park and wanted me to be present as I was to have command of a company. In less than half an hour I was on parade assisting in what may be considered an historic ceremony. The men were roughly divided into groups as follows: public school men; civilians with no knowledge of soldiering; and men who had previously served with the 1st Battalion. Companies were made up 1/3rd from each group, so that all started level. Lieut.-Col. A. R. Berry, T.D., was in command; Lieut.-Col and Hon. Col. A. S. Barham, C.M.G., V.D., 2nd in command, and Lieut. L. H. Martin, Adjutant. Nearly all the senior officers had served together before and so were acquainted with each other's peculiarities."

For the first few months London was the home of the battalion, the parks and commons forming its training-ground. On the 1st October it was inspected in Hyde Park by Major-Gen. Sir Francis Lloyd. Without rifles and uniforms, the men, who numbered 1,065, were drawn up in two extended lines along which the inspecting general rode, and afterwards the men marched past the saluting base in columns of companies.

At the conclusion Sir Francis Lloyd congratulated the battalion on their bearing, their physique and the progress they had made. " You are a magnificent battalion," he said, " all you require is training. Remember that the moment you are fit you may be called, if the King so thinks, into the field to fight, and there you have got to uphold the magnificent record which our troops in France are now showing and have shown to the whole of Europe."

The battalion left London for Crowborough on November 23rd, 1914, and at once went into strenuous training, from time to time sending drafts of well-seasoned men to the 1st Battalion in France as well as supplying many men for commissions in other regiments. All ranks speak very highly of the kindness and hospitality extended to them by the people at Crowborough, who set apart recreation rooms for them, allowed them the use of their bathrooms and in a hundred and one ways showed their gratitude to the boys who had come forth to fight in defence of King and country. Many acceptable and seasonable gifts, too, were received at Christmas time.

Rumours of early departure for active service were rife and at least one false start is on record, but at Crowborough the 2nd Q.V.R. remained until the spring of 1915. The next training station was Ipswich, where the men were billeted until August, when they went under canvas at Bromeswell Heath, near Woodbridge. On the very night of their arrival they fired " their first shot in anger " at some Zeppelins which had come over and did considerable damage to the town. " This," says Lieut.-Col. Langworthy Parry, " made our blood boil." Every few weeks the battalion " stood to," drew small arms ammunition, etc., but nothing eventuated. In November a return to Ipswich was made, the men going into billets as before and so remaining until Easter, 1916, when they moved to their old camping-ground on Bromeswell Heath. " We had stood by for over a week," says C.S.M. Lott, " the limbers had been lined up and packed all ready, and off we went to our old camp ! Next day we had a taste of what later on we were to get quite used to in France. Full kit ; two blankets, and 120 rounds of S.A.A. we marched to the coast at Alderton. It was quite an active service affair. We had outposts in the Martello towers. One company put barbed wire between the breakwaters, but were careful not to interfere with the bathing parades. One company commander told us that the first we should know of the Germans having arrived would be when we heard their boats grating on the beach ! Another gave order to ' dig in ' in the sea wall, but next day the local authorities objected and so we had to fill in the holes again ! "

In July the brigade, now under the command of Brig.-Gen. De Winton, was moved to hutments at Longbridge Deverill, Salisbury Plain, where it completed its musketry course, received the final polish and the approval of the powers that be for transference overseas. But though the men began to think they were really going to France at last, the time was not yet ; they had to wait a little longer. Brig.-Gen. H. C. Jackson, D.S.O., now took over the command of the brigade, the 175th, the battalion being still under the command of Lieut.-Col. A. R. Berry, T.D. The other officers were as follows :

Second in Command	Major P. E. Langworthy Parry, T.D.
Adjutant	Capt. E. P. Cawston.[1]
Quartermaster	Hon. Lieut. F. Judge.
Medical Officer	Capt. G. Eustace, M.D., R.A.M.C.
Bombing Officer	2nd Lieut. H. Samuelson.
Transport Officer	Lieut. A. N. Philbrick.
Lewis Gun Officer	Lieut. E. W. G. Hodgkinson.
Signalling Officer	2nd Lieut. H. S. Prince.[1]
Intelligence Officer	2nd Lieut. W. A. McAdam.[1]

" A " Company	" B " Company
Capt. W. H. Stronge.	Capt. Graham B. White.
Capt. B. G. Bailey.	Capt. G. F. Griffith.[1]
Lieut. Richmond.[1]	Lieut. H. S. Blackwood.
Lieut. C. H. Rose.[1]	2nd Lieut. R. M. Fletcher.
	2nd Lieut. G. C. Allen.

" C " Company	" D " Company
Major W. P. Wilton.	Capt. K. W. Johnson.[1]
Capt. W. N. Carter.[1]	Capt. W. F. Russell Jones.[1]
Lieut. H. S. Walker.	Lieut. A. K. Rice.
Lieut. S. Wightwick.[1]	2nd Lieut. J. L. Worlledge.[1]
Lieut. D. Herbert.	2nd Lieut. R. B. Crosbie.
	2nd Lieut. A. D. L. Harington.

[1] Had seen previous service with 1st Battn.

Regimental Sergeant Major . H. G. R. Tomlinson.
Quartermaster Sergeant . E. F. Jacob.

The 58th Division to which the battalion was posted was constituted as follows :

173rd Brigade	174th Brigade
2/1st London Regt. R. Fus.	2/5th London Regt. (L.R.B.)
2/2nd ,, ,, ,,	2/6th ,, ,, (L. Rifles.)
2/3rd ,, ,, ,,	2/7th ,, ,,
2/4th ,, ,, ,,	2/8th ,, ,, (P.O. Rifles.)

175th Brigade
2/9th London Regt. (Q.V.R.)
2/10th ,, ,, (Hackney R.)
2/11th ,, ,, (Finsbury R.)
2/12th ,, ,, (Rangers.)

It was not until the end of January, 1917, that the long awaited order came. On 27th there was a false start. Half way to Warminster Station the battalion was turned back and passed another two days in camp, but on 29th it actually entrained for Southampton, where it spent the four succeeding days in the notorious " Rest Camp."

The 2nd Queen Victoria's Rifles embarked in the s.s. *La Margarita* on Saturday, February 3rd, 1917, the Channel crossing proving as uneventful as was that of the 1st Battalion two years and three months earlier. " A very steady boat, a smooth sea and a lovely moonlight night," according to one of our diarists. Life belts were served out immediately the men went aboard and strict orders were given to keep them on for the whole voyage. There was an escort of two destroyers whose encircling evolutions aroused much interest. The lights of Havre loomed up long before the French coast line could be seen, and shortly after the harbour patrols came out to pilot the transport into harbour on the morning of Sunday, February 4th. The first thing that met the eye was a newly arrived Red Cross train alongside the quay and the men watched the transference of a long line of wounded men to a hospital ship with mixed feelings. " The rest camp at Havre," says Lieut. Col. Langworthy Parry, " five miles from the docks is not a pleasant place on a cold winter's night with twenty-five degrees of frost, and I can candidly say that it was the most uncomfortable night I spent during the whole time I was in France. The weather was vile and altogether it was not an encouraging experience."

We have other testimony to the same effect. A sergeant writes that " the water froze as we used it," while an imaginative rifleman declares " it was so cold the bolts froze in the rifles ! " A companion (E. E. Snoswell) entered in his diary : " It was so cold yesterday that there was even ice on the sea. This is no fairy tale, but absolute truth."

On February 7th the battalion moved up by rail by half battalions to Auxi-le-Chateau, and then by road to Sus St. Leger, a march of seventeen miles. "The march was one which will never be forgotten by anyone who performed it," says Sergt. Ingram, " C " Company, " the roads were like glass and we were all awfully tired, we saw some fusiliers in a village we passed and inquired where the Vics were. ' Next village,' was the reply and we continued our journey as giants refreshed with wine. Arrived at the next village we found the 10th Londons, our own brigade, and inquired again for the Vics. ' Next village ' came the cheery response, and so off we went again ; found the 11th Londons and were once more assured the next village was our rightful resting-place. By this time fellows were falling out helplessly on the road-side, beaten to the world. We did arrive eventually though and got to our billets—barns, with the usual numerous openings to allow for fresh air—and here we slept, within sound of the guns and to the news that we had captured Grandcourt on the Somme " (February 6th). There is a conflict of testimony as to the effect of the long march on the men, for C.S.M. Lott says : "The march next day to Sus St. Leger was one to remember, too. The cobbled road was one sheet of ice and we did something like eighteen miles on it. Not a man fell out, which proves that we were fit." He philosophically adds : " Looking back on our first few weeks in France there is no doubt that we had a rough time. It was the first time out for the majority, so of course we took it for granted that it was quite the usual run of things, but it did us good and helped us to appreciate better days, which we had later."

On Saturday, February 10th, the battalion went for a short route march to Beaudecourt and during the return home, according to Sergt. Ingram, " we beheld ever-increasing numbers of small white puffs in the clear blue sky and suddenly realised that we were looking at a German 'plane being shelled by our guns. It was our first sight of actual war and great was our excitement. The machine came on and seemed to pass right overhead, apparently having a good look round, and then turned and went the way it came, still being hustled by the shrapnel, which was at times uncomfortably close to our unaccustomed eyes."

At Sus St. Leger the 2/9th made acquaintance with a new method of billeting. Says Rfn. Snoswell : " We are all billeted in barns and outhouses, but instead of sleeping on straw we have wire spring mattresses ! How's that for active service, eh ? This is no kid. Of course, they are not like the spring mattresses we have at home, but they are more comfortable than sleeping on the ground. All round the outhouse is a wooden framework, about 6 feet from the wall, and from this framework wooden beams go back to the wall, and across these beams wire netting is spread. In between each beam is just wide enough for one to lie, and these are our beds. There are three tiers of these bunks, so that instead of getting about 26 men in one place we get at least 100. That conserves the space a lot. The first night we only had one blanket each and never in my life have I slept so cold. I say slept, but there was very little sleep about it. We had a wood fire in the barn during the evening, but at night it froze hard inside as well as out. Water bottles have practically been frozen hard ever since we landed. Still, so far I am enjoying my experiences. We have not had much to put up with yet beyond the cold ; food will be good here, although so far we have lived on bully and biscuits. We had bread this morning, but it had frozen so hard we had to warm it before we could cut it ! For dinner we are going to have mutton stew and boiled chestnuts. How's that for a mixture ? I understand they don't go so badly, and I am rather anxious to try it and see."

Rfn. Snoswell it may be seen was a bit of a Mark Tapley. He never groused and all his letters to his wife, from which these excerpts are taken, teem with cheerfulness : " We drink coffee here without milk. Plenty of it," he writes. "They sell it in small tumblers at 2½d. a time. We have no Y.M.C.A. or Army Canteen, but the battalion is going to run one on its own as soon as the stock arrives. At present we have to buy everything in the village and things are very high. Woodbines 2½d. per packet as against 1d. in England. Once our canteen starts we shall be able to buy at reasonable prices —in fact, many things will be lower than at home. It is very funny, although I can change English silver or postal orders, yet they won't change notes. I have been broke the last two days with a 10s. note in my pocket. Of course, I shall be able to change it when our canteen starts, but until then I am working on Arthurs' (his brother's) money. I owe him 3½ francs already."

CHAPTER II

FIRST EXPERIENCE OF THE REAL THING

ON February 13th the battalion occupied the trenches in front of Berles-au-Bois and Bienvillers, facing Monchy-au-Bois. As this was the first time of their going into the line they were brigaded with two battalions of the Staffords. "Most men remember their first spell in the trenches," says C.S.M. Lott. "The 2/9th went in near Bienvillers. On the march up to the line we were halted in the snow and told to rub our feet with whale oil. It was issued with good intention, no doubt, but I don't think it had the desired effect." This incident seems to have made a deep impression, for nearly all our record keepers, officers as well as men, make some reference to it. Sergt. Ingram says: "We rested for a while in a large field through which ran a single line of railway and obviously we could find no better place to dump our kits and seat ourselves than the sleepers. There were some three inches of snow on the ground, and our rather cramped positions in the buses in which the first part of the journey was made had made our feet horribly cold. Imagine then our feelings when a rumour went round that we had got to rub our feet with whale oil! At first we thought it a huge joke until we saw that it was a fact, and then there was a scramble to dodge doing it. It was of no avail though, so we removed our putties, boots and socks and solemnly rubbed the beastly, greasy, cold, clammy oil into our feet. We were commencing to replace our footwear when everyone was startled by the loud blasts of a locomotive's whistle, and looking up we beheld bearing down upon us at some speed a large engine, out of the cab of which leaned a man who frantically waved to us to get a move on. We moved amid a hustle, men grabbing parts of their equipment and their rifles, or other men's equipment and rifles, or stood and raved because they had to walk through the snow barefooted or in their socks. The incident though cheered us up quite a lot, and our spirits rose considerably."

The further adventures of the day and the spell in the trenches are admirably described by Rfn. Snoswell : " There is no doubt," he says, " that this (whale oil) is good stuff, but seeing that we had to do it in the open air it was a trifle chilly. However, that was nothing. It was getting dark by then and we moved off in small parties for a four- or five-mile march and eventually reached a little village where we were supplied with hot cocoa. I found out this was supplied by the regiment who was looking after us and putting us in the way of the trenches. They were very good to us in most ways. After the cocoa we moved up to the trenches. It was a bit exciting going in the first time, but after all it was nothing to get excited over. Once we got a machine-gun turned on to us, but no damage was done. It took us well over the hour to get to where our post was, and instead of going into the supports our platoon was right up in the front line. However it was real quiet there—in fact, I think that no one got the wind up at all. Honestly I don't think we had a single shell fall near us. I should not have thought it possible that any part of the front could have been so quiet. It was hard to realise that we were in the real thing. We could put our heads above the trenches in the daytime without much risk. It was almost hard to realise at times that there was a war on, except that on either side the guns were going very heavily. As long as we were in the trenches we were quite safe. It will show you how safe it was in that our only casualty was caused by one of our own men handling a rifle carelessly. We had not been in the trenches above an hour or so when Arthur (his brother) was told off to go out with others on a wiring party. He was out for a good two hours, but it was quite quiet. The Germans sent up several star lights, but did not discover them. On the whole we are not so badly off for grub, but when we have had one or two more trips it will no doubt improve. It was not so much shortage as the meals sometimes being an hour or two late. During the night we had an issue of soup and tea, and also, of course, a rum ration. Rum is horrible stuff, but I had it each time, as I believe it is really good for one and gives a little extra strength. We were very fortunate in that the trenches were dry owing to the cold, and it certainly was cold. Once it thawed, and without any exaggeration we were ankle deep in mud and water, and this without any rain falling. What the trenches would be like after a week's rain it is impossible to imagine. After the first night the other regiment was relieved and four of us managed to win a dug-out to ourselves. This made it much nicer. It was a pity there were not more dug-outs, only the trouble was that we could not use them much. The whole of the night every man had to be out in the trenches, but from twelve o'clock those who were not on sentry-go could sleep if they wanted to, or, I should say, if they could. After half an hour's sentry-go it was necessary to stamp about a bit to get warm. The whole time I was in there I only had six hours' sleep together: Six hours out of four days is not much, but it is surprising what you can stand when you have to. Of course, it was tiring and also inclined to sour one's temper a bit, but I think, taking it all round, we did very well. I was on sentry-go most of the time ; in fact, we all were, and our platoon is only half strength owing to some of them being in isolation when we left England. All the machine-gunners were separate, and I don't believe I saw Arthur more than twice or three times all the while I was in the trenches. Of course, he is quite safe although they dropped a couple of rifle grenades rather close to them. The cold was very intense and on the third night one fellow was absolutely crocked up and I was asked if I would lend a hand at taking him down on a stretcher. It was a very tiring job as we were all tired out before we started, but we managed to get him down though we were sniped at once whilst crossing the open ground. The sniper, however, got no bull's-eyes, only misses. The last night I was there I was one of a party told off for a patrol in No Man's Land. We had to parade at 4 a.m., but did not actually get out until after 4.30. We were out about an hour, but saw nothing. We went close enough to hear a German blow his nose, but that was all. It is remarkable how soon you may lose your direction out in No Man's Land. I could not have told whether we were going to the German line or to ours. Of course, we were under an officer who has had plenty of experience, so we were all right. We were originally to come out Friday, but later we heard we should be in till Saturday and then that it would be

Sunday, but eventually we were withdrawn on the Saturday. It was a fearfully tiring time, but as an experience it was new. We came back to billets immediately behind the trenches. We had not had a wash for five days or nights, or a shave; covered from head to foot with mud and all pretty well done up."

Sergt. Ingram apparently did not find trench life quite so safe and placid as the last writer. "We were soon introduced," he says, "to the delights of dug-outs and other places of abode, but the weather was severely cold and the trenches dry and hard. By keeping on the move, and with the aid of a little rum we kept warm and had a really good time. There was no incident during the first three days and we were happy and satisfied, but on the morning of the fourth day we were moved back to the support trench, where we were housed in a huge, deep dug-out. That morning one of our trench mortars exploded, or was hit by a Jerry shell, and Jerry concentrated a great number of guns on the spot for some minutes under the impression that he had found a nest. That night, too, he sent over some gas and we had a delightful game in scrambling up some forty steps wearing our gas masks. We lined the trench and listened to the din. It was our first experience of hearing our own guns speak, and the shells whistled overhead in shoals while we watched their vivid flashes of fire as they burst on the enemy lines. We survived it all and on Saturday morning we were going out. During the night a thaw set in and one sank nearly to his knees in the oozy mud of the trenches. A ration party was sent down with dixies, etc., to a central dump, there to await the arrival of the outgoing men, and while at this dump we had an exhibition and proof of the qualifications of German snipers. A corporal came from the gas office near-by with a pole having on top the points of the compass and also a wisp of threads to indicate the direction the wind was blowing. He got up on the top of the parapet, planted the pole in the ground and jumped into the trench. He had hardly made the leap when there was heard the vicious snap of a bullet and the pole was chipped. This was an obvious instance of luck, but it would have been bad luck for the corporal had he delayed his jump two seconds longer."

The night of the relief was spent at Bienvillers and next day the battalion marched to billets at Grenas—another of those trying marches " that not a man who took part in it will ever forget." Rain had set in, the roads were heavy with mud and everyone was done up. The battalion remained at Grenas until February 26th doing ordinary training, getting fitted out with Lewis Guns and being generally overhauled so as to be ready to take a section of the line on its own responsibility the next time of entering. During this time the battalion had the enjoyment of having its first bath since arriving in France, and needless to say after three weeks " sans " baths it was greatly appreciated although according to the details furnished the experience was quite unique in the way of baths.

On 26th a move was made to Gaudiempré, where the night was passed, and on 27th through Baillemont and Riviere to Wailly. The next day the trenches opposite Blaireville were occupied.

On March 1st the battalion relieved the 1/5th West Riding Regiment in the trenches, and while holding the front line underwent a bombardment from trench mortars, suffering a few casualties. A Lewis Gun team of "D" Company were buried in their shelter and Rfn. Smith and Bonner[1] were dead when extricated. Our friend Snoswell on this occasion remained behind on fatigue duty, his special job being to clean some dirty trench waders, " and when I tell you that it takes a day for two of us to clean 30 pairs and there are 300 to 400 of them to do you can guess what it means. It is some job, I can tell you ! " He goes on to tell us that " The boys came out of the trenches on Sunday morning (March 4th), tired and weary, of course, but still smiling, and they certainly are feeling much better this time than last, even though they did not get much more sleep, and in some cases even less than last time. Not only that, but they had a good lot of shell-fire as well. At last they have begun to realise what war is, and no one is struck with it. Of course, I have not come under shell yet and don't know what it is like, but the only thing that strikes me, and constantly does so, is the appalling waste of this war. Everything is waste : time, money, munitions, even lives are nothing else but waste. Don't ever talk to me of the ' Glory of War.' I can't see it. All I see is waste, waste, waste, and nothing else.

[1] Both killed in action 28/2/17.

It is awful. Just think of the millions of lives that are being absolutely thrown away on practically no advantage to anyone, also the millions of hours spent in turning out munitions that are literally thrown away. It is appalling to me. I can see no sense in it. To think that in these so-called enlightened days men can't find some more sensible way of settling their difficulties. One thing, I think this will be the last war on this earth as the majority of the men who have been out here will be dead against any war except as a very last extreme. It is too awful for words. However, these are only my opinions and thoughts on the war, and I must say I cannot see any glory at all in it. I am quite ready to don civilian attire whenever the time comes without any regrets." Alas, for him that time never came and he was also destined to make closer acquaintance with the waste of lives.

While our rifleman was thus soliloquising (March 6th), No. 1 Platoon of the 2nd Q.V.R. was going into the trenches again, being led by a guide and Sergt. Borsberry when both guide and sergeant were instantly killed by a trench mortar.

"On 9th," says Sergt. Ingram, "there was some heavy shelling on our left, but we remained immune except for one or two 'Minnies,' but on 10th we were bumped all day with 'T.M.'s.' Some sensation! One hears the report of the gun and all eyes are turned heavenwards endeavouring to locate the shell. Presently someone yells, 'There she is, coming here,' and there ensues a wild scramble along the trench to the shelter of a friendly traverse, and this with a foot of soft mud like syrup in the trench requires some effort."

"We went into the trenches on Saturday night (March 10th)," records Rfn. Snoswell, "right up in the front line, and after a quiet, lovely moonlight night, we had quite settled down. Of course, Sunday is the same as every other day of the week, and work has to be carried on just the same, but this Sunday I shall never forget. It was the first time I had ever been under shell-fire, but that did not affect me much. It was just after dinner that Fritz commenced by giving us twenty or thirty Minnies, as the shells from their minnenwerfers are called. These mostly fell on our right, but did no damage. They were, however, too close to be pleasant. Just after tea, about 5.30, I went along to where Arthur and the rest of the machine-gun

U

team were. I stood talking to three of them in their dug-out for a minute or two when the gas alarm was given. I doubled back and passed the alarm on to Arthur and the remainder of the team, but could not stop to say more to him as I had to get back to my post. The 'Gas Alarm Off' was given after about a quarter of an hour and almost immediately Fritz started sending more Minnies over. One of these it was that did the damage. It fell in the trench Arthur and one other was in and killed Arthur instantaneously. Thank God for that. There could have been no suffering on his part at all. The other chap was only wounded, but rather badly, sufficient to send him home to England. The whole trench collapsed upon Arthur, but they are digging him out and he will be buried in the cemetery in rear of the trenches. They kept the news from me for some hour or two until something definite was known, and then one fellow in error said it was hard luck to have my brother missing and this while I was on duty. Immediately after I was relieved I went along to see our platoon officer and he told me Arthur was missing and that they were digging the trench out. He thought he was not there but had shell-shock and had wandered further down the line, as he was the extreme end man of our platoon. They sent a patrol out to look for him, but just after the patrol returned to say they could find no trace of him, they began to uncover his body. This was about 2 a.m. They gave over then as there were some tons of earth on him, and there was no possible chance of life in him. They waited till daylight and are having a special party up to dig him out carefully. Our platoon officer and sergeant are most cut up about it, and both they and all the fellows have been most kind to me. Our company officers also were very helpful to me."

At 7 p.m. the funeral took place in rear of the trenches all the guns on that particular sector of the line joining in a last grand salute "the shells going over our heads by the hundred."

Arthur Cecil Snoswell was in his twentieth year when he was killed. On the outbreak of war he joined a Cadet Corps and transferred to the Q.V.R. in the early part of 1915. He was in the Lewis Gun team and his officers, Lieut. J. L. Worlledge and Capt. Kenneth Johnson both spoke very highly of him in letters advising his parents of his death.

CHAPTER III

OCCUPYING THE OLD GERMAN LINE

IT will be remembered by those who have read the records of the 1st Battalion Q.V.R. that the great German strategical withdrawal began on the night of March 16th, 1917. From 11th to the 17th of the month the 2nd Battalion remained in the neighbourhood of Riviere and Grosville, being alternately in the trenches and in billets, opposite to them were the Germans who were holding Blaireville. Concerning this place Lieut.-Col. Langworthy Parry says : " It was not until March 18th that Blaireville fell, and during that time the battalion was holding the line, half being in at a time and half out. The line was far more pleasant than the rest billets at Riviere just behind, for the Huns were always searching for our guns in that quarter, so that the comparative peace usually associated with the word ' rest ' was conspicuous by its absence. We had several casualties during this period, but the Hun was, as it turned out afterwards, making his preparations to retire, which he did very cleverly, finally clearing out of Blaireville on the night of March 17th/18th. He had kept up his fire almost to the last, and it was about 10 p.m. on 17th that I received orders—being then in command—to send a patrol across No Man's Land to find out if the place was occupied or not. 2nd Lieut. H. Samuelson was detailed to take the patrol over, and after an anxious wait duly reported ' all clear,' then followed ' C ' Company under Major W. P. Wilton who made a still further reconnaissance with the same result. At about 6 a.m. on 18th the battalion was in occupation of the enemy's lines—everyone very pleased with himself. Of the Hun we could see nothing except fires burning in the distance and his usual legacy of booby traps, which, however, did no harm to anybody. By the evening of

18th we had the road cut clear to our old line so that the guns and transport could move forward. The following days were spent in holding the new line and in salvage work, for which the battalion was highly commended."

"Just before the German retreat of March, 1917," says C.S.M. Lott, "the 2/9th were in trenches opposite Blaireville. Our line was very thinly held and we used all sorts of schemes to 'bluff the Hun'—a saying famous in the battalion and started by Capt. Graham B. White who commanded 'B' Company in those days. During the day previous to our 'going over' to occupy Blaireville we heard explosions and at night huge fires were burning. That night 'C' Company under Major Wilton went over to reconnoitre and occupy Jerry's front line. Early next morning the remainder of the battalion went over. For a long time afterwards our boys claimed to have gone 'over the top' though it will hardly count as a battle honour. Our company went through No Man's Land in anything but battle order; it was go as you please, and nearly every man carried a brazier and sandbags full of 'buckshee' kit. Personally I remember having to carry a number of S.O.S. rockets and flares which would get in the way as I floundered through the broken wire, etc. The belt of wire in front of the German trenches was 100 yards deep and very thick, being made of knife-rests all fitted closely together. The trenches themselves were wonderful in many ways. The front-line trench was at least 15 feet deep and paved at the bottom with bricks with a well-made drain. The revetting was done with huge logs, at least 1 foot 6 inches in diameter and all fitted together with thick wire. Steps were made up to the parapet in which were steel snipers' posts and at intervals were steel turrets for machine-gun posts. The dug-outs were splendidly built and quite an eye-opener to us. From the front trench back for about 500 yards a tunnel was built through which ran a railway. In the tunnel was a big and well-fitted cookhouse and aerated water factory ! The German Officers had a tennis-court and very fine dug-outs in the reserve line, and apparently they had a good time at Blaireville generally."

"We were put in the large quarry at Blaireville," says Sergt. Ingram, " and we spent a never-to-be-forgotten night there. Jerry had destroyed all his dug-outs and we had to make

LT.-COL. ANDREW REGINALD BERRY, T.D.

shelters out of trees and waterproof sheets. Everyone got thoroughly drenched, but we were all exceedingly interested in the defensive works which we were in possession of. The huge dug-outs and tunnels which one could explore if one chose to take the risk of booby-traps which abounded everywhere ; the trenches, too, were huge in comparison with our own and exceptionally wide, built up with immense posts and girders, with concrete emplacements for machine-guns and snipers, and, at one place a tunnel leading from the front line into No Man's Land, where there was a trap-door so that a gun could be mounted there at any time and no track be left whence the occupants came or went. Another thing in Blaireville itself was what appeared to be a smashed house, but when one came near one saw that it was of solid concrete reinforced with steel girders and iron which had been built inside a house so that the roof when it fell would camouflage the observation post effectually.[1] From this point—and many mounted the rickety ladder to see—one commanded a view over the whole of our battle area for miles and it was possible to observe everything that took place in our trenches. We all wondered, had we known the complete observation of our lines the enemy possessed, whether we should have wandered about as we did, and do, more or less carelessly."

On March 24th the death occurred in hospital at Birles of Lieut.-Col. A. R. Berry, T.D. He had been suffering for some time with a very severe and trying cough which he had contracted while on duty in the front-line trenches opposite Blaireville. On 17th he saw Dr. Eustace, the battalion M.O., who finding that he had a high temperature advised his removal to hospital. When the order was carried out next morning he was unconscious and although every care and attention was given to his case he succumbed to pneumonia six days later. His unexpected death came as a great shock and surprise to his battalion, and his old friends and comrades felt it very keenly after their long association with him. He was buried in the Hospital Cemetery at Birles, not far from Arras, the sad ceremony being attended by Lieut.-Gen. Sir Ivor Maxse, K.C.B., commanding XVIIIth Army Corps, Brig.-Gen. H. C. Jackson, commanding 175th Infantry Brigade, Major (afterwards

[1] A very common method of making the famous German Mebus.

Lieut.-Col.) P. E. Langworthy Parry, and those officers and men of his battalion whose duties permitted them to be present.

Lieut.-Col. Andrew Reginald Berry, T.D., was born in Bristol on April 25th, 1868, and was the son of the late Mr. James de la Tour Berry, of Bristol and Weston-super-Mare, a member of one of the oldest Devonshire families which has contributed many members to the Navy, Army and other professions. He held his first commission in the 19th Middlesex R.V.C. (St. Giles' and St. George's, Bloomsbury) which on the formation of the Territorial Force in 1908 was amalgamated with the Victoria and St. George's R.V.C. as the 9th County of London Battalion, Queen Victoria's Rifles. Major Berry who at that time was second in command succeeded Col. W. M. Tanqueray, V.D., in command of the regiment on 4th of March, 1911, resigning on 11th December in the following year. On the outbreak of the war he was appointed to the command of the 2nd Battalion and went to France in charge of it on February 4th, 1917. Lieut.-Col. Berry married Miss Rosie Shackleton, a cousin of the distinguished explorer, who with an only daughter survive him. His death came as a shock to all, and his old friends in the Q.V.R. felt it very keenly.

Following the " capture " of Blaireville the battalion acted independently, for some weeks, being engaged in finding working parties in various sectors. On 22nd it was at La Couchie, then in the old line opposite Monchy-au-Bois, where it occupied some of the dug-outs and trenches in which they found themselves at the first. Some of the companies had to bivouac in improvised shelters, and the men generally learned a lot in the way of looking after themselves. About this time Rfn. Snoswell says : " We have been wandering to and fro, up and down the country, no one seeming to want us." On March 31st they were at Agny, near Arras, where they met a few of the 1st Battalion, which was stationed about a couple of miles off, but unfortunately the majority of them were doing a turn in the trenches and could not get over to see their friends.

C.S.M Lott likewise makes reference to the apparently aimless wanderings of the battalion which continued through the following month. " During April, 1917," he says, " our battalion and the division generally seemed to be wanted by no one. We did odd jobs everywhere and were always on the move. Just before the big battle of Arras (April 9th/30th) we met the 1st Battalion at Agny and many old friends met, unfortunately for the last time, for the 1st Battalion was destined within the next few days to take a big part in the big battle. After an interesting walk through the battlefields of the Somme we reached Miraumont (April 10th) and did good work on roads and railways combined with training." Miraumont was at that time merely a rubbish heap but few semblances of the former buildings being left. " We were accommodated in billets," says Col. Langworthy Parry, " in most cases very hard to find, but as there was plenty of loose timber in the place, in spite of the cold weather everyone was comfortable. Battalion H.Q. was in the Railway Hotel, which had been the target for more than one gun and bore evidence of the fact ; given a gale of wind and the consequences would have been unpleasant for its occupants, but we were lucky and the flimsiest supports held. We did a lot of improvement work to the town and on April 16th moved up to Achiet le Petit, where we were accommodated under canvas and shelters. Here we stayed until May 4th, putting in some useful work training. Here also the pioneers erected a four-roomed cottage for the officers, made from timber and corrugated iron taken from Hun dug-outs. It was really quite well made, the building comprising a dining-room, reception-room, kitchen and bathroom. Real doors, windows and stoves were found in some neighbouring ruins, also canvas for the walls, so the cottage was quite a success. Doubtless when the Hun retook Achiet in 1918 he occupied it—but not for long. The policy of improving every place one comes to is, I think, to be commended, and Queen Victoria's Rifles, I fancy, established a reputation for themselves in this."

Just behind the Battalion H.Q. at Achiet was a huge crater, 150 feet deep and quite 80 to 100 yards in circumference. It was supposed that a dump of German munitions had been blown up here, for no known shell could have made such a hole. This crater was utilised for every conceivable purpose, as a church, a concert room and as an arena for boxing competitions. Rfn. Snoswell describes it as arranged for a concert held on May 1st : " ' The Goods,' a concert party belonging to the division, entertained us and it was great. One of the best concerts I have been to for some time past. It was a sight to see. Imagine a great hole in the earth, big enough to seat 4,000 to 5,000 men, gradually tapering from a hole about 100 yards in diameter down to a small circle of about 10 yards. All around from the bottom upwards were men wherever one looked. Half-way up one side was a platform on which the concert party were. I have seen some strange scenes in my time but nothing to come up to this. Fritz little knew when he made that hole to what uses it would be put."

The Big Crater at Achiet.
Q.V.R. Boxing.

CHAPTER IV

BULLECOURT

ON May 4th the 2/9th moved to Favreuil, en route for Lagnicourt, when the brigade took over from the Australians. The day was very hot and a young and lately joined subaltern, writing on May 5th, says: "We had an awful march here yesterday afternoon, about seven or eight miles in a broiling sun, the troops falling out like flies. I only had two fall out from my platoon. I'll tell you what I had to carry: Pack, inside a trench coat; some socks, mess tin, iron ration, towel and washing materials, and a box of chocolate; forty-eight rounds of ammunition in my pouches, and, of course, all the straps and belt of pack which cut into one's shoulders; haversack containing crowds of maps, flask full of rum, books, aspirins, which I found very useful for the platoon after the march as some of them got a touch of the sun; electric torch, my ordinary khaki hat—I wore my steel helmet; then a full water-bottle, and slung round me at odd corners a revolver, a box respirator—a big thing—a gas helmet, pair of field glasses and a compass. I was jolly glad to get into camp." So we should think.

"That night we rested in tents," continues Sergt. Ingram, "and just after it became dark we were all disturbed by a sudden outburst of anti-aircraft fire immediately over our heads, and it was found that a Jerry 'plane was gliding over the tent tops. There was a horrible 'wind up' for five minutes, but the plane got away."

The position held by the battalion consisted of a series of sunken roads (S.E. of Lagnicourt) with trenches in front on the slopes looking towards Queant; these trenches could only be approached after dark and were more or less hastily dug. During a week spent in support and in the line there were

16 casualties, 1 killed and 15 wounded, 2 of the latter being reported to have died later. Early on Sunday morning, May 13th, the 2nd Q.V.R. were relieved by the 29th Australian Infantry and returned to Favreuil.

An interesting account of this turn of duty is given by Rfn. Snoswell : " We can't say we have had a bad time of it, although there has been plenty of shelling ; we certainly were not hard up for sleep this time. After being three days in a sunken road in a hole in the side, we had to take our turn in the line. It was altogether different to our other turns. Instead of walking up miles (seemingly) of communication trenches to get to the front line, we had to go over the top right across the open and drop into a little narrow trench. There were no dug-outs, or not as dug-outs are known, but one slept in holes cut into the side of the trench near the floor. These were not quite long enough to allow us to lie down comfortably ; in fact, they were very like that cartoon of Bairnsfather's where the conversation runs somewhat as follows :

" New hand : ' Had a good night's rest ? '

" Old hand : ' Not so bad. I had to get out a few times to rest.'

" We had to get out occasionally to rest, or rather to stretch. Still it might have been worse. Of course, we had to work or do sentry-go all night, but there are only about six hours of darkness, so it isn't so bad this time of year. Also it was about full moon, which improved things considerably. I was out in No Man's Land each night. The first night I was on a three hours' turn in a listening post in a small shell-hole about 200 yards in front of our line. The next two nights I was out wiring in front. We had no wire at all in front of us and our job was to start putting some up. This had to be some 10 yards in front of our listening post, so it was a bit of a ticklish job. However, we safely returned to our trench each night, although on the first night we had hardly got in before Fritz began dropping shells just about where we had been working, so we were in luck's way. The second night's wiring was perfectly peaceful and we had no trouble at all. During the day we had to keep perfectly quiet and still in our trench as Fritz did not know where we were exactly ; the only men on duty during the day were one sentry from each section. As we had only five men in our section for the first day, and four after that, we had one hour's sentry-go and four hours off, and finally one hour on and three off. A platoon consists of 64 men, but very rarely gets to more than 50; ours has been 25 to 30 men ever since we came out here. The time off we spent in eating and sleeping mostly; it was too uncomfortable for writing letters and we did not feel like doing anything else; watching at night is tiring work and the days were fearfully hot. Taking it all round I think we had quite a cushy time of it. For all Fritz's shelling he did very little damage, so we had nothing much to grumble about. At night time it was really a grand sight to see the shells bursting over the enemy trenches and Fritz was continually sending up white, green and red coloured lights and a species of golden rain. It is remarkable what a number of these lights Fritz uses and yet we hardly use one. It is quite an unusual thing for us to send up a light and never coloured ones except in the case of emergency. Looking from our trench it was quite a Brock's Benefit on a large scale. One thing, in these lights, Fritz certainly excels, but as this is the only thing in which Fritz does excel, and as that is far from a vital thing, it does not matter. As to artillery, aircraft and such vital things, Fritz is easily outmatched to-day. We were relieved last night (May 12th) by Australians (29th Infantry) and had to march to this camp (Favreuil), where owing to delays we arrived about 6 a.m. We had a cup of tea and turned in as we were, as a whole absolutely done to the wide. We had breakfast at eleven and then went into the village, where I enjoyed the luxury of a wash down from top to toe. It was the first wash I had had for a week, and I was lucky in that as most had not had a wash for a day or two more. We had none of us shaved the whole week, so that when we marched into camp we looked like the finest collection of tramps you ever saw."

During the period in which the 2nd Q.V.R. were in the support line at Lagnicourt No. 15 Platoon had a shell fall right in its midst, killing a lance-corporal and a rifleman and wounding 5 or 6 others. Originally very small in numbers, at the time it was relieved this platoon could only muster about 9 men.

From Favreuil, where the succeeding four days were passed in rest *and* training, the 2/9th moved to Bihucourt, arriving there on May 15th and remaining until the 20th, still doing the everlasting training. On that day, after church service the battalion moved up to the Noreuil-Longatte Road before Bullecourt, taking over the line at the latter place on May 22nd from the 2/7th. " We held Bullecourt," says Lieut.-Col. Langworthy Parry, "for seventy-two hours, the shelling being almost continuous ; the enfilade fire from Queant was the worst and we suffered 123 casualties, or about 20 per cent of our strength during that time. The Hun made no actual counter-attack, and while we were there we considerably improved the position."

" We now get on to the time," says C.S.M. Lott, " when the 58th Division made its name at Bullecourt. The latter place this time was about the hottest shop on the whole front I think the night ' B ' Company first went into the line at Bullecourt was one of the worst we ever had. It was pitch dark and raining. The route up to the front line was a mass of craters and shell-holes and we were heavily laden too, being in Full Marching Order and carrying two days' rations, extra bombs, etc. All the way dead English and Germans were strewn about and the enemy was very active with his artillery Also we were hampered with numbers of our wounded coming back, including Capt. Bailey of ' A ' Company. Practically no trenches were left—just mud holes. The 8th Londons had that evening been attacked and had in turn counter-attacked so there was no formal relief—we just took up a line on our own. During the next four days no actual attack took place but there was heavy artillery work on both sides and we had over 100 casualties. The stench in Bullecourt was awful, and I shall never forget Capt. White going about with a large drum of creosol trying to improve matters, but with little success Bullecourt brought the 2/9th its first medals, four men receiving the M.M., Rfn. Stroud of ' B ' Company was one, and he later on won the D.C.M."

" On the 24th," says Sergt. Ingram, " happened one of those heroic acts which somehow are rarely seen. Cpl. Butler of 3 Platoon discovering that there were wounded men out in front of our line, went himself and brought in one man of the

2/6th Londons and another of the 2/7th, both of whom were severely wounded and had been lying out in shell-holes in No Man's Land since their costly advance two or three days before. The first man was got away on a stretcher and Cpl. Butler was himself attending to the other in our lines when a shell burst right on top of the group, both Cpl. Butler and the rescued man being killed. It was a severe blow, for he had been such a steadying power in the inferno we were in and everyone expected he would get distinction, but it never came through. Everyone was more or less on edge when Lieut. Harper turned up straight from leave and Piccadilly. He was as cool as though he was still in town, and in the midst of the heavy shelling walked to the various groups of men, chatting and laughing with them and infusing into them part of his wonderful pluck. Hooper, too, a stretcher bearer, did most praiseworthy work in the course of his duty and was awarded the M.M., but the strain told on everyone."

Amongst others mentioned for meritorious conduct were :

No. 392020 Lce.-Cpl. S. C. Collier.
„ 391744 Lce.-Cpl. W. Treasurer.
„ 392000 Rfn. A. R. Sutherland.
„ 391352 Rfn. F. Roper.

" These two N.C.O.'s and man," wrote Capt. K. W. Johnson, O.C. " D " Company, " proceeded on patrol in daylight to the German lines (Bovis Trench) to report whether it was occupied or not. They were well aware of the danger of their task, but carried their duty out efficiently bringing back the required information. Unfortunately Rfn. Sutherland was killed while performing this work. No. 392001 Rfn. A. Seward, Section Commander, 15 Platoon, Lewis Gun team, on May 25th while in charge of a post a H.E. shell burst wounding all the men and burying them. Although wounded in three places and his arm broken, this rifleman helped to extricate the wounded, and before reporting himself a casualty he returned to the post and looked for the Lewis Gun and ammunition which had almost been completely destroyed. He then made a report on the destruction of the gun and offered himself to take it on to Battn. H.Q. He refused to have his wounds dressed until his section was attended to. Lieut. Keeson, 2nd-Lieut. Worlledge and 2nd Lieut. Crosbie carried out their work most efficiently and were particularly calm while the company was under very severe shell-fire, H.E., and when there were a number of casualties. By their example they were instrumental in keeping all ranks perfectly steady."

Lce.-Cpl. Collier, Rfn. Hooper, Rfn. Seward and Rfn. Stroud were all awarded the M.M.

The battalion remained in the position until May 26th. "On that day," says Sergt. Ingram, "there seemed to be a concentration of all the horrors of the preceding three all thrown into one, and very few were optimistic enough to think they would ever come out. When it became dark the shell-fire intensified and we gave up our last hope of relief, but they came up, the 2/10th Londons, through everything and took over, and we hastily withdrew to the Ecoust sunken road again ; thanks to Lieut. Harper, No 4 suffered no casualties." At Ecoust St. Mein the Battn. H.Q. and a good many of the men were accommodated in the large caves below the church. Referring to these Rfn. Snoswell, who had been acting as a stretcher bearer for the past few days, says : "We stayed two nights and two days in some catacombs. There are large numbers of these in the districts round about here and they are attributed to the time of the Huguenot persecution. We must have been over 100 feet underground. Some of the passages were so low that we had to bend nearly double to get along. Our beds were stone slabs along either side of the stairway and passages and were rather bumpy and hard, but after coming out of what we had been through it was a treat to get where we were in perfect safety. The Germans had, of course, used the place for their troops and had blown up the entrances, but our people came across the place whilst sinking a well. Only a small part has as yet been opened up, but it is reckoned if the whole was cleared thousands of troops could be accommodated down there. We managed to get a good amount of rest although it was rather stuffy. One drawback was that we were short of candles and yesterday we were nearly in darkness as there was no means of renewing our supply."

At a later date he adds : "Life in this place is pretty slow. We never know whether it is night or day—we live by candlelight all the time. I, for one, shall not be sorry to get out of this crypt as the atmosphere is not so fresh as it might be."

The 29th saw the battalion at Mory, where it was reorganised and where a large draft awaited them. Most of the new-comers were posted to "A" Company, which had sustained over ninety casualties during the four days it was in Bullecourt. It remained at Mory until June 3rd, on which day it returned to Bullecourt. In the four days spent here only four casualties were recorded, due, according to Lieut.-Col. Langworthy Parry, to "better accommodation and less shelling." On 7th a return was made to Ecoust, where the cave-cellars were again occupied. On 8th the C.O., Col. Langworthy Parry, went on leave to England for ten days. Now ensued a quiet and comparatively peaceful time ; the war diary contains little of interest and other sources of information are dry. The former says : " The 173rd Brigade had a raid at 11.38 p.m. No response from the Boches and all quiet and normal on our front. They took one prisoner, who gave much information." June 10th : " Same formation. All companies working day and night. Much improvement made in the approaches to Battalion H.Q. which was inaugurated at lunch time." June 12th : " Two prisoners of 119th Regiment brought in about 3 a.m. Both tired of the war and given themselves up. One or two shells near our B.H.Q. about 7 a.m. Work on new mess nearly completed. Several of our own 18-pounder shells bursting short in village in 10th and 12th support lines. Situation otherwise normal ! " On the night of 14th the battalion moved to Mory, the movement being completed by 2 a.m. " with only one casualty," one man of " D " Company being slightly wounded. Another period of "intensive training" followed, varied on 20th by the battalion being " out digging Pelican Trench." From Mory the battalion moved on Sunday, June 24th, " to a most delightful camp at Logeast Wood, S.W. of Ablainzeville," where it once more went into training until July 5th, when it went by road via Bancourt and Ypres to Havrincourt Wood, an entirely new sector, but a most interesting one from every point of view. "In the Havrincourt sector," says C.S.M. Lott, " during June and July the battalion had in many ways a good time. Our line ran through the village of Trescault and from what remained of the gardens of the houses in the village our boys gathered fruit of all kinds and did themselves well. It was a very quiet sector, but we did our best to stir things up, and our patrols at night did a deal of work, but occasionally suffered casualties. Each battalion of our brigade carried out a raid, and that of the Q.V.R. was very successful."

MAP No. 12.

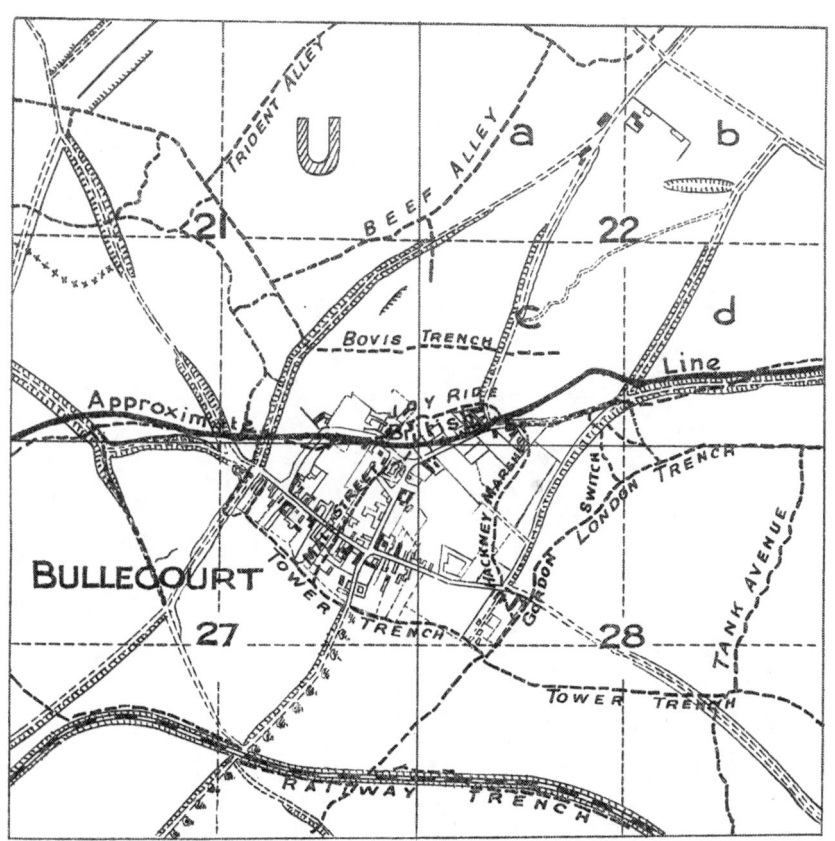

BULLECOURT MAY 1917.

CHAPTER V

THE RAID ON MOW COP

THE famous raid made by the 2nd Q.V.R. on "Mow Cop" deserves a chapter to itself. It was considered of sufficient importance to have mention in the Commander-in-Chief's daily bulletin. On Monday, July 23rd, Sir Douglas Haig telegraphed : " We also raided the enemy's position during the night south of Havrincourt and in the neighbourhood of Bullecourt and Hollebeke. Additional prisoners were secured by us ; a number of the enemy were killed and his dug-outs were bombed."

The raid demanded great skill and care in its preparation and execution as the orders issued will show. They were given by Major W. P. Wilton, temporarily in command of the battalion, the C.O. having gone on a course.

2/9th Battalion London Regiment (Queen Victoria's Rifles).

INTENTION (1). To raid position called Quarry Post at K.33.d.55.08 and rifle pits 50 yards each side of it on July 22nd by creeping forward as a formation until discovered, then rushing with bayonet to overpower any resistance.

COMPOSITION (2). Four officers (2nd Lieut. Prince in command, 2nd Lieut. J. L. Worlledge, second in command, Lieut. Samuelson and the Medical Officer, Capt. Eustace), and 81 Other Ranks composed as follows :

 40 N.C.O.'s and men (in sections of 8 including N.C.O.),
 8 Flankers,
 6 Scouts,
 1 Connecting man,
 2 Runners,
 6 Lewis gunners with 2 Lewis Guns,
 4 Men for gaps in wire,
 12 Stretcher bearers,
 2 Engineers.

EQUIPMENT (3). Steel helmets, rifle with bayonet fixed and darkened; 50 rounds in bandolier tied round waist; 2 bombs in breast pocket. Badges, helmet covers and identity discs removed. Wire cutters.

POINT OF DEPARTURE (4). Fire bay on right of block in Lancashire Trench at Q.3.b.60.86 on a magnetic bearing of 342″.

POINT OF RETURN (5). To point of departure on a magnetic bearings of 162″.

TIMES (6). Party to be in Lancashire Trench at 8 p.m.
Party to leave Lancashire Trench at 10 p.m.
Party to advance at Lancashire Trench at 10.30 p.m.
Party to arrive at Quarry Post at 10.45 p.m.
The first shot of barrage is signal to advance.

FORMATION (7)—

Scouts. Three pairs of scouts at 20 paces interval and 20 paces distance called right centre and left scouts respectively. The centre scout carries a compass.

Connecting Man. Will be from centre scout to front line.

Main body. Two lines of half sections of 4 men in file, 5 half sections in each line at 10 paces interval and 10 paces distance. The N.C.O. in charge of each section will be in rear of front half section.

The centre section will have the N.C.O. in front and he will carry a compass and be the directing point.

Officers. Second in command 2nd Lieut. Worlledge will be between first and second lines in centre.

O.C. party, 2nd. Lieut. Prince, will be in rear of second line.

Lieut. Samuelson will be where Lancashire Trench crosses Shropshire Spur.

Capt. Eustace will be at advanced Aid Post.

Lewis Guns. A Lewis Gun and a team of 3 men will be on each flank. The right flank gun will move on a bearing of 51″ magnetic from point of departure, i.e. parallel to Shropshire Spur, and on arriving at 150 paces from point of departure will act as a standing patrol. The left gun will be 5 paces from centre of No. 5 section on left flank.

The 2nd/10th Battalion will be asked to have a Lewis Gun in Lancashire Trench covering Shropshire Spur Road. All the raiding party are warned not to use this road on any account. Flankers. Four men on each flank in file ; the right flank acting as covering party to the right Lewis Gun. The left flankers will be 15 paces interval from the left Lewis Gun.

ACTION (8). (*a*) *Scouts.* Scouts numbered from right, centre and left on location of enemy halt and pass to front line (by one man crawling back) their information. The centre scout passes word by his connecting man.

If Quarry post is unoccupied scouts push on as far as edge of Mow Cop. Scouts are not to fire at any enemy on sight and after enemy is located wait until absorbed in front line.

(*b*) *Main Body.* On location of enemy crawl forward and on word " Go " (from Sergt. Thorpe, Lieut. Worlledge or O.C. party) rush with bayonet, but on no account to proceed further than the edge of Mow Cop.

(*c*) *The Four Men left on our Wire under Lieut. Samuelson.* After party has gone forward 2 gaps will be cut in our wire by these men who will remain near gaps to guide parties back. Lieut. Samuelson will remain in trench to fire red Very lights if required at 11.30 p.m. The gap men are to count number of men returning through the gaps and report to Lieut. Samuelson, who will be where Lancashire Trench crosses Shropshire Spur. They will have electric torches.

(*d*) *Lewis Guns.* Will cover flanks and engage targets where offered and will cover withdrawal.

CASUALTIES (9). Twelve stretcher bearers will be in Lancashire Trench and will evacuate wounded as far as advanced Aid Post to be established at Q.3.d.05.85 under Capt. Eustace. They will not go beyond our wire to bring in wounded. From thence they will be carried to Q.3.c.9.3 by 2/10th stretcher bearers. They will evacuate stretcher cases ; over the top walking cases will use Ashton Alley.

WITHDRAWAL (10). Order for return will be given verbally and a red Very light fired in direction of enemy by O.C. party. This will be repeated from trench by Lieut. Samuelson. Two red Very lights will also be fired from point of departure by Lieut. Samuelson at 11.30 p.m. as signal to return, in case party has not returned by then. Men will return by Ashton Alley immediately and rendezvous by sections by Battalion H.Q. at Alfred Road Q.3.c.9.4.

PASSWORD (11). Rats. Answer: Rabbits.

ARTILLERY (12). The artillery will bombard Quarry Post and right and left of it for 5 minutes at 10.30 p.m.

WATCHES (13). Watches will be synchronised with artillery at Brigade H.Q. at 12 noon and 6 p.m. on July 22nd.

(Signed) H. S. WALKER,
Lieutenant and Adjutant,
2/9th London Regiment
(Queen Victoria's Rifles).

In conjunction the following instructions were given to the artillery:

HEAD-QUARTERS, 58TH DIVISIONAL ARTILLERY

(1) The following scheme for the artillery support of a raid on Femy Wood, in the vicinity of Mow Cop, to be carried out on night 22nd/23rd inst. is forwarded for your approval.

Zero to Zero plus 3 minutes.

210th Bde., R.F.A.

15/18 pounders K.34.c.0.1½.
1 howitzer K.34.c.3½.½.
1 howitzer K.34.c.5½.3.
1 howitzer K.34.c.2½.4½.
1 howitzer K.33.d.9½.8.

(2) Heavy artillery if possible to fire a few rounds into Boggart Hole.

(3) In addition to create a diversion—
  1. Heavy T.M. to fire on Dean Copse.
  2. Heavy T.M. to fire on Etna—K.26.d.9.1.

(4) *Rate of Fire.*
  18-pdrs. 3 rds. per gun per minute, shrapnel.
  4·5 Hows. 2 rds. per how. per minute.

(5) Support mentioned in Para. 1 to be repeated upon the signal of 3 red Very lights sent up by the infantry.

(Sd.) A. BIRTWISTLE,
Lieut.-Col., Commanding
210th Brigade, R.F.A.

19/7/17.

On the day the raid was to take place the brigadier called in at Battalion Head-quarters to see that everything was progressing well. He was so pleased with the details furnished that he sent the following letter to 2nd Lieut. Prince :

"H.Q. 175th Infantry Bde.
28/7/17.

"My dear Prince,

"I was sorry not to find you in this afternoon when I came over to wish you the best of luck.

"I know how well you have planned the raid and trained your party, and how much the success, which I am certain will attend it, will be due to you personally.

"Kill what you can't bring in, but bring in as many as you can.

"The best of luck to you all.

"Yours sincerely,
"H. C. Jackson,
"Brig.-Gen. Commanding
"175th Infantry Brigade.

An official description of the raid was drawn up by Capt. (Brigade Intelligence Officer) E. P. Cawston and issued for the information of the troops by orders of Gen. Jackson, O.C. 175th Infantry Brigade.

"During early hours of night 22nd/23rd July, a party consisting of 2nd Lieuts. H. S. Prince and J. L. Worlledge, Sergts. Briggs, Thorpe and Jeffreys, and 61 O.R. and 2 R.E., carried out a raid on the enemy outpost line on the west slope of Shropshire Spur-Havrincourt Wood.

"Lieut. H. Samuelson, 12 stretcher bearers and 4 O.R. formed a special party to assist withdrawal after the raid by clearing wire and other obstructions, checking numbers and evacuating wounded and prisoners.

"Dress. Steel helmets with camouflaged cover. Tunic and trousers with plain buttons. Bandolier round waist. P.H. helmet. Two bombs in breast pockets. Rifle with bayonet blackened and fixed.

"All regimental buttons, papers and other means of identification were removed before the raid. Each man had a plain envelope with his name on to expedite checking on return.

"The area raided was the whole of the scrub on the west side of Shropshire Spur, which previous reconnaissance and patrols have shown to contain a line of pits occupied at night and constituting the enemy outpost line which has continually impeded our patrols. The centre of the objective was the quarry in the centre of the scrub, Q.33.d.55.15, from which trench mortars and M.G. activity have been of nightly occurrence. The area to be dealt with was limited to the scrub. The isolated fire bay in the open ground, north of the scrub and protected by substantial wire entanglements, was excluded from the objective.

"The raid was entirely successful and this was due largely to the detailed arrangements for, and practice of, the stealth which was to characterise the operation.

"Our casualties were: 1 officer slightly wounded (Lieut. Worlledge), 3 O.R. slightly wounded and 2 O.R. (of whom 1 has since died) severely wounded.

"The losses inflicted on the enemy must have been considerable as evidence was obtained of 9 killed and 10 wounded, while 2 were taken prisoner.

"At dawn on 22nd 2nd Lieut. Prince and Sergt. Briggs, who had previously carried out several day and night reconnaissances of the approaches to the objective, passed down telephone wire from Ashton Saphead for 50 yards along the route to be taken.

"The raiders took up their position in Ashton Saphead at 9 p.m. and at 9.55 p.m. commenced to crawl out towards their objective in 2 lines of 5 files of 4 at 15 paces interval and distance, covering a frontage of about 70 yards and preceded at 20 yards by 3 pairs of scouts covering a frontage of 50 yards ; the centre pair following the laid wire and then guiding further advance on a compass bearing and laying a tape. The advance was covered by the sound of our machine-guns which fired intermittently across the objective from positions in the rear.

"At 10.26 p.m. the whole of the party had reached, unobserved, a position 100 yards from the objective and was ready for advance under barrage as arranged at 10.30 p.m., at which hour a light barrage of 18-pounders fell on the objective, while one battery of 4·5's opened on various usually troublesome points, in the enemy outpost line in rear and on flanks of the objective. The 18-pounder barrage lasted from 10.30 to 10.33 p.m. the 4·5 battery carried on intermittent fire on its targets until 11.15 p.m., by which time it was arranged that the patrol should have withdrawn.

"Immediately on the opening of the barrage, the party continued its advance and at 10.33 p.m. was within 40 yards of the outpost. The enemy sent up two white lights during the barrage but was otherwise unaware of the raiders' approach.

"On the scouts reaching the enemy wire in front of the outposts, the leading line of raiders deployed, cut gaps through the wire and took up positions on the far side. The order was then given to get ahead. The party thereupon proceeded to clear Mow Cop and was met with rifle fire, rifle grenades and stick-handle grenades from the outpost line, and heavy rifle fire from the line of fire bays in the open ground north of the scrub ; the fire from their comrades in rear appeared to have had a not altogether encouraging effect on the enemy outposts. Hostile machine-gun fire came from both flanks ; one firing from the vicinity of Oxford Valley and another from the right of Shropshire Spur Road. These guns were engaged by the raiders L.G. sections placed on both flanks for this purpose. Our men were occupied until 11.15 p.m. in close fighting, clearing the scrub to its north and west boundaries. Seven of the enemy were left dead in the Quarry and two were killed on our left. A party of eight Germans under a corporal attacked our men on the right, but were wounded and cleared off and the corporal and one Other Rank were taken prisoners unwounded.

"The Quarry is a small excavation about 15 feet deep and has a boarded floor. There was no T.M. or machine-gun in the Quarry, but what appeared to be an emplacement had been damaged by our barrage, and there was nothing to justify the raiders making use of the explosive charges taken with them for demolition.

"The seven timber piles round the Quarry are arranged in a circle about 25 feet in diameter.

"The rifle pits are shallow excavations, like small shell-holes, suitable for listening posts. Two enemy were seen dead in one of the pits.

"At 11.15 p.m. the scrub had been cleared of all living Germa[n] and a signal for withdrawal—three red lights—was fired. Th[e] signal appears to have puzzled the Germans in the rear—[a]s previous to this no lights beyond the usual intermittent whi[te] lights had been fired—and heavy machine-gun fire was opene[d] by the enemy in rear positions upon our trench system and i[ts] approaches. This lasted about ten minutes.

"The withdrawal was covered at a distance of 40 yards b[y] 1 detailed party of 8 men and by the flanking L.G. The who[le] party including the wounded was back in our saphead an[d] names checked by 11.40 p.m.

"With the exception of the usual intermittent M.G. fi[re] on both sides the rest of the night was quiet."

The next morning the following letter was received b[y] Lieut.-Col. Langworthy Parry :

HEAD-QUARTERS,
23rd *July*, 1917.
No. B.W.F. 9/14,
175TH INFANTRY BRIGADE.

OFFICER COMMANDING
2/9th Battalion, Queen Victoria's Rifles.

The Brigadier wishes to congratulate you and your battali[on] on the success of the raid last night.

He considers that the plan was well thought out, and th[at] the excellent training of the party by 2nd Lieut. Prince l[ed] entirely to the way in which it was carried out from beginni[ng] to end without the slightest hitch or confusion.

The Brigadier has forwarded the names of 2nd Lieut[.] Prince and Worlledge and a proportion of the N.C.O.'s a[nd] men for award.

In addition he considers great credit is due to Lieu[t.] Samuelson, who by good organisation was able at once to che[ck] the return of the party and within a few minutes report th[at] they were all in.

The medical arrangements of Capt. Eustace seem to ha[ve] been excellent.

J. A. G. WYLDE,
Captain, Brigade Major,
23/7/17.   175th Infantry Brigade.

THE RAID ON MOW COP

For this exploit 2nd Lieut. Prince was awarded the Military Cross and the Belgian " L'Ordre de la Couronne." In the order conveying the Belgian decoration it was stated : " This officer has shown great initiative and disregard of personal risk throughout. On several occasions, particularly when in the trenches opposite Monchy in March last, and at Bullecourt, May 23rd/24th, he superintended and helped the laying of wires under heavy shell-fire, and set a splendid example in every way to his men. He has also done particularly well at reconnaissance work on more than one occasion."

2nd Lieut. Worlledge was mentioned in dispatches.

Our Tapleian friend, Rfn. Snoswell, relieved from stretcher bearing and turned rifleman again, took part in this raid, but makes very little of it in his letter home : " We kid ourselves we are some soldiers now, as we have had an ' over the top ' stunt since last I wrote. I could not write about it earlier as we were not allowed to say anything about it for fear it might get over to Fritz. This was the reason why I and a party have been separated from the battalion ever since we came from the line. Most of the party were from our company ; in fact, they wanted all from our company, but we are not strong enough, so one or two others were drawn in from other companies. We practised the stunt for the few days before we went over and last Sunday night about the time you go to church we left our billets for the line. We got into position just about dark and after a three minutes' barrage we went over. It was only a raid on some advanced post of Fritz and we were a party of about 100 (?). It was nothing like such a fearsome time as I thought. It did not worry me in the slightest and I think it was the case with most of the fellows. It was just the same as if we were doing another practice. The raid was a success. We came back everyone, with two prisoners, having inflicted casualties on the enemy. We had one or two casualties ourselves, but very few, and everyone is pleased with us over it. Personally I saw no one, and did not fire my rifle at all, so I still have to fire my first shot in this war. So you see I have now been over the top and came through quite all right except for a few scratches from barbed wire, etc. As I say the experience was nothing like what I anticipated it would be and I did not feel windy at all. So you need never worry about me. Not that this was the same as an attack in force, but it was a fresh experience. I suppose our next turn will be a proper attack and we shall have reached about the limit in experience of warfare. We are made quite little gods of by the rest of the men and are living on the fat of the land. Fancy, we have just had boiled rabbit for dinner, followed by a cup of tea ! We have had tea after dinner all the while we have been in this stunt."

In a subsequent letter, "feeling more rested," he gives a more detailed account of the affair. "We left our billets in the wood (Havrincourt) with the lightest possible equipment and marched to the edge of the wood. From here we had to crawl a distance of anything from a half to three-quarters of a mile to our old Battn. H.Q. This was no easy job, and very tiring. We went in little parties of three and four, as for the whole distance we were under observation once we had left the wood. However, in spite of all we arrived safely, Fritz not even troubling to bump us at all. Arriving there we proceeded by trench to the front line, from hence we had to make our raid. We got to our position in the trench and were due to start about ten o'clock, but it was not dark enough; but about that time we got out of the trench, crawled through our wire and formed up in our position ready and waiting. It was no easy task to get through our wire going out, but quite all right coming back, as four men spent the time we were out cutting the wire, so that we had a decent gap to get through on our return. As soon as we were in position our artillery gave a three minutes' barrage on Fritz's position and we moved forward under it. It was a grand sight to see our shells bursting considerably less than a hundred yards from us, but personally I felt no fear at all, which surprised me a lot. It was one of the finest firework displays I have ever seen. Of course, there was danger in it, as all the shells were passing over our heads, and if one happened to drop short we should have caught it—in fact, one or two chaps did catch small pieces, but nothing serious. By the time the barrage was finished we were right on to his position. Our particular group, with two others, had to examine a large shell-hole where Fritz was known to be, but when we got there he had cleared off, which perhaps was lucky for us. Our main object was to find out what

MAP No. 13.

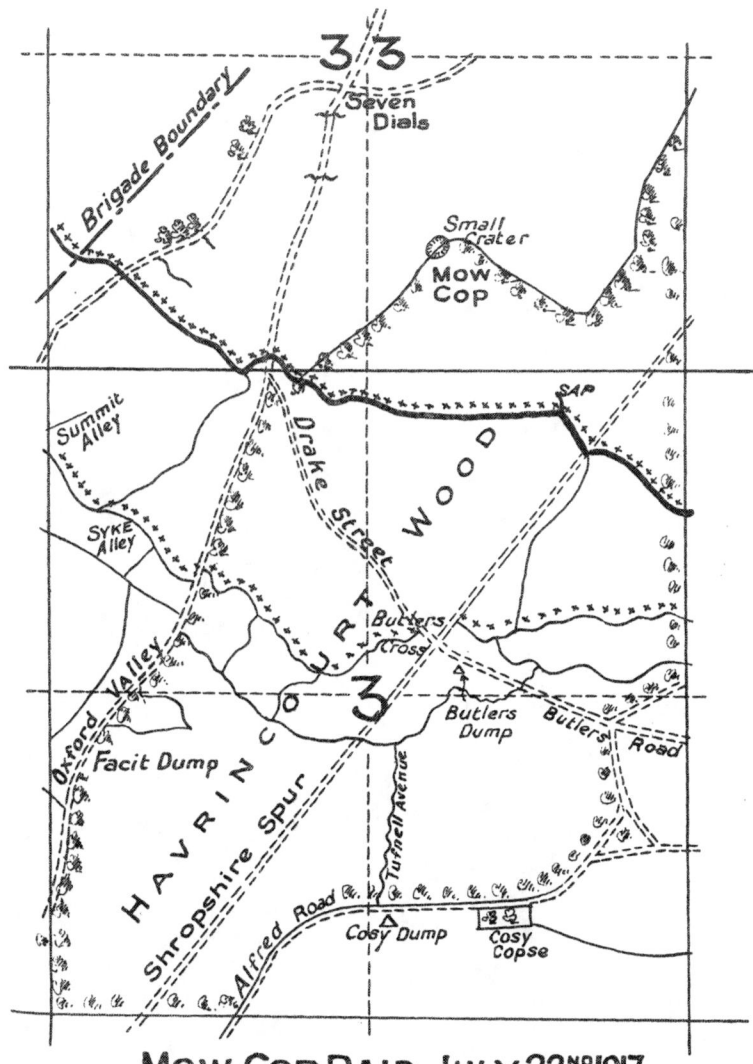

Mow Cop Raid July 22nd 1917.

the ground was like in front of our position and how Fritz held it. Also to get hold of prisoners to find out who was opposite. Contrary to what we had been led to expect we found barbed wire round our post and in trying to get over it I slipped and fell head first over. All the time machine-guns were going on both sides of us, so that any noise we made in moving about was easily drowned. We examined our post well and started moving forward, when on the right of us a little scrap was observed and one or two bombs were thrown. However, two prisoners were captured at our position just then, and we were just forming up to go and assist on the right when three red lights were sent up as a signal to return. We did not need a second telling, but made for our trench as quickly as possible. We were out all told about half to three-quarters of an hour. We did look a motley crowd when we went over. All our steel hats were covered with sandbags, and then rubbed in mud and black from the cookers, and daubed with green paint. All our buttons had to be taken off, as they are regimental buttons, and our jackets were all fastened with safety-pins. Everything had to be left out of our pockets, and all marks of identification had to be removed, even our identity discs had to be left behind. The idea was that should any dead be left behind Fritz would not be able to get any information. Of course, we had no intention of leaving anyone out, and we did not, every member of the party being accounted for. Taken all round it was a most successful turn, and we can consider ourselves very fortunate to have come off with as few casualties as we did."

The one fatal casualty was that of Rfn. Lewthwaite who was shot through the lungs and died a few hours after he was carried back to the lines.

CHAPTER VI

LIFE IN THE SALIENT

ON July 27th the battalion left Havrincourt Wood, which had been its head-quarters since 8th, and journeyed by Betincourt en route for Dainville, near Arras. "The first part of the journey," says C.S.M. Lott, "was made on a light railway. The day was very bright and the enemy's observation balloons were up and evidently they spotted us as we ran alongside the Canal du Nord. Artillery opened on us and the engine driver put on top speed. The train swayed from side to side and we expected every minute to fall into the canal many feet below. Near the big slag heap, which became famous in subsequent fighting, a shell hit the railway line and smashed it. We had orders to scatter and get cover. Shrapnel and H.E. were sent over at us and I stopped a piece in my eye and in consequence spent the next few weeks at a Casualty Clearing Station near Bapaume. The battalion reached that town many hours late for the journey to Dainville, but arrived there safely the following day." At Dainville some very useful training was done. On 10th August there was a brigade "Assault at Arms" in the morning, preceded by the presentation of appreciative cards to officers, N.C.O.'s and men of the brigade recommended for gallant action. Brigade sports were held in the afternoon. The "Assault" consisted of inter-battalion competitions in machine-gun work, platoon and physical drill, signalling, bomb throwing, rifle grenade firing and every kind of specialist training. Says Rfn. Snoswell: "Our battalion did not do at all well in these, so I can see us going through it." A similar assault took place on August 18th, and it is satisfactory to learn that the battalion on this occasion made a better show. Concerts were held frequently in which the Divisional Concert Party, "The Goods," particularly distinguished themselves. And so the time passed until August 24th, on which day the battalion entrained for the "Salient," arriving at Brake Camp near Ypres next day. Its more familiar name was "Dirty Bucket Camp."

During the journey the train conveying the 2nd Battalion into the Salient passed a train on which the 1st Q.V.R. were going out for a rest period. Both trains stopped, but unfortunately about 100 yards separated them, so that there was no opportunity for chatting or fraternising. This was actually the first occasion on which the two battalions came in so close contact.

The day after their arrival at Brake Camp the Brigadier, the Officers Commanding battalions, together with other officers of the brigade went by motor bus to Essex Farm on the canal bank and from there reconnoitred as far as the famous Pilkem Ridge overlooking St. Julien. "We had a good look at the ground with which we were to become so familiar during the next few months," says Lieut.-Col. Langworthy Parry.

"The life of the Salient," moralises the Colonel, "was not without its fascinations, its vivid contrasts, comedies and tragedies, in those days, as all who were there will remember. The roads from the Canal Bank, Buffs Road, Boundary Road, Admiral's Road towards St. Julien, crowded by day and almost deserted by night, presented many a picture. An atmosphere of uncertainty and activity prevailed, men, horses and motor lorries feverishly moving forward or returning, no one staying to pass the time o' day with an acquaintance but all intent on their job and to get it over as soon as possible. It was a study to watch the faces of men returning to the canal bank, if there was any shelling which was generally the case, much or little ; the tenseness of each man's features, the strained look in the eyes showed to what state the nerves were tried, though they were under control ; the blocks in the traffic, the road broken here and there by the burst of a shell and mended with timber ; frequent heaps of shells dropped by some carelessly laden mule and pushed on one side ; here a little party, silent and stern, in fighting order, going up to relieve some post in the line ; men and vehicles laden with all sorts of material : wire, beams, rations and so forth ; parties mending the track or scraping the mud to one side or the other, just as one sees in Piccadilly ; here a sad little procession carrying something covered up on a stretcher ; there a wounded man walking to a dressing station ; next an ambulance in a hurry to get back with its load ; transport of all kinds ; and above all the hum of distant artillery fire, the deafening roar of our guns posted close to the road and the noise of bursting shells ; not a place to linger in unnecessarily, but if one had business there, well, it had to be done and was all in the day's work. It was a picture that indelibly printed itself on the memory and one to which only a master in the art of word painting could do justice."

On August 29th the battalion moved to an adjoining camp at Brown's Farm, described by Rfn. Snoswell as "the best camp I have ever been in. Plenty of room round each tent and plenty of room in each tent. At first we had 10 men in ours, then two were taken out and no more put in, so we had tons of room for everyone. Eight to a tent after 12, 13 or 14 is a treat." Alas for the comfort of our friend. A further move was made the very next day to Dambre Camp, which, he says, was the very opposite to Brown's, with 19 men in his tent and 21 in an adjoining one ! It was a case, he adds, of "When father says turn the whole 19 pairs of feet had to turn." Three days later the battalion marched to dug-outs on the Yser Canal bank preparatory to moving up into the line in the neighbourhood of St. Julien, where it finally arrived on September 5th, but not without suffering some casualties while on the canal bank.

"Almost immediately on our arrival in the Ypres Sector we had a piece of bad luck," writes Lieut. H. Samuelson. "The battalion was living in the dug-outs and galleries on the canal bank just south of Essex Farm near Bridge 4. The Boches evidently knew this particular locality was a centre of activity and his high velocity or "rubber" guns always threw a few over each day. At a quarter past seven one morning the usual shriek of an arrival was heard and this particular one landed right on a dug-out occupied by 'C' Company. There were 15 men in the dug-out, of whom 6 were killed and 8 wounded, the sole survivor being blackened from head to foot and badly shaken. The dead were buried in the afternoon in the cemetery some half-mile south of Essex Farm."

From the same source we gather that "It was not far from

here, namely, at Regiersburg Camp, that an unusual incident took place which unfortunately resulted in the death of Sergt. Matthews, then acting C.Q.M.S. of Head-quarters Company. Several of us were watching one of our observation balloons being shelled—very ineffectually—by the Boches long range guns. The nosecap or some portion of one of the shells fell, striking Sergt. Matthews in the head and killing him almost immediately. This took place within a few hundred yards of where his brother had been killed a week or so previously by an aeroplane bomb."

CHAPTER VII

THIRD BATTLE OF YPRES

ST. JULIEN, like all the villages within the battle area, was a heap of ruins, but scattered about were a number of the type of concrete buildings made by the Huns and known by name as "Mebus," or "pill-box." In one of these, which was not much knocked about and known as Hackney Villa (after the 10th London Regiment), were housed the Battalion H.Q. It was capable of holding about 100 men. The line taken up by the 2nd Q.V.R., as described by Lieut.-Col. Langworthy Parry, faced N.E., the left forward position resting on Springfield and extending as far as Spot Farm, the right company occupying sectional posts N. and S. of the St. Julien-Winnipeg Road. "C" Company, under Capt. Griffith, was on the left; "B" Company, Capt. Walker, on the right; "A" Company, Capt. Stronge, at St. Julien; and "D" Company, under Lieut. Richmond, in support further south at Cheddar Villa. Late on September 5th Col. Langworthy Parry received orders for the battalion to capture and hold Jury Farm and the Cemetery and to establish the line of the Winnipeg-Cemetery-Springfield Road (from D.7.C.17) to the existing post Spot Farm on the night of September 8th.

Orders were issued as follows :

2/9th Battalion London Regiment (Queen Victoria's Rifles)

ORDER NO. 1

Ref. Map *September 7th*, 1917.
Poelcapelle
1/10,000

INFORMATION (1). Enemy, strength unknown, reported to be occupying Jury Farm and the ground immediately east of the Cemetery, all situated in C.12.d.

THIRD BATTLE OF YPRES

INTENTION (2). The 2/9th Battalion will capture and hold Jury Farm, C.12.d.8.6, and the Cemetery, C.12.B.8.0 and establish the line at the Winnipeg-Cemetery-Springfield Road from D.7.C.1.7 to Spot Farm on the night of September 8/9th.

INSTRUCTIONS (3).

(a) *Companies immediately engaged in the attack.*
" B " Company—No. 7 and 8 Platoons.
" C " Company—No. 10 and 12 Platoons.

(b) *Assembly.*
" C " Company jumping-off place, Springfield.
" B " Company jumping-off place, C.12.d.5.5, St Julien-Winnipeg Road.

(c) *Time.* 9.30 p.m.

(d) *Order of forming up, as per plan attached.*

(e) *Zero Hour.* 9.45 p.m.

(f) *Objectives :* " C " Company, Cemetery, C.12.b.8.0.
" B " Company, Jury Farm, C.12.d. 8.6.

(g) *Method of Attack.*

At zero hour the attacking platoons will advance simultaneously from the north and west, two platoons attacking astride the Springfield Road, two platoons astride the St. Julien-Winnipeg Road.

The two platoons of " C " Company, one on each side of the Springfield-Winnipeg Road, will advance in column of sections with scouts in front taking the road as their direction mark.

No 10 Platoon south of the road will go straight to the Cemetery and the Mebus immediately south of it, mop them up and hold them.

No. 12 Platoon north of the road will act as covering party to the other, advancing at the same time, sending on one section to Spot Farm at dusk beforehand, the permanent garrison having been withdrawn for the gas.

No. 12 Platoon will drop another section north of the road immediately east of the Cemetery and the remaining two sections will take up a position north of the road about C.12.d.9.9, and will co-operate in the capture of the objective.

When the objective has been captured the right platoon No. 10, will establish themselves at about C.12.d.8.8.

The left platoon will continue to guard the left flank till one hour before dawn, when it will withdraw to C.12.d.2.9. As soon as the attacking platoons move off at 9.45 p.m., No. 9 Platoon will occupy Springfield and No. 11 Spot Farm, where they will remain as garrison.

"B" Company, Nos. 7 and 8 Platoons, jumping off from C.12.d.5.5, one on each side of the St. Julien-Winnipeg Road, will advance in column of sections taking this road as their direction mark, with scouts in front.

No. 7 Platoon, south of the road, will advance direct on Jury Farm, occupying the whole of it and consolidate it. It will send one section as a forward post to the cross roads D.7.c.0.8.

No. 8 Platoon, north of the road, will advance at the same time, two sections being specially detailed to assist in the taking of Jury Farm and will also mop up any of the enemy found in the western fork of the cross roads. They will then obtain touch with the "C" Company post at C.12.d.9.9. When Jury Farm is consolidated No. 8 Platoon retires to C.12.d.3.5.

(h) *Flanks.* "C" Company will take special care with regard to the protection of its flank (left).

"B" Company will have special care of its right flank.

(i) *Consolidation.* Will take the form of making platoon strong points, utilising the best ground available.

(j) *Screens.* Platoons will push out screens to their front while consolidation is in progress.

(k) *Direction and Distance.* One N.C.O. and one man per platoon will be detailed to see that the direction is kept and the distance to be traversed is not overrun.

Tapes knotted at every 50 yards will be used.

2 N.C.O.'s will be detailed at Company Head-quarters for the same purpose.

Everyone must know the general direction, compass bearing and the general plan and object of the attack.

(l) *Dress.* Fighting Order as laid down, with the following modifications : Every man, except Lewis gunners, will carry either a pick or a shovel. Every man, other than Lewis gunners, will carry 170 rounds S.A.A.

THIRD BATTLE OF YPRES

(m) *Food and Water.* Each man will carry twenty-four hours food rations and 2 bottles of water.

(n) *Dumps.* Dumps for tools, bombs and ammunition will be established at each strong point.

(o) *Synchronisation of Watches.* Company Commanders will arrange to have their watches synchronised at Battn. H.Q. at 6 p.m. on September 8th.

(p) *Wounded.* " C " Company will be evacuated down the Winnipeg-Springfield Road to the R.A.P. " B " Company down the Winnipeg-St. Julien Road.

(q) *Prisoners.* Will be sent under escort to Battn. H.Q. via same route as wounded.

(r) *Password and Distinguishing Marks.* Each man will wear a piece of white tape tied round above the elbow on each arm. The Password for the night will be " Bully."

(s) *Notification of Capture of Position.* Companies will immediately notify Battn. H.Q. when positions are captured.

(t) *Gas.* Provided the wind is favourable on the afternoon of September 8th there will be a projection of gas from " Livens " projectors on the area to be attacked. Following precautions will be taken with reference to this :

The two forward posts of " B " Company and the two forward posts of " C " Company will be withdrawn at dawn on September 8th to positions previously selected.

All companies except " D " Company will have their box respirators in the alert position from 1.45 to 1.55 p.m. when they will put them on and wear them until 2.15 p.m.

(u) *Artillery.* To assist in the enterprise the heavy artillery will shoot on Jury Farm and the Cemetery on September 8th between the hours of 2 p.m. and 4 p.m. and 5 p.m. and 6 p.m. Up till 9.45 p.m. the artillery will also fire on the area objectives.

At zero hour there will be a " crash " for four minutes and the field artillery will then put down a standing barrage on the line D.7.c.00 to D.7.c.47.68, D.7.c.57.68 to D.7.a.12.53.

RATES OF FIRE. From zero plus four minutes to zero plus fourteen minutes 3 rounds per gun per minute. Then cease fire, but guns will stand to, to shoot on the same lines if called for until zero plus two hours.

VICKERS' GUNS. No. 1 gun at C.12.d.7.4 at zero hour to zero plus four minutes will open covering fire on Jury Farm and afterwards on Winnipeg.

No. 2 gun at C.12.d.1.5 will fire on Mebus at C.12.d.8.8 from zero to zero plus four.

Nos. 3 and 4 guns at Springfield will fire from zero till zero plus 6 covering our left flank in the Springfield-Winnipeg Road.

(v) *R.A.P.* (*Regimental Aid Post*), C.18.a.2.9.

(w) "*A*" *Company will remain in its support position.* "*D*" *Company at dusk on September 8th will send one platoon to Battn. Head-quarters.*

REPORTS (4) To Battalion Head-quarters.

(Sgd.) A. D. HARINGTON,
Captain and Adjutant,
2/9th London Regiment
Issued at 2.10 a.m. (Queen Victoria's Rifles).

SUPPLEMENT TO ORDER No. 1

September 7th, 1917.

Ref. Map Poelcapelle, 1/10,000.

(1) MAP OF DISPOSITION AFTER BATTLE. This is enclosed. "D" Company will fill in the No. of the platoon.

(2) "A" COMPANY. At 9.40 p.m. on September 8th "A" Company will move its advance platoon from the St. Julien-Poelcapelle Road in support of Springfield to position held by former garrison of C.12.a.9.4. This platoon will be withdrawn as soon as it is relieved by "C" Company's platoon, or in time to enable it to return to its original position before dawn. (Verbal instructions already given to Capt. Stronge.)

(3) GUIDES. O.C.'s "A" and "C" Companies will make the necessary arrangements regarding guides for "C" Company on the night of September 8th/9th.

(4) RELAY POSTS. "C" Company will find one relay post consisting of four men at Springfield and one at "C" Company's rear H.Q. on the St. Julien-Poelcapelle Road. These relay posts will be in position by 9.30 p.m.

"B" Company will establish a relay post consisting of four

men at Mebus, C.12.d.4.5. This relay post to be in position by 9.30 p.m.

(5) "B" AND "C" COMPANIES PRIOR TO MOVING OFF FROM ASSEMBLY POSITIONS TO ATTACK. As soon as it is dusk tomorrow, 8th September, a section of "C" Company and a Vicker's gun must be rushed up to Spot Farm and a section of "B" Company must also be rushed up to forward post vacated by its platoon at the same time.

(6) COMMUNICATIONS. Communications will be established as follows :

CEMETERY ATTACK. "C" Company Springfield to "C" Company H.Q., St. Julien by lamp direct.

Cemetery to "C" Company H.Q., St. Julien. "C" Company H.Q. to Battn. H.Q. by lamp and "Fuller."

RUNNERS. Relay runner posts will be established at Springfield. Post at C.12.a.8.4. "C" Company H.Q., St. Julien.

JURY FARM ATTACK. Runners from Jury Farm to Border House (M.G. Head-quarters). Border House to Battn. H.Q. by runner. Lamp and wire.

Battn. H.Q. to Brigade, usual channels.

Note.—No copies of orders will go further forward than Company H.Q., Border House and St. Julien.

(Signed) A. D. HARINGTON,
Captain and Adjutant,
2/9th London Regiment
(Queen Victoria's Rifles).

SUPPLEMENT No. 2 TO OPERATION ORDER No. 1
8/9/17.

"A" Company. "A" Company will place two platoons at the disposal of "C" Company this evening to be under the order of Capt. Griffith.

2nd Lieut. Chudley, the Commander of No. 1 Platoon, will report to Capt. Griffith at four o'clock this afternoon for instructions, his platoon being intended for the garrisoning of Spot Farm. This platoon will leave its present position immediately it is dusk and proceed to Spot Farm via Springfield in rear of the covering troops.

2nd Lieut. Day, the Commander of No. 2 Platoon, will

report to Capt. Griffith at 4 p.m. this afternoon, and No. 2 Platoon will move to the gun pits in rear of Springfield and hold the position until relieved by a platoon of " C " Company when it will retire to " C " Company Head-quarters, C.12.C.4.5.

No. 4 Platoon, as soon as it is dusk, will move from Cheddar Villa to " A " Company Head-quarters at St. Julien.

(Signed) A. D. HARINGTON,
Captain and Adjutant,
2/9th Battalion the London Regiment
(Queen Victoria's Rifles).

The operation was duly carried out in accordance with these orders. Capt. Griffith of " C " Company was in command of the force detailed to seize the Cemetery and Capt. Walker, " B " Company, of that ordered to capture Jury Farm and Winnipeg, the plan being roughly to advance on two sides of a triangle and linking up at the apex. Both forces moved off from their positions to time.

Lieut. G. Spenser-Pryse gives the following account of what took place :

" 9.45 p.m. Right Party advanced and captured objective without trouble, together with 7 prisoners (2 wounded). Finding the farm completely demolished by our heavies they consolidated about 50 yards beyond.

"Left Party started handicapped as 12 men from one platoon had been gassed in the afternoon. Our barrage was somewhat short and the platoon experienced some difficulty in getting ahead. Lieut. Wightwick and his platoon sergeant were hit at this time and the platoons unable to reach the Mebus withdrew, leaving a small garrison under 2nd Lieut. Spenser-Pryse, south of the road a short distance from the Cemetery.

" ' B ' Company, finding they were being fired into from the back by the Mebus ' C ' Company had failed to take, returned bringing another 6 prisoners and leaving about 2 more badly wounded Germans behind.

"CASUALTIES. Right Party. Capt. Walker was hit in the thigh and has since died, 1 O.R. killed and 3 wounded.

"German : 13 prisoners, 2 wounded left behind.

"Lieut. Macadam accounted for one himself with the bayonet, another was killed for certain, possibly more.

"Left Party. Lieut. Wightwick died of wounds, 4 O.R. killed and 19 wounded and 9 gassed.

"Next day Lieut. Spenser-Pryse's post killed 3 Germans who were relieving the Mebus.

```
                                    |  |
                                    |  |   Winnipeg.
                                    |  |
              † † †                 |  |
              Cemetery   □ Mebus    |  |   □ Jury Farm
    Left Party ———→                 |  ↑
                                    |  |   Right Party.
```

In a more detailed account Lieut. Spenser-Pryse says:

"Operations at the Cemetery, St. Julien, September 8th/9th, 1917:

"The night 7th/8th September I spent with my platoon at Springfield; my men distributed in adjacent shell-holes to be ready for the attack at nightfall. It had been arranged for our artillery to shell the Cemetery with gas during the afternoon of the 8th. Unfortunately their ranging was to some extent inaccurate and nine of my platoon were sent down wounded and gassed at dusk as the result of one shell burst actually on their position. I therefore asked for and received reinforcements.

"The attack was preceded by a bombardment culminating in a barrage which would lift from the Springfield-Cemetery Road on to a line 150/200 yards E. of that road. Lieut. Wightwick and I were to advance under cover of this barrage to our objectives.

"We moved out at 9.40 p.m. The operations of posting my flank guard presented no difficulty. I then proceeded to the Cross Roads and awaited events. As eleven o'clock approached and Jury being still in enemy hands, although the volume of fire was decreasing from both sides, I realised that Capt.

Walker's attack had not developed satisfactorily. Finally, on hearing that Lieut. Wightwick's attack on the Cemetery Mebus had failed, that he himself was a casualty, and that his platoon sergeant had decided to retire, I came to the conclusion that my position at the Cross Roads was untenable with the forces at my disposal and Lce.-Cpl. Chapman and four survivors of the two sections that had gone forward. It was evident that our success in attaining the objective and in remaining so long in that isolated position, was entirely due to the exceptional darkness of the night. Our further presence there would serve no useful purpose.

"I thereupon withdrew to high ground immediately N. of the Cemetery Mebus, and took charge of the entire operation, countermanding the order to retire and sending out parties to collect our wounded. Having decided to consolidate I selected a position commanding both the Mebus itself and the enemy communicating trench, through the Cemetery, at close range. At this stage invaluable assistance in rallying the men, who were withdrawing in some disorder, was rendered by Lce.-Cpl. Chapman. Without his aid it would have been impossible to carry through a scheme of fortified shell-holes, facing east, south and south-west. In the thick darkness Lce.-Cpl. Chapman crept from one detached group to another, advising and cheering the men, and as a result when morning broke a rough circle of communicating shell-holes had been established in a dominating position.

"During the day 9th September we were able to prevent all enemy movement and to inflict severe casualties on his attempting to relieve the Mebus garrison at dusk.

"At about 7.30 an enemy attempt to outflank our left and cut us off from Springfield was foiled with further loss. At nine we were relieved without incident by the 12th London Regiment via Springfield. A considerable proportion of the men went into the attack suffering from the effects of gas. The whole were greatly exhausted. From dawn till dusk we were entirely cut off from the battalion and there was a shortage of water on the second day. Except for the brief confusion which followed the failure of the first assault on the Mebus the men's demeanour was beyond criticism. It is impossible to speak too highly of the eagerness with which they volunteered to go out under direct M.G. fire to bring in our wounded."

Lieut. McAdam (" B " Company) says : " During the afternoon the artillery gassed the Mebus, Cemetery, Jury Farm and Cross Roads, but unfortunately Spot Farm was also gassed and caused several casualties to ' C ' Company. At zero hour No. 7 Platoon of ' B ' Company advanced along the left side of the road running from Janet Farm to Jury Farm, and No. 8 platoon on the right side of the road. The barrage here was excellent and as we entered Jury Farm we were almost in the barrage itself. Here 7 Boches were taken prisoners and others were accounted for by the bayonet and 2 were shot by Capt. Walker (then in command of the company). After Jury Farm had been dealt with, the attack proceeded to just beyond the Cross Roads, where we dug in. A strong right defensive flank had been established and also a couple of M.G. posts were put out about 70 yards in front. A patrol of an N.C.O. and 8 men were sent out in the direction of the Cemetery to get in touch with ' C ' Company. This patrol returned after about forty minutes stating there was no sign of ' C ' Company and that the Cemetery was still held by the enemy's M.G.'s, therefore it was evident that ' C ' Company had not reached its objective. It was then decided that we should make good Jury Farm. We got back to the farm and tried to dig in. It was impossible, however, to enter the dug-out as it had been blown in by the barrage and it was equally impossible to dig in round it owing to the state of the mud and shell-holes filled with water. On the way back Capt. Walker was unfortunately hit through the thigh by a sniper's bullet from the Mebus, and owing to the enemy's accurate M.G. fire it took two stretcher bearers (Rfn. Bryant and Harold) over an hour to get him to a place of safety. I may mention that both these men well deserved their Military Medals. We heard four days later that Capt. Walker had died in hospital near Poperinghe, which was not only a great blow to the company, but to the whole battalion. While the men were occupied in digging in at Jury Farm they came under cross-fire from M.G.'s from the Mebus on either side which made it impossible to hold the farm as there was absolutely no cover, and even if the men attempted to remain in the shell-holes they would sink in the mud. The company was thereupon ordered to return to its former positions. While on the way back from Jury Farm we suddenly heard a noise, and as we approached the place whence it came someone shouted out, ' Ach, don't shoot. We are two Swiss gentlemen.' Then suddenly appeared from goodness knows where six Boches, whom we escorted back to Battn. H.Q. They had evidently come forward at the beginning of the attack in order to escape our barrage. We reached our positions as the dawn arrived. The total number of our prisoners was 13, and several more were accounted for during the fighting, while many were found dead round and about Jury Farm who had been killed by the barrage or gassed during the afternoon. Our casualties in ' B ' Company were : Killed, 1 officer, 2 O.R.'s ; wounded, 7 O.R.'s."

The following additional details are furnished by Rfn. A. E. Mills who was severely wounded in the chest : "Two platoons of ' B ' Company, and the whole of ' C ' Company were taking part in the operations, and ' B ' Company succeeded in accomplishing their task. Capt. Walker called for a volunteer party of four (presumably he wished to know what was happening to ' C ' Company on our left), and Rfn. Farmer, Ellis, Mills and Wainwright went with him. Capt. Walker stopped to talk to a wounded German and it was then discovered that something had prevented ' C ' Company from carrying out their programme. In rapid succession Mills, Ellis, Capt. Walker, and Rfn. Farmer were hit from a machine-gun which ' C ' Company would have mopped up had they been able to advance. Capt. Walker then sent Rfn. Mills forward to the platoon for assistance, and when he returned Ellis was dead and Capt. Walker was being got on to a stretcher. This gallant gentleman died shortly afterwards in hospital. I shall never forget his action after he was wounded ; he lay on the stretcher directing us (his local knowledge seemed to me wonderful) and we dragged him over the rough ground, just two stretcher bearers and myself, until we were back to our starting-point, where my wound was dressed. One could not judge from his quiet and decided manner whether he suffered any pain, but the rough ground and the shaking he got must have been all against him."

The failure of " C " Company was principally due to the number of casualties including Lieut. Wightwick and his platoon sergeant at a critical juncture. Lieut. Wightwick was carried to a dressing station, but died before he arrived there.

On the following day Brigade Head-quarters issued the following comment on the operations :

Secret.

B.H.F./11/.

ACCOUNT OF ATTACK ON CEMETERY AND WINNIPEG ON NIGHT OF SEPTEMBER 8TH, 1917

1. From personal reports of Capt. Griffith, commanding the Springfield Company, and Lieut. McAdam, commanding the leading platoon of Janet Farm Company in absence of Capt. Walker, the company commander who is wounded, the following appears to be a statement of the facts :

2. The troops engaged were—

" B " Coy. (Capt. H. S. Walker) attacking from Janet Farm.
    One platoon (Lieut. McAdam) attacking north of the Jury Farm-Winnipeg Road—objective Winnipeg crossroads.
    One platoon (Lieut. Russell-Jones) attacking the south of the road—objective Jury Farm.
    One platoon holding post " A "-Janet Farm.

" C " Coy. (Capt. Griffith) attacking from Springfield.
    One platoon working down east of the Springfield-Winnipeg Road to cover flank of platoon (Lieut. Spenser-Pryse) on west of the road with orders to get into touch with Lieut McAdam's platoon at Winnipeg cross-roads.
    One platoon (Lieut. S. Wightwick) attacking west of the road—objective Cemetery and large concrete emplacement at C.12.d.8.8.
    One platoon Spot Farm.
    One platoon Springfield.

3. The two platoons of " B " Company left Janet Farm at zero hour working one on each side of the road, taking Jury Farm and 13 prisoners. Lieut. Russell-Jones' platoon finding

that Jury Farm was completely demolished presumably as a result of the direct hit by a 9·2 reported yesterday afternoon, proceeded to consolidate 50 yards in front of the farm.

Lieut. McAdam's platoon pushed on to Winnipeg cross-roads, and commenced to dig in on the east side of it, putting out posts on three roads to their right, left and centre. They thus gained the whole of their objectives. Capt. Walker, the Company Commander, went forward to see the consolidation at the cross-roads and ascertained the situation, but on his way back to Company H.Q. was hit in the thigh.

During the process of consolidation enemy machine-guns' fire was brought to bear on these two platoons from the concrete emplacement at C.12.d.8.8 and from about C.7.c.5.3. It was now obvious that the Springfield Company had failed to take the concrete emplacement at C.12.d.8.8. The orders of this platoon had been to retire to the concrete emplacement at Jury Farm before dawn, leaving a post at the cross-roads. As this concrete emplacement was non-existent, and as they were being shot into in the back from concrete emplacements from both flanks, it appeared that the position would be untenable in the daylight. A withdrawal was therefore ordered. This I consider was justified under the circumstances. These two platoons captured 11 unwounded prisoners and 2 wounded prisoners of the 414 I.R. They left behind at Jury Farm 2 other wounded prisoners.

Lieut. McAdam himself killed one German with the bayonet. One other German was killed for certain, and probably more. The casualties to this company were Capt. H. S. Walker wounded, 1 man killed and 3 wounded.

I consider that this company was exceedingly well handled.

" C " Company were not so successful. At dusk, when the Company Commander arrived at Springfield, he found that 8 of the garrison (Lieut. Spenser-Pryse's platoon) had been gassed by our gas shells, and had to be evacuated. Lieut. Wightwick's platoon had lost 9 men the previous night during a company relief, and had to be reinforced by a section from another platoon who did not know the ground at the last moment. They thus started seriously handicapped. In addition, our barrage was very short on this flank, H.E. bursting behind the road, though as far as I can ascertain no casualties were caused by it. The barrage on the right seemed excellent.

As soon as the attacking platoons reached the Cemetery and the ground east of it, they were heavily fired at from the Cemetery and from the large concrete emplacement at D.7.a.0.0.

Lieut. Wightwick and the platoon sergeant were both hit at this time. This platoon appears never to have got beyond the Cemetery, although it is stated that 5 men actually got up to the concrete emplacement at C.12.d.8.8, though this I have been unable to verify. It was recognised from the start that the whole success of the operation depended on seizing the emplacement at C.12.d.8.8, as it holds at least 20 men, is on a small eminence which gives it a command on all sides, and is armed with 3 M.G.'s which can fire to the north, the east and the south.

It is questionable whether if at this time Capt. Griffith had sent forward the platoon from Spot Farm to reinforce this platoon, this point might not still have been captured. It must, however, be remembered that Spot Farm was a most important post covering their rear and line of retirement, and that Captain Griffith would have been running a grave risk in withdrawing it. I do not, therefore, in any way blame him for not doing so.

A post has been established astride the Spot Farm-Winnipeg Road at about C.12.b.8.1.

I consider that the failure of Lieut. Wightwick's platoon to take this strong point chiefly due to the fact that he and his sergeant were both hit at the same time.

Although it failed in execution, I consider that the plan was a good one, and had Lieut. Wightwick's platoon succeeded in capturing its objective, it would have been a complete success, and in two days' time I propose to take this strong point with a fresh battalion. It is hoped to-night to push out a post from Janet Farm to Jury Farm, which will be held by night. I do not think it advisable to hold it by day owing to the command which the two forementioned concrete emplacements have over it.

GAS. The Livens projectors were discharged at 2 p.m. The wind appeared favourable and the direction and range of the projectors to be accurate. The results appear, however, to have been negligible, as I myself saw 5 men within an hour get up out of crump-holes and run like rabbits to the strong point, and no trace of gassed men were found about Jury Farm or the cross-roads. Presumably information about the gas will be forthcoming from the prisoners.

I attach a map showing objectives.

With the exception of the above-mentioned post established at C.12.b.8.1, the attacking platoons are now back in their original posts.

I much regret that this attack should have so nearly succeeded, and yet failed, but I am confident that we will succeed next time.

Brigadier-General, Commanding
175th Infantry Brigade.

9/9/17.

Lieut.-Col. Langworthy Parry describes the loss of Capt. Walker and Lieut. Wightwick as a serious one for the battalion. No two officers, he says, were more highly esteemed and loved by all ranks, and they were indeed very gallant gentlemen. General Maxse commanding the XVIIIth Corps afterwards congratulated the colonel on the very near success of the action. Lieuts. McAdam and Spenser-Pryse were each awarded the Military Cross for the conspicuous gallantry they had shown in this affair.

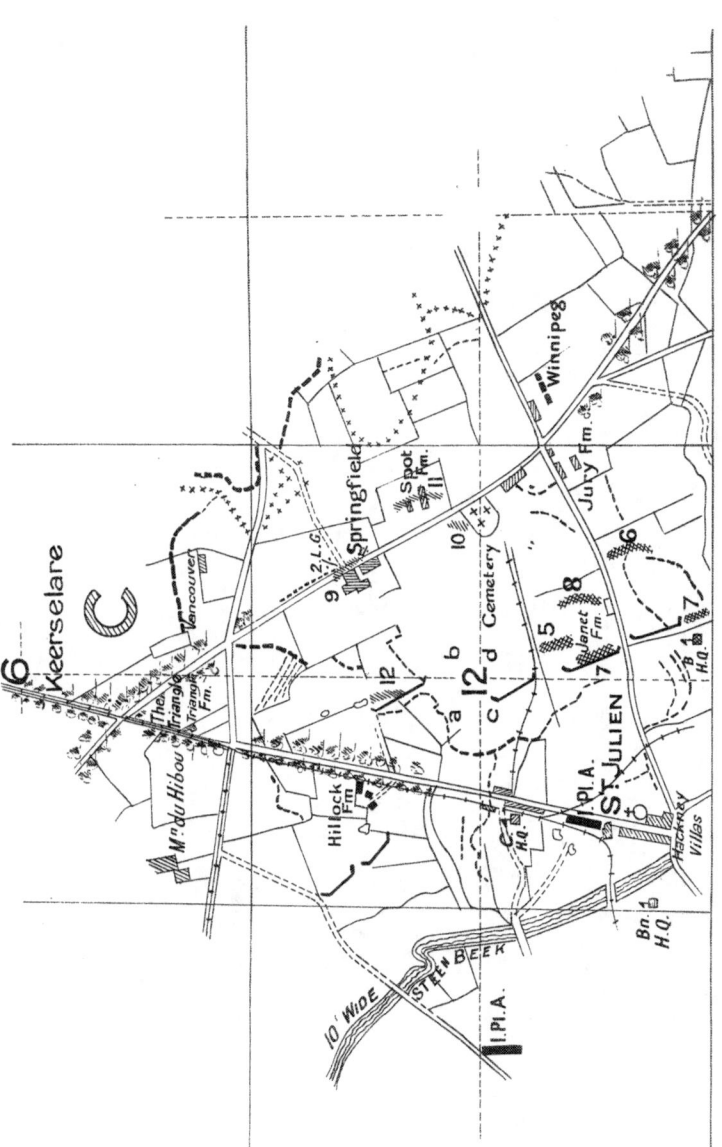

CHAPTER VIII

THIRD BATTLE OF YPRES—(*continued*)

OPERATIONS AT AVIATIK AND WURST FARM

ON the evening of September 9th the battalion went back to the Canal Bank and on 11th was at Brake Camp, remaining there until 19th, when it moved to Reigersberg Camp. In the interval the men were engaged in practising the attack for the coming fighting. This took place on September 20th, but on this occasion the 175th Brigade was in reserve, the 173rd and 174th being the attacking force. The work allotted to the 2nd Q.V.R. consisted of two companies ("A" and "D") being detached to carry ammunition for the heavy guns while "C" and "B" acted as stretcher bearers under Capt. Eustace, the M.O. "Both tasks were well done," says Lieut.-Col. Langworthy Parry, "though not without casualties, and I received very congratulatory reports from the A.D.M.S. and the C.R.A on the behaviour of the men and the excellent discipline they had shown."

So highly was the work of the London men appreciated at home that the Lord Mayor, Sir William Dunn, on September 25th sent the following telegram to Sir Douglas Haig : "September 25th. The citizens of London offer their warmest congratulations to you and your gallant troops on the brilliant successes recently attained. They are proud the London Regiments afforded such effective assistance." On September 27th Sir Douglas Haig dispatched the following reply : "On behalf of all ranks of the British Armies in France, I thank you and the citizens of London for your warm message of congratulations. London regiments did good work again in yesterday's battle." As will be seen in that battle the Q.V.R. had an important task assigned to them.

A promise had been given that the battalion should have a

show on its own and it was fixed to take place on September 26th. It is generally known as the Aviatik and Wurst Farm Operations. On September 21st the battalion had moved back to the Canal Bank and busily occupied itself in rehearsing the attack.

"The Corps Commander and the Army Commander," writes Lieut.-Col. Langworthy Parry, "came to watch the rehearsals, and Gen. Maxse, the Corps Commander, told me he wished the show to be a 'Queen Victoria's one,' but I was to have a company of the 12th attached to me, and that the attack would be preceded by the heaviest artillery preparation ever known in the British Army. I told him I knew the Queen Victoria's Rifles would do well, and he wished us the best of luck and every success."

On 24th September the following orders were issued (they are inserted as an example of the enormous amount of detail to be considered in launching an attack at this period of the war):

2/9TH BATTALION LONDON REGIMENT (QUEEN VICTORIA'S RIFLES)

Ref. map, part of Poelcapelle, 1/5,000. Order No. 1., 24/9/17. As per copy marked "A" attached.

(1) INFORMATION. The brigade will attack and capture the Green Line in conjunction with a large attack being made further south on Z day, which has been communicated verbally to those concerned.

Zero hour will be notified later.

A brigade of the 59th Division is to attack on our right, on our left there will be no attack, but a demonstration with dummy figures is to be made to draw the enemy's fire.

The task allotted to this brigade will be carried out by the 2/12th London Regiment on the right and the 2/9th London Regiment on the left. The 2/10th London Regiment will be in support and the 2/2nd London Regiment will hold that portion of the brigade front on which no attack is being delivered. Objectives and boundaries are shown on the attached map marked A.

For purposes of this operation one company 2/12th Battalion

will be detached from its unit and will be under the orders of O.C. 2/9th Battalion from 11 p.m. onwards on Y day.

(2) INTENTION. The 2/9th Battalion and "B" Company of the 2/12th Battalion will capture and hold the area enclosed in the green line marked on the attached map on the morning of zero day : zero day to be notified later.

(3) INSTRUCTIONS. (a) *Assembly.* Companies will assemble in front of their areas to be attacked as indicated on attached map, reading from left to right as follows :

"D" Company. "C" Company. "A" Company with "B" Company in rear of it. "B" Company 2/12th Battalion. Order of forming up as per attached plan. Time to be notified later.

Company Commanders will arrange to send one officer tomorrow, 25th inst., to Lieut. Underhay and the Engineer Officer at Hackney Villa, St. Julien, at 4 p.m. These officers will each take an N.C.O. with them. These officers will take with them luminous discs bearing the number of their platoons. On arriving at St. Julien they will be shown the tape line and will affix luminous discs where the left of each platoon will rest, all discs being numbered. These discs will be drawn from the Orderly Room.

These officers and N.C.O.'s will eventually act as guides to lead the companys on to the lines. These guides will meet the battalions at the aid posts on St. Julien-Wieltje Road at 11 p.m.

(b) *Order of March :* "D," "C," "A," H.Q., "B."
   "B" Company 2/12th.

(c) *Route.* Essex Farm-Buffs Road-Tin Hut to St Julien.

(d) *Time of Starting.* The leading platoon will pass the starting-point at the point where the Canal Bank meets the Essex Farm-Buffs Road at 10 p.m.

Intervals of 100 yards between platoons, 200 yards between companies.

(e) *Objectives.* "D" Company the area shaded yellow. "C" Company A.70.95. "C" Company the area shaded green. "A" Company the area shaded red. "B" Company the area shaded blue. "B" Company 2/12th the area shaded in pencil.

(f) *Method of Attack.* At zero hour the leading platoons of each company will advance simultaneously on their objectives in the formation shown on attached plan B. Each company commander will detail a specific area in his sector as the objective of each separate platoon, and sections must also have definite work allotted to them. The advance of the battalion will conform with the creeping barrage. A halt will be made for twenty minutes on the dotted red line as shown on attached map A.

" D " Company will establish three strong points on its left flank and one in the neighbourhood of Company H.Q.

" C " Company will establish one strong point on the N.E. corner of its sector (the defensive flank) and the other three platoons will also establish strong points in the areas allotted to them.

" A " Company will establish a strong point at Aviatik Farm and three others in the areas allotted to the remaining platoons.

" B " Company will establish a strong point at Boetleer and one on the company left sector. The remaining two platoons will also establish strong points on their sectors.

" B " Company 2/12th, whose special duty it is to guard our right flank, will establish strong points as indicated in blue on the attached map.

(g) *Screens.* Platoons will push out screens to their front while the consolidation is in progress.

(h) *Direction and Distances.* One N.C.O. and one man per platoon will be detailed to see that the distance is kept and the distance traversed is not overrun. Tapes knotted every 50 yards will be used. Every man must know the general direction, the compass bearing and general plan and object of the attack.

(i) *Bearing of the Attack.* 130" magnetic.

(j) *Dress.* Fighting order as laid down.

(k) *Food and Water.* Each man will carry forty-eight hours' food ration, one bottle of water and one bottle of tea.

(l) *Dumps.* Dumps for tools, bombs and ammunition will be established at each strong point.

(m) *Synchronisation of Watches.* Company Commanders will arrange to have their watches synchronised at Battalion H.Q. at Canal Bank at 8 p.m. on 25th inst.

THIRD BATTLE OF YPRES

(n) *Flanks.* SPECIAL ATTENTION MUST BE PAID TO THE PROTECTION OF THE LEFT AND RIGHT FLANKS.

(o) *Barrage.* The advance will conform with the creeping barrage. The attack will be preceded by a two hours' hurricane bombardment of all available heavy and field artillery, and will be made under cover of:

    (i.) A creeping barrage.
    (ii.) A searching barrage.
    (iii.) A box barrage.
    (iv.) A back heavy artillery barrage.
    (v.) A machine-gun barrage.

A barrage map will be issued later.

The creeping barrage will open 150 yards in front of our forming-up line, and will move by lifts of 50 yards. The first lift at 0 plus 3; succeeding lifts for first 200 yards 50 yards in two minutes. After that the barrage will move in lifts of 50 yards every three minutes. (See addenda order, No. 1, "Barrage.")

(p) *Situation Reports.* Situation by priority message will be forwarded at zero hour and after zero hour every half hour.

(q) *Signal for Gaining Objective.* As soon as each company has gained its final objective lights will be fired as follows:

"A" Company	1 Very light.			
"B" Company	2 ,,	lights, in quick succession.		
"C" Company	3 ,,	,,	,,	,,
"D" Company	4 ,,	,,	,,	,,
"B" Company 2/12th	5 ,,	,,	,,	,,

All fired in the direction of Battn. H.Q.

Companies will also notify Battn. H.Q. by runner immediately their objectives have been taken and their dispositions.

(r) *Medical.* R.A.P. at Janet's Farm. C.6.d.30.40.

All wounded will be cleared and left at Cluster House or Arbre and will be evacuated from there to the R.A.P. by R.A.M.C. bearers. This does not apply to walking wounded who will go straight to the R.A.P.

(s) *Vickers Guns.* As soon as the objectives have been gained 8 Vickers M.G. will be moved forward for defensive purposes. Two guns will be moved to Winzig, 2 guns to Boetleer, 2 guns to Mebus south of Boetleer, and 2 guns to Aviatik Farm.

(t) *Reserve.* As soon as the two rear platoons of " C " Company (Nos. 10 and 12) and the two rear platoons of " A " Company (Nos. 3 and 4) have mopped up their sectors, Nos. 10 and 12 will establish themselves near Clifton House and Nos. 3 and 4 near Wurst Farm and will be under the orders of the Battalion Commander for the purpose of counter-attack. Capt. Griffith will report personally to Battalion Head-quarters as soon as the disposition is complete.

(u) *Appendices.* Appendices regarding artillery barrage, aeroplane co-operation and machine-gun barrage will be issued separately.

(v) *Reports.* Up to zero hour the Battalion H.Q. in Chester House.

(w) *Prisoners.* Any Prisoners captured will be sent back by the companys capturing them to Hackney Villa, C.12.C.10.20, where they will be handed over to the 2/10th Battalion and a receipt obtained.

Arms and ammunition only will be taken from prisoners.

In the case of officers all documents will be taken from them and handed over to the 2/10th Battalion by the escort and a receipt obtained.

(Sgd.) A. D. HARINGTON,
Captain and Adjutant,
2/9th Battalion London Regt.
(Q.V.R.).

2/9TH BATTALION LONDON REGIMENT (QUEEN VICTORIA'S RIFLES)

Addenda to Order No. 1.

25th September, 1917.

BATTLE POLICE. Stragglers' posts will be established at the Cross Roads, Triangle Farm, Ref. C.6.c.65.10, road junction St. Julien, C.12.c.30.20.

BARRAGE. (o) page 2, last line. Delete last sentence starting with the words " After that the barrage." Lifts after the first 200 yards have been covered will be 50 yards in three minutes until the dotted red line has been reached. Subsequent lifts will be at the rate of 50 yards in four minutes.

WARNING. The word " Retire " will not be used on any account. Anyone using this word will be treated as an enemy and shot. This is to be explained to all ranks.

INFORMATION. The enemy is from all accounts somewhat disorganised after our recent attacks. It is difficult to state his order of battle. During the last two days prisoners of eight different regiments have been captured by this brigade.

CONTACT AEROPLANES. A contact aeroplane will fly over the objective at :
> Zero plus one hour.
> Zero plus two hours.
> Zero plus three hours.
> Zero plus four hours.

and at other times not yet fixed.

Troops will be ready to light red flares at these hours, but will not do so unless called for by Klaxon Horn or by dropping white lights.

It will be thoroughly impressed on all ranks that it is to their own advantage and safety, and that their position is not given away to the enemy by so doing IF THE FLARES ARE LIGHTED IN SHELL-HOLES.

Contact aeroplanes will be marked with two black rectangular panels (2 feet by 1 foot 3 inches) attached to, and projecting from, the rear edge of the lower plane on each side of the fuselage.

A counter-attack machine will be also in the air from dawn to dusk. It will draw the attention of the attacking Infantry to any signs of the enemy counter-attack developing by :—

(a) Sounding long blasts on Klaxon Horn.

(b) Then discharging a smoke bomb, which will burst about 400 feet below the machine into a white parachute flare, which descends slowly leaving a long trail of brown smoke about 1 foot broad behind it.

FORMING UP. Platoons will be met at the St. Julien Aid Post on the St. Julien-Wieltje Road by guides at 11 p.m. and

will be led straight to their positions on the tape. ALL THE
MEN SHOULD BE WARNED 5 MINUTES BEFORE ZERO HOUR
TO GET READY TO MOVE INSTANTLY.

(Sgd.) A. D. HARINGTON,
Capt. and Adjutant,
2/9th Battn. London Regiment
(Queen Victoria's Rifles).

We will begin our account of the operations with a few
individual experiences. C.S.M. Lott states, "We had splendid
luck in reaching the line without casualties for we were heavily
'bumped' on the way up. The night passed quietly until
about 5 a.m. when a heavy bombardment started. At 6.50 (?)
the barrage dropped and it was wonderful in its intensity and
accuracy. The dawn was very misty and we went over not
being able to see many yards ahead of us. As has so often
happened both before and since direction was very hard to
keep, especially over the rough ground. We had gone 200
to 300 yards before meeting any opposition other than M.G.,
but our boys found the enemy and many prisoners were taken
and incidentally many 'souvenirs' obtained. Aviatik Farm
was found to be non-existent, and things did not pan out exactly
as intended. Snipers caused us a lot of trouble and many a man
was shot through the head by them. Not satisfied with
getting his man the German sniper kept on all day firing at the
bodies of those who had already fallen. I finished up in a shell-
hole from which I could see no less than 10 'B' Company
men who had been killed. No one during the day, which turned
out a very bright one, dared show an inch. To do so was fatal,
as was proved. Rfn. Cattell, the signaller, known amongst
his pals as 'Polly,' was in the same shell-hole as I, and, chancing
his luck to have a peep over during the afternoon, was shot
clean through his head and died instantly."

Rfn. Read (391283), "C" Company, says, "We were so
weak that I only had another man besides myself in my section,
the Bombers' Section, so I told him to do exactly as I did.
We went over in great spirits as our barrage was splendid,
reached our objective, where I chose a rather large shell-hole
for our position. Unfortunately it had water in it as well as
a dead German, but in times like that it was no good being

squeamish. We had been reinforced by then, so that in the end we had 12 men altogether and a Lewis Gun, which came in very handy as we had 7 counter-attacks that day, all of which were beaten off. The position was so dangerous and we had so many casualties that we were relieved the same night. The company came out of this stunt 28 strong."

"About four o'clock in the afternoon," says Lieut. Samuelson, "observers in the shell-hole which served as Company H.Q. to 'D' Company on the left reported some movement on left flank, and a certain number of Boches were seen to be trickling up in twos and threes to a bank. Within 20 minutes of the release of the pigeons we had brought with us, our heavies opened up and no counter-attack developed on that flank though the battalion on our right were driven back a short distance. Lce.-Cpl. Ives won the Military Medal for pulling in a wounded man across a very exposed piece of ground. Very nearly two platoons of 'D' Company got lost in the fog that day. 2nd Lieut. Marshall was last seen disappearing in the fog about 6 a.m.

"On the right 'C' Company lost one platoon under Lieut. Browett, who found themselves surrounded and fought to the last man."

Rfn. Browning, 9 Platoon, "C" Company, mentions that his company "was at very weak strength and several fellows did not like the idea of an attack with so few men, but on the whole they were quite cheerful and hopeful of pulling it off. We moved off from the Canal Bank roughly at 10.0 p.m. The night was fine and stars were shining, but it was rather cold. My platoon got up safely until we had reached the support line when we ran right into one of Jerry's Strafes; they were falling pretty heavily, and one shell knocked me and one or two more over and wounded one man in the hand. After he had had it dressed he rejoined us. We arrived on the tape about 1.0 a.m., cold and tired after the long march, and I for one was feeling rather fed up and did not care much what happened. Capt. Griffith, our O.C. was killed in this attack, and Lieut. Browett, who went over with the first wave, was also killed. At 5.50 the barrage started and a minute or two later Sergt. Dawe came along and told us to be up and over, after speaking a few words of good cheer which considerably livened us up. I was next to the right-hand man of 'C' Company, and we were given orders that on no account must we lose touch with the company on our right, which was, I believe, 'A.' After we had covered a considerable distance I noticed that the remainder of 'C' Company on my left seemed to be moving off half-left, and I heard later that Lieut. Browett, lost direction, told his men so, and asked them if they should surrender or fight on, and with one accord they answered fight on. I still kept an equal distance between my left- and right-hand men until it got so great that I decided to still keep in touch with the right as ordered ; this was after I had called to the left man telling him and asking him where he was going. Dodging from shell-hole to shell-hole we reached our objective, and I got in a shell-hole with a Lewis Gun team of a section of 'A' Company. Nos. 3, 4 and 5 were in a shell-hole behind, and No. 1 asked me to tell them to pass some ammunition. Not getting an answer after repeated calls, I threw some dirt to attract their attention, and still not getting any answer it suddenly dawned on me that the three of them had been killed. This rather upset me for a while as it was only my second time in the line. Five minutes or so after we had settled down an aeroplane came flying very low over, and having no flares I attracted his attention with a red handkerchief until answered so as to give him our position. During the day and following night we consolidated, making passages between shell-holes. After coming out I had quite a shock on finding that Rfn. Wheeler and I were the only two left of No. 9 Platoon. About ten days later another fellow, Rfn. Beecham, turned up after having spent seven days in a shell-hole by himself with practically no food. He has since been reported missing at Hangard Wood."

Another Rifleman writes : " Up to this time I had always laughed when reading in the papers about how the fellows got so cheerful at such times, yet you can take it from me, it is quite true. One funny sight in the middle of the stunt was a wounded fellow in 'B' Company. He was wounded in the arm and leg, yet he came limping in, obviously in pain, with 4 Boches in front of him, laughing at what he called his ' bag,' and he informed me that he had given more than he received."

In a letter to a comrade written a few days after the battle,

Rfn. S. B. states that "the Battalion Signallers up till then had been very fortunate in that, although they had done such good work, they had had practically no casualties, but this last time they lost three of our really good men. They were a lot of real chums, all the whole bunch, and had been together for such a long time that a loss like this, and they were all killed, not wounded, hits them very hard."

Lieut. Spenser-Pryse, M.C., who was in command of two platoons of "C" Company, in a report to Capt. Johnson, says "as a subaltern of 'C' Company my original orders were first to select a suitable H.Q. for the company in immediate contact with Battn. H.Q. Second, at zero hour to go forward with the two platoons entrusted to me as far as Clifton House, 250 yards E. of the take-off tape. Third, having done this and established my platoons, to rendezvous with Capt. Griffith, my company commander, and receive further orders. As it appeared important to know the ground in advance I asked for and obtained from Capt. Griffith permission to go up the line the day preceding the attack with Capt. Swift, the Battalion Intelligence Officer. Owing to the state of the country we found it difficult to fix positions on the map with certainty. However, I was personally satisfied that the Mebus chosen for Battn. H.Q. was that at 7.C.25.15 named Hut. The power buzzer we found at Cluster Houses. I selected a small shattered Mebus at 7.C.45.40 for Company H.Q. This position stood high, overlooking the countryside east as far as Albatross and Kronprinz, and although in advance of the positions then held yet seemed capable of conversion into a strong Keep. Capt. Swift expressed the opinion that the take-off tape laid for the attack curved backwards towards Tirpitz Farm, so that the left company would start 100 yards in rear of their take-off position as shown on the map. We were on our way back to reach the battalion when Capt. Swift was struck by a M.G. bullet. While his wound was being dressed he asked me to transmit such information as we had obtained to Lieut.-Col. Parry on his arrival.

"The battalion came up before midnight, and I accompanied Lieut.-Col. Parry along the tape pointing out to him the various positions so far as it was possible in the darkness. When everything was clear and after Lieut.-Col. Parry had personally inspected all companies established on their take-off tape, rejoined my company commander. As dawn approached heavy fog lay about us so that the C.S.M. creeping along th[e] tape with the rum ration could hardly find men who were onl[y] a few yards away. Almost as soon as our barrage opened th[e] enemy replied. At zero hour Lieut. Browett moved out with th[e] two platoons of 'C' Company, which were to go forward i[n] full depth of our advance. I followed with the remainin[g] two platoons. It had been arranged for us to lay independen[t] tapes on the line of our advance, Lieut. Browett moving ou[t] 50 yards N. of my line. As we went forward in the fog I too[k] frequent compass bearings. Two hundred and fifty yard[s] from our take-off we first encountered enemy, who ran befor[e] us. I now found myself in the homestead of Clifton House easily identified by the pollard trees running along th[e] ditch which once surrounded it. As we had encountere[d] no serious resistance I decided to go forward another 20 yards, as far as the apex of Vale Trench. This trench containe[d] enemy who bolted as we came up, though few, I think, go[t] away, the mist being now less dense. As I had gone forwar[d] beyond my assigned position I decided to consolidate here sending a runner to inform B.H.Q. of my position as arranged[.] As the air cleared the enemy became visible to our immediat[e] front. Having handed over my platoons to Cpl. Chapman [I] returned along the tape to meet Capt. Griffith, only to lear[n] that both he and the C.S.M. were casualties. About that tim[e] also I learned that Lieut. Browett was killed and that onl[y] a few survivors from his platoons were creeping back. Th[e] original intention had been that my platoons should act as [a] reserve. In the circumstances, however, I saw that I mus[t] quickly establish what I held. The enemy M.G. fire, which wa[s] increasing in volume particularly from the S.E., led me t[o] believe that the other companies had not fully attained thei[r] objectives. I therefore concentrated all stragglers on th[e] position chosen for Company H.Q. and arranged to consolidate[.] Cpl. Chapman having been killed I placed Cpl. Kingswell i[n] charge of my two forward platoons and myself set out fo[r] Battn. H.Q. in response to an order from Lieut.-Col. Parry.

"At B.H.Q. I was informed that the other companie[s] claimed to hold all their objectives except Boetleer. At th[e] same time enemy activity appeared on the increase and the position gave rise to some apprehension. The plan to establish a Keep at 7.C.45.40 covering B.H.Q. was approved. Col. Parry asked me to make the new Keep my H.Q. It was also decided to regard it as forward O.P. for the battalion. On returning to ' C ' Company I found them well established. As the morning passed numerous stragglers crept in from the N. and S.E. belonging mainly to other companies. It became evident that the attack had gone partly astray in the fog, spreading out like a fan, and that in front of Vale Trench I had to deal with undisturbed enemy positions. It was clear, however, that he had suffered severely. In every direction his stretcher parties were gathering in wounded. As the afternoon passed the enemy gun fire became intense. About four o'clock Col. Parry sent for me and told me that he had received information of enemy massing for a counter-attack in the neighbourhood of Albatross. I was able to assure him that those movements had been under my observation for some time and that I considered them to be nothing more serious than an attempt to replace his casualties. At the same time I agreed that the enemy was in strong force on my immediate front; that he kept up constant fire on my advance post in the neighbourhood of Aviatik (although I could not localise the farm and could only judge by the compass bearing from Clifton House), and that the intensity of his bombardment was causing us continual heavy casualties. It was therefore decided to inform Brigade H.Q. of the position.

"It was only afterwards that I learned of the exact nature of the steps that were taken by brigade. So far as my own front was concerned, however—and I could cover the whole position eastward as far as Kronprinz—no massed movement took place. The largest force I saw was about 70 strong moving from Kronprinz to Albatross at dusk. These would be an ordinary relief. I do not mean, however, that the position was stabilised, nor do I mean that there was not much scattered fighting going on. I was better able to judge the state of affairs than B.H.Q. because I could see with my own eyes from my Keep. For this reason, I think, Col. Parry sent for me again on the arrival of the 10th London Regiment in support. It was, of course, a most unhappy thing that the

Intelligence Officer should have become a casualty at such a time.

"At 11 p.m. I was summoned to B.H.Q. to meet Col. Barham of the 12th London Regiment, on whom the command of the entire operation had devolved, and informed him that there was considerable uncertainty as to the position at Aviatik which must be cleared up. I was therefore instructed to proceed with Capt. Bowran of the 10th London Regiment to the neighbourhood of Aviatik, having first warned a company of the 12th London Regiment, lying near Olive House, to be in readiness if called upon. If, in the opinion of Capt. Bowran, acting as an independent authority, the position at Aviatik was unsatisfactory he was immediately to take the necessary steps with the troops at his disposal. Although we went beyond our most advanced posts, nothing that could be identified as Aviatik could be discovered. Capt. Bowran decided that further action was undesirable and I rejoined the battalion which by this time had been relieved and was moving off."

In the course of the day Lieut.-Col. Parry had visited Lieut. Spenser-Pryse at the forward H.Q. in order to personally judge of the position. The post itself commanded a wide view of the scene of operations. He supplies a very interesting account of the battle :

"The plan of the whole operation, which was a big one, roughly resolved itself into an attack E. by the 175th Brigade, the 2/9th Battalion and one company of the 2/12th on a frontage of 750 yards, forming the attacking troops. The 175th Brigade formed the pivot, the advance being made from the high ground above Von Tirpitz Farm, not very far from an old position at Springfield. From our starting-point it was easy to understand the difficulties of holding our former objective of September 9th, viz. Winnipeg, which was well commanded from the ridge on which we now were. The battalion duly reached the tape line in good time and with very few casualties, a piece of luck, and I felt a great relief on returning to Battn. H.Q. after having seen that everyone was in position on the tape, that all was well so far, and that, barring accidents, the battalion would advance at zero hour as one man. The men had a cold wait, however, in shell-holes, before the attack was made, but a dessert-spoonful of rum and a dessert biscuit served out to each man by the section commander 15 minutes before the ' flag went down ' cheered them up. This amount of rum, no more and no less, was prescribed by the doctor, and it was undoubtedly a very excellent thing.

"One incident I feel I must mention. I was waiting at the old aid post at St. Julien—the rendezvous for the guides—for the Head-quarters party, with whom I was going up into the line, when two men came up to be attended to, very much shaken and cut about. They had been knocked over and damaged by a high explosive shell bursting and presented a very bloody appearance. Some little time before zero two breathless and bandaged figures appeared out of the darkness and asked me if I could direct them to ' C ' Company. I did so, and asked them if they were not the two men I had seen at the aid post some hours before. They replied ' Yes,' but had come on as they did not want to miss the show! I told them they were very gallant men and directed them to ' C ' Company. One, I believe, was killed early in the fight and the other wounded. I wish very much that I had taken their names, but I took an opportunity of reciting the incident to the divisional Commander at a later date, for I was very proud of them, and I believe they showed the spirit that animated the battalion. Anyway they set a splendid example.

"The battalion fighting strength was approximately 400 all ranks, including 14 officers. Of the latter, five were among the killed—Capt. Griffith, and Lieuts. Browett, Marshall Blackburne and Rolason, and Lieuts. Swift and Chudley wounded. This, in spite of the fact that all officers were dressed like the men to avoid undue difference in appearance. My Intelligence Officer, Lieut. Swift, was wounded just before we arrived on the tape, so there were only myself and my Adjutant, Capt. Harington, left at Battalion Head-quarters.

"The troops moved off from the tape at zero hour, 5.50 a.m., at which time there was a thick mist, increased by the smoke and dust, so that it was difficult to see many yards ahead. The right and centre objectives were in due course reported as having been taken—the higher command having decided that the village of Boetleer was not to be held—but information was long delayed in regard to Winzig on our left, one of the objectives of 'D' Company. This was a small salient in the line which was never reached, the platoon detached for its capture, being wiped out almost to a man in the attempt. Some very gallant work was done here by Lieut. Browett who was killed fighting to the last. Of prisoners we captured about 90, but some of these were killed by the Hun fire on their way to St. Julien, and the most welcome sight of the day was to see the first batch of about 30 arriving at Battalion Head-quarters.

"A strong counter-attack was made by the Boches, the 100th Reserve Grenadiers, at 10.30 a.m. on our right, but was repelled. Another counter-attack was made on our left at about 2.30 p.m. with the same result. In spite of the heavy preliminary artillery fire, the opposition we encountered was serious, our casualties amounting to 180 out of the 400 engaged, and the loss of 7 officers out of the 14, as already described. During the afternoon some of the 10th Battalion were sent up in support, for as I had been ordered to hold the positions gained at all costs, and my casualties being heavy, I had asked for another company to strengthen my line. There were now the depleted 9th Battalion, and part of the 10th and 12th Battalions on the spot, so the brigadier decided to form them all into one battalion under the command of Col. A. S. Barham of the 12th Battalion, the senior colonel there, which was accordingly done. The enemy shelling was pretty continuous all day, though it slackened towards evening, the positions the men occupied being mostly shell-holes.

"The Brigadier came up to Battalion Head-quarters in the evening, just as the plan of redistribution was being formed, and a little later a congratulatory telegram on the day's success was received from Gen. Maxse, commanding the XVIIIth Corps. It was subsequently decided, however, that the position of our right objective, Aviatik Farm, had not been consolidated, the line actually held being some little way behind. At the time there appeared to be absolutely no doubt whatever that the point held was Aviatik Farm, and it would not have been difficult to have advanced the post to reach this place had it been deemed necessary to do so. It need scarcely be mentioned that landmarks in this area are very difficult to locate and are often deceptive.

"The men fought gallantly and well, and on making

inquiries later seemed very pleased with their 'Hun bag.' One point struck me very much during the fighting as it had on other occasions, the difficulty of maintaining communications. We had all the usual scientific paraphernalia, power buzzer, telephone, lamps, flags, pigeons, dogs and runners, but owing to various causes the main source of reliance was the runner, as I suppose he was in the Greek wars. One cannot but come to the conclusion that the scientific aids to communications, admirable as they are in theory and on field days, are not sufficiently effective to stand the strain of a modern battle. Anyhow, speaking from the point of view of a battalion commander, one has little confidence in them in times of stress. On a former occasion I had rather pinned my faith on dogs, but on 26th our dogs simply ran round in circles or failed to start, one dropping his message, which we picked up. The pigeons were not bad but would not fly after dark."

Describing this action as " one of the most bitterly contested in the Ypres salient," the *Times History of the War* goes on to say : " On the extreme left an advance of only 1,000 yards or so along the Gravenstafel Spur had been ordered by Gough. With the Germans still holding almost the whole of the Wallemoden Spur to its north and the valley of the upper Haanebeck to its south, it would have been courting defeat to have pushed in the direction of Gravenstafel beyond Aviatik Farm and the hamlet of Boetleer. The redoubt and the fortified ruins of the hamlet had been badly hammered by our guns, and the Saxons of the 23rd Reserve Division defending them offered but a feeble resistance to the London Territorials and North Midlanders entrusted with the reduction of the strong points above mentioned. Some of the enemy were discovered in open order, apparently about to assault Wurst Farm. They were sent flying eastwards across the fields. Nearly 200 prisoners were captured. . . . Later the Germans concentrated all their artillery in that region on the Londoners and drove them back. But our men returned to the charge and recovered the positions they had evacuated. In honour of their achievements the western end of the Gravenstafel Spur was thenceforth called 'London Ridge.' South of the London Ridge from between Schuler Farm and Hill 37 the North Midlanders and other English troops pushed forward west and east of the Ypres-

Paschendaele Road. The ground had dried since September 20th, but, as before, it was a waste of shell-holes, among which rose up the towers of numerous field forts. From Abraham Heights, just west of Gravenstafel, and from other points on the southern face of the Spur, machine-guns played on our men ascending or descending into the valley of the Haanebeck. The right flank of the British was enfiladed by the Germans on Zonnebeke, and when Zonnebeke fell, by the garrisons of the dug-outs in the Ypres-Roulers railway. Beyond Dochy Farm there was very stiff fighting and the English were twice heavily counter-attacked. Here our line was advanced about half a mile."

Col. Langworthy Parry's comment upon the above is that neither " the feeble opposition encountered " nor the " driving in of our line " applied to the 2nd Q.V.R.

Capt. Geoffrey Foster Griffith, who was in command of " C " Company, was the second son of Dr. W. S. A. Griffith, M.D. 96 Harley-street, W. 1, and had served with the 1st Battalion in the early days of the war. He was invalided and returning to England was, on convalescence, transferred to the 2nd Battalion.

2nd Lieut. Reginald Browett, also of " C " Company, was the second son of Mr. and Mrs. H. L. Browett, of Lower Kingwell, Longdown, near Exeter, and with a younger brother Archie, went out with the 1st Battalion in 1914. He was in the fighting on Hill 60 in April, 1915, and in the battle of the Somme on July 1st in the following year. It is said that finding himself surrounded by the Germans he asked the men of his platoon (No. 11) if they wished to surrender or would fight to the last with him. With one accord they shouted " no surrender " and fought on till the last man fell.

Archie Browett was later given a commission in the Machine gun Corps and was killed two months later during the great advance on Cambrai.

" C " Company also suffered the loss of their sergeant-major Skipper, who was shot through the lungs and died from hæmorrhage later in the day.

2nd Lieut. Blackburne went out with the 1st Battalion in 1914 as a rifleman, was promoted to corporal and came home wounded in 1915. He was given a commission in the 2nd

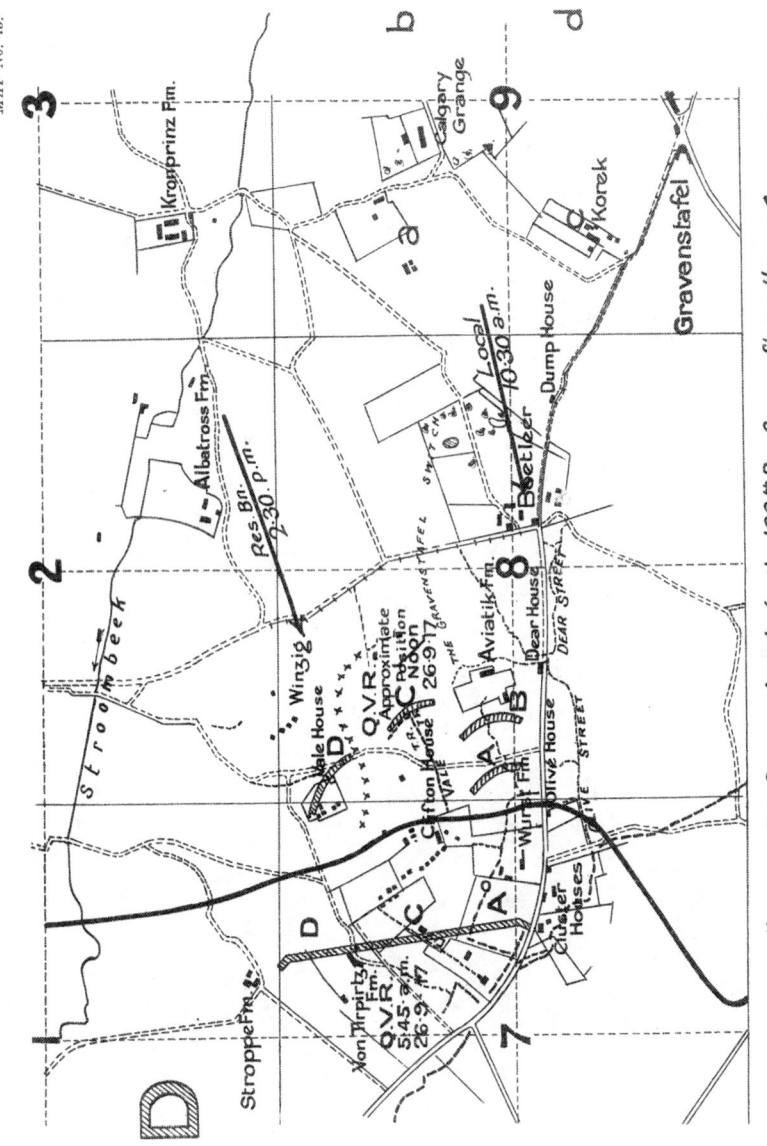

THE FIGHT FOR PASSCHENDAELE. SEPT 26TH-27TH 1917.

Battalion, which he rejoined during the fighting round Bullecourt in May, 1917.

Lieut. John Marshall was among those reported " missing." He was last seen disappearing in the fog about 6 a.m., and no further trace was found of him.

Lce.-Cpl. Chapman, who only gained the Military Medal on September 9th, was shot through the head and killed on 26th.

The following telegram was received at Battalion H.Q. on the evening of September 26th : " Wire from Corps Commander begins a a a Please convey to Brig.-Gen. Jackson, Lieut.-Col. Parry, Lieut.-Col. Barham and to all ranks of Queen Victoria's Rifles and the Rangers my hearty congratulations on their very successful attack this morning a a a ends."

The message was addressed to " Ulick," the code name for the 2nd Q.V.R., and signed " Umpire," the code name for the 175th Infantry Brigade. The Corps Commander was Sir Ivor Maxse, O.C. XVIIIth Army Corps, an old acquaintance of the Queen Victoria's and Commander of the 3rd London Infantry Brigade prior to the war.

CHAPTER IX

The Close of 1917

FOLLOWING their relief the 2nd Q.V.R. reached Reigersberg Camp early on the morning of September 28th, glad of a rest and change, which this time was to be of long duration. October 2nd found them at Zutkerque and neighbouring villages, where they put in the time training and reorganising till they were sent up to the line again at Road Side Camp (St. Jean Ter Biezen), which they reached on October 21st. Reinforcements arrived from a number of units and the companies had hard work in getting into shape. Referring to this our old friend Rfn. Snoswell, who had been away for a month in hospital at Havre and rejoined on October 13th, writes: " I have settled down now in the platoon and there is plenty of work going. The battalion has such a lot of new men with us that we have to work hard training them. Most of them have been in the Army for a year or so, but in the cavalry or A.S.C., so have to get into the ways of infantry. They are a mixed lot both as to men and in that they come from all parts of England. As you go round the battalion you hear all sorts of dialects and it is strange after the old boys—Manchester, Yorkshire, Scotch, Devonshire, etc. As a whole they are a good lot, but they don't come up to the old ones. Most of them will be new to the trenches, but perhaps they will do all the better for that."

On October 17th the battalion paraded for the presentation of ribbons by the G.O.C. Division (Gen. Cator) to officers and Other Ranks who had been awarded decorations in the course of the recent operations. These included Lieut. Prince, M.C., Croix de Guerre (Belgium) and L'ordre de Couronne; Capt. Spenser-Pryse, M.C., and Capt. Eustace, M.C.

At this period Capt. K. W. Johnson had taken over the

adjutancy of the regiment, Capt. Harington being given the command of a company.

Training continued until October 30th, when a move was made to their old quarters on the Canal Bank preparatory to going into the line at Poelcapelle. At this time one-third of the men had never yet been in the line. The battalion paraded at 2 p.m. on October 31st and proceeded by route march to the line, taking over from the 174th Infantry Brigade the portion from Helles House through Poelcapelle village to Tracas Farm. Battalion H.Q. were established at Norfolk House. The very name of the place recalls to everyone who was there the awful and ubiquitous mud ; mud, thick, slimy and glutinous, and nothing but mud. " I doubt if there was a more desolate place anywhere along the front than Poelcapelle," writes C.S.M. Lott. " The trip to the line from Kempton Park, the reserve position, was up about six miles of duck-board track over shell-holes. Naturally at this time of the year the nights were usually very dark and the mud also was at its worst. Being in the Ypres salient we came in for plenty of attention from the enemy's artillery. 'Meunier House' suggests something in the way of cover but it actually was merely a bump in the ground which became visibly less each time we visited it. The mud in the neighbourhood of Meunier House was the worst any of us had seen or have since seen. It was more like an Irish bog and sucked men down. An exhausted man in full kit and carrying a rifle or perhaps a Lewis Gun, went through hell in trying to get along and it took in many cases hours to traverse a hundred yards. On one occasion the company who relieved us, many hours late, arrived with no L.G.'s or ammunition, their rifles all choked with mud and the men absolutely whacked by their awful struggle with the mud. There is no doubt that the mud in the Poelcapelle sector was the direct cause of many a good fellow being killed owing to his helplessness."

" Mud ! Well, I thought I had been through some since I came out here," says Rfn. Snoswell, " but it was absolutely clean to what it is here. You have seen the mud carts in London ; well, if you thickened that up to the consistency of paste you would have something like what it is here, but in some parts it is much thinner than that. To go into it up to one's knees is nothing unusual and if one gets stuck in it—it is awful to get out again."

Various types and sizes of the German Mebus, and known to us as "Pill boxes," lay scattered about, and such as were habitable were made use of as shelters for the men; the others had to put up with shell-holes. The former gave a feeling of security which the shell-holes, open to the air, lacked. "In every Mebus nearly we found wounded men. Tommies in every case," says Rfn. Snoswell, "who had been wounded in the push and had crawled into them for shelter. Some of them had been there for days, but others only the day before we got there."

Only three days were spent in the line. It was impossible to stay longer owing to the horrible conditions. The relieving battalion was the 2/12th London, but unfortunately they lost their way coming up and arrived some hours late. The journey out is described as being performed under conditions worse if possible than the going in. Fritz put plenty of gas shells over and gas masks had to be worn. "Our casualties while in the line," says Lieut.-Col. Parry, "were not heavy, but we rescued about a dozen poor fellows of other regiments who were lying out and who had been unable to be moved previously on account of the mud. There had been a lot of fighting round here and the unburied dead were very much in evidence. However, I don't think we left a single wounded man about, but to show the difficulty of bringing them in : it took 12 men with two stretchers more than ten hours to bring in two wounded men to the Aid Post, a distance of about 500 yards."

On November 2nd the battalion was gratified by the receipt of a message from the Divisional Commander through Brigade Head-quarters, saying :

"The following is an extract from a letter received by me to-day from Lieut.-Gen. Sir Ivor Maxse, K.C.B., C.V.O., D.S.O., Commanding XVIIIth Corps, and should be distributed for the information of all ranks.

1st November, 1917.

'To-day I have been so busy handing over that I could not make an opportunity of calling personally upon you and your Brigadiers to express to them and to all ranks my appreciation of the splendid work they have put in throughout the months they have been in this Corps. Their spirit has been magnificent throughout. On the 20th September they won the best battle yet fought in this Corps—and we have had thirteen battles in Flanders. I consider the 20th September as the Red Letter Day of the Corps and the capture of Wurst Farm was a real feat of arms—even in this war. Having captured that ridge the 58th Division not only held their ground, but they defeated no less than five Hun battalions which counter-attacked them during the afternoon. They and the 51st Division were highly tried on that day, and the enemy was so beaten that he has never once counter-attacked us in strength since that date. I beg you will convey to your people how greatly I have appreciated their services and how sincerely I bid them farewell.'

(Sgd.) A. B. CATOR,
Major-General,
2/11/17.   Commanding 58th Division."

Two days later the battalion marched to Kempton Park on the Pilkem Ridge, and on November 6th, Lieut.-Col. Langworthy Parry, the O.C., went on leave, Major W. P. Wilton, M.C., taking over the command. On November 7th the battalion went up into the trenches again for a short spell. It was much the same as in the last turn except that instead of being in pill-boxes the men were in a short trench or rather ditch. Nothing very important seems to have occurred. Then commenced another period spent in moving from one mud camp to another, the state of each being worse than the other, if such a thing could be possible. From November 8th to 13th, Siege Camp was occupied, and on 14th a move was made via Elverdinghe and Proven to Purbrook Camp. Petworth Camp was reached on 17th and Coulomby on 27th.

A few days previously Lieut.-Col. Langworthy Parry had returned from England and writes : " The time had now come for me to leave the battalion I loved so well. I suppose the strain of the campaign which lately had been rather great, was beginning to tell upon me, and although I was still prepared to carry on it was decided that a job less strenuous than commanding a battalion in the field under the conditions then existing should be found for me. I was accordingly recommended for the command of a battalion at home, and on January 1st, 1918—after a most welcome rest—assumed command of the 8th (Reserve) Battalion, London Regiment, the Post Office Rifles, then quartered at Blackdown, which command I had the honour to hold until the termination of the war."

In the battalion Orders of November 25th appeared the following:

"COMMAND.—On relinquishing the command of the battalion the Commanding Officer wishes to express his most sincere thanks to all ranks for the loyal and hearty support they have always given him, and for the cheerfulness and keenness they have invariably shown in whatever task they may have had to undertake, no matter what or how unpleasant the circumstances attending it may have been. He trusts they will continue to show the same soldierly spirit, and thus maintain the high traditions of the regiment.

"It is with deep regret that the Commanding Officer takes leave of the battalion, after having served with it since its formation in September, 1914, and commanded it since March, 1917, but wishes it every success and Godspeed for the future."

He adds: "Of my officers I would specially recall the names of Maj. Wilton, M.C., than whom no commanding officer ever had a better second in command. Capt. Eustace M.C., R.A.M.C., my medical officer, who did his duty nobly, and to whom the battalion owed more than they knew of. Of my successive Adjutants, Capt. Walker (killed), Harington and Johnson; of Capts. Graham White, Prince, Hodgkinson and Spenser-Pryse; and Lieuts. Samuelson and MacAdam; also of R.S.M. and Acting Quartermaster Tomlinson. They all worked hard and did their best for the battalion, and a 'good best' it was. I feel very grateful to them indeed, and to all those, and they were many, who so loyally supported me and to whom the 'game was the thing.'"

"As to the men, who can ever sing their praises too high? The expression 'the men were splendid' has been used so often that its significance has been largely lost sight of, but having seen the British Tommy at work in front of the enemy—and he always was in front of the enemy—I have the very greatest

Lt.-Col. P. E. Langworthy Parry, D.S.O., O.B.E., T.D.

respect for him and I admire him more than I can say. Carrying heavy loads—when was he not carrying them ?—doing willingly and cheerfully all he was asked to do, killing Huns, burying Huns, digging trenches, putting up with all sorts of dangers and discomforts, even in ' rest billets,' sleeping in his clothes, often on hard ground, under fire by day and bombed by night, playing when he could, but always the British soldier and the Man. Let us hope that our country, for which he fought so nobly, will never forget what she owes to her fighting men in this great war."

For the good work of the battalion while under his command Lieut.-Col. Langworthy Parry was awarded the D.S.O. on the 1st of January, 1918.

In January, 1921, Lieut.-Col. Langworthy Parry, D.S.O., O.B.E., T.D., was gazetted to the command of the 9th London Battalion, Queen Victoria's Rifles, in succession to Colonel Vernon W. F. Dickins, D.S.O., V.D., whose period of service had expired.

About October the 2/9th Battalion officers got up a band, raised largely by subscriptions among themselves and some " unknown " friends. Sergt. Coles, a clever musician, was given the difficult task of selecting the musicians, there being only one or two trained men at his disposal. He accomplished wonders gathering together about twenty instruments and performers and mightily proud did the battalion become of them, and many a pleasant hour was spent in listening to the music they discoursed. On Sunday, December 23rd, each battalion in the brigade held a special Memorial Service for the men who had fallen on that front, and the Q.V.R. band played for the lot.

The little village of Coulomby was left on December 7th, the battalion being conveyed by lorries to Wizernes, thence by train to Elverdinghe, and marching to the old position of Siege Camp. The next day it proceeded to Kempton Park and moved up into the line on the Poelcapelle sector. " A " Company being stationed at Helles House, " B " Company at Meunier House, " D " Company at Tracas Farm with " C " Company in support at Pheasant Trench. They were relieved on December 10th, only to take up the same positions on 14th and on 16th they moved by rail to "Reading," and from thence marched to White Mill Camp. The 24th found them back at Kempton Park in support. On 28th at 5 p.m. they once more moved up into the front line, retaining the position until the night of January 1st when they were relieved by the 2/1st Fusiliers. The Christmas dinner that some of the men had been promising themselves had to be postponed.

Another tale of the mud, told by a young subaltern : " I have had the two worst days of my life. We've been up the line and I had charge of a post—it was the worst post along our front. No shelter except the top three steps, and a dug-out, the bottom of which was flooded, so we had a deal of discomfort. My hole, shared by a sergeant, measured three feet six in. by three feet six in., and we had to cook in it. We were shelled like anything. Coming out last night (December 16th) I had an awful experience. It was pitch black and I was going along when suddenly I sank in thick, very sticky mud. The more I struggled the deeper I sank. I went in up to my thighs and could not move out. Luckily a man came along and hearing me struggling gave me a hand and after half an hour I managed to get out. I felt so weak after it I could hardly stand, but I had to do a six mile walk along the duckboards winding in and out of shell-holes. If the man had not seen me I should have been drowned. I was covered in mud from head to foot and my hands were inches thick in clay. When I had scraped them I found to my dismay that my ring had gone." It was a gold signet ring inscribed with the rank, name and regiment (Queen Victoria's Rifles) of the wearer, who hopes that some day it may be turned up by the plough and restored to its rightful owner. It was a Christmas gift and intended to serve the purpose of an additional identity disc.

The long looked forward to Christmas dinner came off on Saturday, January 5th. " Our Xmas feast is a thing of the past," writes Rfn. Snoswell, " and we had a fine time taken all round. Considering how we were placed up here in the line and the difficulties of transport it was remarkable that we did so well. Breakfast was fairly late and the morning was mainly spent in getting ready. We borrowed tables and forms from the Church Army Hut and it was a real treat to sit down to a table for a meal. At other times we sit on our kits and balance our meals on our knees, but to sit at a table like a civilised being added to the pleasure. The Government supply was roast beef, potatoes, ½ lb. of Xmas pudding and mince pies. Our dinner therefore consisted of a cut off the joint (beautifully cooked) with potatoes *à la* nude (for a change) followed by Xmas pudding with custard and mince pies. There was plenty of everything. Then we had nuts, fruit, etc., cigars and cigarettes, and for drink port wine and whisky and a good cup of tea for others. Crackers were also provided so that we might make fools of ourselves. Tinned fruit and biscuits were also on the board. Of course, mess tins had to be used instead of mugs and plates, by those who did not possess the latter, but things went down all right. Dinner was at three o'clock, but at twelve we had ham sandwiches and a pint of beer per man, so taken all round yesterday was a day of feasting. What added still more to the enjoyment of the day was the news that we were moving out of the line."

www.ingramcontent.com/pod-product-compliance
Lightning Source LLC
Chambersburg PA
CBHW061925220426
43662CB00012B/1804